P9-CJN-526

DATE DUE

NO 8 '01			
NO 27 '01			
NO 1 4 03			
NO 1 4 '08			

DEMCO 38-296

LIVING WITH THE BOMB

Japan in the Modern World

Series Editor:
Mark Selden, Binghamton University

Laura Hein and Mark Selden, eds.
Living With the Bomb:
American and Japanese Cultural Conflicts in the Nuclear Age

Joe Moore, ed.
The Other Japan:
Conflict, Compromise, and Resistance Since 1945
New Edition

Gavan McCormack
The Emptiness of Japanese Affluence
Foreword by Norma Field

AMPO, ed.
Voices from the Japanese Women's Movement
Foreword by Charlotte Bunch

Kyoko and Mark Selden, eds. and trs.
The Atomic Bomb:
Voices from Hiroshima and Nagasaki
Foreword by Robert Jay Lifton, M.D.

NAKAMURA Masanori
The Japanese Monarchy:
Ambassador Joseph Grew and the Making of
the "Symbol Emperor System," 1931–1991
Translated by Herbert Bix, Jonathan Baker-Bates, and Derek Brown

_____

The calligraphy that graces the section title pages is by Kyoko Selden.

LIVING WITH THE BOMB

AMERICAN AND JAPANESE CULTURAL CONFLICTS IN THE NUCLEAR AGE

LAURA HEIN AND MARK SELDEN

EDITORS

Riverside Community College
Library
APR '98   4800 Magnolia Avenue
Riverside, California 92506

An East Gate Book

M.E. Sharpe
Armonk, New York
London, England

An East Gate Book

Copyright © 1997 by M. E. Sharpe, Inc.

D 767.25 .H6 L48 1997

…ook may be reproduced in any form
…he publisher, M. E. Sharpe, Inc.,
…rmonk, New York 10504.

…e used with permission:

Living with the bomb

…urnal of American History, Volume 82, No. 3,
…p. 1124–1135.

…o appeared in the Bulletin of Concerned Asian
…-55, a special issue on "Remembering the Bomb:
The Fiftieth Anniversary in the United States and Japan," under the title "Between Pearl Harbor and
Hiroshima/Nagasaki: A Psychological Vicious Circle."

Chapter 7 by Michael Sherry has appeared in earlier versions in the *Bulletin of Concerned Asian
Scholars,* Volume 27, No. 2, Summer 1995, pp 19–25, and in Tom Engelhardt and Edward Linenthal,
eds., *History Wars: The Enola Gay and Other Battles for the American Past* (New York: Metropolitan
Books, 1996), pp. 97–114.

Chapter 9 by Sadao ASADA is a substantially revised and expanded version of an essay that appeared
in the *Journal of American-East Asian Relations* under the title "The Mushroom Cloud and National
Psyches: Japanese and American Perceptions of the A-Bomb Decision, 1945–1995," Volume 4, No. 2,
Summer 1995, pp. 95–116.

Chapter 10 by Lisa Yoneyama is a substantially revised version of an article of the same title that
appeared in *Public Culture,* 1995, Volume 7, pp. 499–527.

Library of Congress Cataloging-in-Publication Data

Living with the bomb: American and Japanese cultural conflicts in the Nuclear Age /
Laura Hein and Mark Selden, editors.
p. cm.   "An east gate book."
ISBN 1-56324-966-9 (alk. paper)   ISBN 1-56324-967-7 (pbk.: alk. paper)
1. Hiroshima-shi (Japan)—History—Bombardment, 1945.
2. Nagasaki-shi (Japan)—History—Bombardment, 1945.
3. World War, 1939–1945—Japan. 4. Japan—History—1945–
5. United States—History—1945– . I. Hein, Laura Elizabeth. II. Selden, Mark.
D767.25.H6L48   1996
940.54′25—dc 20
96-38664
CIP

Printed in the United States of America

The paper used in this publication meets the minimum requirements of
American National Standard for Information Sciences—
Permanence of Paper for Printed Library Materials,
ANSI Z 39.48–1984.

∞

BM (c) 10 9 8 7 6 5 4 3 2 1
BM (p) 10 9 8 7 6 5 4 3 2 1

For Vinca and Cora, with love.

L.H.

And for hibakusha and civilian bomb victims everywhere.

Contents

Part III: Contending Constituencies

Part IV: Afterword

Acknowledgments

The editors have many people to thank. First among these are the contributors, who graciously accepted the combination of an unusually fast-paced production schedule and double-barrelled editorial demands. Bill and Nancy Doub, the editors of the *Bulletin of Concerned Asian Scholars* helped in many ways, including allowing us to publish slightly revised versions of the essays by Yui and Sherry. They originally appeared in a special issue of the *Bulletin* (27.2), which was organized by Laura Hein and includes five additional essays, some by contributors also represented here. That collection addressed related issues that will be of interest to readers of this volume. The introduction benefited greatly from critical comments from Ken Alder, Jeffrey Hanes, Susan Herbst, George Roeder, and especially Bob Frost, whose trenchant analysis sent us back to work in a new and better direction. The participants at a November 1995 conference at University of California-Berkeley on "Hoping for the Worst: the Planning, Experience and Consequences of Mass Warfare, 1930–1950," organized by Andy Barshay, and participants in May and June 1996 seminars at Hitotsubashi and Meiji Gakuin Universities also helped us develop our ideas. George Roeder participated in choosing all the images and writing the captions. His keen eye and passion for the art of translation of image to prose enriched the volume immensely. Kyoko Selden contributed the calligraphy. Juhani Lompolo provided the two photographs that appear on pages 167 and 170 and Ed Linenthal generously offered the images on pages 55 and 60. Norma Field and S. Hollis Clayson provided Laura Hein with wise guidance on the Afterword, while Hilde Hein and George Hein gave her the text, together with their own judgments, in bits and pieces, over the years.

All Japanese names, with the exception of the author Sadao Asada, are given in Japanese order, family name before personal name, except where citing a work previously published using Western name order convention. Japanese-American names are given in Western name order.

I

Introduction

1

Commemoration and Silence

Fifty Years of Remembering
the Bomb in America and Japan

Laura Hein and Mark Selden

Commemoration, Censorship, Conflict

For more than half a century, the world's peoples have lived with the bomb: in awe of its power, anxious about its destructiveness, and aware that it was used to kill twice and could be used again, perhaps against oneself next time. This knowledge is most vivid, and has been most fiercely debated, in the United States and Japan. Both Americans and Japanese have revisited this issue repeatedly and reinterpreted it through the prism of the intervening half-century. That fifty-year history, including the shifts in United States–Japan relations, rather than the events of August 1945, is the subject of this book.

In both the United States and Japan, an "official story" quickly emerged to shape, but never to monopolize, nuclear consciousness. In each nation, a rich and distinctive body of literary, graphic, and historical work has engaged, documented, commemorated, protested, or mourned the bomb. From the earliest reports of the atomic bombings, Americans have viewed nuclear destruction primarily from the Promethean perspective of the inventor and bombardier. The carefully crafted image of a mushroom cloud spiraling heavenward has represented to most Americans the bomb as the ultimate symbol of victory in a "Good War" that carried the United States to the peak of its power and prosperity. This simple story presented Americans as a brave, selfless, and united people who responded to treachery with total mobilization culminating in a knockout victory. In that narrative, which elides earlier decades of conflict between two rising colonial powers in Asia, retribution was devoid of desire for power or economic gain. The atomic bomb, and the decision to use it twice against urban populations, has been consistently portrayed in the official story as the shining example of American decisiveness, moral certitude, and technological ingenuity in the service of the nation. When the war is remembered as climaxing in the atomic bombs, these are the qualities being celebrated.[1] Beginning in 1945, United States officials prevented wide distribution of most images of the bombs' destruction, particularly of the human havoc it wrought, and suppressed information about radiation, its most terrifying effect. As the "American century" opened, exclusive possession of the bomb instilled confidence in the global deployment of American military power and dramatized the awesome responsibility contingent on possession of such destructive might.

By contrast, from the outset, the official Japanese perspective was from the position of the first, and thus far only, target population. Their focus was on the human victims in the hellfires that consumed Hiroshima, killing 140,000 of its 350,000 inhabitants, and then Nagasaki and 70,000 of the 270,000 people who lived there.[2] The empathy of their compatriots came easily, since nearly all urban Japanese had endured the fire-bombing that had taken a toll of hundreds of thousands of lives and left all but two Japanese cities in ruins. In the official narrative, the bomb conjured images of death and fortitude amid destruction. It soon became the symbol of both national defeat by a cruel and powerful foe and stoic endurance.

Two documents were critical in defining the official story of the bomb for Americans. Both were carefully crafted justifications for its use on the populations of Hiroshima and Nagasaki. One was also the first news most Americans had that such a weapon existed: President Harry Truman's official announcement, in the form of a 1,160-word press release, that the United States had dropped an atomic bomb on Hiroshima. Truman solemnly warned the world of the bomb's unparalleled might: "It is an atomic bomb. It is a harnessing of the basic power of the universe."[3]

From the opening sentence, Truman's announcement was designed to fend off criticism by describing Hiroshima as "an important Japanese army base." This was technically true, but the military base on the outskirts of the city was not the bomb's target. Nor was the main target an industrial site. Rather, the bombardiers were instructed to look for a distinctive bridge in the center of the city. They also had primed the bomb to explode in the air, in order to maximize damage. Their mission was to annihilate the population and destroy the city in a terrifying demonstration of U.S. power.

The principal justification Truman gave for the bomb was vengeance: "The Japanese began the war from the air at Pearl Harbor. They have been repaid many fold." He said much less about inducing surrender and nothing at all about saving American lives. Hiroshima was forever after paired with Pearl Harbor in an official story of innocent victimization and righteous revenge. By treating the bomb as the necessary and appropriate response to Pearl Harbor and subsequent Japanese atrocities, this official narrative erases all the small and large American acts of revenge that went before: mutilation of Japanese war dead, the "take no prisoners" philosophy that frequently prevailed among U.S. forces in the final battles of the war, and especially the systematic bombing of Japan's civilian population. Although most of the major combatants, including the Japanese, bombed cities over the course of the war, in the end Americans far outdid all others in aerial destruction, setting a standard that would only be surpassed by U.S. bombardment of Vietnam twenty-five years later.[4]

The second highly influential document that shaped the official story and silenced critics was the 1947 *Harper's* magazine article by Henry Stimson, secretary of war from July 1940 to September 1945. Stimson added several key elements of the official line when he argued that that Japanese surrender had been elusive until the United States "administered a tremendous shock which would carry convincing proof of our power to destroy the empire." The only credible alternative, he held, had been an invasion that might have "cost over a million casualties in American forces alone," with additional Allied losses and many more enemy casualties.[5] This was the original statement—that is, the invention—of the 1 million casualty figure that would provide the centerpiece for subsequent defenses of the use of the atomic bombs.

Because Japan was a defeated and occupied nation, its framing of an official story of the atomic bomb and war's end was necessarily muted and indirect. Nevertheless, the emperor's Imperial Rescript announcing surrender on August 14, 1945, set the outlines of a Japanese official story. This radio broadcast, the emperor's first direct address to the Japanese people, emphasized the inhumanity of the Americans, the unity of "the entire nation . . . as one family," and the role of the emperor himself as peacemaker, architect of the postwar Japanese state, and purveyor of progress.[6]

The Japanese official story about the bomb complemented the American one in several important ways. It, too, emphasized the awesome power of the bombs and their unparalleled might. It also stated that atomic bombs were an important cause of the surrender. The devastation of Hiroshima and Nagasaki provided an opportunity for the emperor's advisers to solve their most pressing problem: how to save the emperor system and end the war at the same time. The bombings allowed them to begin reshaping the image of the emperor as an advocate of both peace and science, since the surrender was issued in his name. The emperor announced the agreement to end the war, now that "the enemy has begun to employ a new and most cruel bomb, the power of which to do damage is indeed incalculable, taking the toll of many innocent lives."[7] The emperor also used the occasion to exhort his subjects to "work with resolution so as ye may enhance the innate glory of the Imperial state and keep pace with the progress of the world." The bomb and the emperor formed a pair. The elements of the emperor's rehabilitation in postwar Japan—his association with peace, democracy, science, and a residual sense of cosmic awe—all echoed the concurrent American associations with the atomic bomb. The American and the Japanese official stories have collaborated to recast these two agents of destruction as peacemakers ever since 1945.

Japanese officials also paired Hiroshima with Pearl Harbor, but with a slightly different goal than the one Truman had in mind. Rather than using the parallel to justify harsh reprisal, they used it to suggest that Japanese aims in going to war were in no way aggressive. "We declared war on America and Britain out of Our sincere desire to assure Japan's self-preservation and the stabilization of East Asia, it being far from Our thought either to infringe upon the sovereignty of other nations or to embark upon territorial aggrandizement." This would become a major defense argument at the International Military Tribunal for the Far East. Attorneys there argued that Japan had acted in self-defense and the United States had been the aggressor both in its demands that Japan withdraw from China and in its fortification of Pearl Harbor. Near the end of the war, the Japanese leaders were very concerned about protecting themselves and the emperor from indictment as war criminals, as had happened to Kaiser Wilhelm II after the First World War.[8] The Imperial Rescript both argued that Japan had legitimate defensive reasons for going to war and asserted that the emperor had the unique authority to maintain peace and stability in a postsurrender Japan.

The rescript brilliantly anticipated and preempted charges of war crimes by claiming that, because of its greater technological power, the United States had engaged in a larger atrocity than anything Japan could muster. The emperor suggested this when he told the Japanese people that further resistance in the face of the atomic bomb could bring not only the "obliteration of the Japanese nation, but also . . . the total extinction of human civilization." Kiyose Ichiro of the wartime Greater Japan Political Association (and later defense counsel at the Tokyo Tribunal) said as much in the *Asahi Shinbun* on August 14, 1945, on the eve of Japan's surrender. Pondering the fact that so inhuman a bomb had not been used against "white" Germany, he argued that the Americans must have deliberately reserved the atomic bomb for the Japanese, whom, he stated, they regarded as a lower race akin to monkeys. He concluded that vengeful racial prejudice lay behind its use.[9]

Nuclear debate in the United States and Japan over the subsequent half-century would directly or indirectly engage the premises of each nation's official story. Both of these dominant narratives were established early, and both quickly came to define the two national officially sanctioned "etiquettes" of bomb discourse, to use Lane Fenrich's term. In the United States, this etiquette required depersonalizing the victims (the view from the mushroom cloud rather than from the streets of the cities in flames), recalling Americans who died earlier in the war, framing the issues of the decision to bomb in terms almost exclusively of preventing the loss of *American* life, and suppressing inquiry into the relationship between the use of the bombs and subsequent Soviet-American conflict. In Japan, "etiquette" required treating the atomic bombings as uniquely traumatizing events isolated from discussion of Japan's own aggressive colonialism and the war responsibility of the emperor. In other words, American commemorations of the bombings leave out Japanese victims, whereas Japanese ones leave out the victims of Japanese aggression. The Americans falsified the arithmetic of suffering and loss by silencing the voices of *hibakusha* (atomic bomb victims), while the Japanese silence on the larger issues of war preserved the image of a virtuous nation of innocent victims.

Nonetheless, despite the efforts of censors and other guardians of orthodox patriotism, the fabric of these official stories would rip and tear over the years. In both countries, the cold instrumentality of the official story fared badly against a broad humanist vision. Beginning just after the first reports of the bomb's use, a number of American critics—notably scientists, political activists, and religious leaders, but also leading generals and politicians—expressed horror at the slaughter of civilians in Hiroshima and Nagasaki and queried whether, in battling the ruthless Axis powers, Americans had come to resemble them. The broad popular response to John Hersey's evocation of the lives of six Hiroshima residents as early as 1946 showed that such questions and doubts spread far beyond rarefied policy-making circles. In the writings of Hersey, Norman Cousins, Robert Lifton, John Dower, and many others over half a century, the human face of the bomb's victims has been repeatedly invoked against the official U.S. story. Others have questioned the oft-repeated assertion that the atomic bombings were necessary to end the war quickly.[10] The bomb also evoked deep fears of annihilation, strengthened by subsequent nuclear proliferation, the arms race, and Soviet-American and Chinese-American conflict. Indeed, it is precisely this unsettling juxtaposition of celebration and critique that made so intense the American cultural-political battle fought over the heritage of the bomb on the fiftieth anniversary, particularly in the 1995 debate over the eviscerated exhibit on the bombings at the Air and Space Museum of the Smithsonian Institution.[11]

For Japanese, if defeat and occupation were bitter, peace nevertheless held the promise of a better life for a nation in ruins. The atomic bombings marked the end of a conflict that had taken 3 million Japanese lives. Japan's leveled cities—above all, Hiroshima and Nagasaki—symbolized the great sacrifices demanded by the wartime leaders as well as the technological achievements of the democratic foe. Many Japanese drew from the bombings the lesson that their own society needed to change and that postwar Japan had to become democratic, pacifist, technologically adept, and above all, humane.

Japanese writers, artists, and critics have repeatedly used the bomb as a vehicle for questioning not only Japanese colonialism, aggression, and atrocities but also the postwar Japanese political system, including rearmament, within the United States–Japan security relationship. The most sustained and influential such effort has been the succession of mural paintings by the artists Maruki Iri and Maruki Toshi that memorably link the bombing of Hiroshima and Nagasaki to the slaughter by Japanese military forces in the Nanjing massacre and also by the Nazis at Auschwitz.[12] The poet Kurihara Sadako, herself a hibakusha, made the link explicit in a 1974 poem, which began with the question, "When we say 'Hiroshima,' do people answer, gently, 'Ah, Hiroshima'?" She instead heard the chorus from Nanjing, Manila, and other "echoes of blood and fire" and sadly concluded that before she could get the response "Ah, Hiroshima," "we need first to cleanse our own filthy hands."[13] As Ellen Hammond observes, the same tensions over assessing Japanese colonialism and the war reappeared in the 1990s at the heart of the Japanese debate over the construction of a War Dead Peace Memorial Hall.

These Japanese and American controversies show that, rather than diminishing with time, memories of the war and bombings remain extraordinarily vivid and politically divisive at century's end. If anything, tensions both within the United States and Japan and between the two nations have intensified over time. Postwar international experiences—the rise and decline of American hegemony, Japan's political and economic isolation from and later reintegration into Asia, along with its rise as an economic super-power and challenger to the United States—have shaped subsequent discussion of the bomb, as have demands for greater racial, ethnic, and gender equity in both countries.

Remembrance and commemoration of the atomic bomb have been extraordinarily politicized subjects since its use in World War II. The symbolic world of commemoration is by no means a free market of ideas. The creation of official stories always involves processes of suppression of some stories and elevation of others. We characterize that process as the creation of silences. Historical silences take many forms. Outright censorship, insistence on lies, misrepresentation of others, refusal to listen, and defining a single representative national experience while disparaging other experiences as marginal or deviant are all acts of silencing. The act of commemoration may be a claim to a right to speak or to silence others. Some feel compelled to censor themselves. This book is littered with different kinds of historical silences, including state censorship and self-censorship in both Japan and the United States. Monica Braw has documented both the censorship imposed on publishing about the bomb in Japan by the 8,734 staff members of the U.S. occupation's censorship organ and the social stigma that imposed silence on the hibakusha after the occupation ended.[14] George Roeder, building on earlier work on U.S. wartime censorship, shows how visual censorship in both Japan and the United States has denied access to the most powerful images of human suffering inflicted by the war, including the bomb.[15]

Memorials and museum exhibits are important sites of silencing and speaking, as many scholars have observed recently.[16] (So are laws, textbooks, and pronouncements by presidents, prime ministers, and other national leaders.) World War II memorials elevate certain parts of the war story in both countries, particularly victories and the sacrifice of the nation's soldiers, and ignore others, such as the nature and number of military and civilian casualties—including those associated with the atomic bombs. In Japan, rightist vigilantes threaten violence to peace museums that try to speak to Japanese wartime aggression or the responsibility of the emperor, as in an exhibit planned for Nagasaki in 1996.[17] This is the crudest sense in which control over commemoration and remembrance is an act of power. But silencing and suppression also occur in more subtle ways in both countries.

The debate about the bomb ranges from the big issues of war to the enduring problems of peace. When either Americans or Japanese talk about the bombings, they are thinking about the meaning of World War II, of

This view of Nagasaki in ruins was one of the very few images of the atomic aftermath available to Japanese in 1945 and, indeed, throughout the occupation years. It appeared in the *Asahi Shinbun* on August 25, 1945. Such a scene, of city and nature destroyed and Japanese people carrying on, could have been taken in nearly any Japanese city in August 1945. The Japanese press did not publish, in the month before occupation censorship forbade it, images that conveyed the vast toll of human life. Nor did the national newspapers do so after the occupation ended, although regional newspapers and magazines did. (Photograph by Yamahata Yosuke, early morning, August 10, 1945. From Ienaga Saburo and Odagiri Hideo, *Hiroshima Nagasaki Genbaku Shashin-kaiga Shusei* (Hiroshima and Nagasaki: the atomic bombings as seen through photographs and artwork) (Tokyo: Nihon Tosho Senta, 1993) 6 volume set, 1.172. Henceforth Ienaga.

subsequent wars, and of prospective conflicts. They are also posing questions of the relationship of citizens to their own state, the meaning of democratic participation, and the state's prerogatives to make war. In both Japan and the United States, discussion of the bombings has always resonated with visions of the future as well as judgments about the past.

In the end, the official stories are wholly inadequate to capture the lived experience of all the people of either nation or to grasp the ongoing global significance of the dawning nuclear era. The Japanese case has always been more complex, both because of the overlapping authority of American and Japanese government censors during the occupation and also because Japanese politics has long been dominated by American security policy, including its "nuclear umbrella." But many Americans also feel disenfranchised by the bomb orthodoxy. Some, such as Sodei Rinjiro's Japanese-American atomic bomb victims, have difficulty finding a place for themselves within either nation's official story. His title "Were We the Enemy?" highlights their dilemma whether read from the perspective of Japan or the United States. Neither the American government's adamantine defense of the bombings nor the Japanese criticism of them as "contrary to civilization and humanity" can capture what Jay Winter has called "the vigorous and stubbornly visible incompatibilities" of history.[18] This volume explores various forms of commemoration and silencing, as well as conflicts that occurred as Americans and Japanese have grappled with problems of living with the bomb.

The Bomb as Emblem of American Justice and Japanese Innocence

Much of the bomb's specific cultural resonance is with national narratives of the war that define patriotism, power, and honor. In the United States, the most sensitive aspect of the 1995 atomic debate centered on implications that Americans were other than kind, generous, decent, and honorable in all aspects of the war. The conflict over the *Enola Gay* exhibit at the Smithsonian was touched off when critics denounced the exhibit for casting doubts on these premises. The Pacific War, culminating in the atomic bombings, has most often been remembered as a victory for American civilization over Japanese barbarism, unlike the political battle against European fascists. As John Dower has observed, this way of looking at the conflict dates back to wartime propaganda, which highlighted the innate treachery and inhumanity of the Japanese far more than their undemocratic political system or colonial oppression.[19] Portraying Japanese as vicious and even subhuman is subsidiary (but indispensable) to this scenario, which emphasized the virtues of American culture.

American use of the bomb has been associated in official statements since Truman's announcement with reasoned and judicious capital punishment. That image is also preserved to this day in popular attitudes about potential future deployment of atomic weapons. Hugh Gusterson notes that the nuclear scientists at Livermore Laboratories are committed to the idea that anger is dangerous and inappropriate for those who control nuclear weapons. Meanwhile, Gusterson argues, peace protesters challenge the scientists on precisely this point, believing that repression of anger at the production and use of nuclear weapons is far more dangerous. The protesters challenge the claims both to rationality and to justice made for the American nuclear program.

Since 1945, in Japan, the bombs' victims have stood for the wartime suffering of all Japanese. However, this focus is the single point of congruence for several very different Japanese positions on issues of war, peace, and Japan's global role. Although Japanese who were not at Hiroshima or Nagasaki in August 1945 readily see themselves as part of the "imagined community" of victims of the atomic bomb, it is far less common for postwar Japanese to identify either with their forces rampaging across the Asian continent or with the Asian victims of Japanese colonialism. One reason why the simple human tragedy of the bombed emerges so powerfully in Japanese consciousness is that it is among the few aspects of the war on which all Japanese can agree.

Japanese nationalists have focused on the suffering of the bomb's Japanese victims in part to obscure Japan's aggressive war and the predatory character of the empire. In their invocation, the bombings veil Japanese wartime atrocities, including the Nanjing massacre (and many smaller ones throughout China and Asia), the conscription and cruel treatment of military sex slaves ("comfort women"), brutality toward both POWs and civilian conscripted labor in the empire, and the chemical and biological human experiments of Unit 731.[20] The second major elision in the official Japanese story is the repressive nature of prewar society itself. When Japan's leaders evaded inquiry into specific responsibility for war crimes, they did so by displacing blame onto the Japanese people as a whole. They, too, blurred the line between military perpetrators and civilian targets at Hiroshima and Nagasaki, in order to draw attention away from similar distinctions in other battles.

The atomic blasts have never been an easy subject for Japanese nationalists, however. Emphasis on the immense power of atomic weaponry underlines wartime Japan's technical inferiority and thus the stupidity of Japan's leaders in provoking war. Here the contrast with Nazi Germany is fruitful. Where postwar German leaders could simply distance themselves from the Nazi era, the continued political role of the emperor and of many other prewar officials precluded such options for Japanese leaders. At the same time, because Japan was defeated and its wartime military elite and colonial pretensions discredited (with the important exception of the emperor), two powerful and contradictory Japanese narratives of the war and the Japanese wartime state have been sustained since 1945: nationalist celebration and pacifist critique.

Thus, while memories of wartime privation and suffering have served as a basis for nationalist celebration of the unique "Japanese spirit," they also have been the main rallying cry for humanist antinuclear and antimilitary movements. Memories of those bleak years still provide the most powerful imagery for the deep-rooted pacifism that runs through postwar Japanese consciousness and politics. Japan's antinuclear movement has long been linked to international visions of a peaceful future that found powerful resonance and

Residents of Hiroshima and Nagasaki spent the first weeks after the bombings franti-cally searching for family members. This notice, lying in the ruins of a large china shop in Hiroshima, records the fate of one family and the attempts of surviving members to contact others in a city with no telephones, no mail service, and almost no recognizable landmarks. It informs the reader that Tsunoda Hatsugoro is dead. Tsunoda Juichi (38), Tsunoda Denzaburo (30), Tsunoda Fusayo (58), Tsunoda Fumie (27), Tsunoda Midori (21) are all missing. Tsunoda Fusako and Tsunoda Tadashi are at an address in Itsukaichi town. (Photograph by Hayashi Shigeo. No date. Ienaga, 1.36.)

legitimation in the no-war clause (Article 9) of the postwar Constitution.

Official narratives about the bomb as the final act of the war have only imperfectly captured and commemorated visions of wartime American jus-tice and Japanese innocence. Both have been repeatedly disrupted by histor-ical attention to the conduct of the war. Yet divisive as those issues of wartime behavior overseas have been in both countries, issues of democ-racy at home have been even more explosive. The most enduring battles over the bomb in both the United States and Japan have been about citizen-ship and postwar political power.

The Bomb as Enforcer of Postwar Orthodoxies

The insistence on American moral purity in official commemoration of the bombings and the end of the war has had enormous domestic as well as international implications. Every American president from Harry Truman to Bill Clinton has publicly rejected the idea that there could be any moral ambiguity regarding the killing of the civilian populations in the atomic bombing of Hiroshima and Nagasaki, still less an obligation to apologize for that act.[21] This certainty is hard to sustain in light of the devastation and loss of civilian life caused by the two nuclear bombs. Military critics of the Smithsonian exhibit on the fiftieth anniversary of the bomb showed their awareness of that fact when, mindful of the moral weight of a child's charred lunch box set off against the gleaming superfortress bomber, they would accept nothing short of total victory (however Pyrrhic): in the end, the lunch box and other personal artifacts, as well as any doubts about the necessity of dropping the bombs on civilians, were eliminated from the exhibit, and the B–29 *Enola Gay* fuselage was displayed nearly alone and with virtually no explanation of the event. The military critique could not tolerate the presentation of any evidence of the destructive impact of the bomb on city and society. Here again, commemoration required extensive censorship.

The vigilance of the military critics sprang from the fundamental assumption that the war represented two national cultures in conflict.[22] If American culture won the war and safeguards the peace, then criticisms of that culture today—or of the memory of World War II—are not just alarming but directly jeopardize national defense. This assumption lay behind the emotional reaction to the *Enola Gay* exhibit by proponents of orthodox patriotism and the extraordinary level of vitriol hurled at the exhibit designers. Michael Sherry traces those anxieties back to the war itself, locating their social roots in "a lasting interaction between national security and social change" extending to profound shifts in gender and race relations.[23] And as Sherry argues in this volume, this quest for moral purity has both mutated into one for cultural and ideological purity and turned inward to attack other Americans who are perceived as polluters of pristine American life.

The presentation of the bomb in state mythology as a symbol of American moral unity ushered in a world in which many Americans were driven to the margins of citizenship. Those marginalized included racial and religious minorities and gays, a theme to which we return below, as well as political dissenters, Americans whose political ideals were deemed too dangerous to tolerate in the postwar nuclear world. The postwar search for atom bomb spies went public as early as 1948, when the House Un-American Activities Committee charged the scientists at the Berkeley Radiation Laboratory with harboring Soviet spies. But the search for disloyal citizens fanned across the nation, until at least 13.5 million Americans underwent investigation in the course of applying for jobs. One agent working out of Chicago calculated that the only place big enough to put all the local suspects the FBI planned to arrest in a crisis was the football stadium, Soldiers' Field. People were investigated as security risks for inter-racial friendships and homosexuality as well as more overtly political stances, such as a history of support for republican Spain or protest against nuclear testing. [24]

That postwar world was the one created by the bomb, not by the war against fascism. Indeed, in the era of anticommunist witch hunts, adherence to the political ideals of the war era had become grounds for investigation as a subversive. Outspoken commitment to antifascism, anticolonialism, democratic expression, the contributions of a diverse citizenry, and internationalism all became emblems of dissent rather than of a healthy democracy. In that climate, memories of the war against barbaric Japan resonated far better with daily life than did those of the antifascist and anti-imperialist war against Germany and Italy. Moreover, as Yui Daizaburo notes in his essay in this volume, that memory of World War II as a cultural war, rather than a fight between democrats and despots, has been far more appealing to postwar Japanese nationalists as well.

The emphasis on the bomb also dimmed memories of the contributions and sacrifices of America's allies, notably those of the Soviet Union. If the atomic bombs ended the war, then the Soviets contributed nothing to victory in the Pacific. Most Japanese historians argue that the Soviet entry into the Pacific War, together with the atomic bombs, was critical to Japan's surrender. By August 15, the Soviets had routed Japan's Kwantung army in Manchuria. The presentation of the bomb as a superweapon with the capacity to assure total victory without a single U.S. casualty minimizes the extent to which the war was conducted—and its outcome determined—the old-fashioned way, through long, grueling years of conflict that took between 50 million and 80 million lives globally, including 3 million Japanese and 300,000 Americans.[25]

The bomb and the threat of future atomic warfare have been a source of great anxiety or, as Saito Michio has put it, "the ghost that haunts Americans."[26] In contrast to the intensely specific and personal quality of Japanese discussions of the bomb, both celebratory and critical American discussions of Hiroshima and Nagasaki often have been simultaneously anxiety-ridden and oddly vague and abstract. That abstraction went hand in hand with the tradition of ignoring the historical Japanese men and women who actually experienced nuclear warfare, and as Lane Fenrich shows, it stretches back to 1945. Americans often have expressed the effects of the bomb in terms such as "man's inhumanity to man" or have repopulated the landscape of death with imaginary American victims. As Norman Cousins, an early critic of the bombs, put it, the bomb raised "the fear of irrational death ... filling the mind with primordial apprehensions," effectively removing the bomb from historical time altogether.[27] Americans have imagined themselves in the roles of perpetrator and of victim, but typically in ways that erase Japanese suffering, indeed any sense of the actual impact of real bombs that were dropped on living people in a specific historical moment. The chapters by Michael Sherry, Lane Fenrich, George Roeder, Hugh Gusterson, John Dower, and Laura Hein explore diverse expressions of that American imagination.

Japanese have also deployed memories of the bomb to settle postwar political disputes at home. Although the bomb has been a problematic symbol for Japanese defenders of the presurrender system, it also has been hard to control by their critics, even though they often have evoked the suffering of the hibakusha to highlight the tragic consequences of Japanese dreams of conquest. There has always been a tension between those who use the bomb to invoke international disarmament and those who use it to highlight Japan's own war responsibility. The antibomb activists' pacifist vision—because it is addressed to all the participants in World War II, victor and vanquished alike—transcends the issue of responsibility of particular nations, societies, or individuals for the war.[28] Moreover, Japanese critics of their war have also had to negotiate the fact that the atomic bombs may have contributed to Japan's surrender and, if so, liberated the nation not only from war but also from leaders who were prepared to sacrifice many more Japanese lives for a doomed cause.

The difficulties many Japanese experienced in reconciling the experience of the atomic bombings with criticisms of wartime society are epitomized in the personal testimony of Maruyama Masao, one of Japan's most influential voices for a democratic polity. Although Maruyama was in Hiroshima on August 6, 1945, as a young soldier, he did not refer to the bomb in his critique of presurrender Japanese fascism. Although not hiding his status as a hibakusha, he never discussed it publicly until 1969, when he expressed regret at his failure to draw on that experience in his thinking and writing. Maruyama was far more concerned about critiquing the institutional structures of presurrender Japan that had led to the war than about American responsibility for events at war's end.[29]

Both Japanese nationalists and pacifists proclaim their patriotism—that is, they present alternative and quite incompatible visions for serving the best interests of the Japanese people. Jay Winter has described "two essential components of ceremonies commemorating war dead," but in Japan, each side has successfully appropriated only one of them. The government and closely affiliated groups such as the Association of Bereaved Families have supplied "the public recognition, and mediation through ritual, of bereavement" for all the Japanese war dead, thereby implicitly or explicitly endorsing the cause for which they sacrificed, but have offered nothing that linked that sacrifice to the future. The antinuclear and peace movements have far more successfully laid claim to "the appeal to the living to remember the dead by dedicating themselves to good works among their fellow men and women."[30] Their commitment to world peace and disarmament is a powerful means to transform mass death into the warning epitomized in their slogan "No More Hiroshimas." Their rituals of bereavement, however, seem to have offered less satisfaction in Japan, both because they remember the victims of atomic bombs as "first among equals" within the legion of Japanese war dead and because of the terrible factional fighting that has plagued the postwar peace movement.[31]

The government's inability to appropriate Winter's second "essential component" was due in part to its support of the United States–Japan Security Treaty (Anpo) directed against the Soviets and the Chinese. The government has been dominated through most of the postwar era by a political party, the Liberal Democratic Party (LDP), that both defends the postwar security alliance with the United States and houses some of Japan's most ardent nationalists, an uneasy though enduring juxtaposition. In contrast, pacifists and antinuclear activists have opposed the military alliance on internationalist humanist grounds. Thus, Japan's biggest postwar protest was against the 1960 revisions of the Security Treaty, which the LDP rammed through the Diet after most of the opposition members had been carried bodily from the building by police. In other words, antinuclear and antiwar protest in Japan has traditionally combined criticism of Japanese militarism before the surrender, U.S. military policy and Japanese complicity in it after that date, and Japanese democratic procedure at home. The most volatile example of antimilitary action in the mid-1990s is the Okinawan protest against both the presence of U.S. military bases and central Japanese government policy supporting them.[32] The conflict is exacerbated by the long-standing official fiction maintained by both governments that nuclear weapons are neither stored at nor transported through the bases.

Japanese antinuclear activists have moved far in recent years to expand their scope from the victims of Hiroshima and Nagasaki to all the victims of World War II, including non-Japanese, and all subsequent victims of nuclear power, such as those of Chernobyl. The LDP mayors of Hiroshima and Nagasaki have distinguished themselves from the mainstream of their party by calling for reflection on Japanese actions during the war and the subsequent neglect of foreign hibakusha.[33] They are part of an ongoing sea change in Japanese historical memory about World War II in the 1990s. For example, in the 1990s, for the first time, a small number of former military sex slaves dared to speak publicly and to file suit against the Japanese government, which had organized and directed their enslavement. Groups within Japan, as well as support organizations in Korea, Southeast Asia, and elsewhere, including the United Nations, championed their cause.[34] The plight of the comfort women and other colonial subjects also has redirected attention to the callousness of the wartime Japanese state toward its own citizens. This is one reason why demands for redress, pressed vigorously by many groups in the context of the fiftieth anniversary of the end of the war, have revived issues of militarism, war, the empire, and the emperor in such volatile ways. Yui and Hammond are pessimistic about the prospects for change in the near future, citing the lack of support within the government for either apology or restitution to wartime victims. But the scope of the debate over war responsibility at a time of turmoil in Japanese politics in the mid-1990s may be a harbinger of change. Perhaps the hibakusha will soon be able to mourn their own dead, no longer troubled by unacknowledged ghosts all around them.

In recent years, the atomic bomb may also have lost some of its symbolic power to give credence to the official Japanese narrative of wartime and postwar history, unlike the American version. As Korean-Japanese hibakusha and others stake their claims to the story, the subtext of racial unity through suffering has weakened. Moreover, as Japanese such as Nobel laureate Oe Kenzaburo and comic book artist Nakazawa Keiji reframe the atomic horror as part of the greater horror perpetrated by Japan's military leaders on their compatriots and the rest of Asia, the bomb works less and less well as an emblem of a united Japan persecuted by the West. Perhaps this is why, in the 1980s, the government censored from textbooks both graphics depicting the atomic bombings and references to Japanese aggression in Asia. Rather, as Ellen Hammond notes, right-wing nationalists now talk about the war and postwar Allied occupation as one unbroken era, hoping to overlay Japanese memories of wartime coercion by Japanese leaders in the early 1940s with memories of the foreign occupiers later in the decade. Finally, in contemporary Japan, perhaps the most technologically sophisticated place on earth, the narrative of capitulation to overwhelming American technological might no longer compels many Japanese.

Silencing History

Both Americans and Japanese now view the bombings through the filters of fifty years of history. This includes all the postwar interactions between

Japanese and Americans, some of which pertain directly to the bombings themselves. Much of the controversy today over the meaning of those acts is over which aspects of subsequent history are appropriately recognized and which resolutely ignored. As argued above, for Americans, this meant recurring battles over the morality and common sense of American foreign policy.[35] For Japanese, recognition of the nation's wartime depredations in Asia was more controversial. In both countries, the experience of the Vietnam War engendered new levels of criticism, which washed back in time to suffuse perceptions of the bombings. Likewise, in both nations, changes in race and gender relations required citizens of Japan and the United States alike to look back at the 1940s with a new perspective on their own history. Often silenced in the process is any critical recognition of the historical distance between midcentury and century's end in each nation.

One way in which history has been silenced is through the official manipulation of the story of the decision to drop the bombs. We now know that bomb memories have been officially constructed in a remarkably consistent way within each country for fifty years. The research of Monica Braw, Barton Bernstein, and James Hershberg has revealed U.S. officials' preoccupation in the late 1940s with combating negative Japanese and American reactions to the use of atomic bombs. Not only did they suppress unfavorable publicity and maintain a U.S. monopoly on nuclear research, they also deliberately published false information and disinformation as a means to defend the moral legitimacy of the U.S. decision to use the bomb. The calculated inflation of the projected American death toll in a land invasion of Japan is the best-documented, but not the only, example of deception.[36]

It is no coincidence that the final collapse of negotiations over the *Enola Gay* exhibit occurred when the curators were forced to deal with the discrepancy between official casualty projections, published following the surrender, and the far lower unpublished ones that military planners used before the surrender. Critics of the exhibit, fearful that lower U.S. casualty figures would undermine the official case for using the bombs, cried "revisionism" to undermine the authority of those who returned to primary sources to challenge official mythologies. The exposure of the history of the invention of "better" numbers undercuts the credibility of government, making official spokespersons seem deceitful, politically motivated, and deeply cynical in their treatment of Americans as well as other people.

The slowly emerging story of the many times when the U.S. government considered using atomic weapons against other populations, notably during the Korean and Vietnam Wars, is another important example of suppression of information. If nuclear strikes had occurred, the planes would almost certainly have left from American military bases in Japan or Okinawa. Many years after retiring as ambassador to Japan, Edwin Reischauer revealed that it was standard procedure then and since for American nuclear-armed submarines to enter Japanese and Okinawan ports and that the Japanese government was aware of this.[37] His revelation directly contradicted decades of official Japanese government pronouncements.

Censorship does not silence only the powerless, the disorganized, the inarticulate, and the hibakusha. As Michael Sherry and John Dower observe, its victims also include ranking military leaders, such as General George Marshall and Admiral William Leahy, and atomic scientists, such as Leo Szilard and James Franck, who all argued against dropping bombs on civilians.[38] Leahy, for example, subsequently compared the bomb to banned weapons such as poison gas: "It is not a bomb. It is not an explosive. It is a poisonous thing that kills people by its deadly radioactive reaction."[39] His opinion, long available in published form, together with all other traces of doubt and dissent, were banished from the Smithsonian exhibit fifty years later.

Postwar American foreign policy, especially nuclear policy, often has affected Japanese public opinion in powerful ways. The outbreak of the Korean War in 1950 and U.S. testing of the hydrogen bomb at Bikini in 1954 combined to intensify Japanese anxiety about nuclear holocaust. When twenty-three crew members of the *Lucky Dragon* tuna boat were contaminated with radiation from the blast, responses included a petition campaign calling for a ban on nuclear weapons that collected 30 million signatures and the convening in Hiroshima of the 1955 World Conference against Atomic and Hydrogen Bombs. Suddenly, to many Japanese, nuclear destruction seemed a distinct possibility in the future rather than just an event in the past.[40] That heightening of nuclear fears helps explain why hibakusha organizations, which joined in the Japan Confederation of A-Bomb and H-Bomb Sufferers Organization (Hidankyo) in 1957, were able to secure for the first time a Japanese government commitment to pay for their medical treatment.[41] Once again, this peace activity embodied a criticism of Japanese official acceptance of the U.S. Security Treaty as much as of the United States.

The Vietnam War was probably the single most important event in reshaping American attitudes toward World War II and the bomb. That costly conflict undermined American moral certainty and cast doubt on the judgment of American military leaders while eroding American economic and military power and credibility. Then, as in 1945 and 1995, the bomb was invoked to reassert American superiority. In 1976, one year after the United States completed its withdrawal from Vietnam, a group calling itself the

Confederate Air Force, whose ostensible mission was to restore World War II aircraft, attacked Hiroshima in simulations staged throughout the United States. *Enola Gay* pilot Paul Tibbets returned to the controls of a B–29 and taught spectators that "the phoenix of future victory" had risen from the ashes of Pearl Harbor and that the atomic bomb overcame "some of the darkest days of America's history."[42] The re-enactment of the atomic bombing of Hiroshima had far less to do with contemporary American perceptions of Japan than with an attempt to restitch the mantle of patriotism that had been tattered by the long battle in Vietnam.

In other words, the emphasis on the "Good War" in the United States over the last twenty-five years was in part an attempt to erase political disunity about Vietnam from national memory. President George Bush admitted as much in 1990 when he proclaimed that the Persian Gulf War would "not be another Vietnam War," a reference not to the destructiveness of the war but to the speed with which he guaranteed victory.[43] When the pilot of the *Enola Gay* trailed off at the end of his 1995 wish that "If people could see the attitude we had, the great sense of patriotism, the sincerity of our beliefs . . . ," he was acknowledging the cultural distance between his generation and younger people influenced by the Vietnam War and the Watergate scandal.[44]

The Vietnam War has had a powerful effect on Japanese thinking about World War II and the atomic bombings as well. Japan and Okinawa provided major staging areas for the American military with the full cooperation of the Japanese government. The war had little support among the Japanese population, many of whom saw it as an example of both American racism against Asians and Japanese willingness to devastate another Asian nation, albeit this time in a role subordinate to the United States. Sadao Asada shows that American conduct in the Vietnam War disposed many more Japanese to assume that racism was a major factor in the decision to drop the bombs twenty years earlier. One of the most influential Japanese journalists to cover the Vietnam War, Honda Katsuichi, expressed both a sense of pan-Asian identity with the Vietnamese in his criticism of American actions there and a sharp critique of Japanese wartime militarism, when he argued that except for Okinawans, Japanese, even those who lived through the atomic bombings, could not fully understand the experience or the determination of the Vietnamese.[45]

In another kind of example, focused on the subsequent commemoration of the two wars, the Vietnam memorial in Washington, D.C.—and the controversy over building it—inspired the Okinawa memorial, erected in 1995 by the prefectural government. The builders of the Okinawa memorial drew on the example of America's Vietnam memorial but extended the theme of commemoration one step further by listing the names of all combatants who died there on both sides of the struggle.[46] The city of Naha, a cosponsor of the memorial, invited U.S. veterans' groups to put up a plaque but rejected their initial proposal because they thought it glorified the war. [47] The Okinawan commemoration of the war dead explicitly rejected nationalism by expressing reverence for the human carnage of war on *all* sides. It is hard to imagine such a government-sponsored monument either in the United States or anywhere else in Japan. The Okinawan monument both undercuts American and Japanese nationalist commemorations of that battle and stakes out a space for an independent Okinawan consciousness, a position that was strengthened by the protest in 1995 and 1996 against the U.S. military bases following the rape of a twelve-year-old Okinawan girl by three G.I.s. Like the Korean-Japanese, whose monument to Korean hibakusha has provided a rallying point for criticism of Japanese discrimination today, as described by Lisa Yoneyama, the Okinawans offer a critique of contemporary Japanese politics and their marginalized place in society through their analysis of the war and its aftermath.

Critics of Japanese militarism and colonialism also have sometimes drawn inspiration from postwar American re-evaluations of their own wartime practices, particularly over the complex issue of apology and restitution. For example, the Bush administration's apology and financial restitution to Japanese-Americans who had been interned during the war encouraged Koreans and Chinese who had been forced to labor as soldiers, guards, miners, factory workers, or sexual slaves to demand reparations and an apology from the Japanese government for its wartime actions. The official American recognition of its own injustice toward its citizens, and its willingness to provide financial restitution, undercut official Japanese assertions that all the major combatants behaved alike during World War II and have justified their behavior in the same ways ever since.

Nonetheless, the atomic bombs are connected to issues of Japanese and American remorse and apology in complex ways, as the example of redress for Japanese-Americans suggests. The two governments have also used each other's postwar pronouncements about World War II as excuses to avoid dealing with their own level of war responsibility. Yui provides an example of two-way United States–Japan interaction at the policy level in the 1995 proposed resolution to apologize for the war. This stalled in the Diet in part because of official U.S. reiteration of the value of the bombings and refusal to consider any form of apology. In turn, the Diet's failure to pass the resolution stiffened American antagonism toward Japan, rekindling discussion of Pearl Harbor and Bataan.

Norma Field has explored the tension inherent in any apology for barbarous behavior, whether or not accompanied by monetary restitution, through the debate over Japanese state responsibility for and recompense to the wartime comfort women. Because decades have passed since the war, mere words cannot provide adequate recompense for lifelong suffering, humiliation, and sorrow. Yet monetary recompense suggests that misery can be tallied in market terms and paid off as though it were merely a forgotten bill, devaluing the verbal apology. For the comfort women, sexual slaves of the wartime Japanese military, payment risks the added danger of shading their experience into a "normal" prostitution transaction. This tension is heightened by the fact that, for a prosperous Japan, restitution looks suspiciously like a debt of noblesse oblige rather than an act to alleviate guilt.[48] Yet without significant restitution, however belated, such as German government payments to Jewish Holocaust survivors and United States and Canadian government payments to the residents of Japanese ancestry they had interned, the apology has a hollow ring. The passage of time imparts added urgency: soon neither money nor apology will offer solace as the remaining victims die. These issues are likely to remain at the heart of disagreements within as well as between the United States and Japan and between Japan and Asia for a long time.

History has been silenced in other ways as well. In both Japan and the United States, orthodox patriots along with the citizenry generally have become sensitive to criticisms that would not have disturbed their counterparts in 1945. Although most Americans preferred a Jim Crow army and few questioned interning all Japanese-Americans on the West Coast in the 1940s, racial integration of the military subsequently became widely accepted. Critics of the *Enola Gay* exhibit demanded that all references to segregated practices be deleted. They feared that the efforts of (white) American fighting forces would be devalued by attention to those policies. That fear was also revealed in their attacks on earlier re-examinations of Christopher Columbus, the American West, and the wartime internment of Japanese-Americans by other museums under the Smithsonian umbrella. Suppressing discussion of institutionalized racism of the 1940s and earlier is a response to sensibilities that developed slowly over the postwar era, not to attitudes of the war years themselves.

Similarly, in Japan, the existence of the comfort woman was not only common knowledge among millions of Japanese soldiers but was not kept secret from civilians either. The desperate lives of these women did not seem so exceptional to wartime Japanese. After all, the comfort women were only one step more miserable than the Japanese daughters who were indentured to brothels by their impoverished fathers. It is a mark of the changes of the last fifty years in Japan that poorer communities no longer often include at least one family whose daughters are working off their father's debt in a brothel.[49] Immediately after the war, the former sexual slaves were stigmatized in their own countries as well as in Japan. The cruelty of their exploiters was ignored, and the survivors faced decades of contempt, isolation, and poverty. Only after feminists in Japan and Asia reconceptualized these attitudes as oppression of women and criticized contemporary activities such as sex tourism in Asia could the comfort women issue explode into public consciousness in Japan and internationally. This recent shift in acceptable social practice explains why the Japanese government in the 1990s tried to deny the role its officials played in procuring comfort women during the war and refused to pay reparations directly while simultaneously encouraging private groups to raise funds that might be considered unofficial recompense.

Finally, bomb "etiquette" suppresses the emotional distance that many Americans have traveled since August 1945. Paul Fussell has spoken for many veterans in insisting that only those who fought can appreciate the need to drop the bombs and they alone are entitled to assess the validity of the decision. But his argument also silences those veterans who have moved beyond their original reactions to the bomb. David Joravsky and Howard Zinn have each told similar stories of evolving attitudes, beginning with the emotion characterized by Fussell as "Thank God for the atomic bomb." Like Fussell, both Joravsky, on a troop train in France, and Zinn, on furlough between assignments in the European and Pacific theaters, thought of the bomb first as deliverance from danger. But unlike Fussell, both later began to reflect on the ethics of the atomic era. For Joravsky and Zinn, as for many other Americans, veterans and civilians alike, the shock of reading John Hersey's understated portraits of individual hibakusha led them toward a lifetime of sustained inquiry into the issues of morality, patriotism, and the bomb.[50] That chain of thought based on empathy and imagination is the target of many defenders of the bombings, who attempt to break it by rejecting empathy as unscientific, by substituting alternate imaginary scenarios in which bombs fall on America, or by insisting that the Japanese were beyond the pale of human sympathy. The argument that any conduct is justifiable to secure American military victory thus silences all reflection based on the fifty-year experience of living with the bomb.

Silencing Hibakusha

Perhaps the ultimate act of silencing has been and continues to be the silencing of the voices of hibakusha themselves. This occurs in many forms, a few self-imposed, most not. U.S. censorship and disinformation in the early postsurrender years included a concerted effort to minimize information about the human effects of the bomb in Japan, as detailed by Monica Braw in this volume and elsewhere. This included censorship of material that was freely available in the United States. John Hersey's *Hiroshima,* for example, was censored for three years before it could finally be published in translation in occupied Japan. Japanese authorities also censored information about the atomic bombings, probably because such images reflected badly on its ability and commitment to protect the people. And there were also more subtle ways in which the hibakusha experience was suppressed.

Yet the history of silencing includes examples of both enduring suppression and almost quixotic exceptions. Although most photographs of Hiroshima were censored during the occupation, the professional photographer Matsushige Yoshito was only mildly rebuked for 1946 publication of five photographs he had taken on August 6, 1945.[51] Nagai Takashi's memoir *Nagasaki no Kane* (The Bells of Nagasaki) was eventually cleared for 1948 publication when the author accepted the censor's condition that it be published together with material provided by U.S. military intelligence on Japanese atrocities in the Philippines, thereby blatantly equating the U.S. atomic bombing of Japan with Japanese atrocities in Asia.[52]

Not only did the censors occasionally allow publication of descriptions of the war and bombings, but the rules of censorship have sometimes changed precipitously. For example, U.S. government concerns about presenting graphic images of the war dead shifted radically in the fifty years since the war. During the debate over the Air and Space Museum exhibit, orthodox patriots complained that there were more photos of dead Japanese in the plans than there were of dead Americans. The critics charged that the curators were deliberately trying to create an image of the Japanese as passive victims of American aggression. Patriotism, they insisted, required emphasizing Americans' supreme sacrifice, not the loss of Japanese life.

This way of thinking about the presentation of U.S. and Japanese casualties reverses official instructions to the press during World War II. George Roeder notes that no U.S. publication ran pictures of dead American soldiers until military policy changed in September 1943. The military had become concerned that U.S. civilians were becoming complacent about the war effort. After that, images of soldiers killed in battle became more common. Still, scenes of mass carnage were routinely censored when the bodies were American, as were pictures of soldiers who died out of uniform. There was no hesitation about publishing photographs of Japanese war dead unless they showed evidence of Americans' treating the bodies with contempt.[53] In other words, the presentation of more images of Japanese dead than Americans and more dead per image—in scenes of mass death—was coded patriotic in 1944 but unpatriotic in 1994. In both cases, U.S. government policies set the tone.

The wartime Japanese government also carefully controlled information about casualties. Photographs, published descriptions of deaths, and even letters home from the front were censored during the war. Japanese officials restricted depictions of death both in battle and on the home front after U.S. firebombing raids. They also printed no photographs showing the devastation wrought by the atomic bombs in the final nine days of the war. Moreover, although the Japanese press denounced the inhumanity of the "new type" bomb, shortly to be identified as an atomic bomb, there were few photographs of the bombed areas and none that captured the human dimensions of the attack in the one to two months from the surrender until the U.S. censorship was firmly in place. The one newspaper that has pioneered information about atomic destruction is Hiroshima's *Chugoku Shinbun,* which lost 113 of its 300 employees on August 6, 1945. The publishers, who also lost family on that day, have maintained a vigorous antinuclear and pacifist editorial policy ever since.[54]

Nor did the postwar press emphasize the human devastation of the atomic bombs. The first photograph in a national paper revealing the devastation inflicted by the bomb appeared in the *Asahi* on August 19, four days after surrender. This shot panning Hiroshima showed one large factory chimney and a handful of building frames left standing while the city itself was a smoldering ruin, leveled as far as the eye could see. No human being was visible. On August 25, the paper printed two photos by Yamahata Yosuke. The first was of several people, some carrying children, walking through a background of devastation in Nagasaki. A second photograph showed several people in front of a deformed tree with smoke in the background. Neither depicted dead or badly wounded victims of the bomb. In the years following, even after the occupation ended, the press provided only a few other photos of the mushroom cloud, the atomic dome, and the bomb itself.

The first close-up photo of survivors in one of the "big three" newspapers appeared on August 6, 1965, the twentieth anniversary of the bombing, in a section in the *Asahi* captioned "Hiroshima Is Praying." Photographs taken in 1965 showed two women hibakusha and a nurse in prayer, the mayor adding names to the cenotaph, citizens in the Peace Park at 8:15 A.M., and a blind hibakusha playing the violin. The most moving photo showed an elderly couple praying for their lost daughter, her photograph above them on the wall. Whether by government censorship or self-censorship, in the twenty years following the bomb, Japan's leading newspapers published not a single photograph that suggested the nature or magnitude of the injuries, suffering, and deaths that the bombs inflicted on the people of Hiroshima and Nagasaki.[55] This was another kind of silence, one that extended beyond the occupation. Although regional papers and magazines published some records of the hibakusha experience, it was decades before the Japanese people gained access to many of the most powerful visual images of the destructive consequences of the atomic bomb. Atomic bomb literature, much of it censored during the occupation, presented the experience and perspective of the hibakusha in print long before a comparable visual record was released. Film footage shot in 1945 by a Japanese crew was censored by the occupation forces, by the post-occupation U.S. government, by a Japanese film company, and by the Japanese government and was not released until 1968 in the United States and 1970 in Japan.[56] American and Japanese authorities, then, each for different reasons, hid from view the great toll of human lives exacted by the bombs and the physical suffering of the survivors.

The immediate aftermath to the bombings, no less than subsequent memory wars, reflected relations of power locally, nationally, and globally. Such relationships of power profoundly affected the context in which hibakusha could speak of their experiences. Some chose to remain silent. As the three essays on hibakusha gathered here show, many have hidden their experience in the face of prejudice. Some hibakusha refused to permit U.S. scientists to use their personal pain as "data" for political or scientific purposes unrelated to treatment of their wounds. Kurihara Sadako expressed this attitude in vivid language when she compared the scientists of the U.S. Atomic Bomb Casualty Commission to "vultures, [who] carried off the corpses."[57] For survivors like herself, silence was rebuke.

The same issues of power have resulted in important differences in the treatment of hibakusha to this day. Among the most wretched victims at Hiroshima and Nagasaki were tens of thousands of Koreans, many of whom were refused emergency medical treatment or were told to wait until all Japanese were treated first. Those who returned to the Korean Peninsula received no expert medical care, subsidy, or understanding. Lisa Yoneyama shows the ways in which Korean and Korean-Japanese hibakusha, marginalized by the Hiroshima authorities who placed their memorial outside the Peace Park, protested Japanese racism while insisting on maintaining the integrity of a separate memorial.

Similarly, Sodei Rinjiro describes the difficulties that confronted Japanese-Americans—including those who enlisted in the U.S. military, those interned in desert camps, and those who ended up in Hiroshima during the war and became hibakusha—seeking to negotiate between the country of their birth and citizenship and that of their parents. As Sodei explains, American Nisei hibakusha likewise were denied federal assistance for medical aid for decades. Indeed, it was only when their case could be combined with that of other Americans who worked on atomic projects and were callously exposed to radiation by their own government that assistance was forthcoming.[58]

Some silences are expressions of experiences that are simply beyond words. The inability of many survivors to testify verbally to the true horror of the experience, and of others to comprehend it, mirrors the experience of concentration camp survivors and even of American G.I.'s and Japanese soldiers who served in combat, especially in the last and most violent year of the Pacific War.[59]

Other hibakusha have disappeared in every sense of the word. One legacy of the atomic bombings was the staggering number of people who died instantly or disappeared in August 1945. Their absence is a powerful silence, and the personal possessions they left behind—belt buckles, wooden shoes, watches—testify to their echoing absence. Eerily, the intense heat of the atomic bombs etched the shapes of people on stone and wood, leaving no other trace. Yet each shadow leaves behind a story, such as the person who was sitting on the steps of the Sumitomo Bank in Hiroshima, waiting for it to open. Was it someone waiting to take money out to travel, perhaps to see a child who had been evacuated to the countryside? To care for parents whose house had been firebombed in Osaka? There are no clues. But their shadows remain eloquent testimony to those lost lives, precisely because they make us wonder about them as fellow human beings.

It was that moment of human empathy that was blocked when such artifacts and photos were barred from view at the Air and Space Museum in 1995. Nevertheless, the silent testimony of one hibakusha, Yasui Koichi, spoke volumes. He attended the opening day of the Smithsonian exhibit, which had been stripped of all visual reminders of the human targets of Little Boy. Standing in dignified silence in front of a life-sized exhibition photograph of the smiling crew of the *Enola Gay*, he reinserted his perspective and that of a generation of hibakusha into the exhibit.

It is in this context that we must look at the acts of censorship and commemoration that continue to shape our memories of the two bombs that fell in Hiroshima and Nagasaki. If the next fifty years are anything like the last, neither Japanese nor American attempts to ignore or minimize the hibakusha experience are likely to be fully successful. Such efforts have not been able to lay to rest the ghosts that have continued to haunt Americans and Japanese.

The stories of individual hibakusha are too powerful and too complex to be denied. They command attention. Eventually, in photographs, films, autobiographies, documentary accounts, drawings and murals, sculpture, monuments, documentary fiction, children's stories, music, and scholarly

Shadow of human being sitting in front of Sumitomo Bank, Hiroshima. Many people disappeared altogether, leaving only the traces of a human form etched onto some sturdier material. The flash and heat of the bomb were so intense that the top layer of the granite steps of the Sumitomo Bank was scoured away, except in the area where some-one was sitting, perhaps waiting for the bank to open. This image derives much of its power from its fusing of individuality and anonymity. One human life ended on this spot at 8:15 A.M. on August 6, 1945, but we will never know which, out of so many. (1948. Ienaga, 2.17.)

accounts, the hibakusha experiences made their way into public conscious-ness with powerfully disruptive effects in the United States and, in different ways, in Japan. The American wish to sustain an image of the bomb as the savior of American and even of Japanese lives faces its most formidable challenge in the pictorial and verbal images of the hibakusha.

These silences have been broken over and over again. Simple things, such as a pocket watch stopped at 8:15 or the story of one person, whose

AUGUST 6, 1945

This life-sized wall poster of the crew of the *Enola Gay*, mounted at the National Air and Space Museum's atomic bomb exhibition, captures the official American presentation of the bombings. Frozen in time, the crew appears young, happy, and relaxed. On the opening day, hibakusha Yasui Koichi restored some of the elements that had been eliminated from the *Enola Gay* exhibition. By standing next to the poster, he reintroduced the hibakusha's perspective on both the bombing of Hiroshima and the passage of fifty years since then. (Photographer Ed Hedemann, June 28, 1995. Used by permission.)

family—described and named—was destroyed in an instant, disrupt the official stories. In their humanity and their pain, they reach beyond narratives of necessity and high politics. Each story is so personal, even though the general outlines of mass death are chillingly familiar. Each is such a private hell within the general one: a story of a child who disappeared without a trace; another of a brother who seemed fine for a while, only to die later; another whose loved ones lingered in agony for months; others who wished they too had died. The stories—of pain, of tragedy but also of small kindnesses by strangers, and most of all, of the irrationality in one person's survival when so many nearby did not survive—are both deeply personal and oddly uniform. These stories—in their evocation of pain, fear, and loss—bring the listener back, not to the moments when the bombs left the plane or even when they exploded above the doomed cities, but to the long years since then, years spent in private mourning and ill health, stretching into five decades of living with the bomb.

Notes

1. On these themes, see *Enola Gay: The First Atomic Mission,* video produced in 1995 by Jonathan S. Felt as part of the final *Enola Gay* exhibit at the Smithsonian Institution.

2. For more than fifty years, atomic casualty figures have been no less contested than those of the Holocaust and the Nanjing massacre. The most comprehensive and reliable discussion of various casualty estimates remains that provided in the Committee for the Compilation of Materials on Damage Caused in the Atomic Bombs in Hiroshima and Nagasaki, *The Physical, Medical and Social Effects of the Atomic Bombs* (New York: Basic Books, 1981), 335–92. The committee concluded that total deaths attributable to the bombings were in the range of 140,000 in Hiroshima and 70,000 in Nagasaki, the great majority of which occurred within months of the explosions. For a recent discussion of Japanese government fatality statistics, see John Dower, "Three Narratives of Our Humanity," in *History Wars: The Enola Gay Controversy and Other Battles for the American Past,* Edward Linenthal and Thomas Engelhardt, eds. (New York: Metropolitan Books, 1996).

3. The fullest discussion of the Truman statement is Robert Lifton and Greg Mitchell, *Hiroshima in America: Fifty Years of Denial* (New York: Putnam, 1995), 8–22.

4. Michael Sherry, *The Rise of American Air Power: The Creation of Armageddon* (New Haven, CT: Yale University Press, 1977); Mark Selden, "The 'Good War': Air Power and the Logic of Mass Destruction," *Contention: Debates in Society, Culture, and Science* 13 (fall 1995): 113–32.

5. Henry Stimson, "The Decision to Use the Atomic Bomb," *Harper's* (February 1947): 97–107. Barton Bernstein's meticulous research revealed that Pentagon planners estimated forty-six thousand U.S. deaths in the event of a November landing in Kyushu and a subsequent landing in Tokyo. Barton Bernstein, "Seizing the Contested Terrain of Nuclear History," *Diplomatic History* 17, no. 1 (winter 1993): 35–72.

6. The announcement was on August 15 in Japan but August 14 across the dateline in the United States. The official English translation of the Imperial Rescript ending the war is reprinted in Edwin P. Hoyt, *Japan's War: The Great Pacific Conflict, 1863–1952* (New York: McGraw-Hill, 1986), 437–38.

7. For the transformation of the emperor at the end of the war, see Herbert Bix, "The Showa Emperor's 'Monologue' and the Problem of War Responsibility," *Journal of Japanese Studies* 18 (summer 1992): 295–363; and Bix, "Japan's Delayed Surrender: A Reinterpretation," *Diplomatic History* 19, no. 2 (spring 1995): 197–226.

8. The Japanese leaders knew by June 1945 that the United States had amassed evidence in order to put them on trial for war crimes. Philip R. Piccigallo, *The Japanese on Trial: Allied War Crimes Operations in the East, 1945–1951* (Austin: University of Texas Press, 1979), 4, 22.

9. Odagiri Hideo, ed., *Shinbun Shiryo: Genbaku* (Newspaper Materials: The Atomic Bomb), vol. 1 (Tokyo: Nihon Tosho Senta, 1987), 13. This two-volume work reproduces the reportage on the bomb from Japan's leading newspapers over two decades.

10. For a recent review of this literature, see J. Samuel Walker, "History, Collective Memory, and the Decision to Use the Bomb," *Diplomatic History* 19, no. 2 (spring 1995): 319–28.

11. Many people have treated this battle over the commemoration of the bomb and the end of World War II in more detail than we do here. See Laura Hein, ed., "Remembering the Bomb: The Fiftieth Anniversary in the United States and Japan," special issue, *Bulletin of Concerned Asian Scholars* 27, no. 2 (April–June 1995); Mike Wallace, "The Battle of the *Enola Gay*," *Radical Historians Newsletter* 72 (May 1995), 1–32; and Edward Linenthal and Thomas Engelhardt, eds., *History Wars: The Enola Gay Controversy and Other Battles for the American Past*. See also the essays collected in *Journal of American History* 82, no. 3 (December 1995), special issue; and the ones in *Diplomatic History* 19, no. 2 (spring 1995), and revised and reprinted in Michael Hogan, ed., *Hiroshima in History and Memory* (Cambridge, United Kingdom: Cambridge University Press, 1996).

12. John Dower and John Junkerman, eds., *The Hiroshima Murals: The Art of Iri Maruki and Toshi Maruki* (New York: Kodansha International, 1985).

13. Translated by Richard Minear, *Bulletin of Concerned Asian Scholars* 23, no. 1 (January–March 1991): 26. A selection of Japanese literary and graphic responses to the bomb is presented in Kyoko Selden and Mark Selden, eds. and trans., *The Atomic Bomb: Voices from Hiroshima and Nagasaki* (Armonk, NY: M.E. Sharpe, 1989); and in Richard Minear, ed. and trans., *Hiroshima: Three Witnesses* (Princeton, NJ: Princeton University Press, 1990). For American poets addressing the bomb and nuclear war, see John Bradley, ed., *Atomic Ghost: Poets Respond to the Nuclear Age* (Minneapolis: Coffee House Press, 1995).

14. Monica Braw, *The Atomic Bomb Suppressed* (Armonk, NY: M.E. Sharpe, 1991); cf. Lifton and Mitchell, *Hiroshima in America*.

15. George Roeder, *The Censored War: American Visual Experience during World War Two* (New Haven, CT: Yale University Press, 1993).

16. See James E. Young, *The Texture of Memory: Holocaust Memorials and Meaning* (New Haven, CT: Yale University Press, 1993); and Edward T. Linenthal, *Preserving Memory: The Struggle to Create America's Holocaust Museum* (New York: Viking, 1995).

17. Cf. "Nagasaki Museum Exhibits Anger Japanese Extremists," *Vancouver Sun*, March 26, 1996, A16; and Nicholas D. Kristof, "Today's History Lesson: What Rape of Nanjing?" *New York Times*, July 4, 1996, A6.

18. Jay Winter, *Sites of Memory, Sites of Mourning* (Cambridge, United Kingdom: Cambridge University Press, 1995), 5

19. John Dower, *War Without Mercy: Race and Power in the Pacific War* (New York: Pantheon, 1986).

20. Yuki Tanaka, *Hidden Horrors: Japanese War Crimes in World War II* (Boulder, CO: Westview, 1996).

21. For suggestions that Truman was privately troubled by the morality of the use of the atomic bombs against civilians, see the chapters by Asada Sadao and John Dower in this volume.

22. An analysis of this theme of cultures in conflict is developed more fully in Laura Hein, "Free-Floating Anxieties on the Pacific," *Diplomatic History* 20, no. 3 (summer 1996): 111–37.

23. Michael Sherry, *In the Shadow of War: The United States since the 1930s* (New Haven, CT: Yale University Press, 1995), esp. 101–12.

24. Between six thousand and nine thousand government employees were fired under the loyalty programs of the Harry Truman and Dwight Eisenhower administrations, and at least eight thousand more were forced to resign. Griffin Fariello, *Red Scare: Memories of the American Inquisition: An Oral History* (New York: Norton, 1995), 42, 96, 131, 176, 508–9.

25. For the role of the Soviets, see Alvin D. Coox, "The Pacific War," *The Cam-*

bridge History of Japan, vol. 6 (Cambridge, United Kingdom: Cambridge University Press, 1988), 375. For a comprehensive discussion of casualty estimates, see Dower, War without Mercy, 294–300.

26. Saito Michio, "Yomigaeru borei Enora Gei: Sumisonian tenshi ronso" ("Reviving the Dead Spirit of the Enola Gay: The Controvesy over the Smithsonian Exhibit"), Chuo Koron, January 1995, 44–55. Also see Paul Boyer, By the Bomb's Early Light: American Thought and Culture at the Dawn of the Atomic Age (New York: Pantheon, 1985).

27. Quoted in Boyer, By the Bomb's Early Light, 8.

28. Although sharp debate has centered on the war responsibility of the emperor, the military, and the state apparatus, there has been little significant Japanese debate over the question of broad social responsibility of the people comparable to debate in Germany. Yuki Tanaka raises the sensitive issue of social responsibility for Japan in Hidden Horrors. See also the chapter by Ellen H. Hammond in this volume.

29. Chugoku Shinbun, August 5 and 6, 1969, quoted in Rikki Kersten, Democracy in Postwar Japan: Maruyama Masao and the Search for Autonomy (London: Routledge, 1996), 283.

30. Winter, Sites of Memory, Sites of Mourning, 97.

31. For a critical commentary on the factional fighting, see Oe Kenzaburo, Hiroshima Notes, esp. chapters 1 and 2, trans. David L. Swain and Toshi Yonezawa (New York: Marion Boyars, 1981, 1995).

32. For a history of the Okinawa conflict, see Norma Field, In the Realm of a Dying Emperor: Japan at Century's End (New York: Vintage, 1993).

33. Seiitsu Tachibana, "The Quest for a Peace Culture," Diplomatic History 19, no. 2 (spring 1995): 329–46.

34. George Hicks, The Comfort Women: Sex Slaves of the Japanese Imperial Forces (Singapore: Heinemann, 1995), xv–xix, estimates the number of comfort women at more than 100,000. See also Yuki Tanaka, Hidden Horrors, 79–100; Watanabe Kazuko, "Militarism, Colonialism, and the Trafficking of Women: 'Comfort Women' Forced into Sexual Labor for Japanese Soldiers," Bulletin of Concerned Asian Scholars 26, no. 4 (October–December 1994): 3–17; and Yamazaki Hiromi, "Military Slavery and the Women's Movement," in Voices from the Japanese Women's Movement, AMPO–Japan Asia Quarterly Review ed. (Armonk, NY: M.E. Sharpe, 1996), 90–100.

35. Interestingly, whereas Japanese debates quickly moved from the bomb to the nature of Japan's wartime practices and on to the nature of Japanese colonialism, the American debate never engaged either the issue of U.S. colonial rule in the Philippines or the nature of the United States–China relationship.

36. Bernstein, "Seizing the Contested Terrain of Nuclear History"; Braw, Atomic Bomb Suppressed; James Hershberg, James B. Conant: Harvard to Hiroshima and the Making of the Nuclear Age (New York: Knopf, 1993).

37. Edwin Reischauer, My Life between Japan and America (New York: Harper and Row, 1986), 249–50.

38. See Michael Bess, Realism, Utopia, and the Mushroom Cloud: Four Activist Intellectuals and Their Strategies for Peace, 1945–1989: Louise Weiss (France), Leo Szilard (USA), E.P. Thompson (England), Danilo Doki (Italy) (Chicago: University of Chicago Press, 1993).

39. William Leahy, I Was There (New York: Whittlesey House, 1950), 441.

40. Americans were also worrying about nuclear war in the 1950s, as manifested in civil defense programs in all major cities. President Dwight Eisenhower provided a vivid example of the way that nuclear preoccupations spilled over into the civilian realm when he launched the U.S. interstate highway program in 1956 in part to prepare national

evacuation routes in the event of nuclear attack. "Weekend Edition," National Public Radio, June 29, 1996.

41. Seiitsu Tachibana, "Quest for a Peace Culture," 174–76. Lawrence Wittner, *One World or None: A History of the World Nuclear Disarmament Movement through 1953* (Stanford, CA: Stanford University Press, 1993), 46–48.

42. Edward Linenthal, *Sacred Ground: Americans and Their Battlefields* (Urbana: University of Illinois Press, 1991), 185–86. For Tibbets's emotional entry in the debate over the 1995 exhibit, see the chapter by Michael S. Sherry in this volume.

43. Quoted in Sherry, *In the Shadow of War,* 468.

44. See *Enola Gay: The First Atomic Mission,* exhibit video, final comment.

45. Honda Katsuichi, *Vietnam War: A Report through Asian Eyes* (Tokyo: Miraisha, 1972), 472.

46. In a sharp break with most earlier U.S. memorials, of which the Iwo Jima memorial is emblematic, Maya Lin's Vietnam memorial focused exclusively on the personal sacrifice of those Americans who died in battle, listing each of their names and eschewing any heroic or patriotic statement about the war and American involvement in it.

47. *Japan Times Weekly,* July 3–9, 1995, 1.

48. Norma Field, "War and Apology: Japan, Asia, and the Fiftieth," manuscript.

49. Kinbara Samon and Takemae Eiji, eds., *Showashi: Kokumin no naka no haran to gekido no hanseiki* (Showa history: The tumultuous and extreme half-century among the Japanese) (Tokyo: Yuhikaku, 1982), 40.

50. Howard Zinn, *You Can't Be Neutral on a Moving Train* (Boston: Beacon Press, 1994), 95–102. David Joravsky, comments at conference on the atomic bomb, Northwestern University, May 6, 1995; Joravsky, "Scientists as Servants," *New York Review of Books,* June 28, 1979, 34–41; and Joravsky, "Sin and the Scientist," *New York Review of Books,* July 17, 1980, 7–10. Cf. Paul Fussell, *Thank God for the Atomic Bomb and Other Essays* (New York: Summit Books, 1988).

51. See Haruko Cook and Theodore Cook, *Japan at War: An Oral History* (New York: New Press, 1992), 391–94.

52. Tachibana, "Quest for a Peace Culture," 174.

53. Roeder, *Censored War,* 1, 14, 18–19.

54. *Look Japan,* December 1995, 34–35.

55. Odagiri, ed., *Shinbun Shiryo,* 17–18, 105–7.

56. Erik Barnouw, *Media Marathon: A Twentieth-Century Memoir* (Durham, NC: Duke University Press, 1996), chapter on Iwasaki Akira.

57. See "America, Land of Mercy," *Bulletin of Concerned Asian Scholars* 27, no. 2 (April–June 1995): 35–36.

58. Carole Gallagher, *American Ground Zero: The Secret Nuclear War* (Cambridge, MA: M.I.T. Press, 1993). Japan has its own history of irradiating unsuspecting workers. Yuki Tanaka, "Nuclear Power Plant Gypsies in High-Tech Society," *Bulletin of Concerned Asian Scholars* 18, no. 1 (January–March 1986): 2–22.

59. For U.S. combat veterans, see Sherry, *In the Shadow of War,* 96–97. For one exploration of the tension between silence and expression of Holocaust testimony mediated through a son's memory, see Art Spiegelman, *Maus: A Survivor's Tale* (New York: Pantheon, 1973).

II

Commemoration and Censorship

2

Triumphal and Tragic Narratives
of the War in Asia

John W. Dower

Fiftieth anniversaries are unlike other commemorative occasions, especially when they are anniversaries of war. Participants in the events of a half century ago are still alive to tell their emotional personal tales. Their oral histories confront the skepticism and detachment of younger generations who have no memories of the war. Historians with access to materials that were previously inaccessible (or simply ignored) develop new perspectives on the dynamics and significance of what took place. Politicians milk the still palpable human connection between past and present for every possible drop of ideological elixir. History, memory, scholarship, and politics become entangled in intricate ways.[1]

All this is predictably apparent in this fiftieth anniversary of the conclusion of World War II in Asia. Where the end of the war against Japan is concerned, however, the contemporary commemorations have become unusually contentious, especially in the United States. Why such controversy now, when for all ostensible purposes we are commemorating the Allied victory over an aggressive, atrocious, and fanatical enemy?

The answer, of course, lies in the atomic bombs and the fact that victory over Japan entailed incinerating and irradiating men, women, and children with a weapon more terrible than any previously known or imagined. Triumph and tragedy became inseparable. At the same time, in the fires of Hiroshima and Nagasaki the so-called total victory of the United States became fused with a future of inescapable insecurity. The bombs marked both an end and a beginning—the end of an appalling global conflagration in which more than 50 million people were killed and the beginning of the nuclear arms race and a new world in which security was forever a step away and enormous resources had to be diverted to military pursuits.

It is a measure of the impoverishment of our present-day political climate in the United States that Americans have been denied a rare opportunity to use the fiftieth anniversary of Hiroshima and Nagasaki to reflect more deeply about these developments that changed our world forever. That opportunity was lost early in 1995 when the Smithsonian Institution, bowing to political pressure (including unanimous condemnation by the United States Senate), agreed to scale back drastically a proposed major exhibition on the atomic bombs and the end of the war against Japan in its Air and Space Museum in Washington.

The exhibition initially envisioned by the Smithsonian's curators would have taken viewers through a succession of rooms that introduced, in turn, the ferocity of the last year of the war in Asia, the Manhattan Project and the unfolding imperatives behind the United States decision to use the bombs against Japan, the training and preparation of the *Enola Gay* mission that dropped the first bomb on Hiroshima (with the fuselage of the *Enola Gay* as the centerpiece of the exhibition), the human consequences of the bombs in the two target cities, and the nuclear legacy to the postwar world. The draft script included occasional placards that concisely summarized the "historical controversies" that have emerged in scholarship and public discourse.

This ambitious proposal proved to be politically unacceptable. The Senate denounced the draft script as being "revisionist and offensive to many World War II veterans." Critics accused curators responsible for the draft of being "politically correct" leftists and rarely hesitated to brand as "anti-American" anyone who questioned the use of the bombs.[2] Confronted by such criticism, and by a conservative Congress threatening to cut off federal funding to "liberal" projects in general, the Smithsonian—like Japan fifty years earlier—surrendered unconditionally. Visitors to the Air and Space Museum eventually were offered only a minimalist exhibition featuring the refurbished fuselage of the *Enola Gay* and a brief tape and text explaining that this was the plane that dropped the first atomic bomb, following which, nine days later, Japan surrendered. The artifact, supporters of this bare presentation declare, speaks for itself.

Artifacts do not in fact speak for themselves. Essentially, the United States government has chosen to commemorate the end of World War II in Asia by affirming that only one orthodox view is politically permissible. This orthodoxy amounts to a "heroic" narrative, and its contours are simple: The war in Asia was a brutal struggle against a fanatic, expansionist foe (which is true, albeit cavalier about European and American colonial and

The *Enola Gay*. Many sought to put this huge bomber, meticulously restored, at the center of American official memory of the war's end in the 1990s. This shifted the focus from the bomb itself to another aspect of American technological might, the attack bomber that delivered it. National Archives, 306-NT–6521v.

neocolonial control in Asia up to 1941). That righteous war against Japanese aggression was ended by the dropping of the atomic bombs, which saved the enormous numbers of American lives that would have been sacrificed in invading Japan. As the Senate's condemnation of the Smithsonian's plans put it, the atomic bombs brought the war to a "merciful" end.

Other euphemisms convey essentially the same simple story line. The heroic or triumphal narrative coincides with the identification of World War II as the last "good war"—a perception reified in American consciousness by the horribly destructive and inconclusive subsequent conflicts in Korea and Indochina. As captured in the title of a well-known essay by the writer and World War II veteran Paul Fussell, who had been slated to participate in the invasion of Japan as a young soldier, the heroic version of the war's end in Asia also finds common expression as the "thank God for the atom bomb" narrative—a memorable incantation that simultaneously places God on the American side and reminds us *pari passu* that the Japanese are pagans.[3] The triumphal American narrative offers an entirely understandable view of World War II—emphasizing the enormity of German and Japanese behavior, eulogizing American "valor and sacrificial service" (in the words of the Senate resolution), and applauding the bombs for forcing Japan's surrender and saving American lives.

But what does this heroic narrative leave out? What are the "historical controversies" the Smithsonian's curators thought worth making known to the public? What might we have learned from a truly serious commemorative engagement with the end of the war in Asia?

There are many answers. To begin, the argument that the bombs were used simply to end the war quickly and thereby save untold lives neglects complicating facts, converging motives and imperatives, and possible alternative policies for ending the war. Such considerations can do more than deepen our retrospective understanding of the decision to use the bombs. They also can help us better appreciate the complexities of crisis policy making in general.

If, moreover, we are willing to look beyond the usual end point in the conventional heroic narrative—beyond (or beneath) the sparkling *Enola Gay* and the almost abstract mushroom cloud—we can encounter the human face of World War II. Humanizing the civilians killed and injured by the bombs, and, indeed, humanizing the Japanese enemy generally, is difficult and distasteful for most Americans. If this is done honestly in the context of Hiroshima and Nagasaki, it becomes apparent that we confront something more than the human consequences of nuclear war. We are forced to ask painful questions about the morality of modern war itself—specifically, the transformation of moral consciousness that, well before the atomic bombs were dropped, had led *all* combatants to identify civilian men, women, and children as a legitimate target of "total war."

To engage the war at this level is to enter the realm of tragic, rather than triumphal, narratives. As the Smithsonian controversy revealed, however, even after the passage of a half century there is little tolerance for such reflection in the United States, and now virtually none at all at the level of public institutions. We have engaged in self-censorship and are the poorer for it.

Critics of the Air and Space Museum's early scripts emphasized what was missing in them—most notably, a vivid sense of the fanaticism, ferocity, and atrocious war conduct of the Japanese enemy. This was a fair criticism. Using the same criteria, it is also fair to ask what the heroic American narrative of the end of the war neglects.

At the simplest level, the popular triumphal narrative tends to neglect

events and developments that are deemed important in the scholarly literature on the bombs.[4] The entry of the Soviet Union into the war against
Japan on August 8, two days after the bombing of Hiroshima, for example,
tends to be downplayed or entirely ignored—and with it the fact that the
American leadership had solicited the Soviet entry from an early date, knew
it was imminent, and knew the Japanese were terrified by the prospect.[5]
Why the haste to drop the bombs before the effect of the Soviet entry could
be gauged?

The nuclear devastation of Nagasaki on August 9 is similarly marginalized in the orthodox narrative. What are we to make of this second bomb?
Why was it dropped before Japan's high command had a chance to assess
Hiroshima and the Soviet entry? How should we respond to the position
taken by some Japanese—namely, that the bombing of Hiroshima may have
been necessary to crack the no-surrender policy of the militarists, but the
bombing of Nagasaki was plainly and simply a war crime?[6]

The heroic narrative also generally obscures the United States military's
timetables as the terrible end game was played out. Of course, American
leaders desired to end the war as quickly as possible and to avoid the huge
casualties invading Japan would entail. Contrary to the impression conveyed by the "thank God for the atom bomb" narrative, however, no invasion was imminent in August 1945, or in September or October. The initial
assault on the main Japanese islands, aimed at Kyushu in the south, was
scheduled for November 1, and it was anticipated that the major attack on
Tokyo and the Kanto area in the main island of Honshu would not take
place until March 1946. This does not negate the argument that United
States leaders were duty-bound to end the war as quickly as possible, but it
does cast the issue of anticipated casualties in clearer perspective.

Shortly after the end of the war, United States intelligence experts themselves publicly concluded that Japan was already at the end of its tether
when the bombs were dropped. A famous report by the United States Strategic Bombing Survey, issued in 1946, concluded that the material and
psychological situation was such that Japan "certainly" would have been
forced to capitulate by the end of 1945, and "in all probability" prior to
November 1, "even if the atomic bombs had not been dropped, even if
Russia had not entered the war, and even if no invasion had been planned or
contemplated." This was an ex post facto observation, of course, but it
raised (and still raises) pertinent questions about the nature and shortcom-
ings of wartime Allied intelligence evaluations of the enemy.[7]

It also became known after Japan's surrender that alternatives to using
the bombs on civilian targets had been broached in American official cir-

cles. Navy planners believed that Japan could be brought to its knees by intensified economic strangulation (the country's merchant marine and most of its navy had been sunk by 1945). Within the Manhattan Project, the possibility of dropping the bomb on a noncombat "demonstration" target, with Japanese observers present, had been broached but rejected. Conservative officials such as the Acting Secretary of State Joseph Grew, the former ambassador to Japan, argued that the Japanese could be persuaded to surrender if the United States abandoned its policy of "unconditional surrender" and guaranteed the future existence of the emperor system. Through their code-breaking operations, the Americans also were aware that, beginning in mid-June, the Japanese had made extremely vague overtures to the Soviet Union concerning negotiating an end to the war.[8]

These developments complicate the simple story line of the heroic narrative. Greater complication, however, arises from the fact that declassification of the archival record has made historians aware of how many different considerations officials in Washington had in mind when they formulated nuclear policy in the summer of 1945. No one denies that these policy makers desired to hasten the war's end and to save American lives, but no serious historian regards those as the sole considerations driving the use of the bombs on Japanese cities.

Although the initial Anglo-American commitment to build nuclear weapons was motivated by fear that Nazi Germany might be engaged in such a project, it is now known that by 1943—long before it became clear that the Germans were not attempting to make an atomic bomb, before Germany's collapse was imminent, before the Manhattan Project was sure of success, and before the lethal Allied military advance on Japan was clearly underway—United States planners had identified Japan as the prime target for such a weapon. Pragmatic considerations may have accounted for this shift of targets, but the change was nonetheless a profound one. The original rationale for moving to an entirely new order of destructive weaponry had evaporated, and the weaponry itself had begun to create its own rationale.[9]

Sheer visceral hatred abetted this early targeting of Japan for nuclear destruction. Although critics of the Smithsonian's original script took umbrage at a passing statement that called attention to the element of vengeance in the American haste to use the bombs, few historians (or honest participants) would discount this. "Remember Pearl Harbor—Keep 'em Dying" was a popular military slogan from the outset of the war, and among commentators and war correspondents at the time, it was a commonplace that the Japanese were vastly more despised than the Germans. As we know all too well from our vantage place fifty years later, race and ethnicity are hardly negligible factors in the killing game.[10]

Apart from plain military and sociopsychological dynamics, the development and deployment of the bombs also became driven by almost irresistible technological and scientific imperatives. J. Robert Oppenheimer, the charismatic head of the Manhattan Project, confided that after Germany's surrender on May 8, 1945, he and his scientific colleagues intensified their efforts out of concern that the war might end before they could finish—a striking confession, but not atypical. Almost to a man, scientists who had joined the project because of their alarm that Germany might develop a nuclear weapon stayed with it after Germany was out of the war. In the evocative phrase of the scientific community, the project was "technically sweet."[11]

Other political imperatives largely extraneous to the war against Japan also helped drive the decision to use the bombs. Documents declassified since the 1960s make unmistakably clear that from the spring of 1945, top-level United States policy makers saw the bomb as a valuable card to play against Joseph Stalin and the Soviet Union—one that would, they hoped, dissuade the Soviet Union from pursuing its ambitions in Eastern Europe and elsewhere. At the same time, shrewd readers of the domestic political winds warned that if the Manhattan Project ended with nothing dramatic to show for its efforts, the postwar Congress surely would launch a hostile investigation into the huge expenditure of secret funds for it. Some policy makers also effectively argued that the new weapon was so awesome that its horrendous destructiveness had to be demonstrated against real cities with real people in them, so that the postwar world would understand the need to cooperate on arms control.[12] From this perspective, the nuclear destruction of Hiroshima and Nagasaki might be seen as the concrete opening demonstration of postwar deterrence theory.

In Japan, as might be expected, popular memory of the atomic bombs tends to begin where the American narrative leaves off. In the heroic narrative, one rides with the crew of the *Enola Gay,* cuts away from the scene the moment the Little Boy bomb is released, gazes back from a great distance (over eleven miles) at a towering, iridescent mushroom cloud.[13] If by chance one does glance beneath the cloud, it is the bomb's awesome physical destructiveness that usually is emphasized. Rubble everywhere. A silent, shattered cityscape. In this regard, the heroic narrative differs little from a Hollywood script.

By contrast, conventional Japanese accounts begin with the solitary bomber and its two escort planes in the azure sky above Hiroshima, with the blinding flash (*pika*) and the tremendous blast (*don*) of the nuclear explosion, with the great pillar of smoke—and then move directly to ground zero. They dwell with excruciating detail on the great and macabre human suffering the new weapon caused, which continues to the present day for some survivors.

This Japanese perception of the significance of Hiroshima and Nagasaki can become maudlin and nationalistic. The nuclear destruction of the two cities is easily turned into a "victimization" narrative, in which the bombs fall from the heavens without historical context—as if the war began on August 6, 1945, and innocent Japan bore the cross of bearing witness to the horrendous birth of the nuclear age. In this subjective narrative, the bombs become the symbolic stigmata of unique Japanese suffering.

It is virtually a mantra in the United States media that what the Japanese really suffer from is historical amnesia. They cannot honestly confront their World War II past, it is said, and there are indeed numerous concrete illustrations of this beyond fixation on the misery caused by the atomic bombs. These range from sanitized textbooks to virtually routinized public denials of Japanese aggression and atrocity by conservative politicians (usually associated with the Liberal Democratic Party, the United States government's longtime protégé) to the government's failure, until very recently, to offer an unequivocal apology to Asian and Allied victims of imperial Japan's wartime conduct.[14]

In actuality, however, popular Japanese discourse concerning both war responsibility and the experience of the atomic bomb is more diversified than usually is appreciated outside Japan. Since the early 1970s, when Japan belatedly established relations with the People's Republic of China, the Japanese media have devoted conspicuous attention not only to exposing Japanese war crimes in Asia but also to wrestling with the complex idea that victims (*higaisha*) can simultaneously be victimizers (*kagaisha*).[15]

This Japanese sense of contradictory identity is not to be confused with the more simplistic notion of righteous retribution that critics of Japan commonly endorse—the notion that the Japanese reaped what they sowed; that having tried to flourish the sword, they deservedly perished by it. Rather, it is a more complex perception that innocence, guilt, and responsibility may coexist at both individual and collective levels. A well-known series, *Atomic Bomb Panels* (*Genbaku no Zu*), painted collaboratively by the married artists Maruki Iri and Maruki Toshi, provides a concrete illustration. After producing twelve stunning large renderings of Japanese nuclear bomb victims between 1950 and 1969, the Marukis took as their next subject the torture and murder of Caucasian prisoners of war by enraged survivors of the destruction of Hiroshima. They followed this with a stark painting depicting the piled-up corpses of Korean atomic bomb victims, being pecked at by ravens.

For the two painters, as for those who viewed their murals, these shocking depictions were a reminder (really a *discovery*) of the fallacy of the traditional victimization narrative. In the painting titled *Death of the American Prisoners of War,* first exhibited in 1971, the inversion was total: the victims were captured American airmen, the individuals who had been bombing Japanese cities, and the ominous victimizers were *hibakusha,* citizens of Hiroshima who had just been the target of the first atomic bomb. In *Ravens,* completed in 1972, the Marukis undermined the victimization narrative in other ways. The terrible mound of Korean corpses forced viewers to confront the facts not only that there were other atomic bomb victims besides Japanese but also that the Japanese people had accepted without question the colonization of Korea and brutal conscription of Koreans as forced wartime laborers. Even after the nuclear devastation, as the mound of corpses suggested (and an accompanying commentary made explicit), Japanese survivors continued to discriminate against Koreans.[16]

Other Japanese have introduced other moral considerations in attempting to come to grips with the meaning of Hiroshima and Nagasaki. Some see the bombs as a plain atrocity—an American war crime, as it were, that cancels out, or at least mitigates, the enormity of Japan's own wartime transgressions. More typically, however—and this was true even in the immediate aftermath of the bombings—anti-American sentiment per se is surprisingly muted. The focus instead has been on using the bomb experience to bring an antinuclear message to the world. As Professor Sodei Rinjiro has reminded us, Oe Kenzaburo, the 1994 Nobel laureate in literature, emerged as a spokesman for this position in influential essays written in the early 1960s. In Oe's rendering, the *hibakusha* were "moralists" because they had experienced "the cruelest days in human history" and never lost "the vision of a nation which will do its best to materialize a world without any nuclear weapons."[17]

Moral reflections of this sort—by Japanese or by critics of the use of the bombs in general—usually are given short shrift by American upholders of the heroic narrative. In their view, war is hell, the Japanese brought the terrible denouement of the bombs upon themselves, and the only morality worth emphasizing is the moral superiority of the Allied cause in World War II. Indeed, one of the formulaic terms that emerged among critics of the Air and Space Museum's original plans (alongside the "merciful" nature

This lunch box belonged to Watanabe Reiko, a high school student. She was with her schoolmates doing construction labor 500 meters from the epicenter of the explosion. Very few of them survived. The lunch box, with its partly burned contents, was found several days later. Reiko's body was never found. Her father, Shigeru, donated the lunch box to the Hiroshima museum in 1970. This was one of the items singled out for criticism and eventually censored from the *Enola Gay* exhibit. (Ienaga, 4.181.)

of the use of the bombs) labeled the nuclear destruction of the two Japanese cities "morally unambiguous."[18]

It was not, and it may well be that the most enduring legacy of the Smithsonian controversy will be its graphic exposure of the moral ambiguity of the use of the bombs—and of Allied strategic bombing policy more generally. Here is where the triumphal story line gives way to a tragic narrative. The "good war" against Axis aggression and atrocity was brought to an end by a policy that the United States, Great Britain, and the League of Nations all had condemned only a few years previous, when first practiced by Japan and Germany, as "barbarous" and "in violation of those standards of humane conduct which have been developed as an essential part of modern civilization." That policy was the identification of civilian men, women, and children as legitimate targets of aerial bombardment. The United States, President Franklin D. Roosevelt typically declared in 1940, could be proud that it "consistently has taken the lead in urging that this inhuman practice be prohibited." Five years later, well before Hiroshima and Nagasaki, this inhuman practice was standard United States operating procedure.[19]

The proposed Smithsonian exhibition threatened to expose this moral ambiguity in the most vivid manner imaginable, by literally visualizing ground zero; and here, I submit, many proponents of the heroic narrative confronted an unanticipated and unexpectedly formidable challenge. For the triumphal story they cherished and the great icon that represented it—the huge, gleaming, refurbished *Enola Gay* Superfortress itself—were overwhelmed by humble artifacts from the ashes of Hiroshima and Nagasaki. It was not so much the numbers of photographs and artifacts that the curators planned to include in the room on "Ground Zero," unit 4 of the planned exhibition, that undermined the heroic narrative, although this was fiercely argued. Rather, it was the intimate nature of these latter items.

Nothing brought this to life more succinctly than the juxtaposition of the Superforttress and the lunch box.

Among the artifacts the Smithsonian's curators proposed bringing to Washington from the Peace Memorial Museum in Hiroshima was a seventh-grade schoolgirl's charred lunch box, containing carbonized rice and peas, that had been recovered from the ashes. The girl herself had disappeared. In the Japanese milieu, this is a typical, intensely human atomic bomb icon; and to American visitors to an exhibition, it would be intensely human too. This pathetic artifact (and other items like it) obsessed and alarmed critics of the proposed exhibition, and for obvious reasons: for the little lunch box far outweighed the glistening Superfortress in the preceding room. It would linger longer in most visitors' memories. Inevitably, it would force them to try imagining an incinerated child. Museum visitors who could gaze on this plain, intimate item and still maintain that the use of the bombs was "morally unambiguous" would be a distinct minority.[20]

This sense of the tragedy of the war, even of the "good war" against an atrocious Axis enemy, became lost in the polemics that engulfed the Smithsonian. Yet it is not an original perception, certainly not new to the more civilized discourse on the bombs that has taken place in previous years. Indeed, in oblique ways even President Harry S Truman, a hero of the triumphal narrative, showed himself sensitive to the tragic dimensions of his decision to use the bombs. The day after Nagasaki was bombed, he expressed qualms about killing "all those kids." Years later it was discovered, in a copy of a book about the bombs in his personal library, that the former president had underlined this quotation from Horatio's famous speech in *Hamlet:*

> ... let me speak to the yet unknowing world
> How these things came about: So shall you hear
> Of carnal, bloody, and unnatural acts,
> Of accidental judgements, casual slaughters,
> Of deaths put on by cunning and forced cause,
> And, in this upshot, purposes mistook
> Fall'n on the inventors' heads ....
> But let this same be presently perform'd
> Even while men's minds are wild; lest more mischance,
> On plots and errors, happen.[21]

Notes

1. I have developed some of the themes in this present essay in substantially differ-ent form in two other articles: briefly in John W. Dower, "Hiroshima, Nagasaki, and the Politics of Memory," *Technology Review,* 98 (Aug./Sept. 1995), 48–51; and in consider-ably greater detail in John W. Dower, "Three Narratives of Our Humanity," in *History Wars: The Enola Gay Controversy and Other Battles for the American Past,* ed. Edward Linenthal and Tom Engelhardt (New York, 1996).

2. *Congressional Record,* S.R. 257, 103 Cong., 2 sess., Sept. 22, 1994, pp. S13315–16. For the text of Senate Resolution 257, see below, "Documents," 1136. Such accusations of "anti-Americanism" came from the ostensibly liberal as well as conservative and right-wing sources; see, for example, Jonathan Yardley, "Dropping a Bomb of an Idea," *Washington Post,* Oct. 10, 1994, p. B2; and "The Enola Gay Explosion," [editorial], *ibid.,* Jan. 20, 1995, p. A20.

3. Paul Fussell, *Thank God for the Atom Bomb and Other Essays* (New York, 1988), 13–37.

4. I offer the points that follow, not as original observations, but to illustrate the "historical controversies" that, essentially a priori, are anathema to the heroic narrative. For basic treatments, see Martin J. Sherwin, *A World Destroyed: Hiroshima and the Origins of the Arms Race* (New York, 1987); J. Samuel Walker, "The Decision to Use the Bomb: A Historiographical Update," *Diplomatic History,* 14 (Winter 1990), 94–114; and the symposium "Hiroshima in History and Memory," *ibid.,* 19 (Spring 1995), espe-cially Barton Bernstein, "Understanding the Atomic Bomb and the Japanese Surrender: Missed Opportunities, Little-Known Near Disasters, and Modern Memory," *ibid.,* 227–73.

5. As Professor Sodei Rinjiro notes, many Japanese accounts weigh the Soviet declaration of war as being as shocking to the Japanese leadership as the Hiroshima bombing; see Sodei Rinjiro, "Hiroshima/Nagasaki as History and Politics," *Journal of American History,* 82 (Dec. 1995), 1119.

6. See, for example, Taro Takemi, "Remembrances of the War and the Bomb," *Journal of the American Medical Association,* Aug. 5, 1983, 618–19. Takemi, later a prominent physician, was a physicist at the time and privy to responses to the bomb at the highest levels.

7. United States Strategic Bombing Survey, *Summary Report (Pacific War)* (Wash-ington, 1946), 26. Cf. United States Strategic Bombing Survey, *Japan's Struggle to End the War* (Washington, 1946), 13.

8. Among prominent critics of the Smithsonian's critics, Gar Alperovitz and Martin Sherwin emphasize the option of the United States abandoning the demand for unconditional surrender and pursuing a negotiated settlement with Japan. See Gar Alperovitz et al., *The Decision to Use the Atomic Bomb—and the Architecture of an American Myth* (New York, 1995). In American political discourse, this argument represents an interesting ideological somersault—now identified as "leftist," it was conspicuously conservative when originally advanced by Joseph Grew in 1945 and was vigorously attacked as such by liberals and leftists at the time. To Grew's critics, the emperor system was the keystone to Japanese aggression abroad and repression at home, and any presurrender Allied promise to guarantee its continuation smacked of right-wing appeasement and would severely compromise the ability of the United States to dictate reformist policies in defeated and occupied Japan. The waywardness of ideological labels is compounded when we look at contemporary Japan. There the political and academic left is critical of the emperor system and Emperor Hirohito's wartime role, and the Alperovitz–Sherwin argument (that the Japanese were trying to surrender and the United States should have cut a deal with the imperial government) is most associated with pro-emperor conservatives and neonationalists. For critical appraisals of the feasibility of a negotiated surrender, see Bernstein, "Understanding the Atomic Bomb and the Japanese Surrender," 238–44; and a study based largely on Japanese materials: Herbert Bix, "Japan's Delayed Surrender: A Reinterpretation," *Diplomatic History,* 19 (Spring 1995), 197–225. I spell out my skepticism of the "conditional surrender" argument in Dower, "Three Narratives of Our Humanity," but I regard the issue as deserving serious consideration. The so-called revisionist historians whom the Smithsonian's critics dismissed with blanket contempt disagree among themselves on various issues pertaining to the bombs and the end of the war.

9. For a recent treatment of this fact, known for some time, see Arjun Makhijani, " 'Always' the Target?" *Bulletin of the Atomic Scientists,* 51 (May/June 1995), 23–27.

10. On the racial aspects of the war, see John W. Dower, *War Without Mercy: Race and Power in the Pacific War* (New York, 1986).

11. For J. Robert Oppenheimer's statement, see Sherwin, *World Destroyed,* 145. For a rueful acknowledgment of how "technically sweet" the project was, see the interview with Victor Weisskopf, *MIT Tech Talk,* Oct. 2, 1991. Only one or two scientists left the Manhattan Project after Germany surrendered.

12. This was one of the arguments used in rejecting a June 1945 proposal by Manhattan Project scientists (in the Franck Report) that the atomic bomb be demonstrated on a noncombat target. See Sherwin, *World Destroyed,* 117–18, 210–19; Bernstein, "Understanding the Atomic Bomb and the Japanese Surrender," 270–71; and James G. Hershberg, *James B. Conant: Harvard to Hiroshima and the Making of the Nuclear Age* (New York, 1993), 293, 818.

13. It remains for psychologists and symbolic anthropologists to tell us what to make of an American airplane named after the pilot's mother delivering a bomb named Little Boy and giving birth to a wildly celebrated new age of destructive capability.

14. On June 9, 1995, the lower house of the Japanese Diet expressed "deep remorse" (*fukai hansei*) for causing great suffering to other peoples, especially Asians, in World War II. Conservative opposition to a stronger resolution not only thwarted a clear-cut "apology" but also led to wording that made clear that Japan was not alone in "modern history" in engaging in colonialism and aggression. On August 15, 1995, however, Prime Minister Murayama Tomiichi offered a clear apology (*owabi*) for the damage and suffering caused by imperial Japan. On August 23, 1993, the then prime minister Hosokawa Morihiro had made a briefer unequivocal apology, generally ignored by the

non-Japanese media. For the Diet resolution, Murayama's statement, documents illustrating the debate about "war responsibility" across the Japanese political spectrum, and a brief commentary, see my contribution to a University of Michigan periodical: John W. Dower, "Japan Addresses Its War Responsibility," *The Journal of the International Institute,* 3 (Fall 1995). The non-Japanese media has also generally failed to report that current textbooks approved by the conservative Ministry of Education speak more frankly about Japanese aggression and atrocities than was the case up through the 1980s.

15. Japanese Marxist and neo-Marxist scholars, many of them associated with the Rekishigaku Kenkyukai (Historiographical Research Association), have been critically attentive to Japan's war responsibility ever since Japan's defeat. Serious mass media treatments of war crimes in Asia, beginning with the Rape of Nanking, generally are dated from reports by the writer Honda Katsuichi beginning in 1970. In the early 1970s another influential writer, Oda Makoto, popularized the notion of a dual victim–victimizer Japanese identity. The death of Emperor Hirohito in 1989 removed some of the lingering taboos on discussion of Japan's war responsibility. Recent issues that the non-Japanese press has seized on as continuing evidence of Japanese war crimes—such as the murderous medical experiments of Unit 731 and the sexual enslavement of non-Japanese "comfort women" (*ianfu*) who were forced to serve the emperor's loyal soldiers and sailors—have been widely exposed in the Japanese media. While conservative Japanese politicians and bureaucrats have undertaken to sanitize this atrocious chapter of Japanese history, the popular struggle to combat such "historical amnesia" has been vigorous.

16. The Marukis went on to address such subjects as the Rape of Nanking, Auschwitz, the Battle of Okinawa (in which Japanese bore grave responsibility for the death of other Japanese), and Minamata (the postwar site of extensive deaths from environmental poisoning). Their paintings are reproduced and discussed in John W. Dower and John Junkerman, eds., *The Hiroshima Murals: The Art of Iri Maruki and Toshi Maruki* (Tokyo, 1985). The belated Japanese acknowledgment of non-Japanese victims of the atomic bombs—including Koreans, Japanese Americans, a few Caucasian American prisoners, individuals from other Asian countries, and Europeans—is a critical part of the unraveling of the Japanese victimization narrative. In the heroic American narrative, it is customary to refer vaguely, at best, to atomic bomb "casualties." By such linguistic leveling, combat and civilian deaths are placed on the same plane.

17. On Japanese responses to the bombs, see John W. Dower, "The Bombed: Hiroshimas and Nagasakis in Japanese Memory," *Diplomatic History,* 19 (Fall 1995), 275–95; and the foreword to the reprint of a classic work, first published in English in 1955: John W. Dower, "Foreword," in Michihiko Hachiya, *Hiroshima Diary: The Journal of a Japanese Physician, August 6–September 30, 1945* (Chapel Hill, 1995), v–xvii. On Oe, see Sodei, "Hiroshima/Nagasaki as History and Politics," 1121.

18. See, for example, the use of this phrase by Richard Hallion, chief historian of the air force, *Washington Times,* Aug. 30, 1994; and by Congressman Sam Johnson and six of his colleagues in a letter to I. Michael Heyman, secretary of the Smithsonian, Dec. 13, 1994, in Air Force Association, "Congressional Correspondence and Press Releases," pt. 8 of "The Enola Gay Debate, Aug. 1993–May 1995," unpaged compilation of documents, available from the Air Force Association, 1501 Lee Highway, Arlington, VA 22209.

19. Dower, *War without Mercy,* 37–41. See also Ronald Schaffer, "American Military Ethics in World War II: The Bombing of German Civilians," *Journal of American*

History, 67 (Sept. 1980), 318–34; Michael Sherry, *The Rise of American Air Power: The Creation of Armageddon* (New Haven, 1987); and Barton Bernstein, "The Atomic Bombings Reconsidered," *Foreign Affairs,* 74 (Jan./Feb. 1995), 135–52.

20. For the critics' fixation on the lunch box, see, for example, John T. Correll, "War Stories at Air and Space," *Air Force Magazine,* 7 (April 1994), 24; and John T. Correll, " 'The Last Act' at Air and Space," *ibid.* (Sept. 1994), 61.

21. Bernstein, "Understanding the Atomic Bomb and the Japanese Surrender," 257; Merle Miller, *Plain Speaking: An Oral Biography of Harry S Truman* (New York, 1973), 248.

3

Between Pearl Harbor and Hiroshima/Nagasaki

Nationalism and Memory in Japan and the United States

YUI Daizaburo
Translation by Laura Hein

Today, fifty-plus years after the Pacific War, crucial differences in the way that war is recalled in Japan and in the United States are coming to light. Of course, even now, when Japanese people criticize the atomic bombing of Hiroshima and Nagasaki, they are met with the rejoinder "Remember Pearl Harbor."

In the United States, debate centered on cancellation of the National Air and Space Museum's exhibit displaying the *Enola Gay* in the context of a reexamination of both the decision to drop the bombs and the effects on their victims. The Smithsonian's decision to cancel the exhibit, leaving only the *Enola Gay*, caused consternation and anger among many Japanese, particularly among older *hibakusha*, who have been suffering the effects of the bombings for the last fifty years.

However, other Japanese stood by the principle that they cannot criticize other governments more than their own. They turned their attention to plans by the Ministry of Health and Welfare on the occasion of the fiftieth anniversary of the end of the war to create a War Dead Peace Memorial Hall. In spite of calls for major changes in its plans by many historians and concerned citizens, the ministry determined to exclude from representation the war victims of foreign countries, including the rest of Asia, and to include only Japanese who were killed in battle and their families. Conservative politicians and the Association of Bereaved Families also strongly resisted a Diet resolution of self-reflection and self-criticism proposed for the fiftieth anniversary of defeat, arguing that such a move would "desecrate the spirits of the war dead who died as martyrs in a national calamity." Their efforts long stalled the resolution, which eventually passed in only a weakened form in June 1995.

Why is it that, after more than fifty years, the gap between Japanese and American perceptions of the war is growing wider rather than narrowing? Why is it that in the realm of economics, national boundaries are becoming less and less important, whereas in the sphere of politics and culture, consciousness of race and national community (*minzoku to kokumin*) are becoming hugely influential? This chapter explores differences in styles of nationalism between Japan and the United States and the gap between memories of the Asia–Pacific War in the two countries.

Americanism and the Struggle over the Atomic Bomb Exhibit at the Smithsonian

On January 30, 1995, the board of directors of the Smithsonian Institution decided to radically shrink the proposed atomic bomb exhibit, which was to have run from May 1995 to January 1996. Although the plan had been to present both a discussion of the decision to drop the bombs and their effects on their victims, the final exhibit consisted mainly of the fuselage of the *Enola Gay* and information about the airplane and its crew. The exhibit also included statements that the bombings killed "many tens of thousands" but in so doing saved lives by causing Japan to surrender immediately. The five-hundred-plus-page script for the exhibit was completely eliminated, ending a controversy in which it had been revised four times.

In the end, the original thinking of the Air and Space Museum curators was almost completely erased. According to a July 1993 draft proposal entitled "The Crossroads: The Atomic Bomb and the End of World War II":

> The primary goal of this exhibition will be to encourage visitors to undertake a thoughtful and balanced re-examination of these events in the light of the political and military factors leading to the decision to drop the bomb, the human suffering experienced by the people of Hiroshima and Nagasaki and the long-term implications of the events of August 6 and 9, 1945. . . . The museum hopes that the proposed exhibition will contribute to a more profound discussion of the atomic bombings among the general public of the United States, Japan and elsewhere.[1]

The curators hoped to contribute to an understanding of those events not only by reflecting the re-evaluations developed through recent scholarship but also by addressing debates, not just among Americans but also among people in other countries, including Japan.

Thus, the original stance of the Air and Space Museum curators was scholarly and comprehensive, and their first script was highly praised by academic specialists. Their decision to present the bombing from the viewpoint of the hibakusha exemplifies their internationalist perspective.

The original exhibit design was severely criticized. The first part, "A Fight to the Finish," began with a kamikaze attack vessel suspended overhead, thereby linking the decision to drop the bombs to the Japanese military's desperate fighting in the final months of the war, especially on Okinawa. This section, which raised issues of American desires for revenge for Pearl Harbor and posed questions of racist motivation, was severely criticized. The museum retreated from its description of a "race war," changed the section title to the more neutral "The War in the Pacific," and added new stress on Japanese atrocities and massacres. The second section depicted the decision-making process, beginning with the Manhattan Project and including references to anti-Soviet strategy and arguments against the bombs' use. After much criticism, this material was revised to reflect the orthodox view that dropping the bombs hastened the war's end and saved U.S. lives that would have been lost in an invasion. The fourth section was eliminated altogether. The curators had planned that the atmosphere would darken as visitors entered "Hiroshima, 8:15 AM, August 6, 1945/Nagasaki, 11:02 AM, August 9, 1945." There, hibakusha would tell their stories on videotape alongside photos of them and of their belongings. This was criticized as too harsh and unbalanced a presentation of war casualties.

The American Legion and Air Force Association, the main critics, also insisted that the exhibit title be changed to "The Last Act: The Atomic Bomb and the End of World War II." Despite long negotiations and accommodation by museum planners on these and other issues, their critics remained dissatisfied. No matter how much the curators softened the content, their efforts to present the dropping of the bomb from scholarly, diverse, and humanitarian perspectives were fundamentally unacceptable to powerful military critics.

The opposition, including the 3.1-million-member American Legion, many of whom are World War II veterans, had fixed views of the bombing. Insisting that the atomic bombs had brought the war to a speedy close, thereby obviating great sacrifice of U.S. soldiers' lives, they would not tolerate an exhibit that included recognition of the suffering of the bomb

Vengeance for the surprise attack on Pearl Harbor was a major theme in the United States throughout the war, coexisting uneasily with the rhetoric of impartial justice. (Courtesy of Ted Przychoda, used by permission.)

victims. This perspective, emphasizing the decisive contribution of the air force in ending the war, explains why the museum's most impassioned critics came from the Air Force Association (AFA). Museum director Martin Harwit noted that AFA leaders, who criticized the exhibit from the moment they learned of it in January 1994, refused to join the American Legion's attempts to revise it.[2]

The AFA produced a scathing attack on the exhibit plan in March 1994, titled "The Smithsonian and the *Enola Gay*," and air force veterans were the core members of the "Committee for the Restoration and Display of the *Enola Gay*." The AFA demanded that the museum "display [the *Enola Gay*] in a patriotic manner that will instill pride in the viewer for the outstanding accomplishments of the U.S. and the *Enola Gay* in ending World War II without the need for an invasion of Japan and without the additional invasion-related casualties."

The AFA claimed that Japanese "losses, particularly to B–29 incendiary bombing, were described in vivid detail while American casualties were treated in matter-of-fact summations." The AFA article disapprovingly quoted a script line that argued, "For most Americans, it was a war of vengeance. For most Japanese, it was a war to defend their unique culture against Western imperialism." The AFA also complained that the museum "[t]reats Japan and the United States as if their participation in the war were morally equivalent. If anything, incredibly, it gives the benefit of opinion to Japan which was the aggressor." In short, the AFA accused the curators of manipulating history.[3] The AFA viewed the exhibit as a challenge to its own patriotic views, which emphasized air force contributions to national defense, when it included analysis of the atomic bombings from the Japanese side.

AFA critics viewed the air war in general and the atomic bombings in particular as a way to avoid a bloody ground war. The sufferings of the bombed were barely visible from their perspective. During the Vietnam War, while the memoirs by U.S. ground forces are frequently tragic, those of many pilots resonate with the aura of "war heroes."[4] In certain ways, it resembles the difference between viewing the atomic bombing of Hiroshima and Nagasaki from the perspective of its victims at ground zero in contrast to viewing the mushroom cloud rising heavenward.

The critics' insistence on patriotism as the standard for judging the exhibit was grist for the politicians. On September 23, 1994, the Senate unanimously adopted Senate Resolution 257, introduced by GOP senator from Kansas, Nancy Kassebaum. Resolution 257 baldly stated that, "the role of the *Enola Gay* during World War II was momentous in helping to bring World War II to a *merciful* end, which resulted in saving the lives of Americans and Japanese," and then resolved that "any exhibit displayed by the National Air and Space Museum with respect to the *Enola Gay* should reflect appropriate sensitivity toward the men and women who faithfully and selflessly served the United States during World War II and should avoid impugning the memory of those who gave their lives for freedom."[5] The Smithsonian was thus enjoined to limit its exhibit to praise for the sacrifices of U.S. servicemen and those who "gave their lives for freedom."

Politicians and veterans' organizations insisted that the fiftieth anniversary was an occasion for praise and commemoration. Where the museum had sought to present a comprehensive and international perspective on the atomic bombing and the war, its critics demanded a patriotic and commemorative exhibit. The clash was inevitable.

The media analyses of the Smithsonian also turned on this debate between a commemorative and a multifocal exhibit. On the day before the final Smithsonian decision, the *New York Times* warned that a group of senators and veterans threatened to "hijack" the museum. Its editorial put it in stark terms: "But the real betrayal of American tradition would be to insist on a single version of history or to make it the property of the state or any group. History in America is based on freedom of inquiry and discussion, which is one reason why Americans have given their lives to defend it." Similarly, the *Wall Street Journal* expressed anxiety about intolerance and ignorance when it assessed the GOP political pressure on the Smithsonian as motivated mainly by a desire to win the November 1994 elections.[6]

On the other hand, the *Washington Post* supported the Smithsonian's decision to all but cancel the exhibit, calling the exhibitors revisionists and denying that their ideas were based on solid history. It editorialized:

> It is important to be clear about what happened at the Smithsonian. It is not, as some have it, that benighted advocates of a special-interest or right-wing point of view brought political power to bear to crush and distort the historical truth. Quite the contrary. Narrow-minded representatives of a special-interest and revisionist point of view attempted to use their inside track to appropriate and hollow out a historical event that large numbers of Americans alive at that time and engaged in the war had witnessed and understood in a very different—and authentic—way.

The *Los Angeles Times* agreed, calling on the Smithsonian to honor those who fought Nazism and Japanese militarism.[7] If the American media were not unanimous, they mainly supported the decision to scale back the exhibit. The fiftieth anniversary of the end of the war would be celebrated in the United States in a nationalistic manner.

Japanese who followed this year long public debate on how to observe the anniversary of the use of the atomic bomb regretted seeing the subjects of the decision-making process and the bomb's terrible effects on victims excluded from the exhibition. Nevertheless, as Robert Jay Lifton, who has studied the psychological effects of the bomb on hibakusha, says, this was "the first national American debate" on the bomb. Clearly, more are needed.[8] Important issues remain unresolved.

The first is the accumulation of historical research. Many scholars have challenged in fundamental ways the official story of the decision to drop the bomb. There is a strong sense that, in the end, the Smithsonian was forced to ignore their evidence. Of course, debate continues on such issues as the role of anti-Soviet policy in the decision to drop the bomb. Nevertheless, few scholars any longer accept President Harry S Truman's claim in late 1945 that he dropped the bomb exclusively in order to save lives in a land invasion and bring the war to a speedy end. Truman's diary, published in

1979, creates real doubts about the official story, and as historian Gar Alperovitz noted, the "consensus among scholars is that the bomb was not needed to avoid an invasion of Japan—and further, not only did alternatives to the bomb exist, but Truman and his advisers knew it."[9]

But this scholarly consensus has not spread to veterans, politicians, or the general public. The public orthodoxy heavily reflects the views of U.S. veterans who saw the bomb as changing their personal destiny. News reports of the controversy invariably highlighted this veterans' perspective.[10] There is a real gap between these two ways of understanding historical events—as historians or as people who lived through the era.

The veterans' organizations and their allies further argued that dropping the bombs on Hiroshima and Nagasaki, by terrible example, helped to control the spread of nuclear war. This is the realist doctrine long promoted by the U.S. government: that the atomic bomb contributed to the subsequent prevention of nuclear war and to maintaining the balance of power. But this argument neglects the problem of why the officials did not consider alternatives to dropping the bomb on populated areas. Indeed, in the earlier stages of the bomb's development, some nuclear physicists argued passionately for a demonstration of its power by selecting a site where there were no people.

The second issue is the perception that the cancellation of the atomic bomb exhibit represents an extremely dangerous attack on academic and museum freedom. The Organization of American Historians (OAH) responded to this issue three days before the Smithsonian's final decision with a letter by President Gary Nash, past President Eric Foner, and President-elect Michael Kammen. They argued that cancellation of the exhibit "will send a chilling message to museum administrators and curators throughout the United States. . . . Doing so would send the explicit message that controversial subjects cannot be examined openly as a part of our democratic civic life" and that some aspects of our history are "too hot to handle." After the Smithsonian caved in, they blasted the decision as "self-censorship" and "historical cleansing."[11]

Finally, this dispute was fundamentally about the tension between nationalism and multiculturalism, as indicated by the AFA's concern over previous multiculturalist exhibits. In the mid-1980s, the Smithsonian had several exhibits on minority peoples and human rights. For example, on the two hundredth anniversary of the Constitution, the Smithsonian's Museum of American History hosted an exhibit on the internment of Japanese-Americans, called "A More Perfect Union." Then, in 1992, the Smithsonian marked the five hundredth anniversary of Christopher Columbus's arrival in

America with a display that described the devastation wreaked by Europeans on the New World.

The 1980s were marked by a conspicuously conservative turn in U.S. politics, including attacks on affirmative action, a movement to make English the official language, and strong attacks on multiculturalism. Nevertheless, when the Smithsonian hosted some exhibits from a multicultural perspective, it was strongly supported by diverse groups within American society, such as racial minorities, liberals, and people concerned with human rights. In contrast, when the Air and Space Museum took up the atomic bombing, academic groups were unable to prevail over politically powerful pressure groups, such as the veterans' organizations, as well as the media and the Congress.

But the curators did not arrive at their decision to include Japanese perspectives on the bombing simply from a multicultural perspective. They also had grasped the importance of Hiroshima and Nagasaki as a symbol of the dangers of the nuclear era. Martin Harwit was influenced by his service during the 1950s at the Bikini hydrogen bomb tests. "I think anybody who has ever seen a hydrogen bomb go off at fairly close range knows that you don't ever want to see that used on people," he commented.[12] In the eyes of nationalists, this perspective overemphasized Japanese suffering. It was simply "pro-Jap."

Given rising patriotic orthodoxy, World War II could only be presented as a symbol of the antifascist "holy war" and "victorious Americanism." But the "good war" has a double meaning. It is also about the way that the war economy brought the United States out of the 1930s depression. In light of the subsequent decline in the United States, memories of that "good America" which emerged from the war reflect present anxieties.

The Fiftieth Anniversary of Defeat and the
Shadow of Neonationalism in Japan

At the same time that the Smithsonian was considering canceling the atomic bomb exhibit, Japan's Ministry of Health and Welfare announced its plans to commemorate the fiftieth anniversary of the end of the war by establishing a Peace Memorial Hall.[13] In a perfect counterpoint to the U.S. debate, it explicitly excluded foreign war victims and was intended to celebrate only the Japanese war dead and their families.

The memorial hall started as a proposal by the Association of Bereaved Families to the ministry in December 1979 for a commemorative hall for the children of those killed in action.[14] The welfare minister set up a private

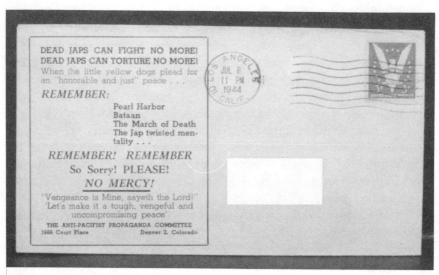

DEAD JAPS CAN FIGHT NO MORE!
DEAD JAPS CAN TORTURE NO MORE!
When the little yellow dogs plead for
an "honorable and just" peace . . .
REMEMBER:
      Pearl Harbor
      Bataan
      The March of Death
      The Jap twisted men-
      tality . . .
REMEMBER! REMEMBER
So Sorry! PLEASE!
NO MERCY!
"Vengeance is Mine, sayeth the Lord!"
'Let's make it a tough, vengeful and
uncompromising peace'
THE ANTI-PACIFIST PROPAGANDA COMMITTEE
1666 Court Place   Denver 2, Colorado

Most white Americans during World War II accepted a level of casual racism that fifty years later had become unacceptable. Recognition of that historical shift was also erased from much of the official 1995 commemoration of the war's end. (Courtesy of Ted Przychoda, used by permission.)

advisory board in July 1985 to study the feasibility of such a memorial hall, which produced a plan in August 1992. According to Welfare Ministry documents, visitors would enter a "prologue exhibition" of 250 square meters. The second room, the 185-square-meter "Road to War," was to have displayed material on the era from the First World War to the Great Depression and Japan's international isolation. The third area, 705 square meters, was dedicated to "Daily Life of the People during the War." This section depicted the mobilization of the whole nation, including sending soldiers to the front, the air raids, and the war's end. The fourth section, 510 square meters, showed "Daily Life during the Occupation." After a 75-square-meter room showing "The Hardships of Orphans Trying to Survive on Their Own," the last section, "Looking toward Peace," 175 square meters, was to introduce viewers to the new Constitution, the peace treaty, and repatriation of Japanese after the war.[15]

These plans devoted only 30 square meters of the display "Daily Life of the People during the War" to Asians in wartime. This was a tiny fraction— .015 percent—of the total exhibit space. Moreover, this section, called "Southeast Asia and China under Japanese Occupation," was not designed to present the perspective of Asians themselves. There was little interest in presenting the viewpoint of foreign, especially Asian, war victims.

On that point, Ministry of Health and Welfare officials responded as follows to questions in the House of Councillors' Welfare Committee in May 1993: "In addition to being a site for people who want to mourn those who were sacrificed in war, our aim is that the War Dead Peace Memorial Hall will support eternal peace by transmitting to younger generations the sufferings of war from the point of view of daily life and the difficulty of keeping body and soul together during and after the war. Given that, our goal is not to apologize to Asian nations."[16] In short, the plan for the Peace Memorial Hall focused squarely on Japanese sacrifice, especially Japanese military dead, and was steeped in imagery of national sacrifice. Indeed, including material on foreign war victims would contradict the basic principle of the exhibit by forcing reflection on Japanese war responsibility and atrocities. Thus, including foreign victims would deeply contradict the goal of commemorating the *Japanese* war dead as desired by the Association of Bereaved Families.

In August 1991, in preparation for commemoration of the fiftieth anniversary of the bombing of Pearl Harbor, the mayor of Honolulu asked that Japanese officials be invited to the ceremony only on condition that they apologize for the war. But the Japanese government spokesman, deputy chief cabinet secretary Ishihara Nobuo, refused, arguing that "the entire world is responsible for the war." He went on to say that "because war could not be avoided, all those involved should reflect. . . . It will take tens or hundreds of years before the correct judgment is delivered on who is responsible for the war." Although this kind of statement, muddying Japan's war responsibility, is a familiar litany from a succession of conservative administrations, it was singled out for harsh criticism by Dutch journalist Ian Buruma. In *The Wages of Guilt,* Buruma noted that Ishihara called for American apologies along with any Japanese ones and commented, "The Japanese had flunked the test. They were not invited. They were still a dangerous people."[17] Actually, the Japanese Diet considered a resolution reflecting on the war in December of that year, but conservative politicians defeated it. In Buruma's terms, they "flunked the test."

Groups such as the Association of Bereaved Families strongly oppose any Diet resolution that either apologizes for the war or takes an antiwar stance. The roster of signatures of one of these opponent groups, the Committee to Act on a National Movement toward the Fiftieth Anniversary of the End of the War, explained why: "Such a resolution would be unique in world history and Japan would become the only nation to accept responsibility for a war as a criminal nation." This would "wound the honor of the state and the Japanese people, profane the spirits of the war dead martyred in a national calamity, and would deal a grievous blow to the future of the nation and the Japanese people."

According to this group, Japan does not bear exclusive responsibility for World War II. Its members believe that "the Greater East Asian war was a holy war [*seisen*], made unavoidable by the international world context surrounding the Japanese state and the Japanese race [*minzoku*] at the time." Thus, they reject Japan's recognition of its own responsibility for a war of invasion. "For Japanese to stick the label of 'a cruel and brutal race' on themselves is to defile the history of their fatherland with their own hands and burden our descendants with a dishonored Japanese race," they insist. They also reject the postwar Tokyo War Crimes Tribunal, which fixed responsibility for an aggressive war on Japan, as nothing but "victors' justice." Thus, they argue, a "resolution of apology" has the character of a "resolution endorsing the assumptions of a Tokyo Tribunal view of history" and is "completely beyond the authority of the Diet."[18] This group's retrograde attitude is revealed by its terminology. It retains the wartime name of the "Greater East Asian War" and sees it as a "defensive war." It was able to collect 4.5 million signatures on a petition against the resolution, and 143 Liberal Democratic Party (LDP) members and 29 Shinsei Party members blocked its passage in the legislature.[19]

The mass media, particularly the four national daily newspapers, were split on the subject of a Diet resolution of apology. An editorial in the February 26, 1995, issue of the *Asahi* insisted that "the no-war resolution indicates political insight," while the *Mainichi* editorialized on March 14 that the resolution was necessary "to obtain a sincere reconciliation with Asian nations." In contrast, in an editorial on March 8, the *Yomiuri* asked dismissively whether the Diet "had the competence to 'decide' among the various views of history." Also, the *Sankei* weighed in with an editorial on February 27 opposing the resolution on the grounds that it was unprecedented for a national legislature to apologize and that wartime problems had been settled by the peace treaty. Moreover, an antiwar resolution might mean relinquishing Japan's right to self-defense.

As the range of editorials makes clear, fifty years later there was no consensus on Japan's role in the Asia–Pacific War. Conservative political parties, such as the LDP, which held power through most of the postwar era, harbor within their ranks right-wing nationalists (*uyokuteki minzoku shugisha*), who affirm the righteousness of the "Greater East Asian War." But at the same time, mainstream conservative politicians have closely followed the American line on diplomatic and security issues, as symbolized by the U.S.-Japan Security Treaty. This congruence has strangely distorted the attitudes toward World War II of LDP right-wing nationalists. Thus, they supported ratification of the San Francisco Peace Treaty, including Article 11, which accepted responsibility for the Tokyo Tribunal verdicts, but on the domestic political stage, they blithely rejected the "Tokyo Tribunal view of history." As Yoshida Yutaka has pointed out, this created a contradictory "double standard" toward the war. The United States, which emphasized anti-Soviet strategy during the cold war era, has long ignored this contradiction.[20]

Nonetheless, in the 1980s, because of economic growth and democratization, as many Asian countries expressed their position internationally for the first time in the postwar era, this double standard became more visible. This development was perhaps best symbolized by the Nakasone Yasuhiro cabinet's metamorphosis. Prime Minister Nakasone was originally known for his nationalistic denial of the "Tokyo Tribunal view of history." On August 15, 1980, he marked the fortieth anniversary of defeat by becoming the first prime minister to pay an official visit to Yasukuni Shrine. However, when China and other Asian countries vigorously denounced this move, he discontinued his formal visits. His Chief Cabinet Secretary Gotoda Masaharu announced that, "given the importance of international relations, we must appropriately consider the feelings of the peoples of neighboring nations." Gotoda also responded to an inquiry in the House of Representatives by reaffirming the cabinet's unified position that Article 11 of the San Francisco treaty specifically expressed respect for the verdict of the Tokyo Tribunal. In other words, ironically, the first Japanese administration to recognize the aggressive nature of the Asia–Pacific War was that of the nationalist politician Nakasone.[21]

This trend continued with the end of the cold war and the death of the Showa emperor, and the tempo increased in the 1990s, along with political reorganization. A symbolic event was the August 1993 statement to reporters by Hosokawa Morihiro, just after he became the first non-LDP prime minister in decades. "For myself, I understand the Asia–Pacific War to have been a war of aggression and a mistake," he said.

This statement was received positively by both the foreign press and many Japanese. According to a November 13, 1993, *Asahi* public opinion survey, 76 percent of those polled were in favor and 15 percent opposed. However, many members of two specific groups were fiercely opposed: conservative politicians and the generation old enough to have fought in the war. Indeed, Hosokawa's statement polarized views of the war. For example, in a September *Asahi* poll, 25 percent of men age sixty or older sharply rejected Hosokawa's statement. Also, published letters from people of the veterans' generation expressed their bitter views along the lines of "If that war was one of aggression, then my friends just died like dogs, meaninglessly."

Some conservative politicians were also very hostile. For example, on October 5, about two months after Hosokawa's statement, LDP member Ishihara Shintaro cross-examined Hosokawa in the Diet:

> Why do you need to apologize to the victor nations who presided over the Tokyo Tribunal? The attitude that the losers were bad and the victors were good is ridiculous. The United States hasn't apologized after losing the war in Vietnam.... Japan does not need in any way to accept its original sin toward those nations that claim to be wartime victors. Any apologies should be mutual. In one blast, 300,000 people were killed by atomic bombs. I have not heard the United States Government express its clear apologies for that.[22]

Ishihara not only rejected Japanese responsibility for war against the Western Allies but also advanced the view that World War II was composed of two separate wars. "We should apologize to the people of the Asian region who were not our enemy but were there in Asia when we encountered the former colonialists," he argued. In other words, Ishihara had begun to distance himself from the official wartime position that World War II was "a holy war to liberate Asia." Nowadays, he separates the Asia–Pacific War into two parts, accepting Japanese aggression against Asia but continuing to argue that Japan fought a "war of self-defense" against the West.

Ishihara is not the only influential LDP member who espouses this theory of two wars. On October 24, 1994, Hashimoto Ryutaro, at the time both president of the Association of Bereaved Families and Ministry of International Trade and Industry (MITI) minister in the Murayama cabinet, made a similar argument in the Diet. "Japanese policy on the Chinese continent did include actions that could be labeled aggression. Moreover, when I look at the history of the Korean peninsula from today's perspective, the choices of previous Japanese political leaders [*waga no senpai kata*] seem imperialist, even though they seemed appropriate at the time. However, I doubt Japan's war with the United States, Great Britain, and the Netherlands can be called a war of aggression." For Hashimoto, the Asia–Pacific War consisted of two separate kinds of war. "Japan never intended to battle the Asian and Pacific peoples but their regions became a battlefield. I believe we truly caused them harm [*meiwaku*] when Asia became a war theater. Nonetheless, it is difficult to use the term 'aggression' there. Perhaps it is a question of semantics, but I think there is a subtle difference."[23]

Hashimoto's recognition of Japan's wartime aggression in Asia but not in general exemplifies the two-war theory. Conservative politicians formerly argued that Japan was "liberating Asia." This shift, indicative of Japan's new Asianism, bears watching as the other side of the coin of anti-Western nationalism. The denial of war responsibility toward Western countries is predicated on the view that the 1930s was an era of imperialist struggle between the "have" and "have-not" countries. The two-war theory provides a nationalistic platform directed against the West for some Japanese in the era of Japan's rise as an economic superpower.

This new Asianism reflects more than simply anti-Westernism. Ever since the stimulus of the Persian Gulf War, Shinsei Party General Secretary Ozawa Ichiro has responded to U.S. demands for military engagement by calling for Japan to become a "normal nation" and by actively encouraging overseas deployment of the Self-Defense Forces. He, too, acknowledges Japan's war responsibility in Asia. In *Blueprint for a New Japan,* he wrote, "Japan is part of the Asia–Pacific and, needless to say, this is the most important region for Japanese diplomacy. . . . However, at the same time, Asian-Pacific people feel a sense of mistrust and vigilance toward Japan, based on 'history.' We cannot deny that in one aspect of past history, Japan was indeed the aggressor there."[24] It is unclear whether this acknowledgment involves genuine reflection on the war or is merely maneuvering for leadership.

In the early 1990s, Japanese conservatives for the first time splintered on the subject of remembering the war. One right-wing group still staunchly affirms all of the goals of the "Greater East Asia War." Another admits Japanese aggression toward Asia but insists that it be understood as including a "self-defense" component in the form of anti-Western Asianism. A third group of moderate conservatives now views the entire Asia–Pacific War as one of Japanese aggression. These divisions made unity on the Diet resolution difficult, although in June 1995, the ruling alliance agreed on language expressing "deep remorse" for actions against Asian nations but stopped short of apology.[25]

Is there validity to the argument that World War II was an unavoidable "defensive war" against the Western nations? Japan argued at the start of the war that hostilities were sparked by "ABCD encirclement"—or economic and military encroachment by American, British, Chinese, and Dutch forces—and that Japan started the war "to defend its existence." In fact, just prior to the outbreak of the Asia–Pacific War, on November 26, 1941, Secretary of State Cordell Hull demanded in the "Hull note" that Japanese troops withdraw from China and Indonesia. He also refused to recognize the Chinese puppet government backed by Japan and called for Japan's adherence to the principles of open access there. The Japanese government saw the Hull note as challenging the very "survival of the Japanese Empire." Thus, it made a historic decision to begin war against the United States and Britain. The contradictions of the "defensive war" thesis are obvious when we realize that it was precisely because Japan had invaded Asia that it came into conflict with the Western nations. Japan started its "defensive" Pacific War exactly when the United States demanded that Japan withdraw from Asia.

Many Japanese, including those who reject the two-war thesis, think it unfair for Japan to be singled out for criticism when the Western powers also behaved aggressively toward their own colonies. Certainly, Japan in the 1930s saw itself as a "have-not" country and demanded redistribution of some of the colonies and overseas markets away from the Western "have" nations. However, the existence of Japan's colonies in Taiwan and Korea contradicts this "have-not" theory. Nonetheless, nationalists argue that nineteenth-century Japan joined the modern global political system at a time when Western nations commonly waged wars for colonies and overseas markets. Japan's survival as a sovereign state, by this reckoning, required it to live by the "survival of the fittest" mentality. Japan was merely the "student" of imperialism, and Europe was the "teacher." Why, then, should Japan be singled out for blame?[26]

But this is a one-sided view. World War II was not just a "war among imperialists"; it was also an "antifascist war." Internationally, both in the West and in the colonies, voices calling for democracy began to restrain colonial activity among the Allied powers. For example, in August 1941, U.S. President Franklin D. Roosevelt and British Prime Minister Winston Churchill signed the Atlantic Charter, which promised to support the principles of "the right of all peoples to choose the form of government under which they will live" and territorial integrity. The charter unambiguously pledged the two leaders to extend these wartime goals to all the Allied countries after the war ended. Of course, it took determined national independence movements in many countries to make these principles a reality. But the United States, itself a former British colony, signed a pact in 1935 promising the Philippines independence in one decade, because of both a desire for open international markets and domestic opposition to holding colonies.

Throughout the postwar era, the United States has maintained military bases all over the world while championing a world structure based on free trade. Also, nationalist movements have triumphed in Asia and Africa, weakening colonial domination. When we consider these two changes, the thesis that we live in a "survival of the fittest" modern world, where it is natural to take colonies based on naked military invasion and territorial occupation, clearly is overdue for revision.

However, prewar Japan, with its sense of inferiority and inequality as compared to the Western "advanced countries," was unable to see that the world was undergoing major change. Trapped by anachronistic thinking, Japan set out to expand its colonies and sphere of power under the self-delusion of "liberating Asia." Nor did Japan experience the long, painful, and divisive decolonizing process experienced by Britain, France, and others after the war, because its colonies were shorn away after military defeat. That fact, together with the burial of Asian concerns embedded in the Tokyo Tribunal verdict, has meant that the colonial mentality is still vaguely present and tied in conservative minds to a "war of self-defense" against the United States and Britain.

At the same time, there is one more reason why conservatives hesitate to recognize that the Asia–Pacific War was a war of aggression—the difficulty in reconciling that admission with their personal memories of those who died, compounded by their feelings, as survivors, of guilt regarding the dead.

This sense of unfinished relations with the war dead is the kernel of literary critic Eto Jun's argument for the appropriateness of official visits by cabinet ministers to pray at Yasukuni Shrine. He has insisted that "the land of Japan, the scenery beloved by the Japanese people, and daily life all co-exist together with the dead in Japan." Left-wing novelist Nakano Shigeharu invented a similar attitude for the ex–middle school principal who was the protagonist of his early postwar novel *Go-shaku no sake* (Five cups of sake).[27] Commenting on the ban by occupation officials on public funerals for the war dead, he said: "If we admit that we can't use public buildings or govern ourselves, then we have let them die like dogs in an aggressive war." Another author, Kobori Keiichiro, supported national prayer for the souls of the war dead because, "The souls of the war dead and others who died untimely deaths, without achieving their full measure of honor, wealth, and authority, must wander between heaven and earth."[28]

Most Japanese have had great difficulty criticizing any actions of the Japanese war dead, given the circumstances of those deaths. It is very dangerous to argue that, if we recognize that the Asia–Pacific War was a war of aggression, then Japanese casualties "died like dogs." Logically, if that were so, the only way to make their deaths meaningful would be victory in a future war. The "dog's death thesis" is the psychological foundation for preparation to push the people into a war of revenge. Such

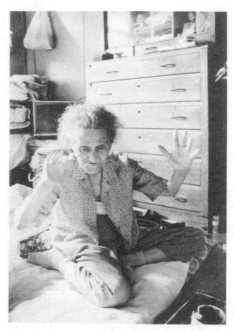

Yun Kap-su, who has survived extraordinary hardships, now lives in Hiroshima. At the age of sixteen, she was taken with other girls from her village in Korea to Japan, where she was sold to a brothel. Later she married a widowed man with five small children. She lost a young son during an air raid in July 1945, when he fell in the river while rushing across a narrow bridge. Her husband and three more children died in the atomic attack a month later. The story of her life inextricably entwines the tragedy of life in Japan under American bombardment and the callous brutality of presurrender Japanese leaders. It fits comfortably into neither the American nor the Japanese official memories of the war. (Ienaga, 3.185.)

thinking has not been dominant in postwar Japan. Rather, showing a skepticism born of their experience of being mobilized by the wartime state, most people feel that the "war brought sorrow," including a sense that—unlike the past, when the war dead were sacrificed to nationalism and warmongering—the future should be built on peace and international cooperation.

There is also a problem with the argument that the nation-state should care for the souls of those who died a "violent and untimely death" in war. Surely, that category includes the Asian people and Allied soldiers who died in the war. How can we look at the Japanese deaths alone as "violent and untimely" or make distinctions based on citizenship within that group? The very same problem emerges among those who discriminate by nationality out of narrow-minded patriotism, when they worship the souls of the Japanese dead at Yasukuni.

In the last half-century, Asia has changed. Many Asian countries have become politically independent and economically dynamic. If Japanese supremacist feelings toward Asia persist, Japan is likely to become isolated in the region. Moreover, in the post–cold war world, economic friction among the advanced capitalist countries is increasing, and alongside that, ethnic sentiments are growing. Thus, the likelihood is strong that most conservatives will shift from their older ideas to the concept that the Second World War was two wars, one of aggression against Asia and one of "defense." It remains hard to judge whether the partial self-criticism in the "two-wars" consciousness is a permanent shift toward splitting a sense of remorse toward Asia from any toward Western countries or just a return to an aggressive old-style nationalism.

In any case, the fiftieth anniversary of defeat brought new levels of nationalism to Japan but also subtle changes in conservative thinking about the war.

Conclusion

Both the United States and Japan turned toward nationalistic commemoration of the war on its fiftieth anniversary, but the forms and roots of that nationalism differed considerably in the two nations. It is with these differences that I would like to conclude.

The first difference, of course, is that one nation was commemorating the war from the perspective of victor and another from that of loser. The United States remembered the antifascist "holy war." It also recalled a complete, unconditional victory in a "good war" that brought the country out of its long-term economic depression. One can say that World War II intensified an American tendency to believe that war is an appropriate way to resolve international conflict. The shock of Pearl Harbor snapped the United States out of the isolationist sense of security that it was a natural fortress, moated by the Atlantic and Pacific oceans, and united the country behind a large, standing military for overseas intervention.

In contrast, Japan lost not only 3.1 million people, including those killed in atomic and conventional air raids, but also all its overseas territories. The home islands were also devastated by the bombings. This is why a broad spectrum of Japanese came to feel that "war brings sorrow." Then, the war crimes trials and postwar purges pinned the main war responsibility on the military, so that the status of the postwar Self-Defense Forces has been and remains extremely low.

Second, there is a huge difference in attitudes toward atomic weapons.

Postwar Japanese are conscious both of the enormity of the suffering at Hiroshima and Nagasaki and of the way that the effects of those bombs differed from the effects of other weapons—such as the lingering, cruel effects of radiation damage. The victims' consciousness that "we are the only nation to have suffered atomic bombs" is strong, as is antinuclear pacifism. This very sentiment, unfortunately, has contributed to the weak sense of responsibility for the Asia–Pacific War. When the danger grew more pressing that atomic weapons might be used again during the Korean and Vietnam Wars, the Japanese government passed the three non-nuclear principles (prohibiting the production or possession of nuclear weapons or their introduction into Japan by another country). This issue transcended left–right divisions within Japan.

In contrast, the United States practiced what can be called "atomic diplomacy." As the sole nation with control over nuclear bombs, the United States entered the postwar era with great confidence. Then, when the United States and the USSR both had atomic weapons, they developed a nuclear standoff to protect each side against potential atomic attack by the other. Even some people within the U.S. peace movement practiced what can be thought of as "nuclear pacifism," arguing that nuclear weapons were a "necessary evil." This, too, helped prevent serious reflection over having devastated Hiroshima and Nagasaki with A-bombs.

Third, the United States also experienced "defeat" in the Vietnam War, but those physical and psychological wounds were largely limited to those who experienced defeat in Vietnam and others of their generation. Of course, the entire nation became wary of getting bogged down in the quagmire of long-term military engagements, as the term "Vietnam syndrome" suggests. Yet there was no general rejection of overseas military involvement itself. And many hoped that the victory in the Persian Gulf War would overcome any lingering Vietnam syndrome. Certainly, the Vietnam War greatly affected the thinking of American scholars and influenced the revisionist New Left in various ways. Probably, the split between academics and politicians in the controversy over the Smithsonian's atomic bomb exhibit in some ways paralleled the great chasm between the effect of the Vietnam War on the academic community and on other areas of American life.

Again, very differently, Japanese concern with the Vietnam War was primarily over avoiding entanglement in the conflict. Nonetheless, Japan's "Vietnam War generation" developed a sympathetic interest in the Third World at that time. When, in 1982, Asian nations protested the whitewash of official Japanese textbooks regarding Japanese predations in Asia in the years prior to 1945, it was mainly this generation that supported them and that has pushed ever since for recognition of Japanese atrocities and compensation to victims.

Of course, there have been other important changes as well. In the 1980s, as they reached retirement age, former Japanese soldiers began to break their silence over their own wartime actions and culpability. Another decisive change is that many Asian countries have successfully democratized, profoundly influencing opportunities for their citizens to speak up about their own experiences, including demands for reparations for wartime atrocities. In 1988, the United States government apologized and ordered compensation to Japanese-Americans incarcerated during the war. In January 1989, the death of the Showa emperor eased the way for more open discussion of war responsibility in the Japanese media. Then, in January 1992, just before Prime Minister Miyazawa Kiichi was about to make a state visit to the Republic of Korea, scholars discovered documents proving that the wartime government and military had directly recruited and managed the former "military comfort women." The Japanese government issued an apology to the affected countries. Since then, the issue of unsettled compensation—not just to comfort women but to other victims, too—has become a major topic of discussion in Japan, in Asia, and throughout the world.

Thus, in the 1980s, the commemoration of World War II in Japan began to change radically in response to both domestic and international events. The fiftieth anniversary of defeat was an occasion for renewed emphasis on nationalism but also marked a shift in the nature of that nationalism and spurred challenges to it. Past commemorations emphasized the difference in outlook between the wartime and postwar generations in very static ways. In both Japan and the United States, the fiftieth anniversary of the end of the war and the dawn of the nuclear era brought to the fore ideas about patriotism that are likely to have long-term and interactive significance for both nations.

Notes

1. National Air and Space Museum, Smithsonian Institution, exhibition planning document, "The Crossroads: The Atomic Bomb and the End of World War II," July 1993, 2.

2. *Asahi Shinbun,* November 29, 1994.

3. Air Force Association, "Special Report: The Smithsonian and the *Enola Gay*," March 15, 1994, 3–4, 13.

4. Ikoi Hidetaka, *Janguru-kuruuzu ni uttetsuke no hi* (Perfect day for a jungle cruise) (Tokyo: Chikuma Shobo, 1987).

5. "U.S. Senate Resolution 257—Relating to the *Enola Gay* Exhibit," unofficial

version of *Congressional Record* (Senate), September 19, 1994, s. 12968. Emphasis added.

6. *New York Times,* January 30, 1995; *Wall Street Journal,* January 31, 1995.

7. *Washington Post,* February 1, 1995; *Los Angeles Times,* February 1, 1995; *Asahi Shinbun,* February 3, 1995.

8. *Asahi Shinbun,* January 23, 1995.

9. Gar Alperovitz, "Questioning Hiroshima," *Boston Globe,* August 29, 1994.

10. *Washington Post,* August 27, 1994; *Boston Globe,* August 24, 1994.

11. *Perspectives,* OAH Newsletter, February 1995, 3.

12. Air Force Association, "Special Report," 10.

13. See chapter 5, by Ellen H. Hammond, for a detailed discussion of the hall.

14. Tanaka Nobumasa, "Nihon Izokukai no Gojunen" (Fifty years of Japan's Association of Bereaved Families), *Sekai,* September 1994.

15. For details, see Arai Shinichi, ed., *Senso Hakubutsukan* (War museums) (Tokyo: Iwanami Shoten, 1994). Also see Heiwa Hakubutsukan o Hajimeru Kai (Committee for Building the Peace Museum), ed., *Heiwa Hakubutsukan o Kangaeru* (Considering the Peace Museum) (Tokyo: Heiwa no Atorie, 1994).

16. Ajia ni Tai Suru Nihon no Senso Sekinin o Tou Minshu Honin Junbi Kai (Preparatory Committee for the People's Court on Japan's War Responsibility toward Asia), ed., *Senso Sekinin, 1-go, tokushu: Kioku no keisho* (War responsibility no. 1: Special issue on succession of memories), 1994, 13.

17. Ian Buruma, *The Wages of Guilt: Memories of War in Germany and Japan* (New York: Farrar, Straus and Giroux, 1994), 294. See also *Asahi Shinbun,* August 16, 1991.

18. *Yamato Shinbun,* February 9, 1995.

19. *Sankei Shinbun,* February 22, 1995.

20. Yoshida Yutaka, "Nihonjin no Sensokan—4" (The views on war of the Japanese), *Sekai,* January 1995.

21. Yoshida Yutaka, "Nihonjin no Sensokan—7," *Sekai,* April 1995.

22. *Shukan Asahi,* December 1993.

23. *Asahi Shinbun,* October 26, 1994.

24. Ozawa Ichiro, *Nihon Kaizo Keikaku* (Tokyo: Kodansha, 1993). This book has been translated by Louisa Rubinfien and edited by Eric Gower as *Blueprint for a New Japan: The Rethinking of a Nation* (Tokyo: Kodansha International, 1994).

25. *Chicago Tribune,* June 7, 1995.

26. There is very little scholarly work arguing this "have-not nation" thesis, but see Gendai Ajia Kenkyukai, ed., *Seikimatsu kara mita dai toa senso* (The Greater East Asian War viewed from the end of the century) (Tokyo: Purejidento-sha, 1991), 309, which notes, "It was believed that Japan had the appropriate and just authority to advance onto the continent based on its natural status as a have-not nation backed up by Asianism."

27. *Five Cups of Sake,* a translation of this novel, appears in *Three Works by Nakano Shigeharu,* trans. Brett de Bary, Cornell University East Asia Series, (Ithaca, NY: Cornell University Press, 1979).

28. Eto Jun and Kobori Keiichiro, eds., *Yasukuni ronshu—Nihon no chinkon no dento no tame ni* (The Yasukuni debate—For the tradition of the repose of Japanese souls) (Tokyo: Nihon Kyobunsha, 1986), 20, 44, 82.

4

Making Things Visible

Learning from the Censors

George H. Roeder Jr.

The atomic bombings of Hiroshima and Nagasaki killed instantly tens of thousands of potential witnesses.[1] Nothing visible remained of many of these initial victims except for cinders. Some left permanent shadows, cast on stone or wood by the bombs' searing flash. Subsequent conflagrations consumed those trapped in debris or too injured to flee. Rivers swept away many who fled to them to soothe burns or escape the heat of converging fires. For reasons of sanity and sanitation, survivors soon burned the remaining corpses. The bombs' intense thermal energy blinded some; smoking fires and rapidly forming clouds of vapor and debris obscured the view for others. In both cities, the enveloping pain and traumatic shock that spread thousands of meters from the hypocenter[2] made comprehension of the magnitude of the suffering difficult even for those in its midst.

Because the bombs destroyed so much of the evidence of their doings, no photographs of long rows of bodies comparable to those taken by Allied liberators when they reached the death camps emerged from these atomic hells. No newsreel footage showed bulldozers burying hundreds of corpses at a time. However, some Japanese and others did record their experiences and observations, visually and in writing, then and later. Choice and circumstance have put limits on access to these testimonies for many years, but they have become increasingly available to people around the world. This chapter uses thirteen images as reference points for discussion of the ongoing struggle to make visible, or to keep out of sight and out of mind, the two bombs' human impact.

As Laura Hein and Mark Selden explain in their introduction, "From the earliest reports of the atomic bombings, Americans have viewed nuclear destruction primarily from the Promethean perspective of the inventor and bombardier. . . . By contrast, from the outset, the official Japanese perspective was from the position of the first, and thus far only, target population."

Only Japan has museums dedicated to keeping alive in historical memory the consequences of using atomic bombs; only the United States has a major exhibition that tells the story of the bombings from the viewpoint of those who dropped the bombs. As Hein and Selden also note, the distinction between the Japanese and American views is not precise and unvarying. Often over the past fifty years, Japanese officials have suppressed evidence of the victims' suffering, sometimes out of fear that it would cast doubt on their own adequacy or threaten the relationship that they sought with the United States. The history of American censorship of the victims' experience began in August 1945 and continues to the present, but so did and does the history of attempts by Americans to make this experience visible.

Many Americans received their first account of individual suffering caused by the bombs when they read John Hersey's "Hiroshima,"[3] which appeared in August 1946 in magazine form and soon after as a widely distributed book. American officials initially withheld photographs and motion picture footage of the bombs' victims that came under their control with the postwar occupation of Japan, but this material slowly became available from various sources. By the late 1960s, the National Archives made public material that included two hours and forty-five minutes of footage taken by Japanese cameramen in the months after the bombings. Eric Barnouw and others working with him shaped sixteen minutes of this footage into the film *Hiroshima and Nagasaki, August, 1945,* which presented viewers in both the United States and Japan a disturbing account of the experiences of bomb victims.[4]

Despite these complexities, it continues to make sense to write of an American "official story" of the bombings as described by Hein and Selden in the introduction to this volume. The Smithsonian Institution's National Air and Space Museum (NASM), which attracts more visitors (10 million in some years) than any other museum in the world, presents this story in its exhibition on the plane that dropped the Hiroshima bomb, the *Enola Gay.* As originally planned, the exhibition would have included discussion of various historical and ethical issues raised by the use of the bombs. It also would have included a section describing the experiences of those at "ground zero." After a prolonged attack on the planned exhibition by the Air Force Association, the American Legion, and the U.S. Congress, the NASM brought the exhibition into line with the narrowest version of the official story.[5] Although much of the controversy focused on the script for the exhibition, critics also objected strenuously to plans to show photographs of dead and horribly injured victims of the bombings. The censored exhibition purposefully excludes all visual reports of what it meant for an individual to be in Hiroshima or Nagasaki on August 6 and 9. The only exception is an eleven-second segment in the video that accompanies the exhibition showing injured Japanese receiving assistance.[6]

A placard in front of the dominant artifact in the exhibition, the gleaming fifty-six-foot-long forward fuselage, poses the question "Is the *Enola Gay* 'Radioactive'?" then gives a reassuring answer: "This exhibition poses no health hazards to museum visitors." No sign asks, "Can this exhibition cause mental sterility?" Yet when visitors regard it as the full story of these bombings, it probably does more to obscure their meaning than any official act since the initial censorship of images and other reports by and about bomb victims.

Because of its limitations, there is much to be learned from the exhibition. It makes easily available information on such topics as the restoration of the *Enola Gay,* the training of its crew, their opinions on the bombings, and the use of humorous, erotic, and sentimental names and "nose art" on American bombers, such as the B-29 that its crew named "Hump Happy Mammy." But the questions created by the bombings never have been easy ones. Visitors seeking a more complex understanding can approach the exhibition as if its real subject were the processes that have rendered invisible the experiences of those on the receiving end of the bombs. By regarding the exhibition's silences as indicators of where they must be most attentive, visitors can transform an instrument of miseducation into one of revelation. This chapter suggests ways to achieve such a transformation. Readers who do not have a chance to visit the NASM can regard that exhibition as representative of the official story and use the strategies suggested here for entering into dialogue with the numerous similar versions of that story presented in other museums, articles, and books.

Many of the issues raised in the controversy over the planned and actual *Enola Gay* exhibition remain open to debate. One point beyond dispute is that critics of the original plan wanted the exhibition to focus on the perceptions and experiences of the crew that dropped the bomb rather than on the people on whom it was dropped or on larger issues of war and peace raised by the atomic bomb. They got their wish. Under pressure from these politically powerful critics, the NASM excluded this photograph and dozens of others like it. Yamahata Yosuke took this picture in Nagasaki on August 10. The site was approximately 700 meters south-southeast of the hypocenter. The burned corpse in the photograph "is presumably that of a mobilized student who was exposed to the atomic bomb while walking along the prefectural highway."[7] (Photograph reprinted from *Nagasaki Journey: The Photographs of Yosuke Yamahata,* August 10, 1945 [San Francisco: Pomegranate Art Books, n.d.] 69.)

The victims are present nonetheless. In the weeks after the bombings, American newspapers and magazines published the only photographs of the bombed cities available to them at the time, aerial views. After American troops occupied Japan, authorities withheld most ground-level images. In the United States fifty years later, public presentations on the bombings, as well as the illustrations in the majority of American history textbooks, continue to feature panoramic views of material destruction. But an entry from Elbert B. Smith's diary can help visitors gain insight from the limited visual information contained in aerial photographs such as the ones of destroyed Hiroshima in the video that accompanies the *Enola Gay* exhibition. Smith headed the crew that would have dropped the third bomb, had it been used. When, soon after the bombings, he saw photographs of Hiroshima, he noted "that rubble for the most part had been literally reduced to powder and sucked up into the cloud, just as had so many of the former inhabitants of Hiroshima."[8] The remarkable evenness of destruction shown in aerial views of Hiroshima testifies to the bomb's ability to cover a large expanse of land with the finely dispersed remnants of buildings, trees, carts, street lights, rubbish bins, automobiles, animals, and people. Critics of the originally planned *Enola Gay* exhibition succeeded in banishing pictures of recognizable corpses, but they failed to recognize photographs such as this one as pictures of an open graveyard, displaying the remains of thousands. (Photograph from National Archives, 434-OR-71, Box 23, Folder 71.)

Censorship of the small number of photographs of victims taken in the immediate aftermath is an especially oppressive act because these few depicted victims must represent so many. The hours after the bombings provided little opportunity for photographs of any sort. Photographer Matsushige Yoshito, attached at that time to the Japanese army, reported how painful it was for him to take even five photographs on August 6. One of the people in this photograph died soon after he took it. Matsushige remembered that "I felt like I was walking through a world of hell." As historian Richard Rhodes wrote, "The world of the dead is a different place from the world of the living and it is hardly possible to visit there. That day in Hiroshima the two worlds nearly converged."[9]

Before or after seeing the *Enola Gay* exhibition, visitors might read the chapter entitled "Tongues of Fire" in Rhodes's *The Making of the Atomic Bomb*. The title comes from Ibuse Masuji's novel of Hiroshima, *Black Rain*: "In my mind's eye, like a waking dream, I could still see the tongues of fire at work on the bodies of men." Visitors also can find testimonies banished from the *Enola Gay* exhibition in Kyoko Selden and Mark Selden, eds. and trans., *The Atomic Bomb: Voices from Hiroshima and Nagasaki*,[10] and in the many other sources listed in the bibliography of that work.

Matsushige noted that in the areas of Hiroshima where he traveled, "other people walked around with cameras, but nobody else took pictures."[11] Unknown to him, a few did record what they saw in Hiroshima. In Nagasaki, Yamahata Yosuke, sent by the News and Information Bureau of the Japanese Western Army Corps, took more than one hundred photographs on August 10, producing the fullest contemporary pictorial record of the suffering and destruction in the immediate aftermath of the bombings in either city. (See pages 10, 76, 80, and 82 above and below.) In the following months, others, including newly arrived Americans, took many thousands of photographs and hours of motion picture footage. Most of these images fell under the control of the country that had dropped the bombs, leaving United States officials with much of the responsibility for deciding who saw what. For reasons that ranged from the avoidance of "public unrest" that might result from stirring up resentment to the wish to avoid "rubbing it in," American occupation authorities in Japan censored visual images as well as printed discussions of the bomb. In Washington, officials made inaccessible to Americans for varying periods of time images of burned, crushed, and irradiated bodies.[12]

The censoring of evidence of the bombs' primary human consequences contrasted sharply with the vigorous efforts of the military to record and publicize the stories of the airmen who dropped the bomb. Colonel Paul Tibbets, pilot of the *Enola Gay*, reported that U.S. Army camera crews and photographers recording the plane's departure for Hiroshima (officials told them that it was on a historic mission, although not that it contained an atomic bomb) were so numerous that he had to urge them to get out of the plane's way so that he could prepare for takeoff. One observer compared the scene to a Hollywood premiere because "amid brilliant floodlights, pictures were taken and retaken by still and motion picture photographers." In its inclusions and exclusions, the *Enola Gay* exhibition continues this celebratory tradition.[13] (Photograph by Matsushige Yoshito, reprinted from *Hiroshima and Nagasaki: The Atomic Bombings as Seen through Photographs and Artwork*, vol. 4, *Let It Never Be Repeated*, 56–57.)

Images presented to the American public during World War II reinforced the idea that the Allied effort contributed to an orderly world. Censors did not allow publication of any photographic images showing civilian victims of Allied bombing. Thus, it did not seem unusual when, even after American occupation of Japan, pictures of Hiroshima and Nagasaki released by the United States government showed the extent of material destruction, but not human victims. The view from afar of the destroyed cities constituted images of order because, for an American audience, the destruction of Japanese war-making capability represented restoration of an orderly world. Because American officials described Japanese cities as military targets, as when President Harry S Truman called Hiroshima a military base in his first publicly released statement on the atomic bombing of that city, Americans could read images of their destruction as a necessary step to bring the boys home.[14] The ending of the war soon after the atomic bombings made this reading seem plausible.

In this context, images of injured Japanese civilians were unacceptable images of disorder. Fifty years later, the Air Force Association saw the same images as disorderly in the context of the story that they wanted the *Enola Gay* exhibition to tell. These photographs, taken by Yamahata Yosuke on the morning of August 10, were two of the several dozen photographs of "ground zero" that would have been in the *Enola Gay* exhibition as originally planned. They are a reminder that the majority of victims of the bombings were women and children. In the United States, as in every other country that carried out aerial bombing raids on civilian populations during the war, all of the top military and political decision makers were men.

In the second paragraph of his August 6 statement, Truman remarked that the bombing "repaid many fold" the Japanese attack on Pearl Harbor. Invariably, Hollywood war movies from the period made reference to Pearl Harbor or depicted some other treacherous Japanese attack on Americans *before* they introduced scenes showing Americans making war on the Japanese. Yamahata's photographs are a reminder that Truman could hardly refer to the atomic bombings as the "Battle of Hiroshima" and the "Battle of Nagasaki." Because the Allies had destroyed most of the Japanese Air Force before August 1945, they encountered no resistance from hostile aircraft as they dropped their bombs on the two cities. The only way to make the bombings seem to be part of a conflict that posed danger to Americans was to look backward to incidents such as Pearl Harbor or forward toward an American invasion of Japan. Truman's reference helped build public support by tapping into the widespread desire for revenge for Pearl Harbor. Yet by using the language of accounting ("repaid"), a rational activity, Truman implied that the bombing of Hiroshima was not a hot-blooded act of vengeance. Acts carried out with too much passion could be irrational and therefore inconsistent with the image of a well-ordered war effort. (Photographs reprinted from *Nagasaki Journey*, 92, 97.)

In the late 1930s, supporters of the Loyalist government in the Spanish Civil War raised funds by sending on tour to various American cities Pablo Picasso's protest painting *Guernica*. Picasso represented the suffering of animals as well as people during the bombing of the Basque city named in the painting's title. Throughout World War II, U.S. officials censored images of animals killed by Allied bombing, potential symbols of the slaughter of innocents.

This photograph, by Yamahata Yosuke, would have been in the planned *Enola Gay* exhibition. In its absence, visitors to the sanitized version of the exhibition might wish to supplement it by seeking out books such as *Nagasaki Journey: The Photographs of Yosuke Yamahata, August 10, 1945,* and a related documentary film also entitled *Nagasaki Journey.* Yamahata went to Nagasaki with two others, including writer Higashi Jun, who reported that at one point, "I found myself walking on something soft and spongy. In the light of the crescent moon I realized to my disgust that I was standing on the corpse of a horse."[15] One Hiroshima survivor remembered seeing "a living horse burning." Other reports from the two cities tell of pets and work animals killed by the bombs and of birds igniting as they flew or hopping about with their wings burned off. (Photograph reprinted from *Nagasaki Journey,* 60.)

During the war, American newsreels and Hollywood movies boasted how such innovations as the Norden bombsight allowed U.S. aircrews to carry out precision bombing, pinpointing military rather than civilian targets. In fact, due to the difficulties of bombing under wartime conditions, bombs typically landed half a mile and more from their targets, eradicating the distinction between munitions factories and hospitals. Unlike most bombs, the one dropped on Hiroshima detonated very close to the intended point, a result of good weather and the lack of antiaircraft activity, as well as of the rigorous training of the crew emphasized in the *Enola Gay* exhibition. In this case, precise targeting placed the bomb over the middle of a populous city. The bomb destroyed some factories and military installations, but a far larger number of residential, educational, medical, cultural, and commercial buildings and their inhabitants. A later American survey, not released to the public, indicated that the bombing had damaged "less than 10 percent of the city's manufacturing, transportation, and storage facilities," which were in outlying districts.[16] Immediately after the bombing, some American newspapers displayed a prewar photograph of an electrical power plant that they speculated might have been the main target for the bombing, although as it turned out, it was one of the undamaged remote buildings.[17] Due to bad weather, the bombardier targeted the Nagasaki bomb a few miles away from the planned aiming point; it also caused mainly civilian casualties and damage. This helps explain why censors in 1945 and 1995 (the year the *Enola Gay* exhibition opened, in commemoration of the fiftieth anniversary of the bombings) suppressed most ground-level images of the two cities.

This is one of the photographs initially censored by the U.S. government, perhaps because it bore too much resemblance to some of the photographs from Nazi death camps appearing at the war's end. There were profound differences between Nazi brutalities and the atomic bombings, but both used modern technology to produce mass death. During World War II, the government censored pictures that depicted Americans as victims or perpetrators of mass death, and the *Enola Gay* exhibition continues this practice of disassociating Americans from mass death. For a more complex view of the issue of mass death, visitors to the *Enola Gay* exhibition should also visit the nearby Holocaust Museum. Here curators have made the respectful assumption that visitors are capable of holding two or more ideas in their mind at the same time. Thus, they explain, accurately, that Americans played a major role in the liberation of concentration camps *and* that anti-Semitism in the United States was strong enough to keep many potential refugees from Nazi terror trapped in Europe.[18] (Photograph from National Archives, 434-OR, Box 24, Folder 78.)

As originally planned, the *Enola Gay* exhibition would have included this watch from Hiroshima. Opponents managed to eliminate from that exhibition anything, including this watch and the child's lunch box mentioned elsewhere in this volume, that served as reminders of the individuality of the bombs' victims. The exhibition once again repeated practices established in the weeks after the bombings. At that time, American newspaper and magazine readers saw overviews of the bombed cities and drawings representing the structure of the atoms whose splitting released the lethal energy. But they encountered few visual reports from the area between these extremes of the vast and the infinitely small, from the human-scale setting where suffering occurred. In the censored version of the *Enola Gay* exhibition, personal attributes are reserved for the American crew, with whom visitors are encouraged to identify. In the video that accompanies the exhibition, Staff Sergeant Robert Caron, tail gunner on the *Enola Gay*, wears a Brooklyn Dodgers cap similar to the one he had on fifty years earlier when a photographer snapped a picture, featured in the exhibition, of the crew before they departed on their mission. (See Figure 1-4.) Personal objects such as the lunch box and the watch had a presence that threatened to make a greater impression on viewers than the massive *Enola Gay* fuselage that the Air Force Association hoped to keep, along with the crew, at the center of visitors' attention.

Further testimony to the power of such objects is found in *Hiroshima Diary*, of Japanese physician Hachiya Michihiko. Dr. Hachiya, injured in the bombing, reported that as a friend bicycled him around the city on August 11, in the midst of all the horrors, "I was disturbed most by the sight of burnt toys in the ruins."[19] Additionally, had the watch survived the critics and remained in the exhibition, it would have encouraged viewers to visit in their imaginations the particular place and time on the ground in Hiroshima at 8:15 A.M. on August 6—where these critics least wanted them to linger. (Photograph from *Hiroshima and Nagasaki: The Atomic Bombings as Seen through Photographs and Artwork*, vol. 4, *Let It Never Be Repeated*, 188.)

At the instant of Hiroshima's immolation, Captain Theodore J. Van Kirk, the *Enola Gay*'s navigator, considered the meaning for his own life: "I thought: Thank God the war is over and I don't have to get shot at any more. I can go home."[20] Millions of American soldiers who learned of the bombing some hours later via Truman's announcement had similar feelings. The *Enola Gay* exhibition continues the practice of using the resources of the United States government to transfer this thankfulness for the bombings—highly understandable on the part of combat military personnel—to the larger public. Of course, in 1945, Americans did not need any government prompting to be thankful for events that they associated with the safe return home of their loved ones, neighbors, coworkers, and fellow citizens. But over time, initial assumptions have been challenged by increased availability of words and images revealing the horror of the bombings and the possibility of bringing about a Japanese surrender by less violent means, and fading of the wartime attitudes that made the bombings seem, in Winston Churchill's word, a "deliverance." Many veterans, upon reflection, developed a more complex understanding of the bombings. Consequently, sustaining the official story as the only possible one has required more concerted effort, as shown by the political maneuvering required of the opponents of the planned exhibition to impose their viewpoint on the NASM.

By insisting that, in lieu of the bombings, the war could have been ended only through an invasion costing many American (and Japanese) lives, the official story has emphasized possible American deaths rather than actual Japanese ones.[21] In a similar fashion, in the days and years after the bombings, government officials and American journalists kept the focus on Americans as potential victims through dramatic predictions of the impact of atomic weapons on American cities. Warnings of this sort can be done in ways that show respect for, rather than distract attention from, those who suffered in Hiroshima and Nagasaki, as in Jonathan Schell's *The Fate of the Earth*. But distraction seemed the more likely result when, in the 1950s, the Atomic Energy Commission distributed illustrations such as this one superimposing the fireball of a hydrogen bomb explosion over the skyline of New York City at the same time that it continued to withhold from public view much evidence of the impact of the actual atomic bombings carried out by Americans. (Illustration from National Archives, 434-SF-1-8.)

Censors also kept out of view photographs that reduced the cultural distance between Americans and Japanese. At a time when President Truman, in announcing use of the bomb, thanked God for putting it in American hands, and a popular song called it the answer to soldiers' prayers, it is not surprising that the government suppressed this photograph from Nagasaki. That city had the largest percentage of Roman Catholics of any in Japan, and the bomb detonated a few hundred meters from the main church, Urakami Cathedral. Several months after the bombings, parishioners held a ceremony that featured eight thousand crosses, one for each of the members of Nagasaki's Catholic community killed in the atomic bombing of that city. The crosses outnumbered the survivors able to attend the ceremony.[22] Although the American government could withhold material in its possession, with the war over, it no longer had complete control over everything coming out of former combat zones. The "Picture of the Week" in *Life* magazine for October 15, 1945, taken by staff photographer Bernard Hoffman, showed a stone head of Christ dislodged by the bombing, with the destroyed cathedral in the background. The *Life* caption suggested that Christians must wonder "whether even the urgencies of war should permit such violation of individual life as the atomic bomb had committed," an issue raised again in a public statement by the Federated Council of Churches early in 1946.[23] Critics of the planned *Enola Gay* exhibition could not tolerate such questions and made it seem as if they had been introduced by "revisionist historians" rather than being present from the beginning. The video that accompanies the censored exhibition continues to enlist divine help in promoting the official story, as Truman did. While the video shows faces of the various crew members, viewers hear the prayer that Chaplain William Downey offered before they departed on "the first atomic mission." (Photograph from *Hiroshima and Nagasaki: The Atomic Bombings as Seen through Photographs and Artwork*, vol. 4, *Let It Never Be Repeated*, 138–39.)

As shown by the previous example, from early on it proved impossible for the American government to keep entirely out of view ground-level visual records of events as immense as the two bombings. In September 1945, a staff photographer for *Life* magazine managed to visit Hiroshima, and the October 8 issue of *Life* published some of his photographs. One showed a family in a Buddhist temple having a memorial service for relatives killed in the bombings. Two others depicted burned survivors, with one showing a mother and child and one showing an older couple.[24] *Life* presented these photographs in a way that protected the official story: "Photographer Eyerman reported that their injuries looked like those he had seen when he photographed men burned at Pearl Harbor." Even with such protective captioning, photographs of victims rarely appeared in American publications until the 1950s or, for most images, later.

The same was true in Japan under the occupation, but this photograph of an injured policeman distributing casualty certificates a few hours after the Hiroshima bombing, which critics succeeded in keeping out of the *Enola Gay* exhibition, did appear. The Hiroshima newspaper *Chugoku Shinbun* published it, along with four other photographs, including the third image in the present chapter, in August 1946. Photographer Matsushige Yoshito explains what happened: "I was summoned to the Occupation GHQ together with the reporter who wrote the article. Despite what we expected, they weren't angry. We were told that it was all right to print those things, since they were facts, but they wanted us to submit them for review prior to publishing them."[25] This was an exception; American authorities prevented publication of most images of bombing victims. Matsushige's photographs first appeared in the United States in September 1952, in a *Life* magazine article entitled "When Atom Bomb Struck—Uncensored." Although such images continue to be banished from the most widely visited presentation on the bombings, they are displayed in others that reach a large public. NASM visitors can counter the disorienting affects of the *Enola Gay* exhibition by walking to the nearby Smithsonian Museum of American History, where they will find the photograph reproduced in chapter 12 of the present volume in the exhibition on "Science in American Life." (Photograph from *Hiroshima and Nagasaki: The Atomic Bombings as Seen through Photographs and Artwork*, vol. 4, *Let It Never Be Repeated*, 61.)

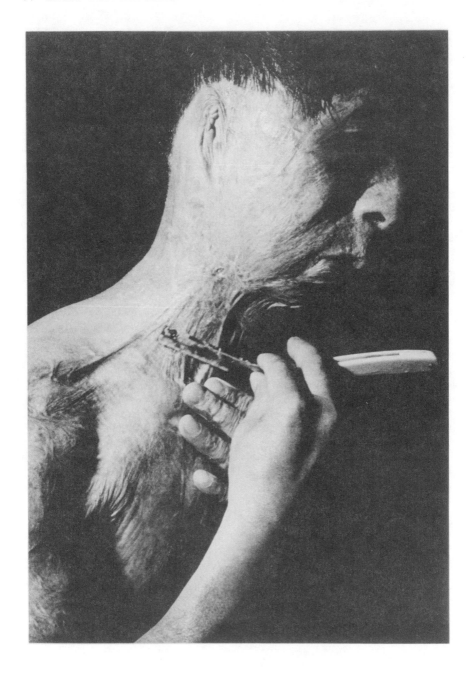

The most lasting type of censorship, and the most difficult to overcome, is that which we impose on ourselves when we choose not to look at distressing images, even when they tell us something we need to know. In chapter 8, Monica Braw explains why in Japan silence is sometimes the sanest response to memories of the bombings, although in Japan, too, silence can be used to avoid confronting difficult issues. Some have used the mushroom cloud to obscure earlier Japanese atrocities, and official Japanese memorializations of the bombings fail to acknowledge that many of the thousands of Koreans who died in Hiroshima and Nagasaki had first been victimized by Japan. In the United States, silence might be an appropriate response to the bombings for some of those with painful personal connections to them, but as an official position, it can only damage attempts to ground public life and public policies in integrity and understanding rather than in deceit and ignorance.

One of the cruelest moments in twentieth-century literature comes when, after a fleeting suspension of disbelief, the reader recognizes the impossibility of the cinematic vision that Kurt Vonnegut offers in his novel *Slaughterhouse Five.* Allied bombers, as they fly backward over burning Dresden, shrink the fires, gather them into cylindrical steel containers, and return them to the United States, where factories operate "night and day" to dismantle them "so they would never hurt anybody ever again."[26] The horrors experienced in Dresden, Sarajevo, London, Tokyo, Leningrad, Pearl Harbor, Phnom Penh, Warsaw, Hiroshima, Nagasaki, and the tens of thousands of other places visited by war in our century cannot be undone. By momentarily luring us in another direction, Vonnegut drives home this harsh truth. If they cannot be undone, they can, at least, be acknowledged.

For individuals, the suffering in Hiroshima and Nagasaki had much in common with that in other bombed cities. But the atomic bombings also were unique, not only in the number of people that they killed instantly, and in the totality of the destruction that the bombs caused, including elimination of support services for those who were injured, but also, because of the effects of radiation on those that they killed weeks, months, and years later. This photograph, and those taken by others such as Domon Ken, have sought to remind viewers that the bombings continued to have consequences after they disappeared from the headlines. (Photograph from *Hiroshima and Nagasaki: The Atomic Bombings as Seen through Photographs and Artwork,* vol. 2, *The Catastrophe and Its Scars,* 180.)

Although the censors had their way with the *Enola Gay* exhibition, for visitors willing to look elsewhere, the resources for understanding continue to grow. Writers in Japan, the United States, and elsewhere have produced many well-researched and analytically rigorous studies of the sort needed to put the visual imagery into context. Building on the small but strong base provided by the photographs that Matsushige Yoshito, Yamahata Yosuke, and others took soon after the bombings, those whose lives the bombings transformed continue to produce visual records of their experiences. Maruki Toshi and Maruki Iri have dedicated much of their lives to producing drawings, large murals, children's stories, and other works expressing the horrors of Hiroshima and then of other events such as the Nanjing massacre, the Holocaust, and the Minamata mercury poisoning tragedy.[27] They reached Hiroshima, where they had relatives, three days after the bombing.

This drawing is from *Unforgettable Fire: Pictures Drawn by Atomic Bomb Survivors*.[28] It is one of the more than two thousand paintings and drawings that the Japanese Broadcasting Corporation (NHK) received after requesting, in 1974, personal recollections of the bombings. The present form of the *Enola Gay* exhibition, as well as restrictions on the presentation of the Marukis' work in Japan,[29] are but two of many examples of continued attempts to keep out of view visual evidence of the human consequences of the atomic bombings. Yet as the publication of *Unforgettable Fire* demonstrated, over the past five decades, the burden on the censors has increased as the volume of evidence has grown larger. Enough is available to give viewers the power to annul any particular act of suppression, if they are willing to assume responsibility for seeing what needs to be seen. The survivor who drew this moment-of-death image wrote, "Walking around the back gate of Shukkeien Garden of Hakushima-cho, I saw an infant boy leaning against the gate and heard him crying. When I approached and then touched him, I found that he was dead. To think that he might have been my son made my heart ache."[30] (Photograph from *Unforgettable Fire: Pictures Drawn by Atomic Bomb Survivors*, ed. Japanese Broadcasting Corporation [NHK] [New York: Pantheon, 1977], 54.)

Notes

1. The combined number killed by the short- and long-term effects of the two bombs has reached the hundreds of thousands.

2. The point on the ground directly under the epicenter, the point in the air where the bomb detonated.

3. For an account of what Americans could read and see of the bombings in 1945 and 1946, see Robert Jay Lifton and Greg Mitchell, *Hiroshima in America: Fifty Years of Denial* (New York: Putnam, 1995), esp. 3–91. Their account is useful but not complete. The authors are unaware, for example, of the early publication of photographs mentioned on page 93. Lane Fenrich's chapter in this volume and his forthcoming *Envisioning Holocaust: Mass Death and American Culture, 1945–1995,* in press, University of Chicago Press, discuss limitations of Hersey's account.

4. For an account of the suppression of this footage and the eventual making and release of the film, see Eric Barnouw, *Media Marathon: A Twentieth-Century Memoir* (Durham, NC: Duke University Press, 1996), 194–217.

5. For discussion of the controversy, see David Thelen, "History after the *Enola Gay* Controversy: An Introduction," and the articles and documents that follow it in *Journal of American History* 82 (December 1995): 1029–1144. Included in this material are a chronology of the controversy and floor plans for the originally proposed and eventually installed exhibitions. For the original script, see Philip Nobile, ed., *Judgment at the Smithsonian* (New York: Marlowe, 1995).

6. The video, released in 1995 and produced and directed by Jonathan S. Felt, with David P. Usher and the Greenwich Workshop as executive producer, is entitled *Enola Gay: The First Atomic Mission* and may be purchased from the Smithsonian Institution.

7. Committee for the Compilation of Materials on Damage Caused by the Atomic Bombs in Hiroshima and Nagasaki, *Hiroshima and Nagasaki: The Physical, Medical, and Social Effects of the Atomic Bombings* (New York: Basic Books, 1981), 12.

8. Gordon Smith, "Diary of a Bomber Pilot," *Chicago Reader,* August 29, 1980.

9. Richard Rhodes, *The Making of the Atomic Bomb* (New York: Simon and Schuster, 1986), 715.

10. Kyoko Selden and Mark Selden, eds. and trans., *The Atomic Bomb: Voices from Hiroshima and Nagasaki* (Armonk, NY: M.E. Sharpe, 1989).

11. Haruko Taya Cook and Theodore F. Cook, *Japan at War: An Oral History* (New York: New Press, 1992), 395.

12. Glenn D. Hook, "Censorship and Reportage of Atomic Damage and Casualties in Hiroshima and Nagasaki," *Bulletin of Concerned Asian Scholars,* 23.1 (January–March 1991): 13–25; and Monica Braw, *The Atomic Bomb Suppressed: American Censorship in Occupied Japan* (Armonk, NY: M.E. Sharpe, 1991).

13. Rhodes, *Making of the Atomic Bomb,* 704.

14. Although Hiroshima was an important site for the assembly and deployment of military personnel and equipment, official U.S. estimates put the number of military personnel killed at approximately 3 percent of the total number of people killed in the bombing. In any case, the bomb's target was chosen to maximize the number of deaths rather than to destroy military equipment. American bombing campaigns had destroyed nearly sixty Japanese cities before the bombing of Hiroshima. Hiroshima was spared prior to August 6 in part because the city was one of those that American officials "saved" for the atomic bomb. But it also seems likely that it was not bombed earlier because it was not considered a priority military target.

15. *Nagasaki Journey: The Photographs of Yosuke Yamahata, August 10, 1945* (San Francisco: Pomegranate Art Books, n.d.), 61.

16. Lifton and Mitchell, *Hiroshima in America,* 24.

17. Ibid., 11.

18. For discussion of these issues, see Fenrich, *Envisioning Holocaust.* See also George H. Roeder Jr., *The Censored War: American Visual Experience during World War II* (New Haven, CT: Yale University Press, 1993), 40–41, 125–28.

19. Michihiko Hachiya, *Hiroshima Diary: The Journal of a Japanese Physician, August 6–September 30, 1945,* trans. Warner Wells (Chapel Hill, NC: University of North Carolina Press, 1955), 50.

20. Rhodes, *Making of the Atomic Bomb,* 711.

21. The official story also denied actual American deaths; for more than thirty years, the American government withheld information that several American POWs, perhaps a dozen, died in the bombing of Hiroshima or in its aftermath. In addition, this story never has had room for the many Americans of Japanese ancestry who were among the Hiroshima victims. The chapter in this volume by Sodei Rinjiro discusses the fate of the Nisei in Hiroshima in 1945.

22. Takashi Nagai, "We of Nagasaki," in *I Have Seen War: Twenty-Five Stories from World War II,* ed. Dorothy Sterling (New York: Hill & Wang, 1960), 269–70.

23. *Life,* October 15, 1945, 36–37.

24. *Life,* October 8, 1945, 27–35.

25. Cook and Cook, *Japan at War,* 394–95.

26. Quoted in Michael S. Sherry, *In the Shadow of War* (New Haven, CT: Yale University Press, 1995), 305.

27. See John W. Dower and John Junkerman, eds., *The Hiroshima Murals: The Art of Iri Maruki and Toshi Maruki* (Tokyo and New York: Kodansha International, 1985).

28. This volume has been published in the United States as well as in Japan. The American edition, edited by the Japanese Broadcasting Corporation (NHK), was brought out by Pantheon (New York, 1977).

29. On these restrictions, see Dower and Junkerman, *Hiroshima Murals,* 24.

30. Japanese Broadcasting Corporation, *Unforgettable Fire,* 54.

5

Commemoration Controversies

The War, the Peace, and Democracy in Japan

Ellen H. Hammond

The controversy over the *Enola Gay* exhibit at the Smithsonian's National Air and Space Museum was closely followed in Japan. When the museum curtailed its original plan in response to criticism from Congress and various private groups, the Japanese media quickly solicited opinions from public figures. Prime Minister Murayama Tomiichi, for example, expressed his regret at the alteration, which he deplored as an affront to the Japanese people.

Interestingly, Murayama's own administration was then embroiled in a similar controversy, one with many parallels to that taking place in the United States. It centered on Ministry of Health and Welfare plans to construct a museum in central Tokyo, provisionally called the War Dead Peace Memorial Hall (*Senbotsusha Tsuito Heiwa Kinenkan*). Although these plans had changed repeatedly since the inception of the project in 1979, the concept that finally emerged in 1993 was of a facility that would function as a memorial for Japan's war dead and an exhibit space dedicated to the war and subsequent military occupation at home. The plan represented the first attempt by the national government to construct a facility dealing with such politically charged issues.

The project was nursed along in secrecy: the first reference to it in the press was not until December 1992. When more details came out the following year, opposition to ministry plans quickly emerged. The critics' key complaint echoed Murayama's criticism of the Smithsonian. They charged that the government plan to commemorate only Japan's war dead was an insult to those in Asia and the Pacific who died as a result of Japanese aggression. Defenders of the project denied any need to apologize to Japan's former enemies or countries occupied by Japan in Asia. They wished only to celebrate the sacrifices made by Japanese during the war. As in the United States, the debate involved, on one side, the attempt to critically examine wartime decisions and actions and their effect overseas (and at home) and, on the other, the attempt to portray such examinations as unpatriotic and an insult to the memory of those who died in the conflict. Whereas this polarization might have been novel to Americans in the context of their participation in World War II (though not Vietnam), it had provided a central theme for Japanese politics for the entire postwar period as the progressive and conservative camps remained deadlocked over the issue of war responsibility. It is precisely this deadlock that accounted for the fact that no nationally funded facility dealing with war issues had yet been constructed.

The controversies in both countries arose in very similar contexts. The generation that had direct knowledge of the war was gradually dying off, while younger generations had little or only distorted knowledge of the period. There was a growing sense of urgency about fixing the meaning of the war in national memory. This intersected with the agenda of a resurgent conservatism in Japan and the United States that stressed patriotism, a sanitized national history, and celebration of a unique national identity. Also, both projects became the subject of national discussion in part because they intersected with the commemoration of the fiftieth anniversary of the war's end. As Yui Daizaburo has pointed out,[1] the trend toward a nationalistic commemoration of this anniversary drowned out attempts to portray events in a more international light. In the United States, the critical perspectives that have emerged from the scholarly debate about the war, the atomic bomb, and Japan's defeat were submerged by the intense criticism of the exhibit at the Air and Space Museum. Likewise, in Japan, the few parts of the museum exhibit that would have stimulated reflection on the actions of the wartime state were eventually censored from view.

In Japan and the United States, those opposed to a nationalistic rendering of wartime history repeatedly emphasized a humanist, internationalist view of the war in their protests. In the United States, attention to what was happening in Japan prior to August 6 and then a detailed look at the human dimension of the suffering caused by the bombs—as intended by the curators who drafted the original Smithsonian plan—would have been necessary to lead exhibitgoers to ponder the bombs' consequences. Such an international perspective would have effectively prevented any drift toward a celebratory tone. In Japan, the most explosive issue was the suffering of Asians under Japanese occupation. For example, during the war, Japanese policies in Vietnam led to the famine of 1945, in which over one million Vietnamese starved to death. Acknowledgment of that history certainly presents Japanese suffering during the war years in a far less noble way.

International perspectives therefore disrupted the view purveyed by museum planners in Japan and the first museum critics in the United States. In Japan, however, the critics took their protest strategy a step further. They extended their discussion from the substantive issues taken up within the exhibits to cautious mention of the structural background to the controversy. By highlighting the organizations and institutions that were attempting to monopolize the planning process and "nationalize" the War Dead Peace Memorial Hall, they were calling into question the very nature of Japan's democracy.

Critics hoped to initiate a more profound discussion, one that not only examined in detail the many controversial aspects of the war and surrender but also tackled the equally important problem of the nation's postwar settlement and other issues of the peace. Japan was not a liberal democracy prior to 1945; just fifty years ago, it was still a highly authoritarian society in which official ideology promoted total allegiance to an emperor-god. Those protesting the nationalism inherent in museum plans were therefore also protesting perceived authoritarian legacies from presurrender Japan and the limits on democracy in postwar society. The Smithsonian's surrender to the critics of its original script suggests that, despite their very different pasts, the United States was confronted with a similar problem of democracy.

This chapter examines the plans for Japan's War Dead Peace Memorial Hall and the attendant controversy, focusing on the linkage between the museum and a nationalist vision of Japan that celebrates many of the central features of pre-1945 society. It then shows how the controversy over these plans paralleled that over the *Enola Gay* exhibit and explores the reasons why the depth and character of the protest against ministry plans in Japan differed from that in the United States. Finally, it suggests why critics in Japan were unable to change the structural factors in the controversy and the implications this has for the effort to end Japan's postwar political impasse.

The Planning Process

The history of the planning process for the War Dead Peace Memorial Hall can be divided into two phases. The first, secret, phase lasted from the genesis of the project in 1979 until the spring of 1993, when details of the plan first emerged during Diet committee sessions. The second phase, the period of protest, began at that point and continues today. In August, 1996, local residents and other critics joined forces to stop the project, suing the government in Tokyo district court. Despite the legal challenge, construction began in October that year.

Plans for the museum have had a chameleonlike quality.[2] The original concept for such a facility came from the Japan Association of Bereaved Families (*Nihon Izoku-kai*), a private organization representing the interests of families of the war dead. In late 1979, the association presented a petition to the government asking for a memorial to the war dead on behalf of children who lost a parent in the conflict (children who are now all in their fifties and sixties). The Ministry of Health and Welfare responded immediately to the group's appeal. In 1980, it appropriated funds for the association to carry out an initial study and formed a planning committee. The committee report, issued in 1984, recommended that the facility function both as a museum commemorating Japan's wars in the modern era and also as a memorial site for the war dead. Although the association backed this concept, dissent within the committee led the ministry to found a new consultative committee the following year.

The report issued by this committee returned to the emphasis on surviving children, with a plan for a War Bereaved Children's Memorial Hall. It suggested that the primary emphasis be put on space for memorializing the dead and consoling their relatives, while exhibits would be dedicated to a history of the war and prayers for peace. This document was appended to the appropriation bill that went to the Ministry of Finance for a budget review in late 1992. During this process, the project gained an enormous budget of 12.3 billion yen ($123 million), of which 2.1 billion yen (more than $20 million) was allocated in 1993.[3]

The museum, however, was restyled yet again during the next few months. It underwent a name change, turning up for the first time as the "War Dead Peace Memorial Hall" in a ministry paper used by government spokesmen for Diet committee debate in spring 1993. The focus on war-bereaved children was missing; instead, the ministry document stressed three other purposes for the exhibit: commemoration of the war dead, description of Japanese suffering during the war and occupation, and testimony to the tragedy of war and need for peace. However, it became clear during the committee hearings that only Japanese war dead were to be honored and that no apology to other Asian countries was intended. Further, the plans included discussion neither of Japan's invasion and occupation of other countries in the region nor of the historical context of the war. These were familiar points of contention between the progressive and conservative camps in Japan and were quickly seized on by critics of the ministry,

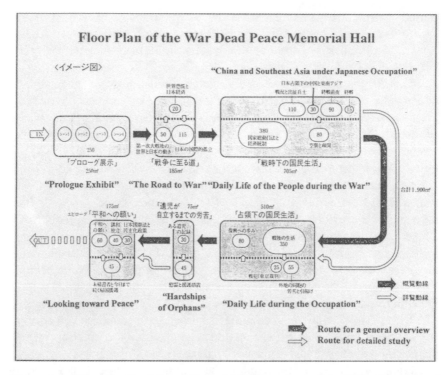

Floor plan of the War Dead Peace Memorial Hall as approved in 1993. This planned museum merged the years of the Asia–Pacific War and subsequent Allied occupation of Japan into a single era of Japanese suffering. Critics charged that it minimized the sufferings of other Asians living under Japanese occupation. Yet even the tiny fraction of exhibit space initially allocated to China and Southeast Asia was struck from these plans, and the current plan is to concentrate only on commemorating the Japanese war dead. (The original floor plan was translated and adapted from Arai Shinichi, ed., *Senso Hakubutsukan* [War museums] [Tokyo: Iwanami Shoten, 1994], by the editors of the *Bulletin of Concerned Asian Scholars*. Used by permission.)

touching off the controversy. The simultaneous announcement that the Association of Bereaved Families was to be charged with management of the facility only added fuel to the fire, for reasons described below.

The Leading Actors

The ministry's conception of the museum was entirely predictable, given the institutions and groups involved. The prime mover in the project, the Association of Bereaved Families, has, for much of its history, been at least as devoted to the restoration of presurrender emperor-centered ideology as to improving the welfare of bereaved families.[4] It was formed in 1947 as the Japanese Association for the Welfare of Families of War Casualties (*Nihon Izoku Kosei Renmei*). For several years, group publications highlighted a commitment to peace and included some recognition that losing a loved one in war was an experience their members shared with many families in Europe, North America, and Asia. However, from the start, the group had close ties to Yasukuni Shrine,[5] the most important site of worship in presurrender state Shinto and the place where Japan's war dead are enshrined. With the end of the occupation, the association grew more conservative, and its focus began to change from the daily concerns of its living members to the need to honor the souls of the war dead.

This shift led the association to wage an aggressive but ultimately unsuccessful campaign to make Yasukuni Shrine a state-supported institution. It was also instrumental in building momentum for the 1982 official visit to Yasukuni by Prime Minister Nakasone Yasuhiro and most of his cabinet. This controversial act involved use of public funds for a religious rite, reviving memories of presurrender state Shinto and challenging the postwar Constitution's separation of church and state. Further, it represented official homage to the spirits of war criminals enshrined at the site, implying approval of Japan's wartime actions. This elicited harsh criticism within Japan and from overseas, including official protest from some Asian governments.

Contemporary association literature asserts that the "Greater East Asia War was a war of self-defense that Japan fought to protect the state, the nation's lives and properties,"[6] and representatives of the group echo wartime propaganda in their claim that the purpose of the war was to liberate Asia. The group therefore issued a strong protest in 1993 when Prime Minister Hosokawa Morihiro stated that Japan had waged a war of aggression. In 1995, it also spearheaded the successful fight against a Diet resolution offering apology for Japan's actions during the war.[7] Association spokesmen such as Vice Chairman Suehiro Sakae vehemently oppose any apology to other Asians and argue provocatively that Japan's history was "interrupted" in 1945, suggesting that only a return to presurrender institutions will allow the resumption of the nation's proper narrative.

The group has had a long, symbiotic relationship with the Liberal Democratic Party (LDP). Since the early 1960s, association chairmen have been LDP Diet members. In return for favors such as periodically augmenting the state allowance paid to bereaved families[8] and privileged access to prime ministers, the association has functioned as a vote machine and fundraiser for the party. It is also linked to the LDP through the minister of health and welfare. For example, the minister at the time the memorial hall was proposed was powerful LDP politician and current Prime Minister

Hashimoto Ryutaro. In 1993, he became head of the association, only step-ping down in November 1995 when, as a potential candidate for prime minister, he was criticized for his close links to the group.

The association's strong ties to those in power assured that its appeal for a facility in honor of the war dead would get a quick response. The group continued to be closely involved in the planning: it received more than $700,000 from the government during the next five years to do the survey and initial planning,[9] and its members served on various planning committees es-tablished by the ministry. This leverage also assured that other groups repre-senting war-bereaved families would have no role in planning. In fact, there are opposing groups, many of them formed by families who objected to the association's continuous lobbying on behalf of Yasukuni Shrine.[10]

It is not unusual for private groups such as the association to establish privileged access to the LDP and the government. The ideological bent of the association is also not unusual; its philosophy is shared with many in the LDP, for example. What is startling in the case of the association is that Japanese taxpayers have been underwriting the expenses of this group for more than forty years. In 1953, the government leased to the group—rent-free—the building known as Kudan Kaikan, a well-known restaurant and wedding hall facility in central Tokyo that also houses association head-quarters. (Profits from the operation of Kudan Kaikan constitute at least 23 percent of the association's budget.)[11] This building was constructed in 1934 by the Imperial Forces Veterans Association (*Teikoku Zaigo Gunjin-kai*) and functioned as a social club for servicemen and veterans until 1945. The government assumed ownership when this group was banned after the war.

The unprecedented decision to confer the property on the Association of Bereaved Families for an unlimited time was a response to aggressive lob-bying by the group and its supporters. During what the group considered the "black winter" of the occupation, families of dead soldiers received no special compensation or allowance, and the prestige accorded to them dur-ing the war years was replaced by the general suspicion the public accorded to the discredited military. The use of the building and quick resumption of allowances were considered by the association to be just recompense for this suffering. The government decision, however, suggests the continuities the association has with the building's former tenants and the postoccupa-tion government's role in supporting groups that have perpetuated pre-surrender ideology.

The leverage of the Association of Bereaved Families also derives from its function as a de facto auxiliary arm of the Ministry of Health and Welfare. The willingness of the ministry to delegate so much authority over the museum planning and future operation to the association is consistent with the history of this bureaucracy. Its actions in this affair offer a revealing but seldom noted example of the way the U.S. decision during the occupation to retain and work through the central bureaucracy encouraged the perpetuation of undemocratic practices. The history of the ministry is integrally tied to the military.[12] It was military concern over the number of recruits failing the military health examination that led the Army Ministry to call for a national insurance plan in 1936. The army made formation of an office for social insurance a condition for supporting the first cabinet of Konoe Fumimaro the following year. The Ministry of Health and Welfare was officially inaugurated in 1938 and began to co-opt existing social welfare organizations, changing the welfare focus from individuals needing special assistance to the needs of the military for healthy recruits. This was closely related to the prosecution of the war; total war was going to necessitate total welfare in Japan. Welfare became a problem of how to ensure that Japan's human resources would be able to produce to the maximum. A national network of insurance offices (*hoken-sho*), which still functions, was established to further the "healthy soldier, healthy citizen" policy.

With surrender, the ministry was essentially charged with binding up the wounds of war; this process has continued to the present day and accounts for what has been called the "concentration of the sense of victimization" within the ministry.[13] This bureaucracy administers the allowances paid to war-bereaved families, sick and disabled veterans, and victims of the atomic bomb. It is responsible for the resettlement in Japan of Chinese citizens of Japanese origin who were orphaned or separated from their families during the chaos of Japan's surrender in China. It coordinates the search for the remains of soldiers who died outside Japan and sponsors pilgrimages by surviving relatives to the countries where their loved ones died. The ministry also erects memorial cenotaphs to the dead soldiers in these locations. In many of these endeavors, it works closely with the Association of Bereaved Families.[14]

The Institutionalization of August 15

The LDP–ministry–association nexus could be seen as an example of the triangular relationships that have functioned so effectively in other areas of Japanese society, the most remarked on being the LDP–Ministry of International Trade and Industry–big-business grouping. The interesting thing about this triangular grouping is that the association seeks gains denominated not only in yen but also in the currency of symbol. As it is primarily interested in symbols circulating prior to 1945, the association also boasts of its links to the emperor system. It sports the chrysanthemum crest of the imperial family as its symbol, and its forty-fifth anniversary celebration was attended by the emperor and empress (as well as then Prime Minister Miyazawa Kiichi). More recently, the group became the recipient of *waka* (a traditional Japanese poem) composed and written by the imperial couple on the occasion of the fiftieth anniversary of the defeat, an honor that had not been conferred on any group since 1918. Such patronage is consistent with the association's efforts to involve the government in funding Yasukuni Shrine, where wartime sacrifice for the emperor is celebrated. It is attempting to revive an image of Japan in which the mystic aspects of the Shinto religion, through the figure of an emperor-god, are melded to state power. Thus, the connections between the association, the ministry, the LDP, and the throne—and the ideological agenda behind the War Dead Peace Memorial Hall—are extremely disturbing. This agenda can best be described by examining a date in Japanese history that is closely connected to museum plans—August 15.

On August 15, 1945, the Showa emperor used the radio to ask all Japanese to "bear the unbearable" and accept surrender. Later, many Japanese invoked that day as a marker of release from a tragic and morally unacceptable conflict and the beginning of a democratic Japan. As shorthand for this postwar ideal of "peace and democracy," August 15 was used by intellectuals during the 1960 crisis over the renewal of the Japan-U.S. Security Treaty to rally antiwar opinion and inspire opposition to military ties with the United States. This date was later eclipsed by the progressives' tendency to focus on August 6 and August 9, the days on which Hiroshima and Nagasaki were bombed. These dates have also been used to support calls for pacifism, although their use for making a general antinuclear statement has partially robbed them of their specificity to Japanese politics.

Despite the paradox of conservatives' embracing the day on which Japan had to admit a humiliating defeat and reverse years of propaganda by surrendering to the enemy, it is actually they who have most skillfully used August 15 for symbolic purposes, transforming it into a day for celebrating the wartime state and those who died for it. The month of August, along with the oppressive heat and monotonous droning of the cicadas, has become inseparable from images of the emperor in Tokyo's Budokan[15] eulogizing the war dead and invoking the need for peace in front of black-suited ranks of government officials, politicians, and Association of Bereaved Families members. In 1982, the LDP government tried to designate August 15 as the "Day to Mourn the War Dead and Pray for Peace." The cabinet passed a resolution in support of this idea, although protest from various groups prevented change in the law to make it an actual national holiday.[16] Instead, the very same concept has come back to life in the memorial hall, which the Ministry of Health and Welfare named the "Hall to Mourn the War Dead and Pray for Peace" in 1993, although it may have planned to use this name from the very beginning.[17] Although the English translation was later simplified, the significance of the Japanese name lies in the linkage to August 15. The building can be seen as an attempt literally to cast in stone interpretations of August 15 that glorify the Japanese war effort.

What were these interpretations as defined by the main actors in the memorial hall planning process? What would be institutionalized with the successful completion of the project as first envisioned by planners? First, the memorial hall planners were attempting to institutionalize their vision of the war and the peace and legitimize it as the central national narrative. This vision, which celebrates the emperor system as the link between Japan at war and Japan at peace, would finally be lifted above the partisan fray in which it had been contested for fifty years. Removed from the controversy over war responsibility vis-à-vis other countries[18] and war responsibility at all levels in Japan, the war and its consequences at home—material deprivation, millions of military and civilian casualties, the physical destruction of many of Japan's cities, occupation by a foreign power   could become simply the uplifting story of how the Japanese bore the unbearable before and after August 15 and somehow survived with their imperial polity still intact.

Second, the museum plans were a conscious attempt to meld the sacred and the secular: public history would be combined with the commemoration of Japanese military deaths as an act of religious veneration (reflected in the use of the character meaning "prayer" in the name). This strategy has great historical resonance with prewar and wartime Japan (as well as with the surrender, which was presented to the Japanese as a gesture of compassion by the emperor). The presurrender Shinto religion, government commemoration of the dead, and a mythical "history" of the imperial cult were all woven into the seamless fabric of the emperor-centered state. This featured a mystical aspect, a nonrationality specifically designed to make historical analysis impossible. Planning documents for the memorial hall have, from the beginning, contained various references to Shinto ritual for consoling the spirits of the dead. One of the main architectural features was a space for this purpose, in order to create an atmosphere that would make any critical presentation of the history of the war impossible. This reflects a right-wing strategy in Japan of manipulating the cultural tradition, which does emphasize the regular, ritual commemoration of the dead. Influential critic Eto Jun, for example, uses the argument that the Japanese "live with the dead" to support his insistence that worship at Yasukuni Shrine is vital to the continuity of the nation.[19]

Understanding the uses to which the war dead are being put is also

The emperor and empress pay their respects to Japan's war dead—symbolized by a mountain of two thousand chrysanthemums—at the August 15, 1995, Ceremony to Mourn the War Dead and Pray for Peace. This government-sponsored ceremony and visits by conservative politicians to Yasukuni Shrine have been skillfully used by conservatives to celebrate continuities with the pre-1945 imperial state, especially the emperor system, and to mute criticism of Japan's wartime actions. Plans for a War Dead Peace Memorial Hall attempt to institutionalize this approach, which emphasizes the nobility of Japanese suffering and ignores the suffering inflicted by Japanese on others. (Used by permission of *Sankei Shinbun*.)

critical in a third meaning of August 15. Carol Gluck has called the emperor system the "ghost at the historical feast,"[20] and it is a specter that hovers around this effort at public history. The emperor's eulogies on August 15—his identification with the suffering of the Japanese people—are the closest the postwar emperor system is allowed to get to the controversial issues of the war. It is politically unthinkable that the present "peace" emperor would ever stand before a group of Imperial Army veterans and offer condolences for their suffering or attend the forty-fifth anniversary of a group of former naval officers. The war-bereaved families, however, mobilized by the association for the August 15 ceremony, are perfect proxies for their dead relatives (and living veterans as well) and help make August 15 a pivotal date for linking the pre- and post-1945 emperor systems and suggesting their continuity. Not only is the peace emperor projected back to presurrender days; the supreme commander of the Japanese soldier and the patriarch—and supreme deity—of the Japanese people are two images subtly projected forward as the emperor gives his August 15 message.

Whereas progressives emphasized August 15 as the demarcation between eras of war and peace, authoritarianism and democracy, museum planners chose to conflate the war and occupation into one long period of Japanese faith and endurance. In this rendering, August 15 marks a key moment in the middle of the era—the emergence of the emperor as representative of peace and democracy. That the emperor could be so cleanly disassociated from the war and the wartime state testifies to the successful efforts made during the first few months of occupation by Japanese elites, who frantically worked to reinvent the emperor system in order to ensure its survival.

The ministry's appropriation of the symbolism of August 15 suggested that one goal of the museum project was the permanent mobilization of an army of ghosts on behalf of the most supreme ghost of all. Association spokesman Suehiro Sakae suggested this when he linked Yasukuni Shrine (representing prayer), the Yasukuni Shrine Museum (representing the Japanese nation's spirit),[21] and the War Dead Peace Memorial Hall (representing the resumption of Japan's interrupted history). In this rendering, the museum was delegated the task of providing ideological support for a vision of Japan that reflects Yasukuni's glorification of prewar and wartime state Shinto, the imperial cult, and wartime sacrifice in the name of the emperor. The ministry decisions to back the project with such a tremendous budget and let the association operate the facility, its efforts to hide the planning process from public view, and its blatant disregard of its critics indicate the importance it attached to the project. These facts suggest that the bureaucrats there were comfortable with the ideology purveyed by the association.

The Protests

The opposition to ministry plans for the War Dead Peace Memorial Hall was quite diverse. The failure of the ministry to inform them about the project angered residents in the neighborhood of the proposed site in Kudan, leading them to form the Association to Protect the History and Scenery of the Kudan Area.[22] This group, in cooperation with the local neighborhood association, mobilized local residents against the project and received the backing of the ward legislative body. Repeated petitions to the ministry finally resulted in four explanatory sessions (required by law) to those living in the area, but questions to ministry representatives failed to elicit much more than vague answers. One bureaucrat claimed that the ministry initially failed to hold public meetings because it did not know anyone actually lived in the area. Both the Kudan association and the ward legislature were disturbed by the fact that little attempt was made to seek their understanding or cooperation; the whole project was unilaterally imposed on them from above. They were opposed to the project for both aesthetic and practical reasons. They felt that the proposed ten-story structure would rob the historical neighborhood of its character and could represent a hazard by raining down glass and debris during an earthquake, blocking access to an evacuation area in the park next to the site. The stance of the ministry was that all legal requirements had been observed and that the project could go ahead at any time.

In fact, it was later revealed that the legal foundation for the project was bogus. The Ministry of Health and Welfare had concluded a secret agreement with the Environment Agency to get around the fact that the proposed structure exceeded local height limitations. In order to remove the plans from local oversight, the Environment Agency agreed to make the area into a national park. However, since regulations also bar such construction in national parks, the agency would only agree to accept the site after the building was completed.[23] This unsavory deal gave the local residents further ammunition in their struggle to influence ministry planning.

The Kudan association resolutely steered clear of the political issues involved in the memorial hall, aside from noting the undemocratic nature of the ministry's maneuvers. All of the other protesting groups were concerned primarily with the political aspects. The Diet committee hearings held in spring 1993 led to a public statement of opposition from thirty-five prominent historians and intellectuals in June of that year. While affirming the need for a nationally funded facility, they argued that the issues of war responsibility (in other words, to recognize not only Japanese deaths but those of Japan's victims as well) and postwar responsibility (to provide financial compensation to those who were used as forced labor or forced into prostitution for the military, for example) would have to be addressed. They questioned the Ministry of Health and Welfare's exclusive control over planning and the decision to have this government-funded facility managed by the Association of Bereaved Families.

The intellectuals made several demands, addressing the undemocratic nature of the planning process and the ideological agenda informing it. They asked for full disclosure of information about the project, postponement until open hearings could be held, transfer of project control from the ministry to the cabinet, consultation with other Asian countries, and canvassing of popular opinion in Japan followed by Diet debate over the purpose of the facility. On the basis of their initial June statement, a cooperative council was established later in the summer; it was composed of major historians' organizations and other groups. This was the nucleus of the Committee to Consider the War Dead Peace Memorial Hall Problem, which continued its opposition with petitions to the prime minister, a signature campaign, and symposia.[24] Statements from the group stressed the importance of apologizing and paying compensation to people victimized by Japan during the war and repeatedly introduced an internationalist perspective to argue that the museum should include explicit recognition of war responsibility. The group also attacked the undemocratic nature of the decision making and asserted that the museum was not the property of one ministry and one association of bereaved families.

These aspects were brought up more forcefully, however, by another group, the National Council of Bereaved Families for Peace.[25] This is also a group of war-bereaved families, but one that formed in opposition to the agenda of the Japan Association of Bereaved Families. The Bereaved Families for Peace, in its criticism, touched on the issues of war responsibility and lack of public disclosure, and also expressly warned against the deepening relationship between the government and the Japan Association of Bereaved Families. It called the proposed museum a "second Yasukuni Shrine," suggesting the dangerous blurring of the distinction between church and state.

Ironically, a latecomer to the opposition, Yasukuni Shrine itself, began to raise exactly the same point for a different reason. Despite the Association of Bereaved Families' decades-long effort on behalf of the shrine, in December 1993, Yasukuni delivered petitions to the Ministry of Health and Welfare and the association, protesting the location of the museum and the fact that the project ignored Yasukuni's own role in commemorating military casualties of the war. Shrine representatives also feared that precisely because it is a public institution, the new museum would not be able to maintain Yasukuni's own adamant stance that Japan has no need to apologize for its wartime conduct. They feared that the government would be pressured into statements of remorse by groups such as the historians, citing as a precedent government acceptance of the verdicts handed down in the Tokyo War Crimes Tribunal. Yasukuni, itself a flash point in the postwar deadlock over issues of war responsibility and the separation of church and state, now pointed with concern to the government's foray into religious affairs (simultaneously substantiating the concerns of more liberal protesters).

Others formerly sympathetic to the ministry's conception of the museum began to desert the beleaguered project. Three members of the internal advisory committee for the planning (scholars Hosoya Chihiro and Hata Ikuhiko and critic Kamisaka Fuyuko) resigned and publicly criticized the ministry for its unilateral decision making. Hosoya was most disturbed by the government's refusal to consider any other than Japanese war dead. It is highly unusual for members of such carefully selected bodies to resign; it also left the committee with no professional researchers or historians.

The growing chorus of opposition finally led the ministry to back down temporarily. In February 1995, it announced that construction would be deferred for two years and that planners would return to the original (vague) concept of a facility for war-bereaved children. In deference to local protesters, it agreed to reconsider the building design. Meanwhile, the Murayama administration, rather than confronting the ministry and the project's powerful supporters, chose instead to inaugurate a rival project. Hosoya Chihiro was asked to head an Asian History Document Center (*Ajia Rekishi Shiryo Senta*), which was to collect documents with an eye to creating a "historical awareness" that would be acceptable both in Japan and overseas. The proposed center's role in documenting war responsibility made it too hot to handle within the government; one bureaucrat described it as the "Old Maid" in a card game that every ministry was trying to avoid having stuck in its hand.[26]

While the new center attempted to find a niche in the bureaucracy, the ministry was taking advantage of its existence to purge the museum project of all references to Japanese aggression. In September 1995, it announced a new concept for the museum exhibits that gave sole emphasis to the hardships and suffering of the Japanese people during war and occupation. Gone was all mention of Japan's road to war, the progress of the conflict, or Japanese occupation policy in Asia. As the health and welfare minister explained, the new policy governing the exhibits was that "any material about the last war that could possibly be historicized" would come within the purview of the Asian History Document Center.[27] The Association of Bereaved Families would remain in charge of the facility, although, in deference to local protesters, the building's height was lowered from 60 to 45 meters.

With this decision, the project planners had completed a circle back to the original wishes of the Association of Bereaved Families. While the new policy begged the question of how the wartime and postwar experiences of the Japanese could be considered without reference to the historical context of a society mobilized for total war, it neatly prevented even the hint of question as to why and for what Japan had gone to war or who might have suffered at the hands of the Japanese. (The subsequent fate of the Asian History Document Center was unclear: although plans were not formally abandoned, they did not get much support in the Hashimoto administration; having served its purpose, the center concept was set to disappear.) In the end, all potentially critical aspects of the memorial hall exhibits were simply eliminated. What remained was a vision of the period that celebrated the sacrifice of fallen soldiers and the heroism of those left behind to face life in the postwar ruins.

Issues of the War and the Peace

The respective denouements of the Smithsonian exhibit and the War Dead Peace Memorial Hall controversies were remarkably similar. In the United States, the restored *Enola Gay* was finally presented to the public, but the history of its use and the consequences were censored. In Japan, as well, the war and occupation experiences of the Japanese were to be decontextualized, and the narrative would be cleansed of any troubling references to "history." In the United States, media accounts frequently featured interviews with World War II veterans who had nothing to do with decisions in Washington and who were generally convinced that the dropping of two atomic bombs was the only way to save lives and guarantee Japan's defeat. The exhibit itself featured the testimony of the pilot of the *Enola Gay,* who is convinced of the righteousness of the bombs' use. In Japan, the war experience was to be reduced to the voices of those who happened to survive the rigors of war on the archipelago. Even a "great man" historical approach looking at elite decision making was too controversial to handle, leading to a bowdlerized social history in which the sincere opinions and actual experiences of some Americans and Japanese were manipulated in order to create a pristine national self-image of sincerity and bravery.

Critics on both sides of the Pacific called repeatedly for exhibit planners to consult with all groups that might have a stake in the portrayal of wartime events. In Japan, where unresolved issues arising from the war have festered for five decades, the stakeholders were defined with a broad stroke. Critics asked the government to canvass public opinion to guide planners, confident that any such sampling would indicate rejection of the ministry's and association's plan. Ultimately, however, as in the United States, only a narrow range of interests was allowed to prevail, and those who questioned the attempt to purvey a single "truth" were outmaneuvered.

Interestingly, the key private groups in Japan and the United States supporting a nationalist vision shared some similarities. One of the few commentators who looked beyond the events of 1994–1995 to analyze the structural background to the controversy in the United States was Mike Wallace.[28] He pointed out that the "veterans' group" that came to dominate planning for the exhibit, the Air Force Association (AFA), represented the interests of not only current and former members of the U.S. Air Force but also 199 Industrial Associates, including the biggest corporate names in military contracting. As the "air wing of what Dwight Eisenhower called the military-industrial complex,"[29] the group, since its founding in 1946, was active in creating an atmosphere conducive to military spending in general and spending on the air force in particular. It was founded by the same man who went on to found the National Air and Space Museum as a bastion for patriotic celebrations of American technological innovation and military prowess. In the past decade, however, changes in the approaches used in U.S. curatorship and new leadership at the Air and Space Museum led to exhibits that provided more context for the military hardware displayed and the possibility of more nuanced and critical perspectives. The *Enola Gay* exhibit became a crucial test case for the AFA, which was determined to reassert control over the museum.

The struggle over the representation of the *Enola Gay*'s mission at the Air and Space Museum was also part of a larger cultural conflict. It became one battle in the "culture wars" that had raged for nearly a decade, featuring attacks by conservatives against a "revisionism" that they viewed as threatening the foundations of American civilization. Neoconservative commentators railed against the "takeover" of U.S. museums, universities, media, and publishing houses by academics influenced by the counterculture and politics of the 1960s and the multicultural approach to U.S. history developed since then. They charged that these academics were "unable to view American history as anything other than a woeful catalog of crimes and aggressions against the helpless peoples of the earth"[30] and were bent on subverting "American values" and destroying the shared culture that had made America great, just as conservatives in Japan criticized independent scholarship in their country as a woeful catalog of crimes and aggressions against the helpless peoples of Asia and a threat to a unique Japanese identity.

In response to this perceived threat, there was a strong push from some conservatives to return to the "traditional" teaching of U.S. history. In the hands of those such as Speaker of the House of Representatives and former history professor Newt Gingrich, this amounted to paeans to American exceptionalism described in a "secularized sacred narrative that flowed from an Edenic past, through a fall from grace in the sinful Sixties, into a degenerate present, and on, hopefully, to future redemption through return to prelapsarian values."[31] This sense of the sacredness of the American past turned up repeatedly in the imagery used in discussions of the controversy at the Air and Space Museum. One journalist called the museum "the central shrine of the military-industrial complex," another, a "temple to the glories of aviation and the inventiveness of the aerospace industry." Also, to veterans, the institution was, perhaps, "more shrine than museum."[32] Here, the religious metaphors suggest the emotionalism generated by the controversy and, in themselves, hint at the way nationalism often appropriates the power of religion for secular ends. They are, however, primarily metaphors, and this indicates one way in which the Air and Space Museum and War Dead Peace Memorial Hall controversies differed.

In Japan, the affair hinged on the fact that religious metaphor constantly skirmished with reality in the form of the still-existing emperor system and the person of the reigning emperor. Critics of the museum were most afraid of the religious overtones in plans for the facility and were afraid that Shinto would be used again, in however subtle a fashion, to relegitimate the emperor as the spiritual head of the Japanese people. They feared that the museum would be used to support a view of Japanese exceptionalism that depended on the centrality of the imperial institution in defining the identity of all Japanese.

Gavan McCormack has written persuasively of the complex relationship that informs the twin debates about Japanese identity and the war.[33] He argues that conservative nationalists are continuing in the path of former Prime Minister Nakasone Yasuhiro, who promoted a neonationalist agenda of restored pride in Japanese identity and attempted unsuccessfully to finally settle the long-running controversy over war responsibility. The nationalists prefer to historicize and relativize the war period—rationalize and explain the events, put them behind, and get on with the primary task of consolidating a positive national identity. However, they want to avoid any attempts to apply historical analysis to the problem of national character because this has been molded around the figure of the emperor and would threaten his transcendental status. The two discussions are inseparable, however, because no analysis of the war is complete without reference to the problem of the emperor's war responsibility, an issue as explosive for conservative notions of Japanese identity as the *Enola Gay*'s payload is for some Americans.

Again, however, this points up the fact that just as pre-1945 Japanese society was very different from American society then, so is post-1945 Japanese society different from American society. The taboos in present-day Japan that chill the atmosphere of free debate are much more potent than those in the United States. For example, every major Japanese newspaper had a representative on one of the early planning committees for the memorial hall, and yet no story appeared in print until the project had become a fait accompli.[34] Right-wing hate mail and nuisance calls aimed at museum critics (and after the ministry failed to push through the plan immediately, to ministry officials) were perhaps an unnecessary reminder that criticism of Japan's war is still dangerous. The attempted assassination of Nagasaki's mayor in 1990 and other incidents of terror are forceful reminders of the violence that can be meted out to any public figures who suggest the emperor bore some war responsibility or who break the unwritten rules about what can be written about the imperial institution. Therefore, although historians' groups and other critics did cautiously expose some of the structural background to the affair, they did not refer to the "ghost" in attendance at this feast for the celebration of public history. This omission forced the controversy back into the old structure of right-wing–left-wing debate over Japan's aggression in Asia.

That museum critics were trying to link the problems of the war and the peace is clear from their insistence on democratic process in resolving the controversy. They constantly criticized the role of the Association of Bereaved Families and the ministry and demanded that the public be consulted as a prelude to debate in the Diet. This response reflects the serious threat to democracy they perceived in the museum project. It is also evidence of the deep divisions in scholarly opinion in Japan, where the presence of historians "in service" to the emperor (*goyo rekishika*) makes any historical consensus impossible. In contrast, the Air and Space Museum's first script for the *Enola Gay* exhibit was reviewed and praised by scholars of various political perspectives. Also in contrast to the United States, public opinion in Japan is much more at odds with official opinion; museum critics could count on support for many of their positions on war responsibility if public opinion was consulted.[35]

In some ways, the struggle over the War Dead Peace Memorial Hall was depressingly familiar. After all, the state has consistently supported conservative notions of Japanese culture, shored up the emperor system, and manipulated portrayals of the war for five decades. What is notable in the present controversy is the strong push by the government to finally fix the meaning of the war in Japanese history and deny Japan's role as aggressor. Instead, the heroism of the Japanese in their military deaths and civilian lives would be used to build a Japanese identity around the figure of the heroic emperor who chose, on August 15, to lead his country into the postwar period. This image is a vehement rejection of the opinion of a significant portion of the Japanese public and much of the rest of the world.

The museum controversy reveals the unabated conflict between the emperor-centered nationalists and the many movements that seek to address problems of the war and the peace. These include movements for compensation for comfort women, forced laborers, and POWs; demands for retroactive payments to former colonial subjects who fought for Japan but were later denied pensions; attempts to document the story of war crimes involving the use of chemical and biological weapons by Imperial Forces Unit 731; and citizens' movements against U.S. military bases, primarily in Okinawa. As in the museum affair, the government has been intransigent. It is conceivable that a powerful catalyst could link all of these movements into a broader popular movement inspired by the vision of "peace and democracy" in the progressives' version of August 15. They wish to celebrate the day as the moment when a break with Japan's imperial past first became possible. The government, however, looks prepared to hold fast to its own interpretation and simply ride out the storm.

Notes

1. Yui Daizaburo, "Between Pearl Harbor and Hiroshima/Nagasaki: Nationalism and Memory in Japan and the United States," Chapter 3 of this volume.

2. Details about the planning process are from Tanaka Nobumasa, "Kokuritsu 'Senbotsusha Tsuito Heiwa Kinenkan' koso o tou" (Doubts about the plan for the nationally funded "War Dead Peace Memorial Hall"), *Gijutsu to Ningen*, December 1993, 22–42.

3. This is at the rate of one hundred yen to one dollar.

4. An overview of association history can be found in Tanaka Nobumasa, "Nihon Izoku-kai no Goju-nen" (Fifty years of the Association of Bereaved Families), *Sekai*, September 1994, 34–52.

5. One of the prime movers during the association's first years was a Yasukuni official, and the liaison office for the group was located at the shrine.

6. Yoshida Reiko, "Planned War Memorial Comes under Fire," *Japan Times*, August 16, 1994, 3.

7. The resolution did pass but in a watered-down form that did not resemble an apology.

8. The association was so identified with these government funds that some families believed that if they quit the group, they would lose their entitlement. See interview in Tanaka, "Nihon Izoku-kai."

9. Tanaka, "Kokuritsu 'Senbotsusha Tsuito Heiwa Kinenkan,' " 28. The figure was 72.8 million yen.

10. Tanaka, "Nihon Izoku-kai," 40. A Christian group was formed in 1969, but most opposition developed in the 1980s. By 1993, fourteen groups opposed to some aspect of the Japan Association of War Bereaved Families' agenda were represented in the umbrella organization National Council of Bereaved Families for Peace (*Heiwa Izoku-kai Zenkoku Renraku Kai*), formed in 1986.

11. Ibid., 45. This information came from an interview with an association official.

12. Background on the ministry can be found in Uda Kikue, Takasawa Takeshi, and Furukawa Kojun, eds., *Shakai Fukushi no Rekishi* (History of social welfare) (Tokyo: Yuhikaku Sensho, 1977).

13. Ibid., 253.

14. Just after the occupation ended, the association succeeded in restoring a special program for veterans' benefits. At that time, the ministry opposed the association, preferring to blend the program into a comprehensive pension plan. See John C. Campbell, *How Policies Change: The Japanese Government and the Aging Society* (Princeton, NJ: Princeton University Press, 1992). Since then, the ministry and association have worked closely together on many projects concerning the war dead, and as seen in the present controversy, the ministry is extremely supportive of association initiatives.

15. Martial Arts Hall; also used for state functions. This landmark forms a geographical and ideological triangle with the War Dead Peace Memorial Hall site and Yasukuni Shrine.

16. The following year, the government sponsored the first postwar "Ceremony to Mourn the War Dead and Pray for Peace." Until 1993, this ceremony was boycotted by Socialist Diet members; they attended their own counterceremony, which commemorated not only Japanese but also those who died due to Japanese aggression. In 1993, however, Prime Minister Hosokawa and Diet House Speaker Doi Takako brought this message into the state ceremony, calling for commemoration of Japan's victims.

17. Tanaka, "Kokuritsu 'Senbotsusha Tsuito Heiwa Kinenkan,' " 36. Although *kinenkan* is a commonly used word for "memorial hall" in Japanese, the first character has been changed to one with the same reading (*ki*) but with the meaning "to pray." Therefore, Prayer Hall might be a more accurate translation. This, of course, is one thing about the plan that disturbed opponents since it suggests government funding for religious observance.

18. Only 1.5 percent of the total exhibit space was to have been dedicated to the Japanese occupation of other countries. See Yui, "Between Pearl Harbor and Hiroshima/Nagasaki," 48.

19. Eto Jun, *Yasukuni Ronshu* (Commentaries on Yasukuni) (Tokyo: Nihon Kyobunsha, 1986), quoted in Ian Buruma, *The Wages of Guilt* (New York: Farrar, Straus, and Giroux, 1994), 220.

20. Carol Gluck, "The Past in the Present," in *Postwar Japan as History,* ed. Andrew Gordon (Berkeley: University of California Press, 1993), 64–95. She wrote: the emperor system "was like a ghost at the historical feast, always in attendance, related to both the past and the present, but elusive and morally and politically charged," 89.

21. He used the term *tamashii*, evoking pre-1945 emperor state ideology, which extolled a unique Japanese spirit.

22. *Kudanzaka no Rekishi to Keikan o Mamoru Kai.*

23. "Heiwa Kinenkan de Koseisho, Kankyocho ga 'Mitsuyaku' " (Ministry of Health and Welfare and Environment Agency conclude 'secret agreement' concerning Peace Memorial Hall), *Asahi Shinbun,* March 13, 1996, 15.

24. The original statement is reprinted in *Rekishi Hyoron,* October 1993, 97–100. Further statements from the group can be found in Sasaki Ryuji, " 'Senbotsusha Tsuito Heiwa Kinenkan' Mondai o Kangaeru Kai no Kessei to sono Seimei ni tsuite"

(Formation of the committee to consider the War Dead Peace Memorial Hall problem and its public statements). *Nihonshi-gaku Kenkyu,* December 1993, 75–80; and "Nihon no senso sekinin to 'Senbotsusha Tsuito Heiwa Kinenkan' ni kan seru—Rekishigaku kankeisha no yobo shomei (shubun)" (Japan's war responsibility and the 'War Dead Peace Memorial Hall'—An appeal for signatures from those in the history profession), *Rekishi-gaku Kenkyu Geppo,* November 1994, 2–3.

25. Heiwa Izoku-Kai Zenkoku Renraku Kai. This group later started the Consultative Committee for the "War Dead Peace Memorial Hall" Problem (*"Senbotsusha Tsuito Heiwa Kinenkan"* Mondai Renraku Kyogikai).

26. " 'Heiwa no Rinkaku' sengo 50-nen" (" 'The Contour of Peace'—Fifty Postwar Years), *Mainichi Shinbun,* August 8, 1995, 22.

27. "Sensoshi-kan no tenji wa Ajia Senta de" (Exhibits with a historical slant on the war to the Asian Center), *Asahi Shinbun,* September 27, 1995, 33.

28. *Radical Historians Newsletter,* no. 72 (May 1995): 1–32.

29. Ibid., 10.

30. Ibid., 25.

31. Ibid.

32. Ibid., 9, 12, 22.

33. Gavan McCormack, *The Emptiness of Japanese Affluence* (Armonk, NY: M.E. Sharpe, 1996), especially chapters 4 and 5.

34. Editorial board members from the *Asahi, Mainichi,* and *Yomiuri* were involved in the planning, as were officials from Kyodo wire service and the business publisher Daiamondo-sha.

35. Various opinion polls taken over the past several years suggest that the Japanese public, unlike its government, is ready to acknowledge Japan's war responsibility. See Yoshida Yutaka, "Nihonjin no Senso-kan" (Japanese views of the war), *Sekai,* September 1994, 22–33.

6

Mass Death in Miniature

How Americans Became Victims of the Bomb

Lane Fenrich

A month to the day after the bombing of Nagasaki, critic and editor Henry Seidel Canby called upon scientists, public relations experts, and even Hollywood filmmakers to "make the atomic bomb real in the imagination of the world's people." Like many postwar columnists, Canby feared that "the world" did not truly appreciate the threat posed by atomic weapons. In part, that concern reflected the little then known outside Japan about conditions in Hiroshima and Nagasaki. At the time Canby's editorial went to print, no non-Japanese reporter had yet filed a story from either of the two cities, although Australian Wilfred Burchett would do so before the piece appeared on newsstands and Japanese reports had long since made their way into American newspapers.

From Canby's perspective, however, such reports were almost beside the point. Unlike Burchett, he looked not to Hiroshima or Nagasaki to demonstrate the reality of mass destruction but to Madison Avenue and Hollywood. Like most Americans, in 1996 as in 1946, he was concerned far less with the reality of Japanese suffering than with the specter of his own. Thus, he turned not to the documentarist but to the illusionist for a way to dramatize what he called "Mass Death in Miniature." Worried that most people were just not smart enough to grasp the dimensions of the threat facing them, he urged: "Let the people see the atomic bomb in action. Let the scientists give us—which should be easy—a miniature bomb." Then, he directed: "Call in the experts of Hollywood to prepare such sets as their imaginations must often have stretched to. Begin here at home with a dozen locations on empty land easily accessible, and let there be built miniature cities carried out to the last physical detail. Mechanize them into movement. Give the illusion, at least, of crowded streets. Put ships in river or harbor, office towers of steel, factories in operation, traffic inbound and outbound, airplanes flying over." With the stage set, spectators could "safely witness . . . the whole of the calamity raised to its highest power." They could even be provided with binoculars, so that no detail need go unwitnessed. When all was in readiness, Canby instructed, "drop the tiny parachute with its bomb."[1]

Canby's proposal was revealing. Rather than directing attention to the victims of Hiroshima and Nagasaki, he urged readers to imagine *themselves* as victims—this at a time when no nation but the United States possessed atomic weapons. And in that regard, his proposal typified the visual and narrative frameworks within which postwar Americans made sense of the bomb, even those most concerned that it not be used again. To judge by much that Americans wrote and said, atomic warfare was something that had to be imagined, not something that had already been waged. After the initial, mostly ecstatic news reports, American attention shifted with breathtaking rapidity away from the atomic attacks on Japan to those which other nations might conceivably launch against the United States.[2]

Americans' lack of attention to conditions in Hiroshima and Nagasaki was not altogether surprising. As historian Michael S. Sherry has established, such reactions were part of a pattern of celebration and evasion that had long structured American thinking about air power, one consequence of which was the ease with which wartime Americans acquiesced in the indiscriminate bombing of civilians.[3] Reactions to the bomb certainly conformed to that pattern. Happy that the war was over, postwar Americans readily attributed victory to use of the bomb and celebrated the good fortune that had made their nation the first to develop it. They acknowledged and even insisted on the bomb's power but without paying much attention to the plight of those against whom that power had already been directed.

At the same time, however, even those most vocal about their hope that the bomb would never again be used groped for ways to imagine the consequences if that happened, as if evidence from Hiroshima and Nagasaki were unavailable or irrelevant. What would happen, they asked, if an atomic bomb were "loosed" on New York, Boston, or St. Louis? They might simply have asked, "What happened to Hiroshima and Nagasaki?" and demanded to see the evidence. However, rather than challenging occupation censors to make available confiscated photographs or motion picture footage, American commentators largely contented themselves with images of bull's-eyes and mushroom clouds superimposed over the skylines of American cities, images as surreal as they were menacing. Only a few—among them, economist and essayist Stuart Chase—proposed the obvious: show people what an atomic bomb actually did, and not in miniature.

Like Canby, Chase worried that people, world leaders in particular, were intellectually unequipped to make sense of what he called the "blinding, shattering force" loose in the world. So, he proposed, let them see it. Politicians, at the very least, should "see the unearthly glare [and] feel the shattering crunch" of an atomic explosion. "They must see, hear, smell, feel—almost taste—a chain reaction," he wrote. "[I]t should be etched forever in the nervous system." Impressed by the suggestion "that the United Nations Assembly be taken *en masse* to watch the U.S. Navy's test of the bomb in the Marshall Islands," he asked:

> Why not carry the idea of first-hand experience much further? Why not expose *all* the outstanding leaders of the world to direct chain reaction? Why not summon every Congressman, the heads of government departments, governors of states, university presidents, important tycoons, the executive committees of the AF of L, the CIO . . . the British Parliament and Cabinet . . . the Pope, the Grand Mullah, Gandhi, a panel of bishops, the chiefs of state of all nations, and all the admirals and generals who carry real weight?

Let them see with their own eyes the potential consequences of their decisions, Chase advised. "Let them stand there and watch: If a few get a little too near and are knocked over . . . that is all right, too. Protect them from lethal rays, but let them get knocked over. That is what they came for." He also proposed "a regular exhibit, say every six months . . . in the Sahara, the Gobi, Death Valley, and other desert areas of the world" where anyone who held high office would see for themselves the forces at their disposal. No one, he argued, should hold high office "without having had at least one first-hand encounter with the event corresponding to $E=MC^2$."

Chase was not a lunatic. He realized—or at least hoped—that, barring outright disaster, most people, especially world leaders, would never see an actual atomic explosion. So, he argued, people should see whatever they could. "All of us," he proposed, "children as well as adults . . . should see such moving pictures or stills of Hiroshima and Nagasaki as are available. . . . We should see the dead, the wounded, the smashed hospitals, the agony." To ensure that people did not forget, those pictures "should be run in every theatre in the world at regular intervals, without soft music. . . . We should take these horrors straight, hard, and unvarnished." Although movies were "not as good as seeing the real thing," he reasoned, they were the best means available for impressing people with the horror of atomic warfare and motivating them to avoid its repetition.[4]

Like Canby's, Chase's proposal was never realized, in large part because

Preparing bodies for mass cremation. Scenes like these were common in the weeks after the bombing but were rarely captured by the camera and still more rarely published. The image of mass death and the "bodies stacked like cordwood" visually recall German concentration camps, much in the news in the months before the atomic bombings and after the war. (Photograph by Miyatake Hajime. No date. Ienaga, 1.15.)

Americans, then as now, had no desire to see the victims of U.S. bombing. That was especially the case in 1945, both because the victims were Japanese and because visual representations of mass suffering had assumed new significance in the months before the bombing of Hiroshima and Nagasaki. Since late April 1945, Americans had been virtually swamped in images of the liberated Nazi concentration camps. For months, many newspapers ran those images on an almost daily basis, ensuring that people became nauseatingly familiar with pictures of corpses stacked "like cordwood," of skeletal survivors staring through barbed wire, and so on. Much the same as Canby and Chase would do regarding atomic destruction, numerous prominent Americans, beginning with Dwight Eisenhower, not only urged people to see for themselves the photographic evidence of Nazi brutality but proposed that civic rituals and educational curricula be constructed around it. The most famous, and successful, measure in that regard was a traveling exhibition of larger-than-life atrocity photos organized by publishing magnate Joseph Pulitzer II that was seen by hundreds of thousands of people in the spring and summer of 1945.

The whole point of an exhibition such as Pulitzer's was to make clear the gulf between good and evil, between Americans and their enemies. At the simplest level, the message was: this was what other people, evil people, did and do. Americans must see this evidence because they are too civilized to comprehend it otherwise. If they do not comprehend it and act on that comprehension, they risk having it happen again. After the bombing of Hiroshima and Nagasaki, many Americans said similar things: Americans, they worried, had to see the realities of atomic destruction for themselves because they were too civilized or sheltered to imagine their peril. For the most part, however, they ignored the visual evidence of Hiroshima and Nagasaki available to them: because they did not want to know and because doing otherwise might taint the emblems they had already chosen to remember the war's meaning.[5]

Another reason Chase's proposal went nowhere was that relatively few motion pictures or still photographs of Hiroshima and Nagasaki were in fact available. They certainly existed: Yamahata Yosuke's photographs of Nagasaki on August 10, 1945, are a powerful reminder of that.[6] However, to the extent that pictures of the destruction, especially of the dead and wounded, came to the attention of occupation authorities in Japan, they were seized, classified, and locked away in U.S. War Department vaults. Some, including Yamahata's, did make it into Japanese and American newspapers before late September 1945, when the Occupation Press Code imposed a blanket prohibition on the publication of anything "which might, directly or by inference, disturb public tranquility."[7] That code, administered by the frankly titled Civil Censorship Division, barred most images of atomic destruction from public view in Japan for most of the seven-year-long occupation. (Some images did make it into print even after September 1945, and the code itself was loosened considerably in 1949.) It also effectively cut off the flow of photographs to the American news media, which passively accepted limitations that Japanese journalists had no choice but to endure. When the occupation ended in 1952, Japanese scholars, journalists, and filmmakers published a flood of previously suppressed images and stories. In the United States, however, it was as if the occupation never ended: film footage confiscated in 1945 remained under government lock and key until the late 1960s—even when identical images were not only available in the United States but widely disseminated abroad—and most Americans, including antinuclear activists, seem to have assumed that the absence of pictures meant they did not exist at all.

As important as the absence of most images of "the dead, the wounded, the smashed hospitals, [and] the agony" was the seeming omnipresence of what editor Norman Cousins called "the classic mushroom," an image that government censors made no attempt to suppress whatsoever.[8] Before and after they saw photographs of the victims, Americans saw pictures and artists' sketches of the clouds over Hiroshima and Nagasaki—and of American cities with mushroom clouds superimposed over them. Indeed, for Americans at least, the mushroom cloud quickly became the most terrifying—and portable—image of the atomic age, one that from the very beginning signified both American might and the possibility that Americans might be next. It is worth noting in that regard that the mushroom cloud is virtually absent in Japanese memories of the atomic attacks. How could it be otherwise? The mushroom cloud is visible only from afar: from the relative comfort of 30,000 feet or of a carefully positioned observation bunker or of a nearby town. Those below the cloud recall instead the flash of the explosion, the *pika* that killed tens of thousands instantly, burned and irradiated thousands of others, and left two cities little more than rubble. More important, although for most Americans the mushroom cloud marks an endpoint, the place where narrative stops, in Japanese accounts of the bombings, the *pika* is just the beginning.

Ironically, the one *picture* of Japanese suffering that did capture American attention was not a picture at all but John Hersey's celebrated 1946 *New Yorker* essay, "Hiroshima." First published a year after the atomic attacks and just a few weeks after much-publicized atomic tests in the Bikini Islands, the story immediately became a sought-after literary commodity. Banded with white wrappers that alerted otherwise unsuspecting readers to the contents, newsstand copies sold out the morning they appeared. Within days, newspapers "from Boston to California" had requested and received permission to reprint the text, and ABC Radio had enlisted popular actors Paul Robeson, Alfred Lunt, Lynn Fontanne, and Katherine Cornell to read the essay live in four half-hour broadcasts. Within a month, the essay was available in book form and had garnered such attention that the *New York Times* issued a "minority opinion" arguing that Hersey's story was "essentially the picture made familiar in history and literature as far back as one can remember," a picture that left what the *Times* called the bomb's "real horror" to the imagination.[9]

As criticism, the *Times'* "minority opinion" underscored the striking degree to which readers discussed Hersey's "eloquent narrative" as if it were not a narrative at all but a *picture,* a way to confront an otherwise supposedly unimaginable reality. Concerned that "Hiroshima" obscured the "direful arithmetic" that distinguished atomic bombing from other slaughters, the

Times and the few critics who joined it in the minority decried not so much Hersey's failure as his success, his skill in making "what happened to a small group of specified individuals" seem real. Paradoxically, the critics charged, that semblance of reality made Hersey's account not only inaccurate but dishonest: by making atomic destruction seem comprehensible, even "familiar," Hersey masked what the *Times* called the "terror" of the event itself.

Critic Mary McCarthy was even more pointed. "Up until August 31 of this year," she argued, "no one dared to think of Hiroshima—it appeared to us all as a kind of hole in human history." Hersey, however, "filled that hole," making it "familiar and safe, and so, in the final sense, boring." In short, McCarthy asserted, "Hiroshima" depicted not the radically indiscriminate destruction of an entire city but only the limited, albeit harrowing, experience of six people, an accomplishment that normalized an event she resolutely refused to consider normal. Not having broken with "the government, the scientists, and the boys in the bomber," the *New Yorker,* McCarthy insisted, could "only assimilate the atom bomb to itself, to Westchester County, to smoked turkey, and the Hotel Carlyle."[10]

Most readers shared neither McCarthy's nor the *Times'* discontent with the adequacy of Hersey's account. On the contrary, in much the same way people the summer before had urged one another to see the photographic proof of German atrocities, many readers fixed on "Hiroshima" as the means to *see* what even pictures could not reveal. The Jesuit weekly *America,* for example, argued that "Hiroshima" brought home the "utter horror" that "miles of print, and endless reels of photographs" had not, an assertion echoed in *Art News'* judgment that the "effects of the atomic bomb must live for us in the words of John Hersey, beyond the reach of the representative arts." In a letter to a colleague, atomic scientist Arthur Squires confided that he wept as he read the *New Yorker* account and recalled with shame that he had celebrated as "the bomb's victims were living through undescribable horror (or rather, describable only in the simple, straightforward reportorial style used by Hersey)."[11]

Other readers also praised Hersey's style, lauding the success with which he had rendered atomic destruction imaginable. Reviewing the essay for *Christian Century,* former naval chaplain Russell Hutchison argued that Hersey had crafted "a concrete picture of what people really mean when they talk glibly and lightly of 'the next war.' This is it," he reasoned, "in miniature. And the miniature paralyzes the imagination." Like Henry Canby, Hutchison contended that Hersey's miniature rendering of mass death had to be seen, that "the facts" about atomic destruction had been lost in explanations of its scientific and political implications. Because it was concerned not with theory but human beings, he contended, "Hiroshima," made one forget "that one is reading about a bomb that fell on a remote city in a strange land. The reader . . . sees his neighbors, his friends, his children, and himself in the grip of catastrophe." In much the same vein, anthropologist Ruth Benedict argued that "Hiroshima" made it difficult to "dismiss the negotiations of atomic commissions as if these statesmen were playing a mere impersonal game of diplomatic chess." For those who read it, she explained, the issue had "become . . . scenes of the burned and wounded staggering endlessly along the roads, of living burial under fallen timbers and rubble, of vomit and suppuration and lingering death." Hersey, she suggested, had "brought home to hundreds of thousands of persons what it meant to drop an atomic bomb on a great city," making intensely personal an experience that other authors treated only in the abstract.[12]

For the rest of the 1940s and for several decades after that, discussions of the bomb's destructiveness, or of the need for world government, international controls, or civil defense, turned to "Hiroshima" for documentation. In 1948, for example, concerned that high school students understand the atomic threat, Pennsylvania schoolteacher Robert Frank prepared a "school edition" of "Hiroshima" complete with study questions, discussion assignments, and unusually, pictures of the six main characters. Two years later, newspaper heir Joseph Pulitzer III could think of no more effective way to communicate the need "to protect civilians in the United States" than to reprint "John Hersey's dramatic, and carefully reconstructed account of Hiroshima." Both men selected Hersey's account from hundreds of available verbal and visual representations, none of which, in Frank's words, conveyed as effectively as "Hiroshima" the "story not printed in the newspapers of 1945, not broadcast by the radio, and not shown by the movies."[13]

Like other readers, Frank and Pulitzer fixed on "Hiroshima" because it seemed definitive, because in some way it enabled readers to *see* what they might not otherwise understand. Pulitzer's memo, for example, began with the admission that he found "stories" on the topic "tough to read," a confession that located Hersey's "dramatic account" beyond the realm of mere narrative. Others agreed. Psychologists Joseph Luft and W.M. Wheeler, for example, studied popular responses to what they called "a picture of the effects wrought in the lives of six people by the first atom bombing." Unlike previous representations, the authors suggested, "Hiroshima" exposed readers to "the human aspects of atomic warfare." Nearly three decades later, historian Michael Yavenditti reached much the same conclusion. Analyzing what he called *Hiroshima*'s "enduring appeal," Yavenditti argued that it "allowed Americans to visualize the actual experience of the Japanese in Hiroshima—the initial surprise . . . the terrible fire

In 1952, residents of Hiroshima were still stumbling on forgotten graveyards full of bomb victims. Three mass graves, hastily dug in 1945, were discovered in April 1952 alone. Two hundred and sixteen bodies were recovered at this site in Sakamachi between July 10 and July 30, 1952. This photo, like the preceding one, is one of the few that conveyed a visual sense of the human scale of the tragedy—mass death, and not in miniature. With the hindsight of fifty years, this photo also is chillingly reminiscent of more recent massacre sites, such as in Cambodia and Rwanda. (Photograph by Chugoku Shinbunsha, July 1952. Ienaga, 4.206–07.)

storm, the devastation of medical services, and the frightened, bleeding, confused survivors." Contending that "Hiroshima" depicted atomic attack "more vividly than all previous publications combined," he reasoned that for "perhaps the first time since Pearl Harbor thousands of Americans confronted Japanese who were ordinary human beings." For Yavenditti, in other words, as for Americans thirty years before, "Hiroshima" was not just effective documentary fiction but a way to "confront" the reality of mass suffering.[14]

Whatever "Hiroshima" might have been, however, it was not a picture. Notwithstanding the merits of the essay itself, and they are legion, the canonical status accorded it as a *picture* of atomic destruction testifies not just to Hersey's talent as a writer but also to the virtual absence of interest among postwar Americans in actual photographs of the suffering he chronicled. Precisely because it was not a picture, "Hiroshima" made it possible to "envision the actual experience of the Japanese" without actually having to look at it.[15] The distinction is an important one. In hailing "Hiroshima" as a picture of events they had otherwise been unable to imagine, Americans disavowed their own agency—in the same way that their reliance on visual representations of Nazi brutality obscured their prior knowledge of mass annihilation in the death camps. Moreover, because it was not a picture, "Hiroshima" enabled people like Russell Hutchison "to see *his* neighbors, *his* friends, *his* children, and *himself* in the grip of catastrophe."[16] As a *picture,* in other words, "Hiroshima" made it possible to "reimage" the catastrophe itself, this time with Americans as victims.[17]

Fifty years after Henry Canby proposed staging "Mass Death in Miniature" so that people might see for themselves the consequences of atomic warfare, curators at the National Air and Space Museum proposed something similar. Rather than turning to Hollywood set designers, however, curators Tom Crouch and Michael Neufeld turned to the survivors of Hiroshima and Nagasaki for physical and photographic evidence of their experience. Doing so violated the more than half-century-old etiquette by which Americans had agreed not to see, and rarely to discuss, the bloody consequences of American war making. Thus, critics responded with outrage rather than mere rebuttal to the substitution of "burnt watches and broken wall clocks" and life-size photographs of their owners for the mushroom clouds that had long screened them from American view.[18] For fifty years Americans had pretended those images did not exist, as if Hiroshima and Nagasaki had simply vanished when *Enola Gay* and *Bock's Car* left the runway on Tinian. Pictures of the destruction demonstrated that that was not the case, that real people, most of them civilians, had suffered and died as a consequence of U.S. actions. Unable to explain those images away—however much they invoked U.S. casualties as an emotional counterweight—critics struggled vigorously, and in the end successfully, for their suppression.

To borrow a word from scholar H. Bruce Franklin, opponents of the proposed exhibition at the Air and Space Museum (many of them veterans or at least claiming to speak for veterans) accused the curators of "reimaging" the conflict, of doctoring the evidence so that Americans looked like the bad guys.[19] That the opposite was closer to the truth, that the veterans' lobby clung to a view of the war that distorted or erased many of its complexities, only made it more difficult for the revisionists, once branded as such, to make themselves heard. Where Crouch and Neufeld relied on often-forgotten archival images to construct a complicated picture of a war in motion, their opponents tapped images familiar for so long that most people took them for the whole truth: images of reluctant soldiers steeled by enemy atrocities, of beaches stormed and taken, of hometown boys dying in one another's arms, and countless other tropes manufactured to commemorate and justify the agonies of warfare. These were images of a war Americans were forced to fight by a treacherous and fanatical opponent, a war in which they simply did what they had to do. To a lesser extent, they were images of the technological might marshaled to break the enemy's *will* and *capacity to continue fighting,* images of planes skillfully evading enemy defenses and dropping their *cargoes* on chessboard targets. They were, in other words, images that not only reproduced an American point of view but that obscured the range of American choices and the consequences for the United States' adversaries.

To the extent that the curators "reimaged" the war, they did so by locating the *Enola Gay* in a trajectory of increasingly indiscriminate attacks on noncombatants—and by including the latter's point of view. The results were startling not because they were inaccurate but because they violated the conventions that five decades after the end of World War II still governed representations of those events. With few exceptions, even in the orgy of fiftieth-anniversary commemorations that coincided with the controversy, representations of "strategic" bombing (in itself an extraordinary euphemism) had depicted it as an impressive but bloodless display of military power and had avoided almost entirely the suffering it caused those on the ground. Thus, when Crouch and Neufeld focused on the civilian casualties of U.S. bombing (as opposed to the more familiar, far less revealing mushroom cloud, which the U.S. Postal Service even considered emblazoning on a commemorative stamp), critics quickly accused them of distorting history, a charge credible precisely because those casualties had so rarely entered Americans' field of vision.

Notes

1. Henry Seidel Canby, "Mass Death in Miniature," *Saturday Review of Literature,* September 8, 1945, 18. As silly as it might seem, Canby's proposal was eerily similar to the Chemical Warfare Service's use of Hollywood set designers during the war to construct—and destroy—scale models of enemy cities as a way to estimate the effects of incendiary bombing. See the discussion in Michael S. Sherry, *The Rise of American Air Power: The Creation of Armageddon* (New Haven, CT: Yale University Press, 1987), 226–27, and photo 14 in the visual essay between pages 146 and 147.

2. For more on people's immediate reactions to the bomb, and especially the rapidity with which they expressed fears of their own victimization, see Paul Boyer, *By the Bomb's Early Light: American Thought and Culture at the Dawn of the Atomic Age* (New York: Pantheon Books, 1985), chap. 1.

3. See Sherry, *Rise of American Air Power,* Chap. 1 and passim.

4. Stuart Chase, *For This We Fought: Guide lines to America's Future as reported to the Twentieth Century Fund* (New York: Twentieth Century Fund, 1946), 116–20. Italics in original.

5. For more on the centrality of visual representation in American reactions to the "discovery" of the death camps, see my discussion in *Envisioning Holocaust: Mass*

Death and American Culture, 1945–1995 (University of Chicago Press, forthcoming 1997).

6. See Rupert Jenkins, ed., *Nagasaki Journey: The Photographs of Yosuke Yamahata, August 10, 1945* (San Francisco: Pomegranate Artbooks, 1995) and the George Roeder essay (Chapter 4) in this volume.

7. Press Code of the Civil Censorship Detachment, quoted in Monica Braw, *The Atomic Bomb Suppressed: American Censorship in Occupied Japan* (Armonk, NY: M.E. Sharpe, 1991), 41. See also her discussion on pp. 17–20 of Japanese reportage in late August and early September 1945. For an example of photographs from Hiroshima and Nagasaki that appeared before the press code went into effect, see "Nagasaki a Month after Blast," *St. Louis Post-Dispatch,* September 17, 1945, 23.

8. Chase, *For This We Fought,* 120; Norman Cousins, "The Standardization of Catastrophe," *Saturday Review of Literature,* August 10, 1946, 17–18.

9. Charles Poore, "The Most Spectacular Explosion in the Time of Man," *New York Times Book Review,* November 10, 1946, 7; "Too Many Warnings," *New York Times,* September 19, 1946, 30. See report of upcoming ABC broadcast, "One Thing and Another," *New York Times,* September 8, 1946, sec. 2, 7. See advertisement for Book-of-the-Month Club, *New Yorker,* October 12, 1946, 111. For contemporary accounts of reaction to "Hiroshima," see "Without Laughter," *Time,* September 9, 1946, 50; Joseph Luft and W.M. Wheeler, "Reaction to John Hersey's 'Hiroshima,' " *Journal of Social Psychology* v. 28 (August 1948): 135–40; and Poore, "Most Spectacular Explosion." For an extended secondary account, see Michael Yavenditti, "John Hersey and the American Conscience: The Reception of 'Hiroshima,' " *Pacific Historical Review* v. 43 (February 1974): 24–49.

10. "Too Many Warnings," *New York Times;* Mary McCarthy, "The Hiroshima *New Yorker,*" *Politics* (November 1946), 367.

11. "*New Yorker* and the Soul," *America,* September 14, 1946, 569; "Spotlight On: George Grosz," *Art News,* October 1946, 80; A. Squires to J. Balderston, September 7, 1946, cited in Alice Kimball Smith, *A Peril and a Hope: The Scientists' Movement in America, 1945–47* (Chicago: University of Chicago Press, 1965), 80–81.

12. Russell Hutchison, review of "Hiroshima," *Christian Century,* September 25, 1946, 1151; Ruth Benedict, "The Past and the Future," *Nation,* December 7, 1946, 656.

13. Joseph Pulitzer III, memo to Joseph Pulitzer II, June 2, 1950, Pulitzer Papers, Library of Congress, vol. 68, reel 54, n.p. See John Hersey, *Hiroshima,* school ed., ed. Robert Frank (New York: Oxford Book Company, 1948).

14. Pulitzer III, memo, June 2, 1950, Pulitzer Papers; Luft and Wheeler, "Reaction to John Hersey's 'Hiroshima,' " 135–40; Yavenditti, "John Hersey and the American Conscience," 36–37.

15. Yavenditti, "John Hersey and the American Conscience," 37.

16. Hutchison, review of "Hiroshima," 1151. Emphasis added.

17. Here, and below, the word *reimage* is one I'm borrowing from H. Bruce Franklin. See *M.I.A., or Mythmaking in America* (Brooklyn: Lawrence Hill Books, 1992), 133 ff.

18. John T. Correll, "War Stories at Air and Space," *Air Force Magazine,* April 1994, 24.

19. Franklin, *M.I.A.,* 133 ff.

7

Patriotic Orthodoxy and American Decline

Michael S. Sherry

Historic changes in America's patriotic culture emerged in sharp relief during the 1990s, especially in the debate over the National Air and Space Museum's (NASM's) *Enola Gay* exhibit. In that debate, as in similar contests, self-proclaimed patriots—the Air Force Association (AFA), the American Legion, and their corporate and congressional allies—sought victory at home, not the extension of military power abroad.[1] As such, the *Enola Gay* controversy signaled the waning of American global power and highlighted the evolution of patriotic culture into a more brittle, nostalgic, and inward-looking orthodoxy.

In the 1930s and 1940s, patriotic culture had been capacious, loosely defined, and outward-looking. Liberals like Franklin D. Roosevelt worked its symbols and themes more successfully than mainstream conservatives like Senator Robert Taft or idiosyncratic ones like aviator Charles Lindbergh. Dissent from national policies in those years often came from conservatives: many criticized use of the atomic bomb against Japan, and Taft inveighed against the nascent imperialism of American cold war policies.

Closely tied to the celebration of the United States as a "melting pot," patriotic culture was also widely inclusive. It welcomed European ethnics like New York's Mayor Fiorello La Guardia. Less easily, it accepted Afri-

Laura Hein, Lane Fenrich, Edward Linenthal, Tom Engelhardt, and Mark Selden provided valuable advice and useful leads concerning this chapter. In addition to them and the sources noted below, I have adapted arguments developed in my book *In the Shadow of War: The United States since the 1930s* (New Haven, CT: Yale University Press, 1995). Earlier versions of this chapter appeared in *Bulletin of Concerned Asian Scholars* 27, no. 2 (summer 1995), 19–25, and in Tom Engelhardt and Edward Linenthal, eds., *History Wars: The Enola Gay and Other Battles for the American Past* (New York: Metropolitan Books, 1996).

can-Americans, who, in turn, linked their aspirations to it: "Are you for Hitler's Way or the American Way?" asked the placards of demonstrators against Washington, D.C.'s racial segregation in 1944.[2]

Shaped by perceptions of totalitarian and technological menace, patriotic culture was expansive, helping to mobilize Americans to wield extraordinary power abroad. The creation of a huge military force during World War II allowed a diverse, though hardly complete, range of Americans to acquire patriotic credentials. Although nearly all Japanese-Americans earlier had been forced into concentration camps by American authorities, by late in the war even Japanese-American soldiers found their combat service for the United States widely hailed.

To be sure, as the incarceration of Japanese-Americans indicated, this patriotic culture had its coercive, exclusionary, and hard-edged qualities. As journalist–historian Walter Millis wrote bitingly in the 1950s: "Since the great mobilization of the First War, a quasi-religious nationalism had been sedulously cultivated in the United States. It had acquired its creed (the oath of allegiance), its icons (the Flag), its ritual observances [promoted by] patriotic societies like the American Legion." As a result, a once unimaginable "degree of regimentation and centralization . . . had by 1941 become no more than a normal and patently necessary order of affairs."[3] Misogyny, homophobia, religious intolerance, racism, and ethnic hatreds waxed and waned in patriotic culture. Peace activism, leftist radicalism, left liberalism, and far-right agitation were extruded from it either when America moved into World War II or when the cold war heated up. As always, patriotic culture served to assert power by some and deny it to others. Still, closely linked as it was to the expansion of American power abroad, it prized an inclusive and varied domestic unity over a divisive, purified order. President Harry Truman's famous order of 1948 banning racial segregation in the armed forces powerfully illustrated that inclusive impulse.

Increasingly under strain, however, patriotic culture split apart during the Vietnam War. Diminishing faith in the necessity and practicality of enforcing American hegemony abroad was the overarching cause: detached from a widely shared vision of American power, patriotic culture changed. Some antiwar protesters angrily opted out of it, equating patriotism with conservatism, while with more effect many conservatives began a quarter-century-long effort to use patriotism to regain power and defeat their real and imagined enemies at home. Subordinate elements of patriotic culture in an earlier era— its exclusionary thrust and brittle posture—now became dominant.

In the wake of Vietnam, patriotic culture devolved into a rigid patriotic orthodoxy—tightly linked with political and cultural conservatism, baldly insistent on a singular version of the American past, crudely celebratory of

America's history of war making. When patriotic culture had been widely inclusive, it had at least partially embraced the idea that many versions of the past were possible. Patriotic orthodoxy insisted on its singular version of that past, which, its proponents claimed, had only one true and unchanging meaning. In that view, the turmoil and radicalism of the Vietnam era disrupted an otherwise singular, stable American history. As Speaker of the House Newt Gingrich put it, "From the Jamestown colony and the Pilgrims, . . . up to the Norman Rockwell paintings of the 1940s and 1950s, there was a clear sense of what it meant to be an American."[4]

In one sense, Gingrich was right. Since the United States had never before so clearly lost a war, patriotic orthodoxy after Vietnam was driven by something new, the determination to redeem a lost cause (as had been true of the white South after the Civil War) and to erase the sting of defeat. Yet in the 1970s and 1980s, few patriotic conservatives—certainly not Ronald Reagan, their symbolic leader—sought redemption through major war making. Instead, they sought it through largely symbolic military actions abroad in places like Grenada and Panama and through the discrediting of foes at home who presumably had caused defeat in Vietnam and later resisted martial renewal. As their reliance on POW/MIA (prisoner of war missing in action) mythology indicated, they leaned heavily on symbols of (or substitutes for) redemption. Rescuing Americans imagined still to be in Southeast Asia would not reverse the Vietnam War's actual outcome, but the fantasy of rescue drew on visions of getting in one last swipe at the commies, humiliating Washington bureaucrats and politicians, reasserting the virtue of America's cause in Vietnam, and rebuking Americans who lacked the patriotic ardor to care about POWs.

As such, redemption in practice meant finding fault at home more than altering history abroad. The POW/MIA mythology was politically unstable stuff: exploited by members of the Reagan administration, it was also turned against them, with George Bush accused of having hidden the truth about POWs he learned as director of the Central Intelligence Agency in the mid-1970s. But for the most part, this mythology extended the politics of Richard Nixon, who had argued that America's greatest enemy was in its midst, not in Hanoi (while the antiwar Left also saw enemies at home). As Nixon put it in 1967, "the war in Asia is a limited one with limited means and limited goals. The war at home is a war for survival of a free society."[5] Given such reasoning, patriotic orthodoxy turned inward, its focus on American power abroad gradually, though never fully, yielding to its quest for victory at home. By the same token, its adherents made culture at home their battleground, demonstrating that the Left was hardly alone responsible for the dominance of cultural politics in American life after the 1960s.

The *Enola Gay* debate dramatized that process. Orthodox patriots sought not just a voice in the exhibit but total victory over domestic foes, as if they were symbolically replaying the total American victory over Japan in 1945. Although the Air Force Association's *Air Force Magazine* acknowledged as early as April 1994 what it called "major concessions to balance" by the museum in its revised script for the exhibit, the AFA remained no less angry. Months later, after more museum concessions, AFA spokesman Jack Giese commented, "We welcome their changes, but they are by no means close to what we've asked for." Indeed, each new concession emboldened veterans' groups to demand more, finally including the resignation of Martin Harwit as the museum's director and abandonment of the exhibit itself (little more than the bomber's fuselage would remain): total victory, indeed, it seemed.[6]

Underlying their demands was an insistence that only veterans could divine the meaning of the atomic attacks. "All we want is for the museum to tell history the way it happened," Giese declared, not how museum curators "thought it should have happened. We're vets, we've actually been in the cold war—they haven't."[7] Giese here echoed a demand on the rise since the mid-1970s and loudly made by critic and World War II veteran Paul Fussell, among others, in the 1980s: the history of World War II belonged solely to those who fought it (although, of course, not all present-day veterans did duty in World War II, as Giese's careful reference to the cold war acknowledged, and many of the AFA's allies in Congress and elsewhere had done no military duty at all).

Patriotic orthodoxy also sought the virtual silencing of views and voices once included within patriotic culture. Before Hiroshima, most military leaders, in secret deliberations on the atomic bomb, had questioned the wisdom or necessity of its use on Japan's cities, although they eventually acquiesced in that use. Army generals like George C. Marshall and Dwight D. Eisenhower had stated major reservations. So, too, had navy admirals, convinced that *their* fleet had already crippled Japan, fearful of air force aggrandizement, or like Admiral William Leahy troubled by the barbaric nature of atomic bombing. Even air force generals like Curtis LeMay, though hardly opposed to the bomb's use, had insisted that their campaign of firebombing was on the brink of ending the war anyway. Civilian officials informed about Japan's secret diplomacy, like Joseph Grew (acting secretary of state until James Byrnes took over in July 1945) and Secretary of War Henry L. Stimson, had hoped that modification of America's surrender terms and/or the Soviet Union's entry into the war (or even its mere signature on the Potsdam Declaration) might alone suffice to end the war quickly. But President Harry Truman and Secretary of State Byrnes, in part for reasons of "atomic diplomacy" against the Soviets, pressed ahead with the atomic attacks. Moreover, after the war, a number of these leaders stated—boldly and publicly in some cases—their reservations about the bomb's use without suffering condemnation as traitors to a patriotic cause. By the same token, such reservations, shared as they were by diverse though not numerous Americans, could hardly yet be seen as the monopoly of "liberals" or "revisionists."[8]

But in 1994, orthodox patriots all but obliterated such reservations, as if embarrassed by them—writing for *Air Force Magazine,* John T. Correll noted their existence only briefly and obliquely—and assailed as "revisionist" those who highlighted the doubts of an earlier generation's leaders. Although the *New York Times* claimed that the *Enola Gay* debate pitted "revisionist historians" against "veterans groups protecting their heritage," in truth, veterans' groups were drastically revising that "heritage" rather than receiving it as an unchanged bequest from 1945. In their new mythology, the decision to use atomic bombs was not only beyond questioning in retrospect, it had not been questioned at the time.[9]

To sustain that mythology, they had to invent new truths, although media accounts usually saw the museum's defenders as the "revisionists." For historians, according to one account, "the atomic bomb has acquired political and emotional baggage in the intervening half century" as "the opening event of the nuclear age" rather than as the climax of World War II. But in fact, that supposedly "academic view of history" had weighed heavily on scientists and policy makers in the summer of 1945, on the air force before and after Hiroshima, and on pundits assaying the meaning of the event. For many officials, the bomb's future implications had consumed more attention that summer than its consequences for the war against Japan. Byrnes pursued its apparent potential to intimidate the Soviets; Stimson urged that it "not be considered simply in terms of military weapons, but a new relationship of man to the universe"; physicist Robert Oppenheimer hoped that showing the bomb's power might avert a future arms race; air force General Henry "Hap" Arnold probed its consequences for interservice rivalries and global peacekeeping. Public commentary after Hiroshima often showed the same emphasis: "[One] forgets the effect [of the bomb] on Japan," according to the *New York Herald Tribune,* "as one senses the foundations of one's own universe trembling."[10]

Thus, it was veterans' groups, not historians, who were adding new baggage to the events of 1945—and stripping them of the load they had once carried. Seeing only a dispassionate and morally simple decision to end the war and save American lives, they wrote out of that decision much that had shaped it: the passion for retribution against Japan, the desire to overawe the Soviet Union, the hope for nuclear mastery, and the fear of a titanic arms race. Taking the invention of new truths even further, Paul Tibbets, the *Enola Gay*'s commander, now claimed that "the urgency of the situation demanded that we use the weapons first—before the technology could be used against us." Apparently, unbeknownst to anyone in 1945 or since, Japan was about to get its own bomb.[11]

Of course, patriotic conservatives hardly had sole power to reshape these matters, as another kind of disappearance demonstrates. Science and scientists, once near the center of debate and images about the bomb's use, were almost wholly absent from the 1990s controversy. As the dog that no longer barks, this disappearance is hard for historians to explain. It may indicate the long erosion of scientific authority in America, for example; or the absence by the 1990s of dramatic, threatening advances in technological warfare; or the loss of that sense of awe felt by an earlier generation about the wondrous or monstrous creations of science. It certainly was not the veterans' doing: the original exhibit said little about science, even though a scientist (Harwit) was the NASM director; perhaps curators thought that other or earlier exhibits dealt sufficiently with this dimension of the bomb's use. Whatever the reasons, that disappearance played into the hands of patriotic conservatives. By erasing another context and set of players, it made it easier to see the 1945 decision as only a simple, straightforward one about how to end the war.

Defenders of patriotic orthodoxy revealed their new priorities by aiming their greatest animus and contempt at the Americans who planned or supported the museum's exhibit. Triumphal and hostile sentiments toward Japan did appear—especially in the indignant, unwarranted claim that the museum treated Japan as America's wartime moral equal—but played a distinctly subordinate role. The case against Japan was short and perfunctory compared to the lengthy, bitter denunciations of the museum, its curators and historians, and its director. Those attacking the museum showed little interest in what Japanese authorities or historians now said about the atomic bomb's use. They wanted to force their view of the war not on the Japanese but on fellow Americans. Just as the once-common rhetoric of a U.S.-Japan "trade war" had generally receded by the mid-1990s, so orthodox patriots rarely linked their views of 1945 to present-day tensions between the two countries. American virtue and victory *were* to be celebrated; that they were revealed in the defeat of Japan was a secondary matter. The diminishing attention paid to Japan was another sign that the enemy at home, not American power abroad, was what now consumed the orthodox patriots.

Likewise, their celebratory version of America's military past was now largely detached from a coherent vision of its military future. In earlier

This cartoon of Martin Harwit, former director of the National Air and Space Museum, surrendering on the deck of the USS *Missouri* captures the sense that the Japanese enemy in 1945 had given way to internal cultural enemies in 1995. (Cartoon by Mike Shelton, reprinted with special permission of King Features Syndicate.)

moments of patriotic revival, such a linkage had been strong. On the eve of World War II, for instance, films like *Sergeant York* got official endorsement as part of efforts to mobilize patriotic sentiment against the Axis powers. And in the 1950s, "under God" was inserted in the Pledge of Allegiance, and the new Iwo Jima Memorial at Arlington National Cemetery was celebrated in efforts to elicit indignation against godless communism and support for amassing American weapons to guard against it. Again in the 1970s and 1980s, patriotic revitalization was closely tied to efforts to expand and update America's nuclear arsenal.[12] To be sure, at every such moment, the advocates of martial revitalization were also jockeying for cultural and political power at home, but that power was at least plausibly linked to plans for exercising military might abroad. In the mid-1990s, the link between the two had all but disappeared. And so had anxieties about and ambitions for nuclear weapons. Earlier controversies about the remembrance of 1945 had been yoked to sharp debate over what the United States and other nations might do with their nuclear arsenals. With the end of the cold war—and of intense nuclear anxiety focused on a superpower enemy—debate about the bomb's use in 1945 was stripped of the resonance it once had with global problems.

Revealingly, the political allies of veterans' groups charted no plausible course for using American military power. Defense policy was a minor concern to ascendant Republicans like Speaker of the House Newt Gingrich; his "revolution" was to be carried out against domestic foes and in pursuit of a new domestic order. Statements like the GOP's 1994 Contract with America did demand greater military spending and specific programs like a revived antimissile defense system. But this was a call to arms with no identified purpose—no particular enemies to fight or threats to counter, only vague talk of a world still troublesome and of the problems that second-rate powers like Iraq or North Korea might pose. Like preparedness advocates before World War I, those of the mid-1990s seemed "more interested in polishing the fire engines than finding the blaze."[13] In fact, their primary mode was to carp at nearly every use of military power that President Bill Clinton pondered or tried—primarily, "peacekeeping" missions of various sorts—and to bemoan the actual or prospective loss of *any* American lives in such operations. As the *New York Times* observed, the October 1993 firefight in Somalia, which left eighteen American soldiers dead, "in many respects had a bigger impact on military thinking than the entire 1991 Persian Gulf war," and that impact enhanced reluctance to deploy American military power anywhere.[14]

Championing that reluctance, the forces of patriotic orthodoxy also borrowed, largely unwittingly, from the rhetoric and concerns of the antiwar culture during the Vietnam era. Although anti–Vietnam War protest had embraced many themes, revulsion at the loss of American life in a needless war had been its most broadly sustained impulse. The response of patriotic forces to the Vietnam War Memorial in Washington, D.C. revealed how much they had come to endorse that impulse by the 1980s. By starkly naming the American dead while avoiding any other explicit message about the Vietnam War, the memorial, at least as it was commonly understood, left the loss of American lives as the war's only widely accepted meaning. Although sometimes protesting the memorial before its completion, conservative patriots in the end embraced that meaning. Their role in the long POW/MIA controversy reflected a similar emphasis: however fanciful its premises, indignation that some Americans remained alive or unaccounted for in Vietnam, like Ramboesque cinematic fantasies of their rescue, valued the saving of American lives above all else. By the same token, most patriots celebrated the Gulf War for its remarkably low death rate among Americans more than for any American geopolitical or moral gains, just as the war's opponents stressed the American deaths they imagined would occur in great numbers. Indeed, by the mid-1990s, the saving of American soldiers' lives, rather than their expenditure in a valued cause, had become a mantra for nearly all American politicians: the dramatic rescue from Bosnia of downed airman Scott O'Grady in June 1995, insisted Bill Clinton, revealed not military failure in a mission but what is "best" about Americans; O'Grady should never have been in harm's way in the first place, responded his critics.

That self-proclaimed patriots would stress avoiding American deaths as the supreme priority—when earlier they had touted the need for sacrifice and excoriated antiwar activists as cowards for refusing to risk their lives in Vietnam—was a striking development. Such a stance left them in no position to entertain the major use of U.S. forces abroad, except in a scenario similar to that of the Gulf War, an anomalous conflict that forecast no pattern for the future.

This revulsion over possible American casualties in any military action fit precisely with the view of 1945 expressed by those attacking the *Enola Gay* exhibit. There were many ways to valorize the atomic bomb's use: it could be said to have ended a terrible war, punished a bestial foe, demonstrated American might, avoided a prolonged Soviet role in the Pacific War, squeezed Stalin out of the occupation of Japan, and showed the Soviets just how formidable U.S. power would be in the postwar world. But among orthodox patriots, those claims were barely noted, brushed aside, angrily rejected, or at best, subordinated to an insistence that, above all, the atomic bomb had saved American lives. Contemporary patriots stressed for 1945 precisely the theme they were sounding for 1995: the necessity of avoiding American deaths in war.

The focal points of their fury drove home that theme. They were outraged at historians' claims that the Truman administration had not expected half a million (or more) casualties in an invasion of Japan and that Japan's surrender had been imminent in August anyway, making the question of the administration's expectations moot. Indeed, it was over the issue of invasion casualty estimates that the final breach between the museum and its critics occurred in January 1995. The museum's opponents insisted that revised, lower figures offered by historians for what American officials had expected in 1945 constituted the final insult warranting cancellation of the *Enola Gay* exhibit. An earlier object of opponents' fury—the museum's plans to display photographs and artifacts dramatizing the carnage wrought in Japan—was also linked to the emphasis on the saving of American lives. Evidence of that carnage might, after all, raise troublesome questions about what it cost to save those lives and challenge the common American notion that it is Asians who hold life in low regard. Thus, veterans' spokesmen scrupulously counted the museum's planned photographs of Japanese casualties, as if each such image somehow diminished the value of the Ameri-

This billboard, located just outside the Oak Ridge nuclear facility, captured the sense of urgency felt in 1945 that the war should end as quickly as possible and that delays meant more American deaths. Visually, it presents violent death of Americans as something out of the normal frame of reference and stresses the links—of blood and affection—between civilians and combatants. After the Vietnam War, this emphasis on preventing loss of American life became the supreme priority in official rhetoric. (Photographer E. Westcott, National Archive series 434–OR.)

can lives saved. To be sure, their preferences also replicated those of 1945, when photographs of Japanese dead were few and those capturing American technological supremacy and the lives it saved dominated American visual culture. But although insistence on the virtue of saving American lives was an old theme, in 1995 it was a singularly overriding one, congruent with a newly dominant view of a military future free of American deaths.

Ostensibly, such insistence honored the sacrifices that American veterans of World War II had made and the value of those lives the bomb had presumably saved. Yet this way of honoring them was, as Robert Lifton and Greg Mitchell have noted, oddly "self-diminishing for the veterans, because it shift[ed] the credit for defeating the Japanese from the military personnel in the Pacific to a small group of bomb makers in New Mexico, and decision makers in Washington." Since Japan was defeated and suing (if ineptly) for peace in July 1945, it was strange that veterans in 1995 would "accept, even promote, the bomb as necessary to end the war when they could, with justification, claim that *they* had already completed the job."[15]

The saving-lives theme came to bear enormous moral weight for some, even allowing them to lay claim to the high moral ground of the Holocaust. In words and images, the Nazi Holocaust and the atomic "holocaust" (as it was often called in the 1940s) had been linked by American commentators from August 1945 on. But in the *Enola Gay* debate, some proponents of patriotic orthodoxy reconfigured that old linkage by suggesting that the bomb's use had averted a holocaust on the scale of Nazi genocide. In August 1994, a commentator in *USA Today* "established a new high for American lives saved [by the bomb]—six million—and claimed that this was 'the consensus view,' " while in 1995 a crewman of the B–29 that had attacked Nagasaki offered the same number (1 million Americans and 5 million Japanese). These claims for 6 million saved had no apparent basis other than their congruence—surely intended—with the number of deaths commonly attributed to the Nazi Holocaust. Thus, absurd claims about lives saved in the past emerged just when willingness to risk American lives in the future diminished to nothing.[16]

If their only vision of the future lay in its risk-free nature, what was the priority of the exhibit's attackers? Primarily, they sought victory over cultural and political foes at home. As Irving Kristol, one of their intellectual godfathers, put it in 1993: "There is no 'after the Cold War' for me. So far from having ended, my cold war has increased in intensity, as sector after sector of American life has been ruthlessly corrupted by the liberal ethos. . . . Now that the other 'Cold War,' is over, the real cold war has begun," one for which "we are far less prepared" and "far more vulnerable."[17] With the cold war abroad over, it was time to win that "real" cold war, the one that Pat Buchanan kept championing, against enemies now deemed far more dangerous than those in Moscow and Beijing had been. The *Enola Gay* exhibit provided an important arena in which to pursue that victory. As one political cartoon had it, replaying the famous scene of surrender on the deck of the battleship *Missouri,* "the Smithsonian"—humbled and professorial—capitulated to military force, with Japanese diplomats (though ugly and caricatured) playing only a background role.[18]

On the most general level, the *Enola Gay* contest echoed earlier struggles over who controlled American culture, who valued the American past, who deserved mention within it, and who controlled federal action that touched on such matters. Bitter controversies had already erupted over a federal amendment against "flag burning," over funding by the National Endowment for the Arts of "dirty" pictures, over the museums that displayed such work, over battle sites like Pearl Harbor supervised by the National Park Service, and over earlier Smithsonian exhibits on airpower and the settlement of the West. Rehashing those exhibits while mounting its case against the *Enola Gay* display, *Air Force Magazine* established its adherents' sense of powerful and dangerous connections among these controversies. Avid historians in their own way, patriotic conservatives felt themselves facing the same domestic enemies—liberals, America-bashing scholars, feminists, gays, racial and ethnic minorities, antinuclear and antiwar activists—in all these battles, as well as in the lopsided contest over American entry into the Persian Gulf War. The nitpicker could point out that the political coalitions in these struggles were complex and shifting: unilateralist queer baiters like Pat Buchanan had railed against the American war in the gulf, libertarian conservatives had inveighed against the flag amendment, and most historians associated with the museum's exhibit were indifferent to the cultural politics of gays and feminists. But there was enough stability in these coalitions for the defenders of patriotic orthodoxy to imagine themselves besieged by the same forces in every contest.

Those struggles also prepared the way for the *Enola Gay* debate by shaping the orthodox patriots' attack on "political correctness," the loose phrase already employed by conservatives claiming to face a rigid, ruthless, ever-growing assault from radical academics and their allies. The historians' and curators' "academic arrogance is beyond belief," insisted the AFA's Jack Giese, and indeed, arrogance is hardly unknown among academics.[19] But as in many preceding struggles, outrage at such arrogance was largely a posture calculated to disguise the grip on cultural power sought by many conservatives, whose claim that only veterans could assess the war's meaning was itself remarkably arrogant. Moreover, those outraged at political correctness conveniently overlooked the fact that much initial criticism of the bomb's use had come from conservatives, Republicans, and military figures. Herbert Hoover, John Foster Dulles, and William Leahy, among others, had weighed in, while Fulton J. Sheen, the prominent Catholic monsignor and cold warrior, had asserted that defending the bomb's use as a way to save lives "was precisely the argument Hitler used in bombing Holland."[20] In any event, quarrelsome leftists and liberals long had been unable and unwilling to impose "political correctness" on their own ranks, much less on the nation. Instead, cultural conservatives (though their cohesiveness, too, was sometimes exaggerated by them and their opponents) were the ascendant force in this regard.

The noisiest of those preceding contests erupted in 1993 about gays in the military. As in the *Enola Gay* struggle, the use of American power in the world was rarely the real issue. Instead, "patriotic" forces momentarily defeated their perceived foes at home while pursuing a vision of purity rooted in a mythology about military manhood. At the same time, however, they revealed how fragile their notions of military manhood had become and how disconnected those notions were from the exercise of American power. Military officials reluctantly had to admit what secret Pentagon studies long had made clear—that lesbians and gay men were fit to serve and long had done so. Defenders of the gay "ban" did claim that the presence of openly gay men would damage military fitness and "unit cohesion," but only because frightened or offended straight soldiers would resign, fail to enlist, or panic in the showers—in short, be unwilling or unable to fight. The orthodox patriots' specter of straight soldiers fleeing in terror from the sexual lust of gay comrades, as women might do in the face of male sexual lust, unwittingly feminized the (straight) American fighting man. It thereby implicitly called into question whether he had the courage and fortitude that war presumably requires and whether the ban's defenders even cared about America's war-making ability.

Indeed, the 1993 debate was largely about citizenship, not marksmanship. Advocates of the ban on gays feared that the military's acceptance of homosexuals would underwrite their fuller citizenship—a fear with foundation, since African-Americans and other social groups had successfully used military service to that end. Ominously in the background was the notorious Tailhook affair, in which male servicemen celebrating victory in the Gulf War had preyed sexually on female personnel, after which navy officials badly botched an investigation of the matter. The Tailhook affair played into the gay debate because patriotic conservatives also feared expanding numbers of and roles for women in the armed forces, against which a formidable weapon long had been the lesbian baiting that the ban made possible. Had the ban's defenders been seriously worried about military readiness, they could have accepted, even demanded, that the military recruit as widely as possible for the best personnel, as some patriotic dissenters like retired Senator Barry Goldwater argued. "You don't have to be straight to shoot straight," he insisted.[21]

That able Americans would be excluded from service underlined how much a vision of purity at home, rather than power abroad, captivated most conservatives, with whom Goldwater, clinging to an older vision of martial virtue, was now badly out of step. They thereby showed the extent to which they had left behind earlier notions of patriotic culture. For much of the century, a wide spectrum of political leaders had viewed the armed forces as an ever more inclusive institution that would meld together diverse Americans, teach them tolerance and teamwork, and broaden citizenship. That dynamic had not officially embraced homosexuals, but it had held the potential to do so. Defeat of Clinton's initiative showed a surging impulse to use the armed forces to mark boundaries rather than erase them; the wagons of military service would be drawn in a tight circle rather than dispatched into new territories of American citizenry.

This debate also foreshadowed the *Enola Gay* controversy through the insistence by "patriotic" forces that military veterans alone (though only straight ones) could judge whether gay soldiers should serve. President Clinton's claim as a nonveteran to have a voice in the debate, and even his right to be commander in chief, were widely ridiculed. Sailors openly mocked him to his face during a presidential visit to one ship, and Congress insisted on legislating, for the first time, in this matter. Indeed, expelling the nonveteran from this arena, as from the *Enola Gay* debate, was another way to attain a new kind of purity at home.

The connection between the gay debate of 1993 and the bomb debate of 1994 was more than temporal and political. It was also imaginative and intuitive. One article on the bomb debate was, for instance, devilishly titled, "*Enola Gay* Baiting," while political cartoonists had a field day with the connection. One cartoon featured the name "ENOLA GAY" with "GAY" crossed out and replaced by "HETEROSEXUAL," while another rendered the bomber sitting at the Smithsonian with "Enola Sexually Undifferentiated" emblazoned on it. Other cartoons added to the mix an incident in which GOP Congressman Richard Armey called gay Democratic Representative Barney Frank "Barney Fag": one pictured a TV reporter "at the Smithsonian to unveil the controversial exhibit of the Enola Frank—I mean GAY!"; another showed Armey commenting "on the proposed commemoration of the Enola Fag."[22] Such material did not trace a precise path connecting the gay and museum debates, but it did powerfully evoke a sense of connection. The name of Tibbetts's mother, "Enola Gay," probably long had sounded odd to many Americans, too feminine for such a mighty deed (though American crews often named their bombers after women) and lacking the ring of an authentic American name. In the wake of the gays-in-the-military debate, that name seemed to tap visceral fears that the America of patriotic memory was succumbing to the dark forces of a feminine, feminized, and homosexualized post-Vietnam era or to a "culture of appeasement," as Norman Podhoretz had complained in the 1970s, cultivated by the "kind of women who do not want to be women and ... men who do not want to be men."[23] To restore that imagined pre-Vietnam America, guardians of patriotic orthodoxy felt they had to defeat Clinton's effort to alter the Pentagon's antigay policy and later the museum's exhibit.

Their subsequent initiatives indicated a similar impulse to defeat foes at home. Emboldened by apparent victory in the *Enola Gay* fracas, the Ameri-

Defenders of patriotic orthodoxy who criticized the *Enola Gay* exhibit were concerned with winning a cultural and political victory over foes at home. "Don't Ask" slyly alludes to the 1993 gays-in-the-military debate, which resulted in a "don't ask, don't tell" policy. It also suggests the censorship of all questions about the decision to drop the bomb, which was far from unanimous in 1945 among U.S. military, scientific, and political leaders. (Cartoon by Ben Sargent. © 1995 *Austin American–Statesman*. [Reprinted by permission of United Press Syndicate. All rights reserved].)

can Legion, backed by 170 House members and 29 senators, launched a new campaign for an amendment banning flag burning. "Nothing disgusts me more than liberals who hide behind the 1st Amendment and want to support people who desecrate Old Glory," commented Republican Van Hilleary of Tennessee, a Gulf War veteran.[24] His language directly echoed earlier charges that liberals hid behind the First Amendment to defend dirty pictures, just as "disgust" captured the feeling of many orthodox patriots toward advocates of the museum's exhibit.

Thus, self-proclaimed defenders of the flag, like foes of the museum's exhibit, revealed how much the new patriotic orthodoxy was both inward-looking and backward-looking, far more focused than midcentury patriotic culture on enemies at home and long-ago triumphs abroad. The fact that it drew so heavily on the reservoir of a half-century-old event suggested as much, a dependence that cannot be attributed simply to some mysterious alchemy produced by fiftieth-year anniversaries. Such moments never carry intrinsic power but instead derive their meaning from current circumstances. In 1968, for instance, no great hubbub among Americans characterized the fiftieth anniversary of victory in World War I: disarray in patriotic culture and anti–Vietnam War fervor made this impossible. The fiftieth anniversary of World War II's end elicited so much attention and controversy because of how it intersected with politics and culture in the 1990s. Champions of patriotic orthodoxy drew on 1945 because, after that date, there was little for them to tap. Korea and Vietnam were useless for such purposes. The most recent case of patriotic glory, the Gulf War, offered little of value: it had been too lacking in gravity of sacrifice, too easy to win, and too ambiguous in outcome—with Saddam Hussein still in power—to establish a new reservoir of patriotic memory.

In part because the reservoir was so dry, victory in the *Enola Gay* debate also rang a bit hollow. The forces of orthodoxy defeated the planned exhibit but got only a puny alternative (to be sure, perhaps all some of them wanted), just as they had achieved, at best, only limited success in other recent struggles over how to memorialize America's military past.[25] They did not prevent withdrawal of a proposed atomic bomb postage stamp that embodied their celebratory view of the bomb's use. They did not stop ABC-TV from showing in July 1995 a biting prime-time documentary ("Hiroshima: Why the Bomb Was Dropped") embracing historians' arguments, condemning the exhibit's opponents, and challenging the celebratory view. In addition, erasing evidence of the bomb's destruction had ambiguous consequences, for that destructiveness, above all, gave visual proof of the magnitude of American triumph. How were Americans to celebrate an event whose effects they could not see, and how long could the celebration go on if entrusted only to the war's aging veterans?

Wounded and reviled in the *Enola Gay* fracas, many curators and historians understandably had trouble seeing such an ambiguous outcome. Some perceived an "unprecedented" assault on intellectuals, on historians' expertise, and on truth itself, carried out by patriotic bullies who used words like *liberal* a bit the way Nazis had once used *Jew*.[26] They were hardly wrong to sense defeat, but little in the assault was unprecedented, as historians of the McCarthy era could have told them. Furthermore, scholarly challenges to patriotic culture were, in the context of public institutions, relatively recent. The Air and Space Museum itself had been founded and long maintained as a celebratory showcase for American technology.[27] Stopping the *Enola Gay* exhibit marked an attempt to turn back the clock, but without recreating the global conditions and American power that had given patriotic culture its meaning in the 1940s and 1950s.

The backward and inward focus of the new patriotic orthodoxy can be exaggerated. Success in such cultural struggles also shapes the future: it bears down on defense policy, orients how textbooks and the media teach Americans to perceive both past and future, and strengthens political and cultural conservatism. The failure of the exhibit's supporters indicated what a free rein patriotic orthodoxy now had in this regard. By the same token, the tight links of the AFA (hardly just a "veterans" group) with the aero-space industry and other allies involved a real political and budgetary agenda. As has long been true, airpower patriots were less "isolationists" averse to the use of American power than "unilateralists" insistent on its unfettered application, just as their version of the atomic bomb's use erased the role of the Soviet Union and other allies in ending the Pacific War. As they saw it, the bomb's use embodied unilateral action, supremely destructive power, and the total absence of risk to American lives—an ideal combination some saw as realized again in the Gulf War and might yearn to replicate in a new crisis. After all, it might be hard to keep "polishing the fire engines" without finding a blaze to justify their existence.

But among most guardians of patriotic orthodoxy, neither the fear of looming crisis abroad nor the will to use American power in any such crisis was apparent, in part because patriotic culture also had absorbed key themes from antiwar culture, especially the horror of losing American lives in war. At least for the foreseeable future, the thrust of patriotic orthodoxy would be to defeat perceived foes at home and advance its vision of American cultural purity, not to do battles with enemies abroad. Its exponents seemed intent on entombing patriotic culture in museums—and making a museum of it—not on projecting it into the world. For them, the proper exhibit was to be a shrine to the past, not a beacon to the future. Far from anticipating new glory for American military power, they seemed more like Englishmen in the early post–World War II years, fondly remembering or angrily defending the lost imperial glory of the pre–World War I era. For sure, America had hardly declined as fast or far as England had, and the Soviet Union's collapse left it the only remaining superpower, but patriots sensed a slower and subtler erosion. They responded less by trying to regain what was lost than by mourning the loss and attaching blame for it. Ironically, the *Enola Gay* debate, and the partial triumph by "patriots" in it, showed that America's great age of military hegemony was drawing to a close.

Notes

1. I call these people "patriots" because that label captures their own sensibilities, but I realize that, as Mark Selden has noted to me, it concedes to them the higher ground

of patriotism when in fact many of *their* opponents saw themselves as no less patriotic. It also reveals the narrowing of patriotic culture, however, that few of those opponents actively laid claim to the term.

2. John M. Blum, *V Was for Victory: Politics and American Culture during World War II* (New York: Harcourt Brace Jovanovich, 1976), 217–18.

3. Walter Millis, *Arms and Men: A Study of American Military History* (New York: New American Library, 1956), 268–69.

4. Gingrich, *To Renew America* (1995), quoted in Joan Didion, "The Teachings of Speaker Gingrich," *New York Review of Books,* August 10, 1995, 8.

5. Stephen Ambrose, *Nixon: The Triumph of a Politician, 1962–1972* (New York: Simon and Schuster, 1989), 126.

6. John T. Correll, "War Stories at Air and Space," *Air Force Magazine,* April 1994, 26. Giese quoted in *"Enola Gay* Baiting," *Washington City Paper,* September 27, 1994, 8.

7. Giese quoted in *"Enola Gay* Baiting," 8.

8. A mountain of scholarship on these points is available, but for the most recent work, see Robert Jay Lifton and Greg Mitchell, *Hiroshima in America: Fifty Years of Denial* (New York: Grosset/Putnam, 1995), and Gar Alperovitz, *The Decision to Use the Atomic Bomb and the Architecture of an American Myth* (New York: Knopf, 1995).

9. Correll, as cited in note 6; "Hiroshima: A Controversy That Refuses to Die," *New York Times,* January 31, 1995.

10. For an account of museum fracas, see *"Enola Gay* Baiting," 8. On dominant frameworks in 1945, see Michael S. Sherry, *The Rise of American Air Power: The Creation of Armageddon* (New Haven, CT: Yale University Press, 1987), chaps. 9–10 (Stimson quoted on 324). For *Herald Tribune,* see Paul Boyer, *By the Bomb's Early Light: American Thought and Culture at the Dawn of the Atomic Age* (New York: Pantheon, 1985), 6.

11. For Tibbetts, see *"Enola Gay* Baiting," 8.

12. Among much scholarship on these matters, see Edward Tabor Linenthal, "War and Sacrifice in the Nuclear Age: The Committee on the Present Danger and the Renewal of Martial Enthusiasm," in *A Shuddering Dawn: Religious Studies and the Nuclear Age,* ed. Ira Chernus and Edward Tabor Linenthal (Albany, NY: State University of New York Press, 1989); Karal Ann Marling and John Wetenhall, *Iwo Jima: Monuments, Memories, and the American Hero* (Cambridge, MA: Harvard University Press, 1991).

13. Thomas Leonard, *Above the Battle: War-Making in America from Appomattox to Versailles* (New York: Oxford University Press, 1978), 148.

14. Eric Schmitt, "Somalia's First Lesson for Military Is Caution," *New York Times,* March 5, 1995.

15. Lifton and Mitchell, *Hiroshima in America,* 240.

16. Ibid., 286, describing *USA Today* commentary. Crewman's claim offered in "Rain of Ruin: Bombing Nagasaki" (PBS, August 8, 1995). On the early history of imaginative linkages between Nazi and atomic holocausts, see Lane Fenrich, "Imagining Holocaust: Mass Death and American Consciousness at the End of the Second World War" (Ph.D. diss., Northwestern University, 1992).

17. Quoted in David Remnick, "Lost in Space," *New Yorker,* December 5, 1994, 86.

18. Original in *Orange County Register,* as reprinted in *Chicago Tribune,* February 11, 1995.

19. *"Enola Gay* Baiting," 8.

20. On this point, see Lifton and Mitchell, *Hiroshima in America* (Sheen quoted on 81), and Alperovitz, *Decision to Use the Atomic Bomb,* 437–44.

21. Goldwater quoted in Chris Bull, "Right Turn," *Advocate,* September 7, 1993, 35.

22. See "Enola Gay Baiting," cited above; "Enola Heterosexual" for the *Arkansas Democrat–Gazette,* reprinted in *New York Times,* January 29, 1995; "Enola Sexually Undifferentiated" by Chip Bok for *Akron Beacon Journal,* also appearing in *Washington Post,* September 3, 1994; Barney Frank–Richard Armey cartoons for *Orlando Sentinel,* circa January–February 1995, and for *San Francisco Chronicle,* January 31, 1995.

23. Quoted in Edward Tabor Linenthal, "Restoring America: Political Revivalism in the Nuclear Age," in *Religion and the Life of the Nation,* ed. Rowland A. Sherrill (Urbana: University of Illinois Press, 1990), 29.

24. "Anti–Flag Burning Drive Begins: Veterans Rally in Support of Constitutional Amendment," *Chicago Tribune,* March 1, 1995.

25. See Edward Tabor Linenthal, *Sacred Ground: Americans and Their Battlefields* (Urbana: University of Illinois Press, 1991).

26. Here I draw on comments made by indignant historians at a session on "The Practice of American History," Organization of American Historians convention, Washington, D.C., March 31, 1995, and on a letter to me recalling that session from Edward Linenthal, July 31, 1995.

27. Advice from Michael Wallace was helpful to me on this point.

III

Contending Constituencies

8

Hiroshima and Nagasaki

The Voluntary Silence

Monica Braw

Since my first visit to Hiroshima in 1969, I have been concerned with the question of knowledge about the atomic bombings of Hiroshima and Nagasaki. I was ashamed to realize that I, a university-educated journalist from Sweden, knew next to nothing beyond the fact that two cities had been destroyed. What I knew least about was the condition of the survivors, both immediately after the bombings and subsequently.

This chapter considers why knowledge of the *hibakusha* and the human consequences of the atomic bombing of Hiroshima and Nagasaki has been so limited. It suggests and assesses the reasons for this, including mechanisms of U.S. and Japanese censorship and self-censorship that have contributed to this silence.

These reasons can be divided into three groups. First are the direct and indirect effects of occupation censorship. Censorship in the years 1945–1949 controlled the dissemination of knowledge, particularly about the atomic bombs, their effects, and even the treatment of atomic injuries. But censorship also had indirect effects. In particular, it discouraged open discussion.

Second, there were social pressures within Japanese society that silenced many hibakusha fears about long-term effects of radiation, led society to shun hibakusha, and forced many into a life of silence, not to say deception about their past. This silence may have been related to silence about the war in general, as both government and people sought to banish the past and look toward a brighter, peaceful future. Moreover, social customs fostering reticence may have strengthened individual hibakusha in their resolve not to speak of themselves and their experiences.

Third, hibakusha had their own reasons for silence, including very human survival needs—that is, the desire to forget and to get on with life—as well as a wish to preserve personal dignity. The latter is relevant not only in their relation to American research at the Atomic Bomb Casualty Commission (ABCC) but also for some as a response to the peace movement's perpetual infighting.

United States Censorship and Its Effects

My initial interest in the silence regarding Hiroshima centered on American censorship. In the 1970s, when I started research among hibakusha, I discovered that they had long been prevented from talking freely about their experiences. In a 1975 meeting I had with the poet Kurihara Sadako, she suddenly responded to one of my questions: "We could never have written about such things during the American occupation." American censorship of the atomic bomb during the occupation became the subject of my research, eventually resulting in *The Atomic Bomb Suppressed*.[1]

In the book, I tried to show the workings of American censorship, which was introduced together with democracy. Censorship covered, among other subjects, all aspects of the atomic bomb, including the personal experiences of the survivors. Reasons for the censorship included the suppression of Japanese anger against the United States and the occupation forces and the U.S. desire to maintain its information monopoly on matters related to the bomb. One result was that, in the immediate postwar years, there was little concrete information in Japan and throughout the world about the terrifying human consequences of atomic bombings and certainly less basis for gauging the effects of nuclear war.

My research showed that, despite an elaborate censorship apparatus, the results were erratic and the execution haphazard. This permitted publication of some "objectionable" material. Nevertheless, American censorship was the main reason why only a trickle of material about the atomic bomb and its consequences was published in Japan from 1945 to 1949 (when the censorship apparatus was dismantled). This is also an important reason why the voices of the Hiroshima and Nagasaki hibakusha seldom reached the world outside Japan at this time. The fact that every foreign correspondent in Japan had to be accredited to the American general headquarters (GHQ) stifled critical reporting. One of few exceptions was the Australian journalist Wilfred Burchett, who traveled alone to Hiroshima on September 3, 1945, and smuggled out the story of radiation. Burchett's trip took place less than a month after the bombing and before occupation censorship was fully organized.[2]

If the American censorship is now history, in some respects there has been and still is silence about Hiroshima and Nagasaki, not least on the part of survivors. This is what I call the voluntary silence. The voluntary silence of the hibakusha is a fact that has to be accounted for in explaining the continued lack of public understanding of the consequences of the atomic bombs. In the immediate aftermath of the bombings, many hibakusha declined to speak. I think it would be a mistake to blame this exclusively on American censorship—or even fear of it. As a matter of fact, only those directly connected with publishing, from newspapers and publishing houses to writers and journalists, were aware of the existence of censorship. Censorship did not take the form of blackened or blank spaces in published works. Precensorship procedures required that material be submitted for clearance prior to publication. Moreover, all printed material was subject to postcensorship, including confiscation and destruction.

This policy led to self-censorship, mainly for two reasons. In the case of precensorship, which entailed submitting a printed copy to censors, the sheer cost of typesetting a manuscript before knowing whether it could be published entailed a financial gamble. Many publishers understandably held back from accepting manuscripts on controversial subjects, and all atomic subjects were controversial. In the case of postcensorship, the risk was further heightened. If a publication was found to contain any objectionable material, the publisher might be prosecuted and fined or otherwise punished. Rumors circulated that penalties even included death. Even the largest mass media, including the national news agency Domei and the newspaper *Asahi Shinbun,* had their rights to publish suspended for some days for having published objectionable information. Domei had disseminated a report that contained the sentence: "Japan might have won the war but for the atomic bomb, a weapon too terrible to face and one which only barbarians would use." *Asahi* had published an article by the future prime minister Hatoyama Ichiro calling the use of the atomic bomb a war crime and a violation of international law. The threat of shutdown of publication or destruction of already printed material forced publishers to weigh carefully the risk of publishing manuscripts on sensitive subjects.

Factors other than censorship kept many hibakusha from relating their experiences immediately after the war. The most direct reasons were probably injury, illness, exhaustion, and the almost unimaginable survival demands they faced. Moreover, for several years, many besides hibakusha suffered from injury and sickness and lived in poverty. Virtually every city had been burned to the ground. Food was scarce. There were no medicines. Hibakusha were fortunate if their radiation burns were treated with iodine. The doctors had nothing else. Trying to scratch together a living under the circumstances in the late forties, few had strength, time, or will to relate experiences that were in any case shared by all around them. For these reasons, for some time after the bombings, many hibakusha would have kept a certain silence regardless of American censorship. For some, this silence became deeply ingrained.

The ABCC and Voluntary Silence

Others found new, compelling reasons for silence. One of the earliest manifestations of hibakusha unwillingness to give information about themselves concerns the ABCC. The United States opened ABCC offices in Hiroshima in 1947 and in Nagasaki in 1948 to research the effects on human beings of the atomic bomb. Hibakusha were examined for their injuries and illnesses. But the ABCC did not treat hibakusha. Furthermore, the results of this research were not made available to Japanese scientists and physicians. In addition, the extensive data relating to both physical and human destruction caused by the atomic bombs collected during the immediate postbomb period by Japanese scientists were routinely stamped "Top Secret." Not only the research reports but even physical specimens were removed to the United States. This included the remains of victims shipped to the United States for further research. In this way, Japanese scientists were deprived of the opportunity to complete or publish their own research. Still less could they see their research findings translated into treatment for Japanese survivors. Few Japanese reports were published during the occupation on the treatment of injuries caused by nuclear war, and hibakusha were left with virtually no support to secure treatment and with a blackout on the dissemination of crucial information such as that regarding radiation and its treatment. Neither the Japanese government nor the American occupation authorities provided significant financial aid for the hibakusha. The limited Japanese disaster relief to Hiroshima and Nagasaki ended within two months of the bombings. American policy then and after was expressly not to help the atom-bombed cities since such aid might imply American guilt about the atomic bombings. There were no funds for hospitals, and there was no support for medical expenses incurred by the survivors.

The ABCC was accused of using atomic bomb survivors as guinea pigs. Hibakusha correctly understood that the research of the ABCC was explicitly not intended to help them but rather to advance atomic research in and for the United States. Bitterness toward the ABCC was widespread. Many hibakusha refused to go there, preferring to keep silent rather than allow their bodies to become objects of American research.

Mistrust of the ABCC was the subject of a novel published in 1954,

Jikken Toshi (Experimental city) by Kajiyama Toshiyuki. He accused the ABCC of using hibakusha as guinea pigs, not for the sake of world peace but for U.S. military purposes. According to Kajiyama, the central cause was racism. U.S. behavior would have been impossible if the Japanese had not been of another race. In the novel, the American director of the ABCC defends the commission's work as a contribution to knowledge:

> We have in our hands a new field of medicine, and we will cultivate this field. Our task is great. At home our people are trying to produce new medicines for treatment, by making use of guinea pigs. And that is being done upon the basis of my findings. Our materials. Other than these, there are no effective weapons. No strike can stop us from getting these materials. This research of ours will enhance the life of humanity in the future. We are right. What else could this be if not humanism? The injured are injured. A historical necessity. Neither Stalin nor Christ, not even Hirohito can change that. Tomorrow is what matters. We are making a contribution to mankind for tomorrow. We are right.[3]

The author comments: "Humanism. Such a concept is excluded from American doctors' concerns."[4]

Kajiyama's novel voiced the fears of many hibakusha. In a 1978 interview, Dr. Nishimori Issei, himself a hibakusha from Nagasaki, sharply criticized the ABCC: "Hibakusha complained because the ABCC only researched and did not try to cure or assist them. The ABCC's way of doing research seemed to us full of secrets. We Japanese doctors thought it went against common sense. A doctor who finds something new while conducting research is obligated to make it public for the benefit of all human beings."

Many hibakusha did not want to be examined by ABCC doctors, not only because they thought that these doctors were treating them like experimental animals but also because the Americans had given them this disease, the "atomic bomb sickness." So even if the Americans had had more sincere motives for examining them, they might not have accepted it.

Discrimination against Hibakusha

Among the saddest victims were young girls whose faces were disfigured by keloid scars. They had virtually no possibility of getting married, an extremely sad fate in Japanese eyes. They were even encouraged to hide themselves in their homes, not to be seen. Not only were they pressured not to speak about their experiences, but they were expected to erase themselves from general consciousness. Simply to see them was perceived as being too harsh, not only for the victims themselves and for the families who bore the sorrow of having been struck by such a fate, but above all for society at large, which would be reminded repeatedly of the terrible past, shocked, and made uneasy at the sight of the disfigurement of these young girls.

Saturday Review editor Norman Cousins arranged for twenty-five of these girls to go to the United States to receive plastic surgery. The American press styled them the Hiroshima maidens,[5] or A-bomb maidens, and much was written about them for several years. A second level of silence was forced on them by this media attention, as their cases were sensationalized. Gradually, they grew despondent over the distortion of facts and with being used for purposes not their own. They withdrew into their private lives, only seldom to break their silence again.

The socially enforced silence of survivors disfigured by the bomb is the extreme example of perhaps the most pervasive silence of all atomic self-censorship: that motivated by fear of discrimination. The hibakusha, including radiation victims who had no visible scars, have had good reason to fear the consequences if their background became known. This has led many to keep silent about their personal history, even to actively conceal it. Some have kept their background secret from all, living a life of deception even with spouse and children. Others have kept a public silence, concealing their background in situations such as job seeking. Still others have refrained from calling attention to their status by avoiding participation in the peace movement, hibakusha rights campaigns, and even atomic bomb memorials.

Deception in marriage and family is the deepest and most oppressive silence to carry through life. In Japan, family background is critical in arranging a marriage. Prior to engagement, extensive research into a prospective spouse's personal and family background, including possible hereditary diseases, is common. Damaging findings may halt a union regardless of the personal feelings of the partners. Hibakusha and their descendants have lived in fear of being shunned as prospective marriage partners. They are thought to fall ill frequently, to die young, and above all, to bear the risk of conceiving malformed babies.

The effects of the radiation from the atomic bomb explosions have been researched extensively. In 1994, the Radiation Effects Research Foundation (RERF; formerly, the ABCC, now including Japanese researchers) reported unusually high rates of nine forms of cancer, especially leukemia, in hibakusha. In a study of 86,000 subjects, the hibakusha were found to have an added cancer risk of 8 to 12 percent. Among 500 unborn babies conceived prior to August 1945, 21 were later born with severe mental retardation, more than four times the norm. However, fears that radiation would affect children not yet conceived at the time of the atomic bombings, or even in future generations, have not been substantiated by research on hibakusha and their descendants. After decades of research on 72,216 children born more than nine months after the atomic bombings, a 1990 report from a Japanese scientist with the RERF found no "significant genetic effects," including birth defects, chromosomal abnormalities, and cancers. Despite a total lack of scientific findings of genetic effects due to the bomb, such fears torment the survivors and their children as they seek to lead normal lives.

This perceived risk, of course, poses formidable problems for hibakusha seeking marriage partners. Data compiled in 1985–1986 by the Japan Confederation of A- and H-Bomb Sufferers' Organization (Hidankyo) reveal deep anxiety among hibakusha regarding marriage. Of the respondents to a Hidankyo survey, 24 percent had worried about marriage because of their A-bomb experience. Of these, 30 percent revealed that they had concealed their hibakusha background prior to marriage. Self-enforced silence for many has taken the form of hiding their atomic bomb experience from family members as well as from society.

Hibakusha status is also hidden as a means to avoid employment and work discrimination. Of the respondents to the Hidankyo survey, 24 percent indicated that they had been worried about finding jobs. Of these, 24 percent hid their hibakusha identity in order to avoid discrimination, and 10 percent said they experienced discrimination after being employed.

The reality and the fear of discrimination have not only been amply documented but have also become the subject for literature. One of Japan's great contemporary writers, Ibuse Masuji, wrote the novel *Kuroi Ame* (Black rain) around the theme of the marriage of a hibakusha girl. It starts:

> For several years past, Shigematsu Shizuma, of the village of Kobatake, had been aware of his niece Yasuko as a weight on his mind. What was worse, he had a presentiment that the weight was going to remain with him, unspeakably oppressive, for still more years to come. In Yasuko, he seemed to have taken on a double, or even triple, liability. That no suitable marriage was in sight for her was a circumstance simple enough in itself. The real trouble was the rumor. Towards the end of the war, it ran, Yasuko had been working in the kitchens of the Second Middle School service corps in Hiroshima City. Because of that rumor, the villagers of Kobatake, over one hundred miles to the east of Hiroshima, were saying that she was a victim of radiation sickness. Shigematsu and his wife, they claimed, were deliberately covering up the fact. It was this that made her marriage seem so remote. People who came to make inquiries of the neighbors with an eye to a possible match would hear the rumor, would promptly become evasive, and would end up by breaking off the talks altogether.[6]

The Politicization of the Hibakusha

The worldview of Oe Kenzaburo, the 1994 Nobel laureate for literature, was profoundly shaped by the atomic experience, a theme that he has explored since the early 1960s. At that time, it was unusual for a writer who was not a hibakusha or a close relative to delve into these areas. Oe's writings raise important questions concerning hibakusha silence. In one essay in *Hiroshima Noto* (Hiroshima notes), written a year before the twentieth anniversary of the bombings, he quotes a letter from a survivor, Matsusaka Yasutaka, on the question of silence:

> People in Hiroshima prefer to remain silent until they face death. They want to have their own life and death. They do not like to display their misery for use as "data" in the movement against atomic bombs or in other political struggles. Nor do they like to be regarded as beggars, even though they were in fact victimized by the atomic bomb. . . .
>
> Almost all thinkers and writers have said that it is not good for the A-bomb victims to remain silent; they encourage us to speak out. I detest those who fail to appreciate our feeling about silence. We cannot celebrate August 6; we can only let it pass away with the dead.[7]

Matsusaka's negative feelings about the antinuclear movement had their background in the fierce political struggle that was then rampant and still divides the movement in the 1990s. That hibakusha started to organize themselves in order both to relate their own experiences to Japan and the world and to demand compensation was a significant development. But from early on, this struggle was marred by ideological quarrels within different factions, quarrels rooted in cold war conflicts that often threatened to overshadow the movement to ban atomic weapons.

In 1961, the Democratic Socialist Party, a right-wing splinter group from the Socialist Party, supported the formation of the National Council for Peace and against Nuclear Weapons (Kakkin Kaigi) in opposition to Gensuikyo (Japan Council against Atomic and Hydrogen Bombs), which was supported by the Communist Party. It criticized Gensuikyo for its "pro-Communist and anti-American" stance. In 1965, several groups split with Gensuikyo after controversies regarding nuclear testing and formed Gensuikin (Japan Congress against A- and H-Bombs), supported by the Socialist Party and Sohyo (the General Council of Trade Unions of Japan, the largest trade union confederates at that time). Many other organizations and grass-roots groups also formed. In 1978–1985, most of the groups joined an ad hoc committee to organize annual world conferences. But the peace movement remains so deeply split that public walkouts at memorial conferences throughout the world have left many hibakusha profoundly embarrassed and suspicious of different peace groups.

Matsusaka brought up another aspect of silence:

> I have long wondered why virtually all of the "A-bomb literature" consists of stories of the miserable people who have not recovered their health, as well as of descriptions of radiation symptoms and the psychology of the A-bomb survivors. Why are there no stories, for example, of families who endured hard times but recovered their health? Must all surviving A-bomb victims eventually meet a tragic death caused by radiation aftereffects? Is it not possible for victims to overcome their illnesses, and their psychological anxiety and inferiority complexes, and thus die a natural death like other people? Must we, instead, all face tragic deaths cursed by radiation aftereffects; and must our deaths then be used as data for opposing atomic bombs? Undeniably, our lives were distorted and tormented by the atomic bomb. Yet many other people, though they did not experience the atomic bombings, nonetheless endured the war and knew suffering of varying degrees. Therefore, I determined not to indulge myself in the victim complex that some A-bomb victims in Hiroshima have developed. Although exposed to the atomic bomb, I wanted my body and soul to recover so that I could live my life and die as naturally as people not bombed by nuclear weapons.[8]

Matsusaka here speaks of silence as a means of overcoming memories of a terrible experience in order to live as normally as possible. He does not want to delve into what has been, both because many people other than hibakusha have suffered horribly from the war and because he believes that it is possible at least to try to overcome these memories, illnesses, and injuries. He goes so far as to say that some hibakusha indulge in a victim complex, a serious accusation that is almost taboo among hibakusha, as well as among all who sympathize with their sufferings and among supporters of the antinuclear movement. However, those who have met many hibakusha must, for the sake of accuracy in understanding human nature, acknowledge that there are those among the survivors for whom relating their experiences has become their raison d'être in ways that may repel others. Such persons may, of course, be found in any group of people, but Matsusaka, in disassociating himself from such fellow hibakusha, presents this as one reason for preferring silence.

Our reluctance to criticize hibakusha as Matsusaka does may also be influenced by the expectations we bring to bear in thinking about Hiroshima and Nagasaki. We do not turn to A-bomb literature in order to read, hear, or see stories of miraculous recovery or even strength and survival. As a rule, we expect to be confirmed in our view of the horror of nuclear weapons. Early attempts by certain writers to minimize the dismal descriptions of

Hiroshima and Nagasaki would never pass scrutiny now that we better understand the effects of radiation. During the occupation, censors who often prohibited the publication of negative descriptions from the atom-bombed cities sometimes permitted more positive news, however ill-founded. For example, a 1947 article reported conclusions of the ABCC that descendants of atomic bomb victims might be "physical monstrosities" and that sterility and altered genetic patterns might be effects of radiation. The censors called this report "pure supposition" and suppressed it. But that year, they passed a report from Hiroshima citing a doctor who said there were no further fears of atomic diseases and that the scars of those who had had plastic surgery had all but disappeared.

New Problems and Perspectives in the 1980s and 1990s

In the late 1980s, *Black Rain* was filmed by Imamura Shohei, showing that the problem of discrimination was still of concern almost half a century after the atomic bombings. Indeed, some hibakusha continue to confront questions of whether they have been too secretive and whether they should now finally reveal their background. Even those hibakusha who were children in 1945 now have their own grown-up children who, in turn, hope to have children. However much radiation research denies the statistical risk of genetic effects among children of hibakusha, concern among potential marriage partners and employers remains widespread. The fear has even deepened among hibakusha, who cannot rid themselves of the anxiety that genetic effects that did not occur in their own children might appear in the following generation. In that case, their grandchildren, who are about to be born, would be at risk.

For hibakusha who have kept silent about the atomic bomb experience until now for whatever reason, the question is whether they have a duty to speak to their spouses and children. The ramifications for their personal lives are enormous, not only for having hidden the truth from children who would then bear the burden of anxiety but also in some cases for having misled or lied to husbands, wives, and in-laws for decades. The agony of hidden hibakusha fifty years after the atomic bombings thus runs deep.

Even those who made no secret of their background but, on the contrary, made it the basis for lifelong work in the peace movement can be deeply shaken over such new and difficult questions. A case in point is a widow of a hibakusha and leading peace worker who suffered no serious illness. She was shaken when her teenage daughter asked whether it would be safe for her, as a second-generation survivor, to have children. This fear of a perfectly healthy young daughter of a hibakusha mother who suffered no serious illnesses, who has been brought up with full knowledge of the atomic bombing of her parents, underlines how even a partial silence, such as avoiding discussion of fears that scientists recognize as unsubstantiated, influences the lives of both hibakusha and their descendants.

During his last years, Ibuse said that he no longer reread his own book *Black Rain*. "Gradually the picture of war is getting faint in my memory," the author said. Like Ibuse, many hibakusha, and not only hibakusha, may no longer wish to remember that painful past. To recall what has been forgotten or hidden in the mind's locked rooms might only awaken old anxieties while others may have said all they wanted to say.

Japanese public television, NHK, reported one such silence in its 1993 program on censorship of the book *Masako Taorezu* (Masako does not give up) during the American occupation. Masako was fifteen years old at the time of the Nagasaki bombing. She wrote about her experiences, and her father, judge Ishida Hisashi, tried for several years to have her writings published. Aware of the difficulties, he devised a strategy that included contacting foreign correspondents so that news of the censorship of the forthcoming book would appear in the American press. He also kept pressure on the censors by writing to and visiting them. In one letter, he assured the censors that the book would not disturb public order or stir animosity against the United States or the occupation forces.

Those two points, disturbing public order and stirring animosity against the United States and its forces, were the primary considerations of censorship during the occupation. Masako's book provides a good example of the issues censors weighed in deciding what to censor. *Masako Taorezu* was in fact recommended for printing by some American censors in the Fukuoka censorship district, which included Nagasaki: "For us to promptly realize the significance of the atomic bomb, to experience vicariously the feelings that so many thousands of Japanese experienced is desirable in these propitious times," wrote Lieutenant Colonel Victor E. Delnore of the Nagasaki Military Government Team in 1947.

In spite of this and of a signature campaign among citizens of Nagasaki, *Masako Taorezu* was banned. Especially offensive were descriptions like the following: "Flesh raw from burns, bodies like peeled peaches . . . the river was filled with corpses, legs. . . . [D]ead bodies of mother and child . . . as if in the Inferno. . . . At last we were defeated in war and I felt mortified. I never could convince myself that it was our sky through which the B-29s carried that devilish atom bomb."[9]

The district censor held that the book would "disturb public tranquillity" and that it "implies that the bombing was a crime against humanity." Perhaps, he added, publication would be possible in the future, "when it would be less apt to tear open war scars and rekindle animosity."

Masako Taorezu was finally published in 1949, a small, thin book that can be found in the Nagasaki Library of Atomic Bomb Materials. The 1993 NHK program about the book documented the sustained effort of Masako's father and brother. The program showed files of a family journal the brother published regularly for members of the Ishida clan and also his photographs from the atom-bombed city. Judge Ishida had hoped to combine Masako's writing with photographs of places she mentioned. The brother took more than one hundred photos, including one of the father and daughter sitting in front of the ruined Urakami Cathedral.

Masako, now the wife of a judge in Tokyo, appears in only one short sequence. Here, she smilingly says that the final permission to publish her book probably delighted her father much more than herself. The film conveys the impression that the whole effort to convince the American censors to allow publication of *Masako Taorezu* had been his. When my book about American censorship, *The Atomic Bomb Suppressed,* was to be published in Japanese, the translator informed Masako about it. She responded that she felt "deep emotion" turning the pages of the book, as she had when she recently visited Nagasaki for the first time in thirty years. That was her only comment.

Having written about her experiences right after the bombings, for personal reasons, Masako subsequently preferred not to discuss the matter further. She seems to have escaped the negative experiences of media attention of, for instance, the Hiroshima maidens. But she does not wish to serve as a public witness to the bomb and her personal experiences. She may, of course, feel that she has nothing to add, either to her own or to others' descriptions. But there are other possible reasons, which would be in line with the socially enforced silence discussed above. Judge Ishida did his utmost to get his daughter's writings about the bomb published. He was unusual, not only as a hibakusha and a father but as a judge, for whom it may have been considered unseemly to engage in public controversies. On the other hand, his social standing carried self-assurance and influence as he challenged the authorities to justify their censorship of the manuscript and subsequently organized a petition campaign among Nagasaki citizens supporting publication. But for Masako, the future may seem far more important than the past. Public identification as a hibakusha and an activist might have damaged her husband's judicial career. Although not denying her past, she had no wish to publicize it. Perhaps Masako felt she had no more to say; maybe she succumbed to social pressure. Whatever the reason, she has maintained virtual silence for fifty years since writing *Masako Taorezu*.

Children of hibakusha attending an anniversary commemoration of the atomic bombing in Hiroshima in the early 1990s. They, too, worry that their health and lives will be forever affected by the atomic bomb. (Photo by Juhani Lompolo. Used by permission.)

Breaking the Silence after Fifty Years?

Among hibakusha who never talked about their personal experience with anyone, not even those closest to them, realization of the significance of their experience may be growing. The peace movement born in the 1950s grew to new strengths in the 1980s and 1990s. Hiroshima again took on meaning for many young people, not least in Europe and the United States. There was a demand for knowledge about the bombed cities as well as the experiences of the survivors that not only brought invitations to hibakusha from many groups and countries but also created a brisk demand for guides and witnesses of the bombings in Hiroshima and Nagasaki. New groups and organizations formed in response. Hiroshima Interpreters for Peace, consisting mainly of housewives and students, served as guides and translators for tourists and also compiled an extensive *Hiroshima Handbook* for interested visitors. Many who had never participated in peace work before joined at this time.

The Chernobyl reactor catastrophe in 1986 also turned eyes toward Hiroshima and Nagasaki. It was not the first time that hibakusha were joined in their experiences of radiation, as witness the Japanese radiation victims of the 1954 *Lucky Dragon* fishing boat incident, the U.S. radiation victims from nuclear tests, and the Marshall Islands test victims. In the 1980s and 1990s, knowledge of the effects of radiation leakage from U.S. nuclear weapons plants spurred an international movement in support of victims of radiation. But it was the Chernobyl disaster, with its immediate and long-range effects spilling out from a sixty-square-mile area and threatening large portions of the Soviet Union and Europe, that above all made the experiences of hibakusha directly relevant to millions of people. Their suffering and the research conducted could now be used to help others. Exchange programs of scientists and doctors as well as visits by patients and survivors from Chernobyl to Japan were quickly arranged.

Not only the possibility of being of use to others but also awareness of the significance of their experiences as a warning of the dangers of nuclear power became obvious to many following Chernobyl. As in other countries, the connection between the anti–nuclear weapons movement and the anti–nuclear power movement was not automatic. Chernobyl strengthened the argument of those who insisted on the linkage. This connection to a controversial contemporary issue, the development of nuclear power in Japan and globally, may have influenced some formerly silent hibakusha to speak.

The fiftieth anniversary of the end of World War II also offered a strong incentive to some to abandon silence. Leading up to the anniversary year of 1995, the climate of public discourse regarding the war years gradually changed. Official public apologies for Japan's wartime conduct left many victims of Japanese militarism dissatisfied. But a wide range of TV programs, articles, and books publicly aired many atrocities. At times, the theme changed from the "Suffering was inflicted on me" type to "I (We) inflicted suffering on others." Even more significant, efforts were made to explore issues of Japanese responsibility for the war. Peace groups had long sought to discuss these questions in the face of official silence and suppression, as in the case of school text censorship of passages relating to Japanese wartime atrocities. In 1995, the climate was more open. The renovation of the Peace Memorial Museum in Hiroshima is a case in point.

Earlier exhibits in the Hiroshima museum—while moving in their depiction of hibakusha experience—provided no political or military context for the atomic bombing. The question of responsibility for the war was completely ignored, nor was there any discussion of the war itself. The new wing of the museum questions both Hiroshima's part in the war effort and Japanese aggression and atrocities such as the Nanjing massacre. Issues of interpretation and responsibility, absent from earlier exhibits, are now raised. Seeing long-standing taboos concerning discussion of the war fall, some who previously were reticent to relate their hibakusha experience may now feel freer to do so.

Other events may have influenced some hibakusha to abandon silence. In an important development, Nagasaki Mayor Motoshima Hitoshi openly laid responsibility for the war on Emperor Showa (Hirohito). Motoshima, who frequently appeared at peace forums all over the world during his time as mayor, in a 1990 interview, explained: "I have always wondered if what we [from Hiroshima and Nagasaki] were saying was being accepted as the truth, and what we should do to make us understood. I think it depends on whether we can honestly search our hearts and face up to our responsibilities for past wars, and if each one of us can live as a 'world citizen.' "

Another example linking hibakusha to contemporary events was the protests against French nuclear testing on the Mururoa atoll in the South Pacific during 1995. Hiroshima mayor Hiraoka Takashi stated that the use of nuclear weapons violates international law, which prohibits the deployment of weapons that inflict unnecessary suffering on human beings. He also severely criticized the extension of the Non-proliferation Treaty for leaving nuclear arsenals intact, whereas the goal should be total abolition of nuclear weapons.

Many of those who have kept silent may also be entering a new phase of their life as hibakusha. Some aging hibakusha were prompted to tell young people about the atomic bomb both because they noticed how little these youngsters knew of the past and because the fiftieth anniversary of the war's end led them to think back on their own lives. Propelled by a feeling of duty to add to the knowledge of the consequences of atomic war, and observing the rapid development of nuclear power in Japan and elsewhere, some started to speak. In the 1990s, as in the 1980s, citizens' movements involving hibakusha and others interested in furthering knowledge of the atomic bomb grew rapidly.

Among groups that have broken their silence or begun to find an audience in the 1990s, the foremost is the Koreans. Of an estimated 48,000 Koreans in Hiroshima in 1945, 30,000 are believed to have died as a result of the bomb; of 30,000 in Nagasaki, 12,000 probably died. In 1995, there remain 18,000 Korean hibakusha in Japan and Korea, only 4,300 of whom have received official designation by the Japanese government, giving them the right to medical treatment at state expense. Korean hibakusha have started campaigns for official recognition as hibakusha, contesting the location of the monument to Korean hibakusha, presently located outside the Hiroshima Peace Park, and addressing broad issues of discrimination.[10]

Conclusion

The silence of hibakusha has been influenced by several factors, beginning with occupation censorship. Another occupation institution, the ABCC, an-

The silence of many hibakusha echoed the general silence about many other important aspects of the war in Japanese society. In recent years, some have begun to speak out of a desire to teach young people about the war era before those who remember it are gone. This photograph was also taken at the Hiroshima anniversary commemoration. (Photo by Juhani Lompolo. Used with permission.)

tagonized hibakusha to the extent that many refused to give information about themselves in any form.

But the survivors were also pressured to be silent from within their own society, particularly by fears of discrimination. This was manifest in the difficulties hibakusha faced in finding marriage partners, which, in its turn, was based on a fear for future generations, which no research seems able to dispel. Their deep feeling of insecurity about life, health, and future, combined with a general reluctance among Japanese to discuss the war years, has discouraged many hibakusha from speaking about their experiences. Although some hibakusha have spoken out and organized, many others have maintained silence, whether because of public pressure, fears, or personal discretion, even extending to the concern not to embarrass others. These factors remain salient to this day.

Despite extensive research and publication in all forms of mass media, from newspapers to books, paintings, theater, film, and comics, despite indefatigable efforts of many survivors, and factors such as Chernobyl and the fiftieth anniversary of the war's end, which encouraged many to speak out, there has been and remains a certain silence about Hiroshima and Nagasaki, including on the part of many hibakusha. Some of the reasons are probably no different for the survivors of the atomic bombs than they would be for survivors of any other catastrophe. What can be said to be different in the case of hibakusha is a certain moral pressure, a sense of duty toward humanity to bear witness in the face of the patent threat to life posed by nuclear weapons.

I believe there is a further reason for hibakusha silence—one that is more difficult to substantiate. In our time and in our Western society, we have a tendency to believe that knowledge, openness, and information are an absolute good. Conversely, silence is suspect, if not evil. Not only the mass media but also the scientific basis for so much of our perception of life and society strive toward a mapping of reality and consequently toward a complete picture. Knowledge is seen as all-important, often regardless of the circumstances surrounding its compilation or the difficulties it may create. Likewise, at a personal level, we encourage openness with expressions like "You will feel better if you talk about it" as we soothingly tell a troubled friend. Psychologists and psychiatrists have encouraged generations to open themselves up in order to find understanding of their own behavior.

This emphasis on openness, so highly prized by Europeans and Americans, finds little resonance in Japan. Neither at the governmental level nor on a personal level is high value placed on openness. Of course, there are many cases in Japanese history of revolts and protests that have exposed and challenged the status quo. In private life, there are naturally cases and situations in which one pours forth innermost thoughts. But reticence and understatement continue to be valued highly. Consider, for example, the different reactions to two recent great catastrophes: the 1994 Estonia ferry disaster, with close to a thousand dead, mostly Swedes; and the 1995 great Hanshin earthquake, centered in Kobe. In Sweden, grief led not only to extensive counseling for survivors as well as for bereaved relatives but also to a drawn-out public probing into the psychological effects on the nation of such a large loss of life. In Japan, on the other hand, after the first shock, the official efforts focused on practical aspects of rebuilding, while the survivors, whatever material help they received, were left basically on their own to cope with the psychological aftereffects. The city authorities encouraged them with the traditional, and to many unbearable, booster slogan: *Gambare Kobe* (You can do it, Kobe).

I believe that the silence of many hibakusha is in part the product of such culturally rooted behavioral norms as reticence, bearing up in the face of adversity, and discretion as well as the more concrete fears of discrimination and the very human wish to try to forget for the sake of living life as best one can. If the silence of hibakusha is in large measure self-imposed censorship, we have no alternative but to accept it.

Notes

1. Monica Braw, *The Atomic Bomb Suppressed: American Censorship in Occupied Japan* (Armonk, NY: M.E. Sharpe, 1991).
2. Wilfred Burchett, *Shadows of Hiroshima* (London: Verso, 1983).
3. Kajiyama Toshiyuki, *Jikken Toshi* (Experimental city) (1954).
4. Ibid.
5. Rodney Barker, *Hiroshima Maidens* (New York: Viking Penguin, 1967, 1985).
6. Ibuse Masuji, *Kuroi Ame* (Black rain) (Tokyo: Kodansha, 1969).
7. Matsusaka Yasutaka, quoted in Oe Kenzaburo, *Hiroshima Noto* (Hiroshima notes) (Tokyo: YMCA Press, 1981).
8. Ibid.
9. Ishida Masako, *Masako Taorezu* (Masako does not give up) (1949).
10. Lisa Yoneyama, "Memory Matters: Hiroshima's Korean Atom Bomb Memorial and the Politics of Ethnicity," *Public Culture* (1995): 7.

9

The Mushroom Cloud and National Psyches

Japanese and American Perceptions of the Atomic-Bomb Decision, 1945–1995

Sadao ASADA

Japan's strongly felt national identity as the first and only country to have undergone atomic bombings gives a unique twist to its perspective on the bomb. It is hardly surprising that Japanese views on the American decision to use the bomb have been markedly different from those of Americans. What deserves to be noted, however, is that, in some respects, the gaps in collective memory have, if anything, widened over the half-century since Hiroshima and Nagasaki. In both Japan and the United States, the A-bomb question is dominated by emotion and, more often than not, surrounded by historical myths and moralism.[1] In the United States until recently, the exigencies of the cold war and imperatives of the "national security state" have defined perceptions of the A-bomb decision in narrowly strategic terms, often clouding the broader significance of Hiroshima and Nagasaki in human history. The psychological and cognitive dissonance over the question has been such that it has constituted a serious irritant in relations

This chapter draws upon some of the findings presented in my earlier essay "Japanese Perceptions of the A-Bomb Decision, 1945–1980," in *The American Military and the Far East: Proceedings of the Ninth Military History Symposium, United States Air Force Academy*, ed. Joe C. Dixon (Washington, DC: United States Air Force Academy and Office of Air Force History, Headquarters, USAF, 1981), 199–219. The early Japanese version is: "Kinokogumo to kokumin shinri: Genbaku toka o meguru Nichi-Bei ishiki no gyappu, 1945–92" (The mushroom cloud and national psyches: Japanese and American perception gaps regarding the A-bomb decision, 1945–92), in *Amerika to Nihon* (America and Japan), ed. Jochi Daigaku Amerika-Kanada Kenkyujo (Tokyo: Sairusha, 1993), 81–107.

between the two peoples as well as in their official dealings.[2]

This state of affairs was suddenly dramatized by the controversy over two events: the United States Postal Service's abortive plan in December 1994 to issue a stamp depicting the mushroom cloud[3] and, more important, the *Enola Gay* as the centerpiece of an exhibition on the atomic bomb at the Smithsonian Institution's National Air and Space Museum. The fiftieth anniversary of Hiroshima and Nagasaki provides an appropriate opportunity to trace and compare the development of divergent perceptions held by the two peoples and to point to the fallacies of their collective memory. Only such a long-term and comparative perspective can provide historical background to the Smithsonian controversy.

The earliest statistics available about Japanese perceptions of the atomic bomb are found in the United States Strategic Bombing Survey, undertaken just three months after Japan's surrender. Questioning some five thousand people in Japan, the survey team found a relatively low level of Japanese hostility toward the United States. Only 19 percent of Hiroshima and Nagasaki residents (and 12 percent of the Japanese people as a whole) registered resentment against Americans for having used the atomic bombs. Rather, they tended to turn their anger against their own leaders, especially the military, which led Japan to war. When asked where the responsibility lay for the atomic bombing, 35 percent of respondents replied that it was Japan's fault; another 29 percent said that neither side was responsible, believing it to be a consequence of war.[4]

As the survey's report frankly admitted, these figures probably underestimated hostility to the United States. The stupor caused by the shock of defeat, the immediate postwar lethargy, and a fatalistic attitude toward war all influenced Japanese attitudes. Many respondents refrained from disclosing their feelings for fear of offending the Americans. The International Military Tribunal for the Far East, which began its investigation in the spring of 1946, exposing one Japanese war crime after another, reinforced the view that Japanese military leaders were responsible for the atomic bomb tragedy.

In the early postwar years, the Japanese people, on the verge of starvation, were in no condition to give much thought to the A-bomb question. Even had they wished to do so, the press code (a euphemism for censorship) of the occupation authorities, which went into effect in September 1945, severely restricted information about the bomb and the devastation it wrought. Yet censorship was by no means total,[5] and as the years passed and the occupation neared its end, foreign publications relating to the bomb began to appear in Japanese translation. Most notably, the translation of

John Hersey's *Hiroshima* was finally able to appear in April 1949.[6] In 1951, the translation of P.M.S. Blackett's *Fear, War, and the Bomb* appeared and quickly became a bible for Japan's left-wing historians, peace activists, and even textbook writers.[7]

In 1952, the year Japan regained independence under the peace treaty signed in San Francisco, a spate of books and films about the bomb appeared. Changes in the international environment—the intensification of the cold war, Soviet acquisition of nuclear capability, the Korean War, the conclusion of the United States–Japan Security Treaty in 1952—had their effect on Japanese perceptions of the A-bomb decision. And the Bikini incident of 1954 (in which Japanese fishermen aboard the *Lucky Dragon* were exposed, with one fatality, to radioactive fallout from an American H-bomb test) ignited antinuclear—and anti-American—feelings, triggering a ban-the-bomb-movement, which spread across the nation from its origins among a group of Tokyo housewives. Now not only the Hiroshima–Nagasaki survivors but the entire Japanese people could see themselves as nuclear victims.

In the late 1960s, the escalating war in Vietnam—with reports of atrocities and "body counts"—gave credence to a racial interpretation of the A-bomb decision. Instances of American brutality in Vietnam intensified the Japanese sense of racial victimization; these events seemed to confirm the view that American racial callousness toward Asians lay behind their use of the atomic bombs. By this time, the Japanese people had long since abandoned their immediate postwar attitude of blaming their leaders, rather than Americans, for the use of the bomb. In time, the new nationalism that accompanied Japan's rise to an economic superpower was to color critical perceptions of the bomb.

With the caveat that public opinion surveys on the A-bomb question are sporadic and unsystematic, we shall make the most of the data available to reconstruct shifting Japanese perceptions. According to a 1970 survey by the *Mainichi shinbun,* 38 percent of respondents expressed resentment against Americans for the bomb; those who blamed their leaders had declined to 19 percent.[8] A year later, a survey of Hiroshima residents by the *Chugoku shinbun* showed that 31 percent criticized the American government and military, including 10 percent who singled out former President Harry S Truman for denunciation, whereas just 10 percent held the Japanese government and military responsible.[9]

Let us compare these changing perceptions with the American reaction. As early as August 9, 1945, President Truman publicly stated that the bombs had been used to end the war quickly and thus save American lives that would have been sacrificed in any invasion of Japan's home islands.[10]

This photo by a Japanese photojournalist in Indochina in 1965 shows pistol-packing U.S. soldiers leading a nearly naked and blindfolded young man to a waiting helicopter for interrogation away from his village on the Lao-Thai border. Such images of casual American brutality shaped Japanese assumptions about the decision to use atomic weapons at Hiroshima and Nagasaki twenty years earlier. They also shaped Japanese assumptions about the Vietnam War. In 1965 almost no such images were available in U.S. media, nor were many Americans then aware of the U.S. military activity in Laos. The Japanese public saw these disturbing images much earlier than did Americans. (Photograph by Ishikawa Bunyo. Used by permission.)

This "official" view—the "Truman orthodoxy" that the decision was necessary and justified by military reasons—became the standard line for American presidents from Truman to Bill Clinton, and it also became the mainstream view of the American people.

When the Pacific War—a "Good War" for most Americans[11]—ended, few expressed remorse or guilt about dropping the atomic bomb, with the exception of a handful of confirmed pacifists and religious leaders. A soldier's reaction to Hiroshima, as recalled by Paul Fussell, was "Thank God for the atom bomb."[12] According to an August 16, 1945, Gallup poll, 85 percent of respondents approved of the use of the bomb. Two months later, a Roper poll starkly registered American feelings on the subject:[13]

1. We should not have used any atomic bombs at all 4.5%
2. We should have dropped one on some unpopulated region, to show the Japanese its power, and dropped the second one on a city only if they hadn't surrendered after the first one 13.8%
3. We should have used the two bombs on cities, just as we did . . 53.5%
4. We should have quickly used many more of the bombs before Japan had a chance to surrender 22.7%
5. Don't know 5.5%

Not only did 53.5 percent endorse the bombing of both cities, but an additional 22.7 percent regretted that the United States had not quickly used atomic weapons to bomb other cities.

In 1946, John Hersey's best-seller, *Hiroshima* brought human dimensions to the issue. His dispassionate yet poignant portrayal of six survivors was a profoundly moving document. Because he refrained from moral criticism, however, readers could seek catharsis in the book while at the same time holding to views supportive of the use of nuclear weapons.[14]

But then a confusion of thoughts and actions intervened. From the beginning of the atomic era, Americans were haunted by nightmares that one day they themselves might become A-bomb victims—fear that became pressing with the successful Soviet detonation of a nuclear device in August 1949. With President Truman's decision a few months later to proceed with work on a hydrogen bomb, a nuclear arms race was under way. In a world of nuclear deterrence, the symbolic meanings of Hiroshima and Nagasaki for humankind were quickly overpowered by the rhetoric of megaton overkill.[15]

There is a dearth of data on American views about the A-bomb decision during the 1950s and 1960s. The available evidence from that time forward shows that Americans overwhelmingly approved the A-bomb decision.

We have the 1965 nationwide Louis Harris survey in which 70 percent agreed that the United States was "right" in dropping the atomic bomb to save American lives; 17 percent "regretted" it.[16] The figures had changed little since the 1945 polls. In 1971, when the *Asahi shinbun* (in cooperation with Harris) conducted its first poll on American attitudes toward Japan, 64 percent of respondents asserted that dropping the bomb "could not have been helped," 21 percent said it was a "mistake," and 15 percent replied "don't know." These findings came as a profound shock to the Japanese people; the *Asahi* writer expressed "great surprise."[17]

In Japan, the assertion that the atomic bomb was dropped to end the war quickly is regarded not as a statement of fact or historical interpretation but as a moral justification of the act and, as such, evokes revulsion. For example, in 1971, Yamada Setsuo, mayor of Hiroshima, said that such a statement was "a political utterance, in which there is not one iota of humanity, and the American people must understand this."[18]

In August 1983, the well-known Japanologist and former ambassador to Japan Edwin O. Reischauer created a furor in Japan by writing in the *Boston Globe* that, but for the bomb, the Japanese would have "fought on to extinction," so that the bomb not only saved millions of lives but also preserved Japan "as a nation."[19] The Japanese overwhelmingly took umbrage at this exercise in counterfactual history, with people remarking that "even Reischauer is justifying the A-bomb!"[20] To "refute" Reischauer, Kawaguchi Kazuko and two other Japanese political scientists, then residing in the Boston area, interviewed fifteen professors at Harvard, MIT, and the Fletcher School of Law and Diplomacy. To their surprise, however, they found that "most of the scholars interviewed seemed to agree with Reischauer and tended to approve of the dropping of the bomb to hasten Japan's surrender." Kawaguchi's reaction is revealing: "I experienced at first a certain amount of culture shock. I recognized how differently the same historical facts could be interpreted by U.S. and Japanese scholars and individuals."[21]

A recent instance of this cognitive gap occurred in December 1994 and revolved around the projected "mushroom cloud stamp" with the legend "Atom bombs hasten war's end, August 1945." The design and caption "irritated the rawest nerve in the Japanese psyche, triggering shock, anger, outrage and threats."[22] Japanese mass media and political leaders, not to mention the mayors of Hiroshima and Nagasaki, joined the nationwide chorus denouncing the stamp as "heartless" and justifying the use of the bomb. After the Japanese government officially protested and President Clinton made his distaste known, the U.S. Postal Service hastily withdrew its plan for the "A-bomb stamp."[23]

It is clear that since the first *Asahi* poll in 1971, American feelings about the bomb changed little and slowly. In a 1986 poll, 67 percent replied that the atomic bombing could not have been helped, and 24 percent said it was a mistake. Women are more critical of the atomic bombing than men. Middle-aged and older respondents are more likely to approve of the use of the bomb than are the young.[24] A 1991 survey of Californians showed that 60 percent approved of the bombing, whereas 28 percent disapproved.[25] The most recent poll, a December 1994 Gallup survey, indicated that 55 percent approved of the bombing and 39 percent disapproved, the highest disapproval rating ever achieved.[26] This Gallup survey confirmed that substantial percentages—particularly among younger, female, and nonwhite respondents—say they disapprove of the bombing. (See appendix A, at the end of this chapter.)

The Smithsonian controversy of 1994–1995 revealed that the majority of American newspapers and especially veterans' groups passionately defended the atomic bombing as the right and necessary thing to do. There were signs to indicate that, as the fiftieth anniversary approached, significant segments of Americans were having difficulty in coming to terms with Hiroshima and Nagasaki.

It is noteworthy that there has always been a minority of Americans who disapproved of the atomic bombing of Japan, and their numbers have increased over the years. The 1971 *Asahi* survey found that about one-fifth of Americans considered the atomic bombing a "mistake."[27] The November 1991 poll conducted by the *New York Times*[28] and the November–December 1994 Roper survey showed that as much as 38 percent of Americans condemned the atomic bombings as "morally wrong."[29] (See appendix B.)

Japanese bitterness toward the United States over the atomic bombing appears to have increased in recent years. In a 1985 poll, 44 percent of respondents replied that they "hold it against the United States for dropping the atomic bombs"; in a 1991 poll, 50 percent felt this way. (See appendix B.)

It is interesting that many Japanese, especially A-bomb survivors, have tended to direct their resentment not to the American people but to one individual, former President Truman. As psychiatrist Robert J. Lifton has suggested in his *Death in Life: Survivors of Hiroshima*, this may have been "a means of avoiding wider and more malignant forms of hatred."[30]

Be that as it may, the Japanese people were baffled, offended, and outraged by Truman's repeated public disavowals of any "remorse" over his decision. For more than a quarter-century, until his death in 1972, he repeated ad nauseam the "Truman orthodoxy" that use of the atomic bomb was necessary and justified to save American lives. "I never lost any sleep over *that* decision."

When Edward R. Murrow asked in a 1958 television interview, "Any regrets?" Truman responded, "Not the slightest—not the slightest in the world." He added that to have a weapon to win the war and not to use it would be "foolish." Truman's statement that he "had no qualm" enraged the Japanese. The mayor of Hiroshima published a denunciation of Truman's remark, and in a letter of protest, the city assembly said that Truman's words were a desecration of Hiroshima's atomic victims. In response, Truman repeated that the use of the bomb was an "urgent and necessary measure." He wondered aloud why the citizens of Hiroshima could not understand this, adding that he had been trying to tell them that Japan's wartime leaders were to blame.[31]

In his *Memoirs* (published in 1955 and translated into Japanese in 1966), Truman flatly stated: "Let there be no mistake about it. I regarded the bomb as a military weapon and never had any doubt that it should be used." He added that, under similar circumstances, he would do the same thing.[32]

Finally, on May 5, 1964, an occasion arose for Japan's atomic survivors to meet Truman, about to celebrate his eightieth birthday, and ascertain his "real feelings" about the atomic bomb. He was to receive the Hiroshima–Nagasaki delegation at the Truman Library in Independence, Missouri. The Japanese peace pilgrims had been led by those close to Truman to believe that he would admit the atomic bombing was a "mistake." Having been told that the former president was suffering from a sense of guilt, they were all the more disappointed by his reiteration of the "Truman orthodoxy" about half a million American lives saved.[33]

The Japanese people, particularly the people of Hiroshima and Nagasaki, wanted and waited for one word—*regret*—above anything else. In Japan, a "sincere apology" has magical power to bring about reconciliation, whereas Americans do not easily apologize.[34] The Japanese people felt that if there was to be true "forgiveness," it behooved Americans, Truman in particular, to take the initiative by expressing "regret." For Truman to apologize, however, was out of the question. This would have meant not only admission of official responsibility—culpability—on the part of the United States government but also the negation of the nuclear deterrence that at that time underlay American cold war strategy toward the Soviet Union. Besides, apology simply was not in Truman's nature.

Materials opened since his death reveal that Truman, contrary to the resolute image he projected, actually harbored secret doubts about his decision. Shortly after Nagasaki, Truman wrote Senator Richard B. Russell, "For myself, I certainly regret the necessity of wiping out whole populations because of the 'pig-headedness' of the leaders of a nation." He added, "I also have a human feeling for the women and children in Japan."[35] When Truman issued an order on August 10 prohibiting the use of a third bomb, he told the cabinet that he "didn't like the idea of killing all those kids."[36]

In public, Truman used to say, "It was just the same as getting a bigger gun than the other fellow had to win a war."[37] But privately, he understood that the atomic bomb had revolutionized warfare. When he was informed of the successful testing in the New Mexican desert while attending the Potsdam Conference, Truman scribbled in his diary: "We have discovered the most terrible bomb in the history of the world. It may be the fire destruction prophesied in the Euphrates Valley Era, after Noah and his fabulous Ark."[38]

Although Truman had grasped the apocalyptic significance of the atomic bomb in human history, perhaps the main stumbling block to his reconciliatory gesture toward the Japanese was Pearl Harbor. A few days after Nagasaki, he wrote privately: "I was greatly disturbed over the unwarranted attack by the Japanese on Pearl Harbor. The only language they seem to understand is the one that we have been using to bombard them." This motif of revenge and retribution had been bluntly expressed in his statement on August 6, 1945: "Japan started the war at Pearl Harbor; she has been repaid many times over."[39]

Such a moral equation between Pearl Harbor and Hiroshima–Nagasaki is familiar to many Americans, including some who visit Hiroshima's Peace Museum and scribble in the register, "No more Hiroshimas, but remember Pearl Harbor!" According to the 1991 *Asahi* survey, half of American respondents still considered Pearl Harbor a psychological "block" in U.S.-Japanese relations.[40]

The Japanese indignantly reject the "Pearl Harbor–Hiroshima syndrome." To them, the atomic annihilation of the two cities by the "absolute weapon" belongs to a totally different category from a raid against naval and army installations in Pearl Harbor—different in terms of sheer numbers of (civilian) casualties, the nature and length of human suffering, and the symbolic significance for the survival of humankind. For most Americans, however, what is important is that the Pearl Harbor raid was a surprise attack, and in peacetime at that. (To reinforce the equation further, President Truman, in announcing the atomic bombing, characterized Hiroshima—inaccurately—as a "military base.")[41]

If, as Truman said, Japan had indeed been repaid "many times over," the reasoning goes, Japan has atoned for Pearl Harbor. Why is it, then, many Japanese ask, that Americans refuse to express official remorse over the hundreds of thousands of civilian lives taken at Hiroshima and Nagasaki? The feeling that the United States must apologize for the two atomic bombings has grown stronger as Japan became an economic superpower, with its attendant nationalism, sensitive to its *amour-propre* and assertive in its trade conflict with the United States.

Truman's successors have repeatedly invoked the "Truman orthodoxy." On August 5, 1985, on the fortieth anniversary of Hiroshima, President Ronald Reagan stated in a press interview, "We cannot now say that those who made the solemn decision were foolish." In addition to chanting "more than one million American lives saved," he offered a more sophisticated argument. He asserted that the nuclear weapon provided essential deterrence that assured "peace for forty years, an unprecedentedly long period."[42] (He did not mention Korea, Vietnam, El Salvador, Angola, etc.)

The fiftieth anniversary of Pearl Harbor in 1991 once again brought into bold relief the Pearl Harbor–Hiroshima syndrome by raising the question of mutual apology. We have a survey conducted by the *New York Times* in November 1991 in which 73 percent of the Japanese respondents said "the United States government should formally apologize to Japan and its people for dropping the atomic bombs." Only 16 percent of Americans felt that way. Americans were then asked, "If Japan apologizes for the attack on Pearl Harbor, then do you think the United States government should apologize to Japan for dropping the atomic bombs?" In response, only 34 percent said that the United States should, whereas 42 percent replied that it should not.[43]

On December 1, 1991, in a televised interview, President George Bush categorically stated that he had no intention of apologizing to the Japanese for the use of the atomic bomb. "No apology is required, and it will not be asked of this President, I can guarantee you. I was fighting over there!" In strong terms, he dismissed such an idea as "rank revisionism." President Truman, he said, "made a tough, calculating decision, and it was right, because it spared *millions* of American lives."[44]

As was to be expected, the Japanese took umbrage at Bush's statement as another American "justification" of the bomb. Hiroshima's atomic survivors expressed strong revulsion, saying that President Bush "failed to understand the historical meaning of the atomic bombing." Protests came from the atomic victims' organizations, and there were sit-ins in front of the cenotaph in Hiroshima's Peace Park. Bush's statement caused such a furor among Japanese leaders (especially conservatives in the ruling party) that it immediately doomed a parliamentary resolution, then under debate, that would have formally apologized to Japan's former enemies for its wartime aggression on the eve of the fiftieth anniversary of Pearl Harbor.[45]

Then, on December 4, the *Washington Post* published a scoop, reporting that Foreign Minister Watanabe Michio expressed "deep remorse" over the suffering in the war that Japan had started with the Pearl Harbor surprise attack. At the same time, he said that the Japanese government "isn't seeking any kind of apology" from the United States for Hiroshima and Naga-

Before-and-after street scene from Hiroshima. The photographer returned to scenes he had previously photographed, including this once-bustling shopping center. This human-scale pair of photographs reveals the transformation of a modern city—complete with electricity, public transportation, and complex infrastructure—into a desolate ruin. (Photograph by Matsushige Yoshito. Ienaga, 1.43.)

saki. This one-sided expression of regret, which left many Japanese dissatisfied, was apparently provoked by concern that the remembrance of the Pearl Harbor attack might prompt increased American bitterness toward Japan, bitterness that had already been aggravated by the trade conflict.[46]

The Pearl Harbor–Hiroshima syndrome surfaced again in June 1994, when Emperor Akihito took a two-week tour of the United States. His original itinerary, submitted to Washington, had included a stopover at the USS *Arizona* memorial at Pearl Harbor. However, it was canceled because of a domestic backlash from Diet members who questioned why the emperor must apologize for Pearl Harbor when no American president had visited and apologized for Hiroshima and Nagasaki.[47]

President Clinton reiterated the official American stand in April 1995, stating that "the United States owes no apology to Japan for having dropped the atomic bombs on Hiroshima and Nagasaki." Concerning President Truman's decision to use the bomb, he chose his words carefully and said, "based on the facts he had before him," Truman's decision was the right one for ending the war. Clinton thus gave support to congressional critics and war veterans in the A-bomb disputes that preceded a ceremony scheduled in Hawaii in the summer of 1995 for the fiftieth anniversary of the war's end. As expected, Japanese political leaders were sharply critical of Clinton's "justification" of the atomic bombings, and the mayor of Hiroshima, Hiraoka Takashi, blamed Clinton for "following the idea of successive presidents."[48]

Thus far, we have compared Japanese and American perceptions of the A-bomb decision in terms of approval or disapproval. The ways Japanese and Americans interpreted the A-bomb decision, of course, had a great deal to do with the motives they attributed to the decision. Without going into the familiar historiographical controversy, we may identify two schools of interpretation.[49] One is the so-called orthodox school, led by the late Herbert Feis, which argues that the bomb was dropped to force a prompt Japanese surrender.[50] The other is cold war "revisionism," led by "New Left" historian Gar Alperovitz, which claims that the bomb was used to intimidate the Soviet Union in the emerging cold war.[51] My own view is close to that of Barton J. Bernstein, who maintains that the United States dropped the bombs primarily to hasten the end of the war but that the bombs had the "bonus effect" of pressuring the Soviet Union.[52]

In Japan, the revisionist thesis of "atomic diplomacy" has carried much appeal, not because Alperovitz is widely read (his *Atomic Diplomacy* has never been translated)[53] but because P.M.S. Blackett's *Fear, War, and the Bomb,* which anticipated Alperovitz's main thrust, was translated in 1951 and has been very popular among Japanese intellectuals, especially on the Left.[54] A British physicist and Nobel laureate, Blackett was not a historian, and his 1948 book lacked documentation. He presented his thesis as a mere "hypothesis," but many Japanese intellectuals have accepted Blackett as an oracle.

There has been no large-scale public opinion survey in Japan as to why the bombs were dropped; we therefore conducted three surveys (January 1976, December 1991, and July 1994) among undergraduate students at Doshisha University, a large private institution drawing students from all parts of Japan.[55] (See appendix C.) Students were asked, "What do you think were the reasons for dropping the atomic bomb?" Supplying seven reasons in our questionnaires, we asked the respondents to rank them in importance. In our surveys, the most frequently chosen reasons were political considerations vis-à-vis the Soviet Union: "To pressure the Soviet Union by a display of power" and "To end the war against Japan before Soviet entry." Other reasons chosen by our respondents, in descending order, were: "To avoid U.S. casualties"; "To justify to the American public the $2 billion spent on the Manhattan Project"; "To pay [Japan] back for Pearl Harbor"; and "To avoid [both] U.S. . . . and further Japanese casualties." Our findings roughly coincided with those of a small-scale survey conducted at Hiroshima University in 1978.[56]

How can we account for the prevalence of the "atomic diplomacy" thesis among Japanese students? One obvious answer, already alluded to, is the popularity of Blackett's *Fear, War, and the Bomb*. In point of fact, students are exposed to the Blackett thesis in their junior high school textbooks. A typical history textbook states that "as the Soviet Union's entry into the war became imminent, the United States dropped the atomic bomb to gain supremacy over the Soviet Union after the war."[57] History readers print an excerpt from Blackett, and teachers' manuals make special mention of his thesis.

Among widely read surveys of contemporary Japanese history, *Showashi* (A history of the Showa period) by Toyama Shigeki, Imai Seiichi, and Fujiwara Akira quotes approvingly from Blackett: "The dropping of the atomic bombs was not so much the last military act of the Second World War as the first major operation in the Cold War with Russia."[58] In a similar vein, *Taiheiyo sensoshi* (A history of the Pacific War), compiled by a left-wing group of historians, charges: "500,000 citizens [of Hiroshima and Nagasaki] were utterly meaninglessly sacrificed for America's cruel political purposes." Here, the sense of victimization prevails over reasoned analysis.[59]

To cite another example, Nishijima Ariatsu's much-quoted book *Genbaku wa naze otosaretaka* (Why were the atomic bombs dropped?) recapitulates Blackett and argues that "the most important thing" was that

Hiroshima–Nagasaki residents were "killed as human guinea pigs for the sake of [America's] anticommunist, hegemonic policy." He concludes with a political appeal that "cognizance of this fact must be the foundation on which to build any antinuclear movement in Japan."[60] Taking this injunction to heart, a leader of an organization for A-bomb survivors recently demanded a public apology from the United States government for the atomic bomb on account of its "diplomatic-strategic imperatives vis-à-vis the Soviet Union" and the "experimentation on human effects."[61]

This is not to say that American scholarship has had no impact in Japan. For example, Herbert Feis's *The Atomic Bomb and the End of World War II* and Martin J. Sherwin's *A World Destroyed: The Atomic Bomb and the Grand Alliance* have been translated. Japanese experts are fully au courant with respect to the writings of their American colleagues, but they simply cannot counter the prevalent atomic diplomacy theory in the mass media.[62]

For one thing, the atomic diplomacy thesis enjoys wide currency in the mass media. For example, in 1975, in serialized articles on the A-bomb question, the *Asahi* stated: "It is now a commonly accepted view that the real purpose of the United States in dropping the atomic bombs was not so much to force Japan's surrender as to coerce the Soviet Union."[63]

The atomic diplomacy thesis even found its way into the most complete scientific study to appear on the subject, *Hiroshima and Nagasaki: The Physical, Medical, and Social Effects of the Atomic Bombings*, prepared under the sponsorship of the two battered cities in 1979.[64] A review in *Time* magazine critically observed that the study "clings to the questionable theory that the attacks were mainly intended to awe Joseph Stalin and the Soviet Union."[65]

It is anomalous, to say the least, that, in Japan, textbook writers, left-wing historians, peace activists, the media, and even scientists have continued to quote approvingly from Blackett's 1948 book, a work that did not even pretend to offer a history. One reason for its continued popularity may be that by dissociating the A-bomb question from the Pacific War, it helps extricate the Japanese from the moral symmetry of the Pearl Harbor–Hiroshima syndrome and shifts the balance in favor of their victim status. Although the atomic diplomacy thesis exacerbates their sense of victimization, it accords with Japanese unwillingness to come to grips with their responsibility for the war and its consequences. Suffering from collective amnesia, the Japanese are reluctant to see the A-bomb decision in the context of the Pacific War. Japanese often assert (as do American revisionists like Gar Alperovitz) that Japan was already prostrate and on the verge of surrender when the United States dropped the bombs. Can the Japanese have forgotten that their military leaders had taken a last-ditch stand to fight to the death against invading American forces, much as their troops had done in Okinawa? After all, it took the two atomic bombs plus the Soviet entry into the war plus the unprecedented intervention of Emperor Hirohito before the Japanese government finally decided to surrender.[66] This suggests that the popularity among the Japanese people of the atomic diplomacy thesis is in part the product of unwillingness to come to terms with their past.[67]

On college campuses, much credence is given to a racial interpretation, which makes a special point of prejudice against Asians as a factor influencing the atomic bombings. Perhaps this is not surprising, given the long history of discrimination against Japanese immigrants and the Nisei that culminated in their internment in "relocation" camps during the Pacific War. About half the Doshisha University respondents in our three surveys asserted that the United States would not have used the atomic bombs against Germany if they had been ready before the German surrender. Since this racial interpretation became more pronounced and prevalent in the late 1960s, it seems to have represented an extrapolation backward of perceptions in Japan that American policy in Vietnam had racist overtones—the My Lai incident, saturation bombings of North and South Vietnam, and other reported instances of racial callousness.[68] A recent right-wing expression of the racist interpretation is found in Ishihara Shintaro's *The Japan That Can Say No*,[69] but the general interpretation cuts widely across political lines.

Some Japanese polemicists, like *Asahi* reporter Honda Katsuichi, have quoted approvingly from Noam Chomsky concerning "official racism," associating the policy of "genocide" in Vietnam with the nuclear holocausts of Hiroshima and Nagasaki; both, they claim, stemmed from the same racist attitude of treating Asians as "less than human beings."[70] In his book cited above, Nishijima states that the Hiroshima–Nagasaki victims and Vietnam War victims were "two of a kind."[71]

A corollary of the racist interpretation is the "human guinea pig theory." A sizable number of Doshisha students responded that the atomic bombs were dropped "[t]o test the[ir] destructive power." On August 6, 1994—the forty-ninth anniversary of the Hiroshima bombing—the Japan Congress against Atomic and Hydrogen Bombs (led by the Japan Socialist Party) issued a public pronouncement that the atomic bombing was "an experiment on human bodies."[72]

Earlier, the *Sankei shinbun* asserted that American physicists who developed the atomic bomb chose the Japanese as guinea pigs precisely for racist reasons. "The technical advisers were keenly anxious to experiment [on human beings]. And it may be that they felt less compunction in experimenting on the Japanese than on white people."[73]

The claim that racism was the decisive or even the only factor flies in the face of the fact that, from the beginning, American efforts to develop the atomic bomb had been a race against German science and technology. But there is no doubt that Truman made his decision in a wartime climate saturated with crudely racist portrayals of the Japanese as subhuman monsters or vermin, as John W. Dower has shown.[74] Yet it is difficult to find direct evidence linking such pervasive racism to the decision to drop the bomb on Japan. Although Truman's private papers contain no trace of overt racism, one might detect racist nuances in a letter he sent a few days after Nagasaki, in which he wrote: "When you have to deal with a beast you have to treat him as a beast."[75]

On the other hand, Secretary of War Henry L. Stimson—an admirer of Japanese culture—was hardly a crude racist. On July 2, 1945, he wrote in an important memorandum to Truman that, after the war, Japan's "liberal leaders" could be "depended upon for her reconstruction as a responsible member of the family of nations. I think she is better in this last respect than Germany was."[76] In the end, racist explanations remain too vague and diffuse. Far more compelling were the issues that were in fact actively debated about the means to secure a swift victory that would save American lives and best position the United States to dominate the postwar world order.

According to a 1991 poll by the *New York Times,* 38 percent of the Japanese respondents but only 8 percent of the American ones supported a racial interpretation.[77] (See appendix B.) In 1994, the curators of the Smithsonian Institution were roundly criticized for implying in the script for their exhibition on the atomic bomb that racism motivated the atomic bombing of Japan.[78] In Japan, as the survey among Doshisha students would seem to indicate, the view overplaying the racial factor in the A-bomb decision is gradually losing support as memories of the Vietnam War fade.

One cannot overemphasize the importance of secondary school history textbooks in Japan in shaping consciousness of the tragedies of Hiroshima and Nagasaki and keeping their meaning alive.[79] During the occupation period, the A-bomb issue was not allowed to appear in textbooks, but as soon as Japan regained independence, a rich variety of excerpts from "A-bomb literature," including graphic descriptions of the *hibakusha* (atomic victims), found their way into textbooks. Textbooks also contained an abundance of statistics on damage and casualties, as well as photographs of the mushroom cloud and the atomic desolation. A ninth-grade textbook in social studies, published in 1952, devoted as many as twenty pages to the atomic bomb and related subjects.[80] Since 1960, the coverage has dwindled.

The treatment in a current high school history textbook is almost perfunctory: "In August 1945, atomic bombs were dropped on Hiroshima and then on Nagasaki."[81] It does not even say which country dropped the bombs! No wonder that about 10 percent of pupils in the Hiroshima and Nagasaki areas do not know it was the United States.[82] The impression the textbook gives is that the atomic bombing just "happened," much like a natural catastrophe. Other recent textbooks are surprisingly similar, indicating how effective the government censorship and self-control are. (In Japan, school textbooks must be "authorized" by the Ministry of Education, and its policy in recent years has been to downplay the horrors of war, including the atomic bombing.)[83]

In 1980–1981, educational experts and editors of schoolbooks undertook a joint "Japanese-American project on social studies textbooks." The American members came to the heart of the matter when they pointed out that Japanese textbooks "omit all explanations of the ethical and moral significance of the atomic bombing of Hiroshima and Nagasaki."[84] The Americans also questioned the atomic diplomacy thesis.

How do American textbooks fare? They all devote far more space than do their Japanese counterparts to the atomic bomb. This is not surprising, given both American official rationalization and criticism of its use by some historians. More simply, it can be explained by the much greater length of American textbooks.[85] Although the majority subscribe to the "Truman orthodoxy," many raise "ethical questions" about the bomb.[86] Some of the better recent textbooks urge students to place themselves in the position of "decision makers" and discuss the pros and cons of the decision to use the atomic bomb. Gary B. Nash's *American Odyssey* quotes the dissenting views of General Dwight D. Eisenhower, Undersecretary of the Navy Ralph A. Bard, and the nuclear physicist James Franck. Students are asked to discuss the "conflict in values" found in these quotations. "Have our values as Americans changed over time, giving new meanings to the events of the 1940s?"[87]

Lew Smith, in *The American Dream*, asks whether the atomic bombing was necessary or justified and presents three excerpts written from totally different viewpoints. The first, from Truman's memoirs, was his usual military rationale. The second account was taken from a school composition by a boy who lived through the Hiroshima blast. After describing hell on earth, he asked, "I wondered why human beings, who ought to be of the same mind, have to make wars; why they have to kill each other like this." The third was a statement by Sakomizu Hisatsune, chief cabinet secretary of the Japanese government, that the atomic bomb "saved the face of the military and provided an excuse to surrender." The students were asked which they think provided "the most significant perspective" and why.[88]

At least one recent textbook—*America: Pathways to the Present* by Andrew Clayton, Elisabeth Israels Perry, and Allan M. Winkler—suggests racism as a possible factor in the atomic bombing of Japan. Overall, this textbook provides a model treatment of "the lasting impact of the Atomic Bomb," discussing a wide range of political, economic, and technological changes that have occurred in the half-century since 1945.[89] It is also interesting to note that at least one new American textbook introduces the students to the atomic diplomacy thesis alongside the conventional interpretation.[90] What characterizes American textbooks is their variety and richness, which stand in sharp contrast to monotonic Japanese treatments. As far as history textbooks are concerned, it appears that Americans are doing a better job of "A-bomb education" than the Japanese.

The influence of schoolbooks may partially account for generational differences: according to the 1994 Gallup survey, less than half (48 percent) of the 18–29 age bracket approved of the use of the bomb, whereas 64 percent of the middle-aged group (45–64) registered approval.[91]

As long as we are trapped in the "victim–victimizer syndrome" and the habit of mutual recrimination, we shall keep talking round and round in circles. As a way of breaking out of this impasse, the well-known historian John W. Hall has urged "a tragic view" of the Pacific War, "one that takes no comfort in scapegoats and offers no sanctuaries for private or national claims of moral righteousness, but rather admits that . . . something very tragic in human affairs is taking place."[92] If one is grounded in such a view of human history, one will be freed from excessively ideological viewpoints and emotional racism. Now that the cold war is over, one would have expected cold war revisionism to decline, yet the sharp public debate of 1995 over the Smithsonian exhibit suggests that issues surrounding the bombs remain divisive in the United States.

The half century since Hiroshima and Nagasaki has been a period of unbroken international tension and local conflict, crises and provocations, which, in the preatomic age, might well have triggered a third world war. There have been genuine scares: in 1948 and 1961, the Berlin crises; in 1953, the Korean War; in 1962, the Cuban missile crisis; in 1967, the Battle of Khe Sanh in Vietnam; and in 1968 and 1973, the Arab-Israeli wars. With the hindsight of history, one might argue that use of the "ultimate weapon" against Japan in 1945, by offering a horrifying warning, helped deter a thermonuclear war.

This, I hasten to add, is not to invoke the logic of nuclear deterrence ex post facto to justify the bombing of Hiroshima and Nagasaki, as President

Reagan and, more recently, Harvard political scientist Philip D. Zelikow[93] have done. The "long peace,"[94] built on deterrence, was a fragile and unstable affair, hanging as it did on an uncontrolled nuclear arms race and punctuated by numerous wars, from Korea to Vietnam to Iraq. With the end of the cold war, new possibilities for nuclear disarmament came to the fore. Robert S. McNamara, once a consummate practitioner of nuclear strategy, made a rather surprising statement in October 1992, on the thirtieth anniversary of the Cuban missile crisis:

> The lesson I draw from the Cuban missile crisis is that as long as we combine human fallibility with nuclear weapons, the world runs a high risk of use of these weapons with the likely destruction of nations and perhaps the risk of survival of civilizations. And there is only one way we can avoid it, and that is to return insofar as achievable to a non-nuclear world."[95]

We may very well call this "the lesson of Hiroshima and Nagasaki." Physicist Ralph Lapp, who had worked on the bomb, protested at the height of the cold war: "Hiroshima has been taken out of the American conscience eviscerated, extirpated."[96] One may hope that the events of the fiftieth anniversary in both America and Japan, proving that this is no longer the case, will help affirm modern memory and the broader significance of the atomic bombings of the two cities.

Appendix A

Gallup Poll

Survey organization:	Gallup Organization
Research sponsor:	Cable News Network, *U.S.A. Today*
Date:	December 2–5, 1994
Sample size:	N = 1,014 (national adult)
Interview method:	Telephone

Q. As you know, the United States dropped atomic bombs on Hiroshima and Nagasaki in August 1945 near the end of World War II. Looking back, would you say you approve or disapprove of using the atomic bomb on Japanese cities in 1945?

Responses:

Approve	55%
Disapprove	39%
Don't know/Refused to answer	6%

Responses by Race

Frequency Col. Pct.	Race of Respondent			
	White	Black	Hispanic	Total
Approve	480.87	45.16	16.71	542.74
	57.36	44.37	57.50	
Disapprove	323.25	45.31	10.18	378.74
	38.56	44.52	35.08	
Don't know/Refused to answer	34.17	11.30	2.13	47.60
	4.08	11.10	7.34	
Total	838.29	101.77	29.02	969.08

Frequency missing = 45.57

Responses by Sex

Frequency Col. Pct.	Gender of Respondent		
	Male	Female	Total
Approve	351.42	208.24	559.66
	71.81	39.64	
Disapprove	121.19	278.02	399.21
	24.76	52.93	
Don't know/Refused to answer	16.76	39.02	55.78
	3.42	7.43	
Total	489.37	525.28	1,014.65

Responses by Age

Frequency Col. Pct.	Age of Respondent				
	18–29	30–44	45–64	65+	Total
Approve	102.85	152.03	189.72	114.12	558.72
	47.91	47.64	64.44	62.82	
Disapprove	97.33	152.07	90.31	58.67	398.38
	45.34	47.66	30.67	32.29	
Don't know/Refused to answer	14.51	14.99	14.40	8.88	52.78
	6.76	4.70	4.89	4.89	
Total	214.69	319.09	294.43	181.67	1,009.88

Appendix B

New York Times/CBS/Tokyo Broadcasting System Poll (Contrasted to a July 1985 Poll)

United States (telephone)
November 18–22, 1991
$N = 1,106$

Japan (in person)
July 7–13, 1985
$N = 1,446$

Do you agree or disagree with this statement: Dropping the atomic bombs on Japan in World War II was morally wrong. (percent)

	Strongly Agree	Agree Some- what	Disagree Some- what	Strongly Disagree	Don't Know/No Answer
7/85					
United States	20	18	30	25	7
11/91					
United States	21	18	27	28	6
Japan	56	28	10	4	2

These days, do you hold it against the United States for dropping the atomic bombs on Hiroshima and Nagasaki? (percent)

		Hold It Against	Don't Hold It Against	Don't Know/No Answer
7/85	Japan	44	47	9
11/91	Japan	50	43	7

Do you agree or disagree with this statement: One of the major reasons that the United States was willing to drop the atomic bomb on Japan was because the Japanese people are not white. (percent)

	Strongly Agree	Agree Somewhat	Disagree Somewhat	Strongly Disagree	Don't Know/No Answer
7/85					
United States	3	4	15	73	5
Japan	9	24	42	20	5
11/91					
United States	4	4	15	71	6
Japan	11	27	38	20	4

Appendix C

Poll of Doshisha Students

Dates:	January 1976	December 1994	July 1994
Sample sizes:	$N = 95$	$N = 209$	$N = 310$
Interview method:	Questionnaires	Questionnaires	Questionnaires

I. Concerning the American decision to drop the atomic bomb, please indicate your support, opposition, or neutrality to the following views.

A. It was right to drop the atomic bomb to save the lives of a vast number of American soldiers who would die in an American invasion of the Japanese homeland.

	1976	1991	1994
Strongly support	0.0	0.0	0.9
Support	1.1	5.7	12.2
Oppose	25.2	25.4	41.7
Strongly oppose	62.1	43.5	31.3
Neither support nor oppose	7.4	22.5	9.6
Don't know	4.2	2.9	4.3
Total	100.0	100.0	100.0

B. For the same reason, the atomic bombing could not be helped.

	1976	1991	1994
Strongly support	0.0	1.0	0.9
Support	2.1	14.4	16.5
Oppose	30.5	21.5	44.3
Strongly oppose	51.6	36.5	26.1
Neither support nor oppose	8.4	23.67	11.3
Don't know	7.4	1.9	0.9
Total	100.0	100.0	100.0

IIA. Even if the atomic bomb had been completed while war against Germany was still continuing, the United States would not have used it in Germany.

	1976	1991	1994
Strongly support	16.8	13.0	14.8
Support	33.7	31.7	34.8
Oppose	16.8	13.5	26.1
Strongly oppose	1.0	17.3	5.2
Neither support nor oppose	11.7	3.3	2.6
Don't know	20.0	21.2	16.5
Total	100.0	100.0	100.0

III. What do you think were the reasons for dropping the atomic bomb? What do you think were the important reasons to the American leaders? Please circle them and then list them in order of importance.

    A. To avoid U.S. casualties
    B. To avoid further Japanese casualties also
    C. To end the war against Japan before Soviet entry
    D. To pressure the Soviet Union by a display of power
    E. To test the destructive power of the atomic bomb
    F. To pay back for Pearl Harbor
    G. To justify to the American public the $2 billion spent on the Manhattan Project

Student Responses

Order	A.	B.	C.	D.	E.	F.	G.
No. 1	22	0	13	26	12	1	2
	(36)	(2)	(64)	(38)	(32)	(2)	(3)
	[31]	[2]	[40]	[13]	[25]	[2]	[2]
No. 2	10	0	15	12	13	5	5
	(36)	(8)	(30)	(51)	(25)	(7)	(17)
	[18]	[5]	[13]	[37]	[26]	[5]	[5]
No. 3	8	0	3	8	20	2	6
	(29)	(5)	(32)	(33)	(33)	(9)	(27)
	[14]	[7]	[17]	[13]	[24]	[10]	[15]
No. 4	5	2	3	2	5	6	4
	(28)	(39)	(15)	(24)	(36)	(42)	(45)
	[12]	[10]	[8]	[11]	[5]	[8]	[11]
No order	13	3	7	14	11	3	7
	(80)	(155)	(68)	(63)	(38)	(149)	(117)
	[40]	[91]	[37]	[41]	[35]	[90]	[82]

1976
(1991)
[1994]

Notes

1. On the "A-bomb question" in Japanese memory, the best collection of sources is Odagiri Hideo, ed., *Shinbun shiryo: Genbaku* (Newspaper materials: The atomic bomb) (Tokyo: Nichon Tosho Senta, 1987–1988), which contains, in two large volumes, a wide variety of clippings from eight major newspapers from 1945 to 1980.

2. See, for example, Asada Sadao, "Busshu daitoryo to genbaku toka mondai" (President Bush and the A-bomb question), *Sankei Shinbun,* December 4, 1991.

3. Asada, " 'Genbaku kitte' ga kataru mono" (The meaning of the "A-bomb stamp"), *Sankei Shinbun,* December 21, 1994. For an English translation, see "The Flap over the A-Bomb Stamp: How Japanese and American Historical Perceptions Differ," *Japan Echo* 22 (summer 1995): 79.

4. The breakdown of the reaction of Hiroshima–Nagasaki residents to the atomic bombing was as follows: fear/terror (47%); fear for own life (16%); admiration—impressed by the scientific power behind the bomb (26%); jealousy—why couldn't Japan make such a bomb? (3%); anger—bomb is cruel, inhuman, barbarous (17%); hatred of United States specifically because of A-bomb use (2%); no reaction indicated (11%). United States Strategic Bombing Survey, *Effects of Strategic Bombing on Japanese Morale, Report on the Pacific War,* no. 14 (Washington, DC: U.S. Government Printing Office, 1947), 3, 91–97.

5. Monica Braw, *The Atomic Bomb Suppressed: American Censorship in Occupied Japan, 1945–1949* (Armonk, NY: M.E. Sharpe, 1991), 92, 102–3, 151. The former members of the Civil Censorship Division of the General Headquarters recently testified that there were relatively few instances of deletion by the occupation authorities. The Japanese media, they said, practiced self-control. *Asahi Shinbun,* May 15, 1994.

6. John Hersey, *Hiroshima* (New York: Penguin, 1946); Japanese translation by Ishikawa Kinichi and Tanimoto Hiroshi (Tokyo: Hosei Daigaku Shuppankai, 1949).

7. P.M.S. Blackett, *Fear, War, and the Bomb* (New York: Whittlesey, 1949); originally published as *Military and Political Consequences of Atomic Energy* (London: 1948); Japanese translation by Tanaka Shinjiro (Tokyo: Hosei Daigaku Shuppankai, 1951).

8. *Mainichi Shinbun,* August 3, 1970.

9. *Chugoku Shinbun,* July 23, 1971.

10. *Public Papers of the Presidents: Harry S Truman, 1945* (Washington, DC: 1961), 203–14. It was only after this paper was published in its original form that I read Robert Lifton and Greg Mitchell, *Hiroshima in America: Fifty Years of Denial* (New York: Grossett Putnam, 1995)—the most detailed and systematic examination of American reaction to the bomb.

11. Studs Terkel, *"The Good War": An Oral History of World War II* (New York: Pantheon Books, 1984).

12. Paul Fussell, "Thank God for the Atom Bomb—Hiroshima: A Soldier's View," *New Republic,* August 22–29, 1981, 26–30.

13. Paul S. Boyer, *By the Bomb's Early Light: American Thought and Culture at the Dawn of the Atomic Age* (New York: Pantheon Books, 1985), 183–84; Spencer R. Weart, *Nuclear Fear: A History of Images* (Cambridge, MA: Harvard University Press, 1988), 106–9. For an overall treatment of the half-century since 1945, see Allan M. Winkler, *Life under a Cloud: American Anxiety about the Atom* (New York: Oxford University Press, 1993).

14. Michael J. Yavenditti, "The American People and the Use of Atomic Bombs on Japan: The 1940s," *Historian* 36 (February 1974): 224–47; Yavenditti, "John Hersey and the American Conscience: The Reception of 'Hiroshima,' " *Pacific Historical Re-*

view 43 (February 1974): 24–49; Peter Schwenger, "America's Hiroshima," *Boundary 2* (spring 1994): 240–41.

15. Michael Sherry, *The Rise of American Air Power: The Creation of Armageddon* (New Haven, CT: Yale University Press, 1987), 245, 351; Sheila K. Johnson, *American Attitudes toward Japan, 1941–1975* (Washington, DC: American Enterprise Institute, 1975), 37–39; Boyer, *By the Bomb's Early Light*, 204–10.

16. *Asahi Shinbun*, August 5, 1965.

17. Asahi Shinbunsha, ed., *Nihon to Amerika* (Japan and the United States) (Tokyo: Asahi Shinbunsha, 1971), 430–32; Asahi Shinbunsha Yoron Chosashitsu, ed., *Shiryo Beikoku ni okeru tai-Nichi yoron chosa* (U.S. public opinion survey regarding Japan) (Tokyo: Asahi Shinbunsha, 1982), 9–10.

18. *Asahi Shinbun*, March 18, 1971.

19. Edwin O. Reischauer, "Hiroshima Bomb Saved Japan from a Worse Fate," *Boston Globe*, August 30, 1983. Reischauer repeated the same view in his memoirs, *My Life between Japan and America* (New York: Harper and Row, 1986), 101.

20. *Asahi Shinbun*, December 16, 1983.

21. Among the professors interviewed was physicist Philip Morrison of MIT, a veteran of the Manhattan Project. Hirose Kazuko et al., "Did Hiroshima Save Japan? 'Reischauer's Interpretation' Reexamined," unpublished manuscript. Portions of this report were published as "Hiroshima wa Nihon o sukutta ka?—'Raishawa kenkai' e no Amerika no kyojutachi no iken" (Did Hiroshima save Japan? American professors' views on the "Reischauer thesis"), *Asahi Janaru*, December 16, 1994.

22. *Chicago Tribune*, December 2, 1994.

23. Asada, "Flap over the A-Bomb Stamp," 79.

24. *Asahi Shinbun*, December 17, 1986; May 24, 1988; Asahi Shinbun Yoron Chosashitsu, ed., *Gurafu de yomu Amerikajin no Nihonkan* (American views of Japan as seen through charts) (Tokyo: Asahi Shinbunsha, 1987), 68. See also *New York Times*, August 6, 1985.

25. *Asahi Shinbun*, November 3, 1991.

26. Gallup poll, December 1994; Frank Newport, "Majority Still Approve Use of Atom Bombs on Japan in World War II," *Gallup Poll Monthly* (August 1995): 2–5.

27. Asahi Shinbunsha, ed., *Nihon to Amerika*, 432.

28. *New York Times*/CBS News/Tokyo Broadcasting System poll, November 26, 1991.

29. Gallup poll, December 1994.

30. Robert J. Lifton, *Death in Life: Survivors of Hiroshima* (New York: Simon and Schuster, 1967), 323–24. John Whittier Treat notes that reference to the United States, not to mention strident anti-American sentiment, is "relatively absent" in the discourse of Japan's A-bomb literature by survivors. Treat, "Hiroshima's America," *Boundary 2* (spring 1994): 233–53.

31. *New York Times*, February 3, 1958; *Asahi Shinbun*, February 3, 1958, August 5, 1958.

32. *Asahi Shinbun*, February 3 and 14, March 15, April 9, 1958; *Tokyo Shinbun*, February 3, 1958; *Sankei Shinbun*, February 8, 1958; Harry S Truman, *Memoirs*, 2 vols. (Garden City, NY: Doubleday, 1955–1956), 1:419.

33. Chugoku Shinbunsha, ed., *Honoo no hi kara 20-nen* (Twenty years since the day of the flame) (Tokyo: Chugoku Shinbunsha, 1966), 197.

34. On the Japanese concept of apology, see Doi Takeo, *"Amae" no kozo* (The anatomy of dependence) (Tokyo: Kobundo, 1971), 51–52; English translation by John Bester (Tokyo: 1982).

35. Barton J. Bernstein, "Roosevelt, Truman, and the Atomic Bomb, 1941–1945: A

Reinterpretation," *Political Science Quarterly* 90 (spring 1975): 61; Harry S Truman to Richard B. Russell, August 9, 1945, Papers of Harry S Truman, Official File, box 685, Truman Library, Independence, MO.

36. John Morton Blum, ed., *The Price of Vision: The Diary of Henry A. Wallace, 1942–1946* (Boston: Houghton Mifflin, 1973), 474.

37. Harry S Truman, *Truman Speaks: Lectures and Discussions held at Columbia University on April 27, 28, and 29, 1959* (New York: Columbia University Press, 1960), 93.

38. Robert H. Ferrell, ed., *Off the Record: The Private Papers of Harry S Truman* (New York: Harper, 1980), 55–56.

39. United States Department of State, *Foreign Relations of the United States: The Conference of Berlin* (Washington, DC: Government Printing Office, 1960), 2:1376.

40. Asahi Shinbunsha, *Amerikajin no Nihonkan,* 66.

41. For a personal exposition of the "Pearl Harbor–Hiroshima syndrome," see Akiba Tadatoshi, *Shinju to sakura* (Pearl and Cherry) (Tokyo: Asahi Shinbunsha, 1986).

42. *Sankei Shinbun,* August 6, 1985; *Asahi Shinbun,* August 6, 1985, evening edition.

43. *New York Times*/CBS News/Tokyo Broadcasting System poll, November 26, 1991.

44. USIS Press Office, December 2, 1991 (emphasis added); *New York Times,* December 2, 1991; *Asahi Shinbun,* December 2, 1991, evening edition, December 6, 1991; *Mainichi Shinbun,* December 2, 1991; *Nikkei Shinbun,* December 2, 1991, evening edition; *Sankei Shinbun,* December 2, 1991, evening edition), December 3, 1991. Regarding the estimate of American lives saved, President Truman had used the figure a quarter-million, but after leaving the White House, he raised the figure to a half-million.

45. *New York Times,* December 6, 1991; *Nikkei Shinbun,* December 5, 1991; *Asahi Shinbun,* December 3, 1991.

46. *Asahi Shinbun,* December 5 and 6, 1991; *Sankei Shinbun,* December 4 and 5, 1991.

47. *Asahi Shinbun,* May 20, 25, and 26, 1994, June 14, 1994; *New York Times,* June 25, 1994; *Washington Post,* May 20, 1994.

48. *Asahi Shinbun,* April 8, evening edition, April 18, 1995; *Japan Times,* April 9, 1995.

49. See Samuel Walker, "The Decision to Use the Bomb: A Historiographical Update," *Diplomatic History* 14 (winter 1990): 97–114.

50. Herbert Feis, *Japan Subdued: The Atomic Bomb and the End of the War in the Pacific* (Princeton, NJ: Princeton University Press, 1961) and *The Atomic Bomb and the End of World War Two* (Princeton, NJ: Princeton University Press, 1966).

51. Gar Alperovitz, *Atomic Diplomacy: Hiroshima and Potsdam* (New York: Vintage Books, 1965; exp. ed., 1985; rev. ed., Boulder, CO: 1994). I have published a critical analysis of "cold war revisionism": "Reisen no kigen to shuseishugi kenkyu" (The origins of the cold war and revisionist studies), *Kokusai mondai* 170 (May 1974): 2–21.

52. See especially the following articles by Barton J. Bernstein: "The Perils and Politics of Surrender: Ending the War with Japan and Avoiding the Third Atomic Bomb," *Pacific Historical Review* 44 (February 1977): 1–27; "Marshall, Truman, and the Decision to Drop the Bomb," *International Security* 16 (winter 1991–1992): 204–21; "The Atomic Bombings Reconsidered," *Foreign Affairs* 74 (January 1995): 135–52; and "Understanding the Atomic Bomb and the Japanese Surrender: Missed Opportunities, Little-Known Near Disasters, and Modern Memory," *Diplomatic History* 19 (spring 1995): 227–73.

53. The reception in the United States of *Atomic Diplomacy* was briefly noted by *Nikkei Shinbun* on July 19, 1965. A brief excerpt from Alperovitz's "Why the United States Dropped the Bomb," *Technology Review* (August–September 1990): 23–34, ap-

peared in Japanese translation in the *Asahi Shinbun* weekly *AERA,* October 2, 1990, 25–28.

54. For an early citation from Blackett, see Osada Arata, "Genshi bakudan wa naze toka saretaka" (Why were the atomic bombs dropped?), *Sekai* (September 1953): 181.

55. The 1976 survey was conducted by Mark Fitzpatrick, who has written an excellent paper for my undergraduate seminar, "How the Japanese View the A-Bomb Decision" (1977, mimeographed in the author's possession).

56. Hiroshima Daigaku Heiwa Kenkyu Senta, *Heiwa kagaku kenkyu tsushin* 2 (June 1978): 1–2. Shono Naomi, ed., *Kaku to heiwa: Nihonjin no ishiki* (Nuclear weapons and peace: Japanese perceptions) (Kyoto: Horitsu Bunkasha, 1978), although based on an extensive survey, is vitiated by its premise that the "atomic diplomacy" thesis is the sole "scientific-historical" interpretation.

57. Kodama Kota et al., *Chugaku shakai: Rekishiteki bun'ya* (Junior high school/social studies—History) (Tokyo: Nihon Shoten, 1986), 297; Kawata Tadashi et al., *Atarashii shakai: Rekishi* (New society: History) (Tokyo: Tokyo Shoseki, 1992), 24; Tokyo horei shuppan kikakubu, *Seikibetsu rekishi shiryo* (Historical materials) (Tokyo: Toho Shuppan n.d.), 113; Blackett, *Fear, War, and the Bomb,* 127. It was not until the early 1970s that the Blackett thesis made inroads into history textbooks.

58. Toyama Shigeki, Imai Seiichi, and Fujiwara Akira, *Showa-shi* (A history of the Showa period) (Tokyo: Iwanami Shoten, 1959), 366.

59. Rekishigaku kenkyukai, compiler, *Taiheiyo sensoshi* (A history of the Pacific War), 6 vols. (Tokyo: Tokyo Daigaku Shuppankai, 1973), 5:363–66.

60. Nishijima Ariatsu, *Genbaku wa naze otosaretaka* (Why were the atomic bombs dropped?), new ed. (Tokyo: Aoki Shoten, 1985), 383.

61. Yamada Hirotami, "Shazai koso kaku zetsumetsu e no ippo" (American apology is the first step toward demolishing nuclear weapons), *Asahi Shinbun,* December 31, 1991.

62. Feis, *Atomic Bomb and the End of World War II* (1966; Japanese translation, (Tokyo: Nansosha, 1974); Martin J. Sherwin, *A World Destroyed: The Atomic Bomb and the Grand Alliance* (New York: 1975); Japanese translation (Tokyo: TBS Britannica, 1978). Political scientist Nagai Yonosuke presents a sophisticated analysis of bureaucratic momentum in the decision to drop the atomic bombs. *Reisen no kigen* (The origins of the cold war) (Tokyo: Chuo Kotonsha, 1978), 147–89. The most recent publication is a massive documentary collection, *Shiryo Manhattan keikaku* (Documents: The Manhattan Project) (Tokyo: Otsuki Shoten, 1993), compiled by Yamagiwa Akira and Tachibana Seiitsu, and translated by Okada Ryonosuke.

The fiftieth anniversary of the atomic bombing of Hiroshima and Nagasaki brought forth a Japanese translation of Lifton and Mitchell, *Hiroshima in America,* and Gar Alperovitz, *The Decision to Use the Atomic Bomb* (New York: 1995), among others.

63. *Asahi Shinbun,* July 30, 1975.

64. Hiroshimashi–Nagasakishi Genbaku Saigaishi Henshu Iinkai, ed., *Hiroshima–Nagasaki no genbaku saigai* (Disasters of Hiroshima and Nagasaki) (Tokyo: Horitsu Bunkasha, 1979), 411–12, quotes from Blackett and Nishijima. Its English translation is Committee for the Compilation of Materials on the Damage Caused by the Atomic Bombs in Hiroshima and Nagasaki, ed., *Hiroshima and Nagasaki: The Physical, Medical, and Social Effects of the Atomic Bombings* (New York: Basic Books, 1981).

65. *Time,* August 17, 1981, 56.

66. The most recent treatment of the subject is Sadao Asada, "The Shock of the Atomic Bomb and Japan's Decision to Surrender," forthcoming. The abridged Japanese version was published in *Sekai* 616 (December 1995): 232–42.

New York Times correspondent David E. Sanger correctly observes that Japanese have long opposed mixing the history of the war with the Hiroshima bombing; in

Hiroshima's Peace Memorial Museum, the devastation of the bomb "has always been presented with only the briefest reference to ... Japan's responsibility for starting the war that the bombing ended." Recently, in the summer of 1994, this began to change, and the museum added new exhibits on Japanese "aggression." *New York Times,* August 4, 1994.

67. Likewise, Alperovitz and other American revisionists do not fully take into account the determination of the Japanese military to fight to the finish. Alperovitz, *Decision to Use the Atomic Bomb.*

68. The impact of Vietnam caused not only Japanese but some Americans to seek hidden racial motives in the atomic bombing. For example, respected Japanologist John W. Hall wrote in 1975: "What are the racial implications of Hiroshima and Nagasaki? Can we imagine that our 'outraged conscience' against Nazi Germany would have as easily permitted the atom bombing of two of Germany's foremost cities?" "Pearl Harbor Thirty Years After—Reflections on the Pathology of War and Nationalism," *Fukuoka UNESCO* 10 (1975): 12.

69. Ishihara Shintaro and Morita Akio, *"No" to ieru Nihon* (Tokyo: Kobunsha, 1989), 38. Its English translation is *The Japan That Can Say No: Why Japan Will Be First among Equals* (New York: 1992).

70. Noam Chomsky, "On War Crimes," *At War with Asia* (New York: 1970), 298–99; Honda Katsuichi, *Korosareru gawa no ronri* (The logic of being killed) (Tokyo: Asahi Shinbunsha, 1971), 17, 33, 156.

71. Nishijima, *Genbaku wa naze otosareta ka,* 384.

72. *Asahi Shinbun,* August 6, 1994, evening edition.

73. *Sankei Shinbun,* August 5, 1985.

74. John W. Dower, *War without Mercy: Race and Power in the Pacific War* (New York: Pantheon Books, 1986), while highlighting racism on both sides, is not explicit on the racist motivations behind the atomic bombing of Japan. See also Sherry, *Rise of American Air Power,* 242.

75. Bernstein, "Roosevelt, Truman," 61; Ferrell, *Off the Record,* 55–56.

76. United States Department of State, *Foreign Relations of the United States: The Conference of Potsdam* (Washington, DC: Government Printing Office, 1960), 1:891.

77. *New York Times*/CBS News/Tokyo Broadcasting System poll, November 26, 1991.

78. Philip Nobile, ed., *Judgment at the Smithsonian* (New York: Marlowe and Company, 1995), 16–18, 21.

79. Frances FitzGerald, *America Revised: History Textbooks in the Twentieth Century* (New York: Vintage, 1979), 17–19, points out that it is often the version of events presented in history textbooks that sticks in the memory of their readers for the rest of their lives.

80. Ishida Akira, *Hibaku kyoshi* (A-bombed teacher) (Tokyo: Hitotsubashi Shobo, 1976), 214–29; *Chuto shakaika* (Junior high school social studies) (Tokyo: 1953), 74–76.

81. Nakamura Hidekazu et al., *Sekaishi* (World history) (Tokyo: Tokyo Shosekin, 1988), 330; Yamada Nobuo et al., *Kihan sekaishi* (Standard world history) (Tokyo: Teikoku shoin, 1990), 345; Besshi Atsuhiko, *Senso no oshiekata: Sekai no kyokasho ni miru* (How to teach about war: Textbooks around the world) (Tokyo: Shinchosa, 1983), 131–32. It would be only fair to mention that more conscientious teachers give special lectures on the atomic bomb in the classroom or take their pupils to the peace museum on school tours to Hiroshima.

82. *Nagasaki Shinbun,* July 20, 1977.

83. Ienaga Saburo, "The Glorification of War in Japanese Education," *International Security* 18 (winter 1993–1994): 113–33; Ienaga sosho shien shimin no kai, ed., *Taiheiyo senso to kyokasho* (The Pacific War and textbooks) (Tokyo: Shiso no kagakusha, 1970), passim.

84. Kyokasho kenkyu senta, *Shakaika kyokasho no Nichi-Bei hikaku* (Comparison of Japanese and American social studies textbooks) (Tokyo: Daiichi Hoki Shuppan, 1981), 59.

85. Carol Berkin, Robert A. Divine, Alan Brinkley, et al., *American Voices: A History of the United States,* Teacher's Annotated Edition (Glenview, IL: Scott Foresman, 1992), 649–65; Henry W. Bragdon, Samuel P. McCutchen, and Donald A. Ritchie, *History of a Free Nation* (Lake Forest, IL.: Macmillan/McGraw-Hill, 1992), 875–76.

86. For an analysis of American college textbooks, see J. Samuel Walker, "History, Collective Memory, and the Decision to Use the Bomb," *Diplomatic History* 19 (spring 1995): 319–28.

87. Gary B. Nash, *American Odyssey: The United States in the Twentieth Century* (Lake Forest, IL: Macmillan/McGraw-Hill, 1991), 415–21.

88. Lew Smith, *The American Dream* (Glenview, IL: Scott Foresman, 1983), 557–59.

89. Andrew Clayton, Elizabeth Israels Perry, and Allan M. Winkler, *America: Pathways to the Present* (Englewood Cliffs, NJ: Prentice Hall, 1995), 682–87.

90. Paul Boyer, *Todd Curti's American Nation* (New York: 1994), 765.

91. Gallup poll, December 1994.

92. Hall, "Pearl Harbor Thirty Years After," 12. A penetrating discussion of the ethical dimensions of the A-bomb decision is Michael Walzer, *Just and Unjust Wars: A Moral Argument with Historical Illustrations* (New York: Basic Books, 1977), 255, 263–68.

93. At a U.N. conference in Hiroshima in June 1992, Philip D. Zelikow created a furor among Japanese delegates by stating that the atomic bombs, by forcing prompt Japanese surrender, "saved more than a million Japanese lives." The Japanese criticized this statement as grossly "insensitive." Zelikow later amplified his statement by saying that "the sacrifice of so many innocent lives" in Hiroshima and Nagasaki saved "millions of other innocents around the world." *Asahi Shinbun,* June 16 and 20, 1992, December 11, 1992.

94. John L. Gaddis, *The Long Peace: Inquiries into the History of the Cold War* (New York: Oxford University Press, 1987).

95. Robert S. McNamara's statement is from the NHK television program on the Cuban missile crisis, October 28, 1992. For an earlier articulation of this view, see McNamara, *Out of the Cold: New Thinking for American Foreign and Defense Policy in the 21st Century* (New York: Simon and Schuster, 1989), 97–99, 102–4.

96. *Los Angeles Times,* August 3, 1994.

10

Memory Matters

Hiroshima's Korean Atom Bomb Memorial and the Politics of Ethnicity

Lisa Yoneyama

There is a battle for and around history going on at this very moment which is extremely interesting. The intention is to reprogram, to stifle what I've called the "popular memory," and also to propose and impose on people a framework in which to interpret the present. . . . Popular struggles have become for our society, not part of the actual, but part of the possible. So they have to be set at a distance. How? Not by providing a direct interpretation of them. . . . But by offering an historical interpretation of those popular struggles . . . to show that they never really happened!

—Michel Foucault

Universal history has no theoretical armature. Its method is additive; it musters a mass of data to fill the homogeneous, empty time. . . . A historical materialist approaches a historical subject only where he encounters it as a monad. In this structure he recognizes the sign of a Messianic cessation of happening, or put differently, a revolutionary chance in the fight for the oppressed past.

—Walter Benjamin

The research and writing of this chapter were supported by the following: the Anthropology Department at Stanford University, Hiroshima Shudo University, a Social Science Research Council–MacArthur Foundation Fellowship in International Peace and Security, a MacArthur Foundation Summer Grant and Write-Up Grant from the Center for International Security and Arms Control at Stanford University, and a postdoctoral fellowship from the East–West Center.

Earlier versions of this chapter were presented on various occasions, including the SSRC-MacArthur fellows' workshop on "Time, Space and the Politics of Memory," at

In the spring of 1994, following newly appointed Justice Minister Nagano Shigeto's public statement that the rape of Nanjing—the Japanese military operation in which somewhere between 155,000 and 300,000 people were massacred—was a "fabrication," the national and international media yet again problemized the Japanese people's amnesia about their war atrocities and colonial aggression toward other peoples in Asia and the Pacific. From the 1980s textbook controversy concerning the Liberal Democratic Party (LDP) Ministry of Education's euphemization of Japanese expansionism by its replacement of *invasion* (*shinryaku*) with a more diluted expression, *advancement* (*shinshutsu*), and incidents in which the conservative politician Ishihara Shintaro has repeatedly denied the rape of Nanjing, in a fashion very similar to that of Nagano, to the more recent administration's concealment of documents that corroborated the military's official involvement in the recruitment of women who were forced to provide sexual "comfort" to the Japanese military—examples of "Japanese amnesia" about the past war and colonialism seem inexhaustible. That the Japanese cannot remember themselves as aggressors but can only remember their self-victimization in the atom bombing of Hiroshima and Nagasaki has almost become a cliché, even in the U.S. news media.

Although this amnesia over Japan's past deeds is unmistakably persistent in certain sectors of society, it is no longer as pervasive or as dominant as claimed by many. Setting aside the matter of the U.S. media's portrayal of "the Japanese" as a monolithic entity and its inattention to the diversity of historical awareness within Japan, what has been missing in most media

the University of California, Santa Barbara (April 1990); the "Memory and Catastrophe" conference at the University of California, Santa Cruz (May 1990); and the "Cultural Borders/Border Crossings" session at the December 1992 American Anthropological Association meeting.

I am grateful to Young-hae Jung, Keisaburo Toyonaga, the members of Hiroshima Mintoren, and many others who generously shared their opinions about the conditions of Korean atom bomb survivors and of *zainichi* more generally. I have also benefitted from the encouragement and critical comments of Harumi Befu, Jonathan Boyarin, Chungmoo Choi, Carolyn M. Clark, James Clifford, Jane Collier, T. Fujitani, H.D. Harootunian, Marilyn Ivy, Dorinne Kondo, Lata Mani, Masao Miyoshi, Lisa Rofel, Renato Rosaldo, Miriam Silverberg, Marita Sturken, Geoffrey White, and Sylvia Yanagisako.

All quotations whose source is not specified from interviews and personal conversations conducted during the research period, 1987–1990.

Japanese and Korean names are rendered with surnames first, followed by given names. Except in cases in which individuals have designated unique ways of romanization, the Korean names are written in simplified McCune-Reischauer style. Most of the individuals mentioned in this article follow this hybrid practice. Pseudonyms are used when necessary to protect individuals' privacy.

coverage is recognition that opinions such as Nagano's are increasingly parochial to the present cabinet and even among conservative politicians. As exemplified by the government's attempts to join the United Nations Security Council, the primary nationalist agenda in the present government is to secure Japan's status in the post–cold war global political economy, when the political, military, and economic reliance on the security treaty with the United States has come under question and is less certain. The Socialist Party's recent approval of the treaty's official standing, despite the party's past opposition to the militarized and quasi-colonial nature of the treaty, paradoxically attests to the increasing uncertainty and waning appeal of the bilateral alliance with the United States. In order to achieve the nationalist ambitions of especially the conservative elites, it is imperative that they carefully resolve past wrongdoings against neighboring countries through apologies or by settling such memories within the "collective" consciousness.

The fiftieth anniversary of Hiroshima's atom bombing and the 1995 commemoration of the "end" of the war in Asia and the Pacific offered an opportunity for those who desired a closure to the contentious discourses on the nation's past. In this chapter on the memorial to Hiroshima's Korean atom bomb victims, I problemize one such recent attempt to contain and domesticate unreconciled discourses on the nation's past.

As we shall see, the Korean memorial has allowed a discursive space for Japan's former colonial subjects. It has contested and denationalized the dominant ways in which Hiroshima memories are articulated—namely, the remembering of Hiroshima's holocaust exclusively as "Japanese" victimization. Yet this memorial, which challenges the silence about Japan's colonial aggression and war atrocities, is starkly isolated from the official commemorative site, the Hiroshima Peace Memorial Park. This chapter explores the controversy that erupted in 1990 over the city's proposal to relocate the Korean memorial within the peace park proper. The memory practices revolving around the Korean memorial and its location constitute a double discourse. They separate the remembered and those who are remembering the event from the rest of Japanese society and identify them as those who are ethnically minoritized by Japan's social and legal arrangements. Yet at the same time, these narratives and practices of memorialization constitute contradictory elements in the production of subjectivities, thereby marking differentiations within the group as well as within each individual.

On the one hand, the ability to perform one's own acts of remembrance—the ability, for instance, to erect memorials, to hold public commemorations, or to write autobiographical histories—serves to reterritorial-ize the cartography of memory, authorizing one's past as differentiated from that of others. The act of inscribing one's own way of remembering onto a society's historical knowledge makes one's presence visible within its public sphere and assures one's voice a place in the production of dis-courses on the past. To possess and demonstrate one's own memories is therefore inextricably tied to power and autonomy.

The erection of the Korean atom bomb victims' memorial in 1970 there-fore ensured the presence of ethnic Koreans in Hiroshima's history and society. The memorial restored the sovereignty of those dead who had been deprived of independent national status under Japan's colonial rule and who consequently were doubly victimized as a result of the U.S. nuclear attack. Among the 350,000 to 400,000 who were attacked by the atom bomb and/or exposed to the lethal postexplosion radiation, at least 45,000 were people from the Korean Peninsula who had been forcibly sent to Japan as mobilized workers and soldiers or who had left their villages following the devastation caused by Japan's colonial takeover of Korea in 1910.[1]

In past official representations of Hiroshima's holocaust, Korean atom bomb victims have been virtually absent. In the official narratives of the Atomic Bomb Memorial Museum, those who suffered the U.S. assault have tended to be cast as a homogeneous victim of the nuclear holocaust, a moment unprecedented in human history. Until 1990, the speeches of politi-cal elites at the annual municipal Peace Memorial Ceremony on August 6 never referred to the at least 20,000 to 30,000 Korean atom bomb dead estimated to have been immediately killed by the Hiroshima and Nagasaki bombings. Among numerous sites commemorating the Hiroshima nuclear holocaust, the memorial for the Korean atom bomb victims is therefore the only visible reminder of the tribulations and suffering of those identified as Koreans.

In this respect, the discourse on the Korean minority's memories of the atomic bomb disturbs the dominant national as well as humanist narratives about the war and the nuclear holocaust, constantly challenging the amnesia and whitewashing involved in official representations of the nation's past. Issues concerning the memorial's location are inextricably intertwined with the question of how the Japanese government faces its responsibilities for colonialism and the war of invasion. The Immigration Control and Refugee Act and the Alien Registration Act, the two laws that presently define the legal status of approximately 700,000 Korean resident aliens in Japan (*zainichi kankoku chosenjin*, referred to as *zainichi* hereafter), have un-doubtedly inherited many of the forms of Japan's colonial policy that treated Korean people and other colonial subjects as second-class citizens. The legal practices that continue to subordinate the Korean minority in Japan include: the requirement that an alien registration card be carried at all times, even by permanent residents; the discretionary power of the Ministry of Justice, which relegates resident aliens to a vulnerable status that makes them subject to possible deportation; the arbitrary naturalization process; and informal administrative pressures to assimilate them and other aliens by imposing Japaneselike family names upon them.[2]

Segregation of the ethnic memorial site from the city's central commemorative space is therefore often regarded as symptomatic of the subaltern status of *zainichi*, who are invariably subjected to legal and administrative practices that are often summarized as those of "discrimination, assimilation, and expatriation." Not only has the memorial provided a ritual space for the annual memorial ceremonies for Korean victims, but by allowing an occasion for the continued rearticulation of past and present knowledge about ethnic Koreans, the memorial and the discourse on its location have also constituted, as we shall see in detail, a critical locus for the identity politics of Korean resident aliens in Hiroshima and elsewhere.

On the other hand, the narratives and practices of memorialization inevitably shape the Korean minority's diverse consciousness about history, ethnicity, and nationality—in other words, about those elements that cannot be entirely subsumed under the totality of collective identity or by what are imagined to be shared communal experiences.[3] Far from merely constituting "sites where groups of people gather to create a common past for themselves, places where they tell the constitutive narratives, their 'shared' stories of the past,"[4] the Korean memorial, and many other mnemonic sites in Hiroshima, often generate contentious interpretations about the past and present while inciting a kaleidoscope of visions toward the future.[5]

The meanings of the memorial, the event it commemorates, and the subject of memorialization are rarely transparent. The acts of remembrance necessarily entail questions regarding the legitimacy and ownership of memory as well as belongingness to the shared past. Who participates in the remembrances at the memorial, what is desired in the remembering, how the commemorated event is construed, and for what objectives—these questions are inherently tied to the issue of communal boundaries and their authenticity. The collisions and elisions of meanings over the memorial, its location, and the event it commemorates occur both without and within the ethnic boundaries, thereby differentiating the members of the Korean minority not only from the rest of Japanese society and history but also from one another.

By exploring the diverse narratives produced by Korean resident aliens in Hiroshima—who are differently positioned through the matrices of nationality (i.e., North and South Korea), generation, region, gender, sexuality, and class (although I cannot discuss them all)—I shall disentangle elements within the web of memories that often collapse diverse referents into the single totality of Korean-ness while at the same time recognizing the critical importance of organizing and mobilizing individuals by their ethnic difference.[6] In doing so, I ask how the Korean memorial continues to be constituted as a site where contestatory representations of Japan's colonial history can be enunciated.

In examining narrative contestations over the Korean memorial, I shall also focus on the tension between attempts to control the contestatory memory of colonialism and resistance to these attempts at domestication. Contrary to the common perception, the hegemonic process within the production of Japan's national history is moving beyond what we currently see as reprehensible—that is, *beyond* amnesia—to a point at which those in power are contriving to "come to terms with the past," through at least partially acknowledging the nation's past misconduct and inscribing it onto the official memoryscape. Yet as Theodor Adorno wrote, the coming to terms with the past (*Aufarbeitung der Vergangenheit*) "does not imply a serious working through of the past, the breaking of its spell through an act of clear consciousness. It suggests, rather, wishing to turn the page and, if possible, wiping it from memory."[7] This process, therefore, necessarily entails the forgetting of that very amnesia, masking the fact that the memories of aggression and discrimination have been deliberately and at times forcibly repressed for almost half a century since the end of the war. As this study of the plight of the Korean memorial hopefully demonstrates, what really is at stake in this time of the proliferation of memorial objects and commemorative practices is to remember this very amnesia, so that we might consider how such a history of forgetting has shaped the subjectivities and the politicized engagements of those who are now being remembered.

Contentious Memorial

The memorial for the Korean atom bomb victims stands northwest of Hiroshima's Peace Memorial Park, across the river that demarcates the park's western boundary. It is located at the foot of a bridge on an approximately fifty-square-meter corner lot, at a narrow four-way intersection. There stands a statue of a mythic turtle, supporting a fifty-foot-high granite column. On the front of the memorial is an engraving of Chinese characters that reads (in Japanese), *kankokujin genbaku giseisha irei hi,* and means "memorial for *kankokujin* [South Korean and/or Korean] atom bomb vic-

Korean-Japanese hibakusha have never been fully incorporated into commemorations of the hibakusha experience, just as they have not been fully included in Japanese society. Kim Nam-Chul, a longtime Korean-Japanese resident of Hiroshima, was sixteen in August 1945. She is standing in front of the monument to Korean hibakusha placed outside the Peace Memorial Park. (From Ito Takashi, *Genbaku Kimin* [Human refuse of the atomic bomb] [Tokyo: Horupu Shuppan, 1987]. Photograph by Ito Takashi. Ienaga, 3.195.)

tims." Next to it is another line, also of Chinese characters but in a different style of calligraphy, which reads, "In memory of Prince Yi U and the other 20,000 or more souls." Below these two lines, written vertically, is another horizontal engraving, in English: "The Monument in Memory of the Korean Victims of ABOMB [*sic*]."

The memorial has incited a number of interpretive contestations in the past two decades. Whether this "monument" memorializes all souls of the Korean atom bomb dead or only those whose survivors are affiliated with the Republic of Korea has been a central issue. The term *kankokujin,* at least in contemporary Japanese usage, refers in most cases to nationals of the Republic of Korea, whereas the other term for Korean people, *chosenjin,* is used either to specifically describe nationals of the People's Republic of Korea or to indicate the ethnological group.

The schism of the homeland—brought about by the history of Japanese colonialism, U.S. cold war hegemony, and the Korean War—also resulted in a chasm in the memorializing of the atom bomb dead. Members of Zainippon Chosenjin Sorengo (Soren, for short), or the General Federation of Korean Residents in Japan, an organization that provides various administrative services for those affiliated with North Korea, contend that they have been excluded from the commemoration at the existing memorial and have been asking the city since 1975 to allow them to construct their own memorial.[8] In contrast, Zainippon Taikan Minkoku Kyoryumindan (Mindan, for short), or the Association for Korean Residents in Japan, an organization for those affiliated with the Republic of Korea, officially holds the view that the memorial stands for both North and South Koreans, based on the grounds that *hanguk,* or *kankoku* in Japanese, was the official name of Korea before the Japanese occupation. For example, the head of the Mindan-affiliated Hiroshima Prefectural Headquarters of the Special Committee for the Atomic Bomb Victims reiterated the understanding that "the memorial stands for the Great Korean People (*taikan minzoku*), with no distinction between South or North."[9] Despite the disputes, the ownership of the memorial appears to be rather self-evident, at least in the eyes of those affiliated with the Republic of Korea. Later, I will return to the question of the memorial's nationalist character.

Another interpretive crisis concerns the memorial's location. As has often been pointed out by the media and many other observers, the memorial stands outside the administrative boundaries of the peace park. The Korean memorial, to be sure, is not the only memorial that stands outside the official territory. Yet although the eastern and southern peripheries appear to be integral to the park due to the spatial arrangement of the extended greenery and paths, the park's northwest end is much more secluded from the central commemorative sites. Over the past decade, visitors to the memorial have construed the site/sight of isolation as indicating synecdochically the alienation of Koreans in Japanese society.

One letter written in 1986 and addressed to the municipal government, by a Japanese man in collaboration with Oh Tokai, a first-generation *zainichi* poet whose activism I will describe later, expressed both perplexity and resentment: "But how could this be? Discrimination even against the dead? Discrimination even among the victims of the atomic bomb? . . . We demand that Hiroshima city fulfill its own responsibilities and obligation to swiftly relocate the present memorial, or to construct a new memorial inside the park."[10] Since the letter was written, voices questioning the memorial's marginal status have become increasingly audible. In response to growing public criticism, the city has up to the present consistently offered three reasons for denying requests to relocate the memorial.

First, the city has insisted that it must observe the regulation it established in 1967 that restricts any further construction of memorials inside the official zone of the Peace Memorial Park.[11] Second, the city has argued that, even if the memorial were to be relocated in the official territory of the peace park, it needs to be a "unified memorial" so that those affiliated not only with the Republic of Korea but also with the Democratic People's Republic of Korea can pay their respects without inciting political controversy. The city administrators have maintained that the peace park is a sacred site where prayers for the peace of all of humanity are offered, and it should therefore not be desecrated by bringing in so-called ideological issues. Third, the mayor and the city administrators in general have contended that the central cenotaph in the peace park enshrines all souls lost to the bomb without regard to nationality or race and that therefore there is no need to have a separate memorial dedicated solely to the Korean atom bomb victims.[12]

At least for those who have problematized the Korean memorial's present location, the way in which the memorial has been treated is understood as an index of ongoing discrimination against the Korean minority and its continuing alienation. The physical location of the Korean memorial, therefore, paradigmatically portrays how official history has suppressed the ethnicity of Koreans through the marginalization of their memories. The visitors to the Korean memorial pass through the park proper, approaching the border greenery as they sense the park's periphery, and then walk across the bridge to arrive finally at this small, cramped corner lot. The memorial's physical isolation reinforces the pilgrims' sense of the very reason for their visit. For them, the memorial confirms and condemns the Korean minority's exclusion from the national memory.

Monument to Homeland

Despite the ever-growing public discontent, some Koreans do not necessarily regard the present location of the memorial as "a sign of discrimination." One such person is Chang Tae-hui, an *Issei* (or first-generation) retired president of a small business, who served as a representative of the committee that both initiated and executed the memorial's construction. In responding to interviews by the media and activists, he has repeatedly asserted that although he wishes to see the memorial placed within the peace park as promised by the former mayor, he does not believe that the present location of the memorial is in any sense "discriminatory," or a "disgrace," as is often suggested by "outsiders." As on numerous other occasions, in responding to my personal interview, Chang reiterated the significance he saw in the memorial's present location: "[The location where the memorial stands today] was the site where the Korean prince [Yi U] was found at the time of the bombing. The river was already filled with dead corpses floating like rafts. There they found one body glittering with accessories. 'This must be someone important,' people thought, and they pulled the body out of the river." A nephew of the Yi dynasty's twenty-seventh king, Prince Yi U was killed by the bomb while serving as a lieutenant colonel in the Japanese Imperial Army. Without a pause, Chang went on to describe how the Korean royalty has been unfairly viewed:

> Unlike the Japanese imperial family, members of the former Korean royal family are not cared for. The Korean kings and their families are regarded as national traitors, [because it is believed that] they actively created a pro-Japanese camp. During the colonial era, the Japanese [in Korea] occupied every position of leadership. They controlled everything from financial unions, farmland registration, and the rice mills [one of which his father owned] to forceful mobilization of the populace. In our prefecture, they built munitions factories designated by the navy under the slogan of "Korea–Japan unification" (*naisen ittai*). When we were preparing for the construction of the memorial, many wanted us to use the word *kankoku,* as [the character *kan*] had been used in *nikkan heigo* (Korea–Japan annexation) [of 1910].

What prompted the designer of the memorial to choose Yi U to represent the Korean people who had fallen victim to the bomb, if in fact the prince is among those who, as Chang indicated, are "regarded as national traitors"? His narrative suggests that Prince Yi U and Korean royalty as a group are victims of Japan's colonial policy, just as much as any other Koreans, including *zainichi* and Korean victims of the atom bomb. Perhaps Chang was projecting onto Prince Yi U's tribulations his own personal history of having formerly been accused of collaborating in Japan's war effort and colonial rule. The choice of Prince Yi U to represent the other Korean atom bomb victims may have been part of his personal effort to restore the good name of many Koreans who were coerced into cooperating with Japan and who have long been disparaged as collaborators. And as the memorial redeems the Yi family and other colonial subjects who presumably shared the same historical destiny, it at the same time, in Chang's interpretation of history, resurrects the essential character *han* (or *kan* in Japanese) of the name of their sovereign country, the name that was forcibly taken from them during Japan's colonial regime.

The nation's name, its language, its history, and the prince, though tarnished, denote the memorial's referent by distinguishing the dead enshrined there from the rest of the atom bomb victims. The althea trees, the national tree of the Republic of Korea, add yet another sign of the homeland. The granite stones and pebbles are also native products, processed in Korea and then shipped to Hiroshima. These material objects from the soil of the home country are said to have consoled the souls of those who died while yearning for their homeland.

Moreover, the memorial, embellished as it is with Korean national symbols, signifies the victories of Koreans who survived Japanese colonialism, the war, and even the atom bomb. The memorial honors the national culture and the existing political regime; it also celebrates paternalistic ties with Korea. For instance, the Republic of Korea's national flag is engraved on the left side of the memorial. Below the flag are the names and titles of two individuals: Yi Hyo-sang, the chairperson of the National Congress of the Republic of Korea at the time of the memorial's construction, who provided the calligraphy for the main inscription, and Han Kap-su, a Seoul University professor who provided the memorial's description about the history of the Korean victims. Referring to this icon of Korean national and anticolonial pride, one of the construction committee members wrote, "Like a [magnificent] stork among a [common] flock of chickens, this solemn memorial, which evokes images of a king's tomb that crystalizes the pure spirits of Shilla, stands absolutely [peerless] among numerous monument stones in the peace park."[13]

In this particular sense, unlike Hiroshima's other memorials, which register defeat in the war, this icon of remembrance bears witness to the victory of the martyrs of independence. The Korean memorial stands for the triumph over Japanese aggression and also signifies the fulfillment of emancipation from colonial injustice. While registering the emotions of grief, atonement, and consolation, the Korean memorial simultaneously serves as a nationalist monument, embodying the pride and glory of the Republic of Korea.[14] It is likely that Chang's way of remembering the Hiroshima holocaust is predominant among first- and perhaps many second-generation Korean resident aliens. Nevertheless, it is certainly not the only way remembrance takes place, even among those who supposedly share a similar generational history.

Oh Tokai, the *zainichi* poet mentioned earlier as one of the writers of a letter criticizing the memorial's location, does not subscribe to the narrative of great Korean national glories. Born in 1919, Oh Tokai considers himself one of the oldest of those who claim to be *zainichi*. Oh is a poet who has earned his living mostly as a construction worker and day laborer. Today, he receives social welfare. Practically homeless, he lives in a corner of a common room in a university students' dormitory. He is also known as the first person who protested against the legal restrictions on resident Koreans in 1973 by publicly burning his alien registration card.

Underlying Oh's notion of being a Korean, radically different from that of Chang and most other Issei Koreans, is the obstinate rejection of any communal boundaries regarding what is assumed to be the shared experience of hibakusha or Korean victimization. At one meeting in Hiroshima, Oh began his speech by criticizing the largest peace and antinuclear organization, the Gensuikin (Japan Congress against Atom and Hydrogen Bombs): "When the [Japanese peace and antinuclear] movement gained popularity, in the cries that called attention to the cruelty of the atomic bomb, I did not even once hear the claim that there are survivors in Korea." His criticism of the Japanese majority's treatment of the Korean atom bomb victims furthermore extends to the general question of postwar reparations. He points to the unfair situation in which former colonial subjects who fought and labored as Japanese imperial subjects before and during the war have not received monetary reparations equal to those given Japanese nationals. He concluded, "In Japan, the object of rescue is always limited to the Japanese. And people don't think it's odd."

While he criticizes the self-centrism in Japan's national memory, Oh at the same time distances himself from those *zainichi* who employ such words as fellow countrypeople, or *doho* in Japanese, or homeland, or *sokoku* in Japanese, in order to reinforce the sense of solidarity with greater Korea. For him, such a tie is illusory and dangerous because it may create yet another boundary of empathy and also because it obscures struggles over hierarchical relations of power within such a boundary. From his point of view, it is hypocritical for Koreans in Japan to identify with Koreans in Korea, as if they shared the same subjective world. As a way to demonstrate his own notion of being an ethnic Korean in Japan, he refuses to pronounce his name in the Korean reading of the Chinese characters, O Tu-hoe, but insists that his name be pronounced in the Japanese reading. He also considers it natural that most Koreans in Japan speak Japanese as their first language. He maintained, "I once told a *zainichi* activist who always summons camaraderie with the Koreans back in the homeland that they shouldn't dare say that Koreans in Japan and Koreans in Korea share the same horizon. We were making money in Japan when Korea was suffering during the [1950–1953] Korean War. Our roads were separated a long time ago. We are Japanized Koreans."

Oh's refusal of the nationalist narrative has also led him to form a critical outlook on the Korean memorial that subverts the established authorities of class and state: "But that memorial itself is in fact quite nonsensical. Why is a specific individual's name inscribed? . . . Moreover, why does only the prince receive special treatment when tens of thousands of other Koreans also died? . . . What does the memorial exist for? That there is only an inscription for the Republic of Korea's national flag [when in fact there are two separate sovereign nations for the Korean people] should also be a matter of controversy."

In concluding his populist narrative—a view that contrasts sharply with Chang's—Oh further cautioned that transferring the Korean memorial into the park proper might result in the municipal government's cooptation of ethnic minority issues: "The fact that the memorial for the Korean atomic bomb victims stands across the river is very suggestive. It expresses the reality of *zainichi*. The fact that it is located across the river from the peace park is in itself very significant. It's important. Isn't it quite natural that the memorial should stand across the river precisely because the *zainichi* exist across the river?"

A *partial* fulfillment of demands might lead to the further occlusion of yet unresolved questions. Oh's narrative, undoubtedly shared by very few Isseis and high-ranking members of Mindan, situates the memorial within the context of the *zainichi*'s current location within Japanese society—that is, in the midst of their ongoing endeavors to build their futures in a society that casts them as others who should be assimilated. Oh's position, one that relentlessly denies yearning for the homeland and advocates a radical politics of difference, resonates curiously with the recent strategies of ethnic politics pursued by many second- and third-generation youth. We will later return to some of the younger generations' narratives on the politics of Korean ethnicity.

Excess of Memory

Shortly before the forty-fifth anniversary of the city's atom bombing, the Hiroshima city government, despite its decade-long refusal to consider any requests for the memorial's relocation, suddenly shifted its position. Unilaterally disregarding the 1967 regulation, the city announced that relocation would be welcomed, provided that the North and South Koreans could agree upon a unified memorial. The spring of 1990 was indeed a time when the speculations and motives of different political constituencies—the South Korean government, the Liberal Democratic Party, the Japanese government, Soren, Mindan, and the municipal government—converged on issues regarding the Korea–Japan relationship. Several incidents staged on the national political scene during the first half of that year, including a visit by President Roh Tae-wu of the Republic of Korea in May, finally brought the long-deferred question to the majority's attention.[15]

Hiroshima city administrators, along with economic and political elites, have also discovered their own interests in relocating the Korean memorial. The city administration's two most pressing matters at the end of this century have been hosting the 1994 Asian Games, an athletic competition involving all of "Asia," and the fiftieth commemoration of the city's atom bombing, held in 1995. To the dismay of city officials, however, visitors from the very Asian countries with which the city has been promoting "international friendship" have become increasingly visible and vocal in denouncing the peripheral state of the Korean atomic bomb victims' memorial. "Discrimination persists even after death?" With headlines such as this, the local news media have unfailingly reported on tourists' outrage toward the city and the Japanese people for their irresponsibility regarding the memorial's marginal status. With continuing exposure of the suppression of memories of Japanese aggression, it appears likely that the city will experience yet more embarrassment at such international events.

The 1990 proposal for the Korean memorial's relocation is symptomatic of the broader nationalist agenda that is currently at work—namely, the attempt to officially come to terms with and officialize memories of Japan's aggression. To secure political and economic stability in the adjacent Asian and Pacific region, it has become necessary for the government to incorporate memories of Japan's colonial and military atrocities into the national history, but in a manner that does not threaten the present order of knowledge. The Hiroshima city government's agreement to grant permission for the Korean memorial's relocation ought to be understood in this broader context.

This process of cooptation, however, could only be effective if the memorial were converted into something innocuous. Following the city's official announcement of the memorial's relocation, an administrative advisory committee consisting of several local celebrities, all of whom were Japanese nationals, stated that in order to unify the memorial for North and South

Koreans, the present engravings should be replaced with a new inscription. In short, the 1990 proposal required a careful tailoring of the Korean memorial's form and content.

After many debates and complications, the details of which I cannot discuss in this limited space, the committee ultimately submitted the following suggestions to the city for unifying the memorial.[16] First, the main inscription on the front of the memorial, the committee suggested, should be changed to *genbaku giseisha ireihi* (memorial for the atom bomb victims), eliminating the term *kankoku* (Republic of Korea) as well as Prince Yi U's name. Second, four Chinese characters, *mango yubang*, which would in Japanese read *banko ryuho*, should be placed above the main inscription. Taken from classical Korean literature, according to the official interpretation the committee offered, this idiom means, "The precious death of the people will remain as a fragrant stream forever in people's hearts." And finally, two small Hangul, or Korean, letters, reading "tribute to the dead," should be added across the top of the inscription.

Despite the initial confirmations from high-ranking members of Mindan and Soren, the attempt to relocate the memorial into the park by August 6, 1990, ultimately failed, due to strong protests from other citizens and members of the two organizations. Those in Mindan and Soren who tentatively agreed to the memorial's alteration certainly had hoped for a positive outcome from unifying and relocating the memorial. Some argued that it would indeed be humiliating for the memorial to remain at the present site and that the memorial's incorporation into the park proper would enhance the visibility of ethnic Koreans in Japanese society in general. Others saw it as an opportunity to eliminate the name of Prince Yi U, a name that for many in Korea does not necessarily evoke favorable memories. Though not without some reservations, many also expressed their desire to see the dream for a "unified homeland" fulfilled, at least in the unified memorialization of those who fell victim to the bomb.

When seen from the official perspective, it may seem as if the opportunity to relocate the memorial was spoiled only because of objections to the proposed alterations to the present inscriptions. However, the plan's failure should ultimately be attributed to city officials' original insistence on making the memorial into a site that they believed could be free of "ideological conflicts." The irony of the matter is, however, that given the imminent fiftieth annual commemoration of the atom bombing, it would have been to the city's advantage to relocate the memorial into the park proper rather than to have it remain where it is, certain to incite further international rebuke. What, then, was at stake for city officials and others that compelled them to obstinately refuse relocation of the memorial as is and to propose controversial alterations that ultimately led to their failure to move the memorial?

The present memorial is central to at least two processes of signification. On the one hand, in the eyes of some, the memorial has served as a site for discursive intervention. It is a location where knowledge about the consequences of Japanese colonial rule in Korea is enunciated by evoking memories of the adversities that faced Korean atom bomb survivors. At one public symposium organized by several citizens' groups in Hiroshima, an invited speaker, Kim Song-won, commended the memorial for its instrumental value in helping to bring to the public's attention the hardships of survivors in Korea. For due to a lack of public understanding regarding the persistent effects of radiation, they have faced great difficulties obtaining financial and medical support. "In that sense, I am pleased that the memorial exists," said this *Nisei* (second-generation) entrepreneur who at one time had served as a member of the memorial construction committee. "For the memorial not only consoles the souls of the victims; it also helps urge people to think about the very fact that there were this many Korean survivors [and] why Korean victims [of Hiroshima and Nagasaki] . . . have been ignored ever since the war's end. I think it is an obvious outcome of the discriminatory policy against us Koreans."

At the same time, from its inception, the memorial has been "a tribute to the dead." As a shrine where the dead are memorialized, as a public grave for those whose souls have never received proper individualized consolations, it has always had qualities that are closely associated with the sentiments for the dead broadly shared by people in general and not limited to the Korean minority. In this regard, the Korean memorial is similar to a number of other memorials in Hiroshima: it is a universal tribute to those who were equally killed by the bomb. After all, it could be argued that the United States attacked and indiscriminately massacred as a collectivity those who were present in Hiroshima on that day, regardless of their military or civilian status or age, class, sex, or nationality. Besides, can there be any differences in the weight of individual human lives, in the sentiments of the bereaved, in their deepest desires to offer proper homage to the deceased?

Yet it should not be overlooked that this universalist understanding of the human attitude toward death often serves to obscure important cleavages, incommensurabilities that are both politically and culturally constituted and therefore need to be addressed precisely in those terms. In the case of the differences between Japanese and Korean atom bomb victims, the second-generation Korean survivors almost invariably recall how their first-generation parents were mistreated by Japanese soldiers and others at the relief stations, even while remembering the shared horrific experience of survival itself.[17]

Moreover, journalist Nakajima Tatsuyoshi, who has written extensively on Korean survivors' issues, has argued that Korean atom bomb survivors, and especially those who returned to Korea and thus endured what he calls "triple afflictions," suffered in multiple ways in contrast to other survivors in Japan. According to Nakajima, the Korean population first of all was concentrated in the city proper and hence was close to the hypocenter. Due to immigration and forcible mobilization, many were confined to an area where munitions factories were clustered together. Second, unlike many Japanese survivors, who sought shelter outside the city through familial and other affiliations, the majority of the Korean survivors had no option but to remain in the city and thus were exposed to radiation considerably longer than most others. And finally, those Koreans who returned to Korea have not been able to receive medical care comparable to survivors in Japan.[18]

Kim problemized the city and committee's 1990 relocation plan by arguing that in order for the memorial to "urge people to think about the very fact that there were this many Korean survivors," the referents of memory—that is, whom the memorial is memorializing—must be obvious. Moreover, he contends that it is insufficient for only those who are the ethnic curators of the memories of the dead to be aware of the nationality of the enshrined. The communicative dynamics of this memorial ought not to be confined to the Korean minority alone but should extend to the broader Japanese society and reach out as far as the Korean Peninsula. The memories it involves must constantly spill over the boundaries of ethnic memory. Kim concluded that, from the newly proposed inscription, "it is impossible to know the nation and the people, as well as the reason, for which this memorial stands."

The existing memorial marks just that kind of difference, a distinctly "Korean" kind of memory. The Korean memorial speaks specifically to the Korean nation's victimization by Japanese colonialism and the war of expansion. It embodies memories that have been collectively reconstituted and distinguished from those of the perpetrators. As such, the memorial stands for the irreconcilable chasm between the colonizers and the colonized, for the disparity of memories that even the sincerest sentiments for the dead cannot easily conflate under a common denominator.

The proposed alteration of the inscriptions would have obscured this incommensurability of memories. As a monument, the present icon not only mourns the victims but also, for the reasons described earlier, celebrates the Korean nation's independence and its emancipation from Japanese colonial rule. Moreover, its messages delegitimize the Japanese government's poli-

Ito Takashi traced 180 hibakusha who had returned to their native Korea, including this elderly man, Lee Meng-hi. One of his compatriots, Son Gin Doo, successfully won a lawsuit against the Japanese government after it refused to make ex–colonial subjects eligible for the subsidized medical service provided to hibakusha. His efforts inspired American hibakusha to petition the U.S. government for similar support. (Photograph by Ito Takashi. Ienaga, 3.179.)

cies toward Koreans in the past and present. By defacing these memories, the city and committee's proposal would have transformed the memorial in such a way that it would have been commensurate with other memorial icons in the Peace Memorial Park. It tried to convert the magnificent, the monumental, and the accusatory to a banal, universalizing "tribute to the dead." What the city and committee would have canceled was precisely such an excess of memory in Japan's official remembering of the Hiroshima holocaust.

Memory Matters: "Minzoku"

The 1990 blueprint for the Korean memorial's relocation was yet another attempt to contain and domesticate one of the many disruptive memories in Japan's historical consciousness. Yet resistance to the 1990 relocation plan demonstrates how struggles over endangered memories are a crucial part of engaging in the politics of difference. Those Koreans and their non-Korean supporters who objected to rewriting the memorial inscription did so precisely because they saw that the city and committee's intervention in their acts of remembering threatened to erase their difference *as* Koreans.

For most Nisei and *Sansei* (third-generation) Korean resident aliens, the memorial issue took on a further significance that did not converge with the narrative of the South Korean nation. In objecting to the memorial's alteration, they resisted containment of the politics of their ethnic memories: they rejected surveillance over the manner in which they remember the past as ethnic subjects (*minzoku to shite*). Concretely, the younger generation of Koreans in Hiroshima regarded the relocation issue as a pressing concern that needed to be addressed in the city's administrative policies, along with a number of other issues relevant to their ongoing civil rights struggles. A Sansei grocer, Kang Song-dok, who is a member of several ethnic organizations, understood the memorial issue as follows: "Those who belong to our generation do not have an awareness of being Korean citizens residing abroad (*kaigai komin*). Precisely because we believe that our future lies here in Japan, we protest such legal discriminations as the Alien Registration Act, and at the same time we wish to retain our ethnic culture in a symbolic manner (*shochoteki ni*). We regard the Korean memorial relocation issue as an integral part of such issues."[19]

Kang's remark succinctly captures the idea of citizenship or civil rights (*kominken*) that is divorced from the concept of nationality. That non-nationals should be treated on equal terms with nationals in local/national communities because they are both residents who share various obligations equally, including paying taxes and taking on responsibility for determining the community's future—such is the emerging awareness that has generally guided the protests of especially the third generation of Korean resident aliens.

In order to create "an environment in which we can live as ethnic subjects (*minzoku to shite ikite yukeru kankyo*)," Kang has pushed the city administration to create conditions in which "the municipal community would approve our membership as community residents (*chiiki jumin to shite*)." He has urged the city to pursue policies that would provide the *zainichi* population with an environment in which all ethnic members would be granted permanent residency unconditionally; there would be community services for minorities, including opportunities for ethnic education; and it would be possible to vote as resident aliens, at least at the local and prefectural levels. He and others believe that eliminating all so-called nationality requirements (*kokuseki joko*) in the city's hiring practices (that is, the requirement that public employees be Japanese nationals) is especially crucial for stabilizing the socioeconomic conditions of resident aliens.[20]

"[Third-generation *zainichi*'s] protests," writes Hong Tae-pyo, "are not so much rebellions against Japanese society as excruciating love calls, in which they probe their own self-being."[21] The Sanseis' assertion of civil rights—especially of voting rights—also differentiates younger Koreans from earlier generations regarding how they conceptualize their sense of belongingness to the nation and their relationship to Japanese society at large. If, for the Issei, the homeland tended to be thought of as the home to which they would eventually return, and the Nisei were obliged to continue to make their livelihood in Japan while generally acknowledging their parents' yearning, for the Sansei, the reality of *zainichi*, or literally "being in Japan," is usually taken as a historical given. On the one hand, the reclaiming of their families' colonial memories—of the origin of their displacement and their present subaltern status—helps third-generation Koreans affirm their difference from the rest of Japanese society. Yet this avowal of difference paradoxically legitimates the sense that their future "lies here in Japan," thereby fueling protests against institutional arrangements that treat them differently from Japanese residents. This protest informs Sanseis' political participation, not in the Korean homeland but in their everyday local communities.

It is particularly important to note that the third generation construes the memorial issue in this context. The awareness that one can be a full citizen of a society while retaining a different nationality severs the memorial's signification from either a strictly Korean or Japanese nationalist narrativization. Rather than providing witness to the collective experience of the national community, the memorial in the third generation's politics offers a plenitude of fragmented memories that need to be articulated and secured "at a moment of danger"[22]—that is, at a moment when the Sanseis' participation in Japanese society and history as incommensurable subjects is threatened by the reprogramming of the knowledge about their struggles.

Although Kang remarked that "ethnic culture in a symbolic manner" is a part of Sansei protests, this notion of culture is quite different from what has generally been regarded in social analyses as a stable, transparent entity that is collectively shared in a coherent manner.[23] What actually constitutes their ethnic culture and what it means to live as an ethnic subject can never be discussed uniformly, even among those who belong to the same generation. Some, for instance, view the Korean language as an indispensable ingredient of their difference. Others claim without hesitation, as one young print shop owner said to me, "We Sanseis do not necessarily have to be competent in our [Korean] language," while believing that an "inner drive," a subliminal ethnic soul (*minzoku no kokoro*), constitutes their difference.[24]

Even while *chesa,* ancestral rites, are regarded by many as a crucial material component of Korean ethnicity, such "traditional" Korean family rituals and the relations they enact are not embraced by some women as markers of ethnic difference. To be sure, although these women do not seek elements of ethnic difference that would entail adoption or retention of what are considered authentic if patriarchal Korean family relations, they are at the same time fully aware of the socioeconomic circumstances and the dominant representations that have created negative stereotypes of Korean men as frustrated fathers or failed husbands. Yet as Sansei sociologist Jung Yeong-hae observes of her interviews with a number of teenagers who refused to be fingerprinted (which was formerly a requirement for all resident aliens in Japan), younger *zainichi* women are beginning to question the conventional notion of ethnicity (*minzoku*) that has in many ways subjugated women and others who do not conform to the dominant Korean gender and family ideology.[25] In other words, they are beginning to challenge patriarchally constructed notions of nationhood and ethnicity, without losing sight of their positions as members of the Korean minority.

Given the extensive variety of regional, economic, political, and gender disparities, the lived reality of Korean resident aliens appears almost as fragmented as that of Asian-Americans who have immigrated in different historical periods and from many disparate countries and class backgrounds. How each individual views his or her difference from other members of society, and the ways in which that person perceives conditions as oppressive and discriminatory, are never consistent. In this sense, the Korean resident aliens' indeterminate idea of Koreanness confirms Michael M.J. Fischer's argument that the ethnic process is a dreamlike work of memory—that is, in the making of ethnicity, fragments of images, stories, and cultural forms are "worked out through, and integrated with, [each individual's] ongoing experience."[26] Conventional sociological studies, unable to capture the fluidity and mutifacetedness of individual ethnic subjectivity, have often dismissed such allegorical dimensions of ethnicity. Rather, they have tended to conceptualize ethnicity as a uniform entity with a coherent social agency that is grounded upon stable and unproblematic linkages with a unified past.

Nonetheless, the construction of ethnic subjectivity, though often differing wildly according to each individual's condition, is not an entirely arbitrary invention. Regardless of what individuals deem appropriate to articulate differences, to live as an ethnic subject means for individuals to live through the ways in which they have been interpellated, to live with that which has been suppressed, with elements that have been consistently and forcibly taken from their lives. The criticalness of the relocation issue resides specifically in the fact that the memorial crystallizes for many people, though in different ways, the elements of difference of which they believe they have been bereft by other memorializations of the Hiroshima holocaust.

The Korean family name is one such element. In responding to the city administrators' official account that the central cenotaph in the peace park enshrines all souls lost to the bomb indiscriminately, Chang, for instance, describes the memorial's relation to ethnic names as follows: "Japanese are enshrined in the central cenotaph, but not Koreans. There are individuals whose names are recognizable as Koreans, such as Kimura or Kanemoto [which are Japaneselike names often adopted by people of Korean ethnic background]; but they are enshrined with their Japanese names. They are [in that sense] indistinguishable."

Most Korean resident aliens use at least two family names: an ethnically Korean name passed on from the paternal lineage, which is read in either or both of the Japanese and Korean readings of the Chinese characters, and a Japanese-like surname—such as Kimura or Kanemoto in Chang's remark— often referred to as the "commonly used names" (*tsumei*).[27] At schools, progressive teachers encourage students to use their "real names" (*honmyo*). But it is often the case in the corporate world or at workplaces that Korean resident aliens are dissuaded from using ethnic names by informal administrative guidance. Above all, the imposition of "commonly used names" upon *zainichi* often evokes the memories of Japanese colonial rule over Korea, when the Japanese government coerced the Korean population into adopting Japanese-like surnames.

In addition to alteration of the main inscription, the 1990 relocation proposal further called for not only the removal of a plaque adjacent to the memorial that explains the background of the memorial's construction in English, Korean, and Japanese but also the erasure of the historical description of Japan's colonial rule that is written in Hangul on the memorial's back side. In place of the present inscription, the new proposal suggested that the following be written in both Hangul and Japanese: "This memorial was constructed in order to enshrine the souls of those from the Korean Peninsula (*chosen hanto no katagata*) who fell victim to the atomic bomb dropped on Hiroshima on August 6, 1945, and also to pray for eternal world peace."

For the younger generation of Koreans, the defacing of colonial memories implied by the elimination of the engravings and also by the proposed removal of the plaque suggested delimiting the possibilities of their politics in the present and the future. Kim, too, angrily contended that "to retain [the present inscription together with the explanatory plaque] means to keep such words as forceful mobilization, civilian war workers, soldiers, and so on—namely, those things that are upsetting and unacceptable for high-ranking city officials. We simply wrote down what is obvious to us (*tozen no koto*). The fact that we are Koreans will be erased. The fact of forceful mobilization will be erased. How could we continue to live here in Japan? It truly makes me feel anxious about our future."

This anxiety of Korean resident aliens regarding their future is a fundamental uneasiness about the fact that their existence is not and cannot be represented in the world. Takeda Seiji, a *zainichi* literary critic, described it as a form of dysphemia or aphasia.[28] Adrienne Rich called such dismay at not being able to find oneself in the authoritative discourse a "psychic disequilibrium."[29] A Korean woman survivor referred to a similar condition of her existence as "ghostly" (*yurei mitai na mon*).

The purpose of retaining the inscriptions on the present memorial was therefore not to pledge loyalty to the homeland. Rather, the purpose of transferring the inscriptions intact onto the official territory of memorialization was to help reverse the very suppression of "the suppressed," of "the excluded," with all the agony and enmity that it might evoke. Moreover, such a move would open up an opportunity to reclaim the materiality of memory—that is, to recover the "matters" of memory, with which individuals might articulate their being. "Their" historical "truths," the irreducible and unassimilable whole of historical self-evidence—Kim's "what is obvious to us"—would be allegorically interjected onto society's memory processes through this space of rupture.

It should be noted, however, that such desires to restore the materiality of difference in discourses on the Hiroshima holocaust do not necessarily mean that these *zainichi* believe that one historical truth must be excavated in order to replace another. Likewise, to say that one believes in the urgency of recuperating certain cultural practices is not the same as to say that there is an authentic and essential cultural heritage that inherently unifies Koreans and differentiates them from others. Perhaps the younger generations of Korean resident aliens themselves most acutely sense the strategic quality of their politics of difference. As mentioned earlier, the Korean women are aware that aspirations for "authentic" Korean familial relations can, in turn, create totalizing and oppressive conditions of male domination and patriarchy. The sociologist Jung, introduced earlier, told me, as many others often did, that "ethnicity" (*minzoku*) has no ultimate significance in life. "Though I may sound contradictory," she claims, "I feel that in order to be able to say that *minzoku* is insignificant, we must first have it."

I want to make it clear that this claim only bears an apparent resemblance to what Gayatri Chakravorty Spivak once called, in referring to feminists' deployment of the category of woman, "strategic essentialism." To mobilize political alliances around a shared narrative about how one has been interpellated historically is not the same as claiming solidarity based on ahistorical categories of difference that are assumed to be naturally and prediscursively given.[30] Nor is it the same as subscribing to the idea that historical knowledge can exist prior to discursive mediations and that past events can reveal their inherent significance in and of themselves. The names, language, ethnic cuisine, ancestral rites, and the recently excavated historical knowledge that has long been concealed—all such materialities of differences matter to the extent that they are endangered and in urgent need of discursive restitution.

Unsettling Memories: Some Concluding Thoughts

As we can see from the controversy over the Korean memorial's relocation, the narrative space of Hiroshima constitutes a discursive border where atom bomb memories are produced by multiple, polyglot elements. It is a site where narratives about the past, the status of self, the condition of the nation, and the future of the world come together and compete. The pilgrims and storytellers transform the Korean atom bomb memorial and other sites of memories into components of history in dialectical praxis. Rather than the sublime object of sacred prayers, or the frozen site of a past catastrophe, Hiroshima is a moving crossroads where things and people ceaselessly intermingle, where the voices of the dead intersect with the outcries of the living. It is a hybrid space where travelers and their heterogeneous voices continue to encounter one another.

Yet the crossings of memory boundaries often entail pain and violence. Immediately after the announcement of the 1990 relocation plan, arsonists attacked the Korean atom bomb memorial. Many *zainichi* perceived this as yet another assault inflicted upon their own physical bodies. Furthermore, just as the choice between remaining a Korean resident alien and naturalizing to become a Korean-Japanese is never understood as a choice between symmetrical alternatives for many ethnic Koreans, border crossings are not smooth and free movements between two or more interchangeable spaces or identically weighted choices.

Like the state forces that police national borders, the boundaries that configure the discourse of authentic memorialization, which exclude and domesticate heterogeneous and ambiguous elements, are invisible to most people until they are encountered directly. But for those in subjugated positions, the boundary walls reveal themselves with clear force and violence. Inasmuch as they are effects of power, any attempt to challenge or blur boundaries is inevitably accompanied by conflict and entails much pain and brutality.

In sum, the politics of ethnic memory over the 1990 relocation issue were intensified by a seemingly paradoxical sense of alarm: the very remembering of the past might be tantamount to closing the possibilities of the present and aborting the future. Protests against the 1990 relocation plan ought to be understood within the context of this particular dialectics of memory—one in which struggles for the future became translated into assaults against memories about the past. Simultaneously, injustices to memories of and about earlier generations in turn become construed as an attack, above all, on the contemporary history of ethnic political struggles. Here, the commonsensical directionality of memory becomes reversed. It is not simply an effort to make the past account for the present; rather, it is an effort in which present attempts to wrest ethnic differences from the homogenizing processes of society work through time to recover memories of struggles against colonial and postcolonial domination. Out of this struggle came an awareness that settling accounts of the past in the manner that the city proposed would produce a conciliatory remembering that would placate the yet critical memories that continue to constitute present ethnic politics and would once again render them invisible to mainstream Japanese society.

Walter Benjamin once wrote about the dialectics of historical knowledge: "[E]very image of the past that is not recognized by the present as one of its own concerns threatens to disappear irretrievably."[31] Those who objected to the 1990 relocation plan sought to situate memories of colonialism and discrimination in official historical representations in such a way that they would be the present's "own concerns"—that is, so that these critical ethnic memories would not become assimilated into the nation's "homogeneous, empty" history of linear progress but would instead "place the present in the critical position."[32]

In May 1996, the Korean atom bomb memorial had not been relocated. The earlier proposal, a plan devised solely by top-level representatives of Mindan and Soren, suggested the addition of three Chinese characters that read *chosonsaram*, or *chosenjin* in Japanese, and placing it alongside the word *hangusaram*, or *kankokujin* in Japanese. The memorial would then explicitly refer to the nationals of two separate countries. The plan was not executed because of disagreements over the rewriting of the memorial's other inscriptions. Yet even if the memorial had been relocated under this latest proposal, if it had not in some way addressed not only the history of Japanese colonialism but, more important, postwar failures to deal with that history, it would once again have contributed to the taming of ethnic memories, effacing critical differences in remembering. In a similar way, no matter how inadequate they might appear to be, the Japanese politicians' recent official admissions of and apologies for Japan's colonial and military aggressions—that is, their attempts to move beyond amnesia and silence—pose serious threats to heretofore marginalized memories. To cope with the current reprogramming and domesticating of popular memories requires a dialectics of memory in which the long-suppressed past can be "redeemed" without compromising its power to challenge yet another hegemony of remembering and forgetting.

Notes

1. See, for instance, Hiroshima-ken Chosenjin Hibakusha Kyogikai 1979.
2. See Kang and Kim 1989; Field 1993; and Lee and De Vos 1981.
3. My critique of the totalizing concept of Korean ethnicity owes much to feminist writers who have examined the essentialist, determinist, and foundationalist notions of "community," "identity," and "subject." They have argued that these politically salient configurations should be conceptualized as, for instance, multifaceted locations for struggles, differentiations, and displacements. See Martin and Mohanty 1986; de Lauretis 1986, 1990; and Anzaldua 1987, among others.
4. Young 1993 (6–7). Despite this Durkheimian overtone in his discussion of collective consciousness, James E. Young's series of studies on the Jewish Holocaust monuments (1988, 1993) nonetheless offers many insights relevant to the study of Hiroshima's memorials. These include an attentiveness to the ways in which the performative dimension of memorial icons intervenes in present politics and the current history-making process.
5. Elsewhere, I discuss various other sites over which there is a tension between attempts to domesticate memories of the Hiroshima holocaust and resistance to such dominant forces. See Yoneyama 1994 and forthcoming.

6. Lisa Lowe (1991) makes a similar argument for the importance of capturing such a duality in ethnic processes in her analysis of Asian-American women writers. Arguing for the criticalness of the dialectical negotiation between an attempt "to organize, resist, and theorize *as* Asian Americans" and the task of warning against "the risks of a cultural politics that relies upon the construction of sameness and the exclusion of differences" (28), Lowe proposes, following Ernesto Laclau and Chantal Mouffe, a coalition politics that can be organized along the multiple axes of oppositions based upon gender, sexuality, class, and other differences.

7. Among the variety of nuances the German expression may convey, I borrow it here to indicate one of the senses to which Adorno draws attention—namely, that coming to terms with the past is a process of domestication. Adorno 1986 (115).

8. For more detail, see especially the booklet published by a voluntary research group composed of journalists and schoolteachers concerned with the issue of minority students' status (Pika Shiryo Kenkyusho and Zenkoku Zainichi Chosenjin Kyoiku Kenkyu Kyogikai 1989; referred to hereafter as "Pika and Zenkoku 1989"). It is the first accessible and sizable resource collection concerning the Korean atomic bomb victim issue, to which this chapter, too, is much indebted.

9. *Chugoku shinbun,* April 19, 1990.

10. Pika and Zenkoku 1989 (55).

11. A local newspaper article, however, revealed that the city has in fact allowed construction of at least seven memorials inside the park since the announcement of the 1967 regulation (*Chugoku shinbun,* May 17, 1988).

12. Pika and Zenkoku 1989 (84–85). This administrative attitude has not changed even under the new mayor, Hiraoka Takashi, a former journalist who had been regarded as sympathetic to Korean atom bomb survivors' issues. See Minzoku Sabetsu to Tatakau Renraku Kyogikai 1991 (13).

13. Pika and Zenkoku 1989 (31).

14. In her sophisticated analysis of the politics of the Vietnam Veterans Memorial, Marita Sturken draws attention to how "memorials" differ from "monuments," in that the former tend to be associated with images of loss. Following other observers of the memorial, such as Arthur Danto and Charles Griswold, Sturken argues that "Monuments are not generally built to commemorate defeats," but rather, "the defeated dead are remembered in memorials. While a monument most often signifies victory, a memorial refers to the life or lives sacrificed for a particular set of values" (Sturken 1991, 118). Arguing against such a rigid distinction, Young (1993, 3) stresses the interchangeability of the two.

15. Unlike the situation at the time of the Showa emperor's expression of "regrets" for the past, the Japanese government was this time assigned concrete and urgent tasks with which to prove that the emperor's public statement had meant something. These included, for example, improvement of the Korean residents' legal status as well as adequate support for and compensation to Korean victims of the Asia–Pacific War, including Korean colonial subjects deserted in Sakhalin and atomic bomb survivors who returned to Korea.

16. See also Hashimoto 1990. I am grateful to Toyonaga Keisaburo for calling my attention to Hashimoto's essay.

17. There are numerous personal accounts and memoirs regarding the mistreatment of Koreans in the aftermath of the bombing. See, for instance, Hiroshima-ken Chosenjin Hibakusha Kyogikai 1979; Hiraoka Takashi 1983; and Chu Soku 1990.

18. Nakajima, public lecture, "Zaikan hibakusha mondai no rekishi to genjo," May 28, 1989, Hiroshima YMCA.

19. *Chugoku shinbun,* August 1, 1990.

20. Cf. Nakai Kiyomi 1989.

21. Hong 1986 (4–5).

22. Benjamin 1969 (255).

23. During the past decade, critics such as Clifford (1988), Marcus and Fischer (1986), and Rosaldo (1989), among others, have criticized the anthropological notion of culture as a bounded and timeless entity that prescribes actions and emotions. See also Dirks 1992 for an important discussion of how the above concept of culture was produced and has functioned in the contexts of colonial rule.

24. It is important to note that I am observing the narratives produced by those Korean resident aliens who are living in an environment in which it is not possible to organize their lives around a sizable and institutionally distinguishable community, such as ethnic language schools or a "Koreatown." See Maruyama 1983 for a historical and sociological observation of the Korean community in Hiroshima.

25. Jung 1986 (219).

26. Fischer 1986 (208).

27. According to a 1984 survey in Kanagawa prefecture, about two-thirds of the Korean residents there usually or exclusively use their *tsumei,* whereas about 20 percent use both, depending on the occasion. The survey also shows that whereas more than 90 percent of Korean residents have two names, more than 80 percent of Chinese residents in Kanagawa use only their Chinese surnames. See Rekishigaku Kenkyu Kai and Nihonshi Kenkyu Kai 1985 (41) and Kinbara Samon et al. 1986 (180). Ethnic Koreans who had been forced to adopt Japanese family names at the time of naturalization recently demanded in a series of lawsuits that the government recognize their ethnic names. See Minzokumei o Torimodosu Kai 1990. This is a path for emancipation envisioned differently from the one I describe here—namely, one that pursues civil rights not as nationals but as non-national residents.

28. Takeda 1989 (13–15).

29. Quoted in Rosaldo 1989 (ix).

30. Elsewhere, Spivak has also referred to the writing practices of Indian subaltern historiography as "a strategic use of positivistic essentialism in a scrupulously visible political interest" (1988, 13). For a further critique of essentialist notions of political identification, see Judith Butler 1993. I am also grateful to Sylvia Yanagisako for providing me with useful suggestions.

31. Benjamin 1969 (255).

32. Benjamin, quoted in Buck-Morss 1989 (338).

References

Adorno, Theodor W. 1986. "What Does Coming to Terms with the Past Mean?" In *Bitburg in Moral and Political Perspective,* ed. Geoffrey H. Hartman, 114–29. Bloomington: Indiana University Press.

Anzaldúa, Gloria. 1987. *Borderlands/La Frontera: The New Mestiza.* San Francisco: Aunt Lute Book Company.

Benjamin, Walter. 1969. *Illuminations.* Trans. Harry Zohn. Ed. Hannah Arendt. New York: Schocken Books.

Buck-Morss, Susan. 1989. *The Dialectics of Seeing: Walter Benjamin and the Arcades Project.* Cambridge, MA: MIT Press.

Butler, Judith. 1993. *Bodies That Matter: On the Discursive Limits of "Sex."* New York: Routledge.

Chu Soku. 1990. *Hibaku chosenjin kyoshi no sengoshi: Saigetsu yo! Ariran yo!* (The postwar history of an atom-bombed Korean teacher: Oh, the passage of time!), Tokyo: Akashi Shoten.

Clifford, James. 1988. *The Predicament of Culture: Twentieth-Century Ethnography, Literature, and Art.* Cambridge, MA: Harvard University Press.

de Lauretis, Teresa. 1986. "Feminist Studies/Critical Studies: Issues, Terms and Contexts." In *Feminist Studies/Critical Studies,* ed. Teresa de Lauretis, 1–19. Bloomington: Indiana University Press.

———. 1990. "Eccentric Subjects: Feminist Theory and Historical Consciousness." *Feminist Studies* 16, no. 1 (spring): 115–50.

Dirks, Nicholas B., ed. 1992. *Colonialism and Culture.* Ann Arbor: University of Michigan Press.

Field, Norma. 1993. "Beyond Envy, Boredom, and Suffering: Toward an Emancipatory Politics for Resident Koreans and Other Japanese." *Positions* 1, no. 3: 640–70.

Fischer, Michael M.J. 1986. "Ethnicity and the Post-Modern Arts of Memory." In *Writing Culture: The Poetics and Politics of Ethnography,* ed. James Clifford and George E. Marcus, 194–233. Berkeley: University of California Press.

Foucault, Michel. 1989. "Film and Popular Memory." Trans. Martin Jordin. In *Foucault Live (Interviews, 1966–84),* trans. John Johnston, ed. Sylvère Lotringer, 89–106. New York: Semiotext(e).

Hashimoto Manabu. 1990. "Hiroshima no heiwa shisei o tou: Hibaku 45 shunen o mukaeta Hiroshima no genjo." (Interrogating Hiroshima's peace administration: Hiroshima's situation in the 45th commemorative year), *Jokyo to shutai,* no. 177 (September): 42–59.

Hiraoka Takashi. 1983. *Muen no kaikyo: Hiroshima no koe, hibaku chosenjin no koe,* (The deserted strait: voices of Hiroshima, voices of the atom-bombed Koreans), Tokyo: Kage Shobo.

Hiroshima-ken Chosenjin Hibakusha Kyogikai, ed. 1979. *Shiroi chogori no hibakusha,* (Hibakusha in white Chogori), Tokyo: Rodo Junposha.

Hon Tae-pyo. 1986. "Josho: Zainichi no atarashii rekishi wo kizamu wakamonotachi no shimon onatsu kyohi," (Introduction: The youths' refusal of fingerprinting creates a new history of the resident aliens). In Jung Yeong-hae, ed., *Ore shimon oshite hennen,* 1–8.

Jung Yeong-hae, ed. 1986. *Ore shimon oshite hennen: Shimonkyohi to jodai no joda: hatsugen.* (I didn't give my fingerprints: Fingerprinting refusal and statements by the teenagers), Tokyo: Akashi Shoten.

Kang, Chae-on, and Kim Tong-hun 1989. Zainichi Kankoku/Chosenjin: rekishi to tenbo (Koreans in Japan: past and future), Tokyo: Rodo Keizaisha.

Kinbara Samon et al. 1986. *Nihon no naka no Kankoku/Chosenjin, chugokujin: Kanagawa kennai zaiju gaikokujin jittai chosa yori.* (Koreans and Chinese in Japan: From the survey of resident aliens in Kanagawa prefecture), Tokyo: Akashi shoten.

Lee, Changsoo Lee, and George De Vos. 1981. *Koreans in Japan: Ethnic Conflict and Accommodation.* Berkeley: University of California Press.

Lowe, Lisa. 1991. "Heterogeneity, Hybridity, Multiplicity: Marking Asian American Differences." *Diaspora* (spring): 24–44.

Marcus, George E., and Michael M.J. Fischer. 1986. *Anthropology as Cultural Critique: An Experimental Moment in the Human Sciences.* Chicago: University of Chicago Press.

Martin, Biddy, and Chandra Talpade Mohanty. 1986. "Feminist Politics: What's Home Got to Do with It?" In *Feminist Studies/Critical Studies,* ed. Teresa de Lauretis, 199–212. Bloomington: Indiana University Press.

Maruyama Koichi. 1983. "Toshi no naka no mainoriti: Zainichi chosenjin no sengo seikatsu to bunka." (Urban minorities: The postwar lifestyle and culture of the resident alien Koreans). In *Hiroshima shinshi: Toshi bunka,* (New History of Hiroshima: urban culture) ed. Hiroshima-shi, 302–90. Hiroshima: Hiroshima-shi.

Minzokumei o Torimodosu Kai, ed. 1990. *Minzokumei o torimodoshita nihonseki chosenjin: Watashitachi no namae/uri irumu,* (The naturalized Koreans who reclaimed their ethnic names), Tokyo: Akashi Shoten.

Minzoku Sabetsu to Tatakau Renraku Kyogikai. 1991. *Zenkoku mintoren nyusu,* no. 56 (June).

Nakai Kiyomi. 1989. *Teijyu gaikokujin to komu shuninken: 70man nin o shimedasu ronri.* (Permanent resident aliens and their rights to hold public office: the logic for excluding 700,000 people), Tokyo: Takushoku Shobo.

Pika Shiryo Kenkyusho and Zenkoku Zainichi Chosenjin Kyoiku Kenkyu Kyogikai, eds. 1989. *Shiryo: Kankokujin genbaku giseisha ireihi,* (Sources: the Memorial for the Korean atomic bomb victims), Hiroshima: Hi no Kai.

Rekishigaku Kenkyu Kai and Nihonshi Kenkyu Kai, eds. 1985. *Koza nihon rekishi,* (Japanese History Anthology), Vol. 13. Tokyo: Tokyo Daigaku Shuppankai.

Rosaldo, Renato. 1989. *Culture and Truth: The Remaking of Social Analysis.* Boston: Beacon Press.

Spivak, Gayatri Chakravorty. 1988. "Subaltern Studies: Deconstructing Historiography." In *Selected Subaltern Studies,* ed. Ranajit Guha and Gayatri Chakravorty Spivak, 3–32. Oxford, United Kingdom: Oxford University Press.

Sturken, Marita. 1991. "The Wall, the Screen, and the Image: The Vietnam Veterans Memorial." *Representations* 35 (summer): 118–42.

Takeda Seiji. 1989. "Kurushimi no yurai," (The origin of suffering). In *Yume no gaibu* (The dreams' exterior), 13–15. Tokyo: Kawade Shobo Shinsha.

Yoneyama, Lisa. 1994. "Taming the Memoryscape: Hiroshima's Urban Renewal." In *Remapping Memory: The Politics of Timespace,* ed. Jonathan Boyarin. Minneapolis: University of Minnesota Press.

———. Forthcoming. *The Dialectics of Memory/Hiroshima.* Berkeley: University of California Press.

Young, James E. 1988. *Writing and Rewriting the Holocaust: Narrative and the Consequences of Interpretation.* Bloomington: Indiana University Press.

———. 1993. *The Texture of Memory: Holocaust Memorials and Meaning.* New Haven, CT: Yale University Press.

Zaikan Hibakusha Mondai Shimin Kaigi, ed. 1988. *Zaikan hibakusha mondai o kangaeru.* Tokyo: Gaifusha.

11

Were We the Enemy?

American Hibakusha

SODEI Rinjiro

At 8:15 A.M. on August 6, 1945, Hiroshima looked bright in the summer sunshine from the B–29 bomber, *Enola Gay*. A moment later, the city would be engulfed in a hellish conflagration. Thousands of American citizens, the children of Japanese parents in the United States, were living there at the time, but there is no evidence that the crew members of the *Enola Gay* had any knowledge of this. The matter had never been discussed among military personnel on the island of Tinian, the launching base of the *Enola Gay,* nor had it ever come up during planning discussions in Washington, where the decision to drop the atomic bomb on Hiroshima was made. The *Nisei* (American-born children of Japanese immigrants to the United States), together with approximately a dozen downed U.S. pilots imprisoned in Hiroshima, were "forgotten Americans."

Among the 350,000 citizens of Hiroshima who experienced the evil fire that humankind itself had created, several thousand suffered an additional tragic irony: the atomic bomb was a creation of the very country of their birth. Of these victims, a great many died immediately or within the first few days. Quite a few nevertheless survived.

Japanese Immigrants in America

How did so many Japanese-Americans happen to be living in wartime Hiroshima? The answer goes back to the late nineteenth century, to the time when Japanese began to emigrate to the United States in large numbers. At that time, and in the decades that followed, Hiroshima Prefecture sent the highest number of emigrants to America. According to 1927 Japanese government statistics, over the years, a total of 67,155 overseas Japanese had originated from Hiroshima. Of these, 22,101 were living in Hawaii, 25,206 in the continental United States, and 5,329 in Brazil.[1]

Japanese immigrants to the United States experienced racial discrimination from the very beginning. Discrimination against immigrants was most severe on the West Coast, where Asian immigration was concentrated. The ever-growing numbers of Chinese and, eventually, Japanese immigrants provoked public protest from the general populace, especially from organized labor. Between 1908 and 1924, only family members of Japanese who had already immigrated were allowed into the country.

Once the immigration law was revised in 1924, emigration from Japan to the United States was finished. In November 1922, two years before immigration was banned, the U.S. Supreme Court ruled in *Ozawa* v. *United States* that "Japanese have no right to be naturalized as U.S. citizens." First-generation immigrants, the *Issei,* thus became "ineligible aliens." And the Immigration Act of 1924, sometimes referred to as the "anti-Japanese immigration law," which prohibited the immigration of all "aliens ineligible for citizenship," virtually outlawed the introduction of new blood into the Japanese immigrant community.[2]

The Issei, although denied the right to be naturalized or to own land—their most important means of livelihood—continued to make efforts to achieve some gains in the United States. Their children who had been born in the United States were growing up as American citizens. Many Issei were also strongly influenced by the culture and spirit of Meiji Japan.

Their desire to communicate in their own native language with their English-speaking children, and to pass on to them the elements of Japanese culture, led the Issei to establish Japanese schools in many Japanese communities. More Nisei girls than boys were sent to Japan to be educated. Issei parents, perhaps fearful of the "Americanization" of their daughters, hoped that they would acquire the "beautiful virtues" of Japan. Indeed, many Issei parents of sons specifically listed "education in Japan" as a qualification for prospective daughters-in-law. A former teacher of the Hiroshima Mission School (Jogakuin) observed that it was widely believed that a girl could "marry into a family one class higher" back in the United States if she could add "excellent education in Japan" to her basic education in the United States.[3]

Issei parents saw little hope for their children's future in the United States when, in the midst of the Great Depression, even American college graduates could not find work. Some, indeed, were selling apples on the street at two for five cents. Not a few Nisei were sent to Japan by parents who sincerely believed that their children would have better employment prospects there after receiving a Japanese education. These "Americans educated in Japan" were called *Kibei* Nisei.

Other Issei also reasoned that their children should be brought up in Japan from the beginning because, unable to find a good future for themselves in the United States, they would eventually go to Japan anyway. The "Kibei Nisei" reached almost 30,000 as of January 1929. Of these 30,000 Nisei, 4,805, or 16 percent, were living in Hiroshima Prefecture. Their ages ranged from one to thirty, but 3,803 of these 4,805 students—that is, nearly 80 percent—were attending elementary and middle schools.[4]

The *Tatsuta Maru,* which sailed for Japan in August 1941, was crowded with Issei going to their hometowns and with Nisei visiting the country of their parents for the first time. Incidentally, Iva Toguri, a Nisei who, as "Tokyo Rose," was later to be charged with treason, also arrived in Yokohama by ship on July 24 of the same year to visit her sick aunt. Few passengers at that time experienced any anxiety that they might be unable to return to the United States. The attack on Pearl Harbor caught them by surprise.

Executive Order 9066, signed by President Franklin D. Roosevelt on February 19, 1942, was to alter the destiny of more than 120,000 Americans of Japanese ancestry on the West Coast. This presidential decree designated the entire western half of the states of Washington, Oregon, and California, as well as the southern half of Arizona, as "military areas" and gave the secretary of war the authority to remove from this region those who did not have permission, based on "military necessity," to be there. Under this order, all those who had "even one drop of Japanese blood" were evacuated from the Pacific Coast. They were shipped off to concentration camps in the desert.[5]

Roosevelt's order applied not only to the Issei, whose classification was changed from "ineligible for citizenship" to "enemy aliens." It also applied to the Nisei, who, as American citizens, should have enjoyed all the guarantees of the Constitution. Lands on which the Issei had built their livelihood were marked "Off Limits," and they were forced to leave their homes and places of business. The U.S. Army, and then the War Relocation Authority (WRA), and often the inmates themselves built camps to confine 120,000 people.

While their "fellow countrymen" in the United States were locked up in the "camps," what must have been the feelings of those Americans of Japanese parentage who were leading *their* lives in the "enemy country" of Japan across the Pacific? Among those who left Japan when they were very young and were still in early childhood when the war broke out, there are

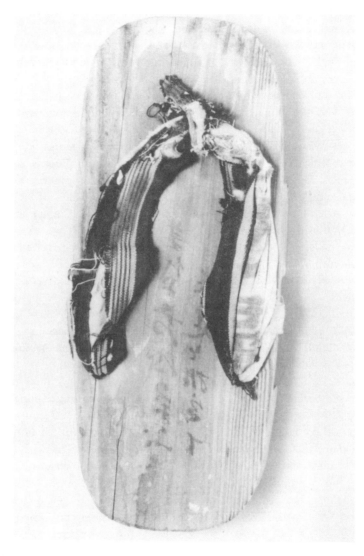

Wooden shoe of Inoue Miyoko, a high school student. Miyoko, like all high school students by 1945, was mobilized for labor. She and her classmates, none of whom survived, were demolishing houses to create a firebreak when the atomic bomb fell. Her mother, Tomiko, searched for her for three months after the bombing but found only her left shoe. The marks of her toes, worn into the wood, are still visible, as is her name. Miyoko was in the same age group as most of the Nisei hibakusha, and probably one or two of her classmates were American citizens. (Kaz Suyeishi and Jane Ishigame were in different Hiroshima high schools at the time.) Inoue Tomiko donated this shoe to the Hiroshima Peace Memorial Museum on July 16, 1963. (Ienaga, 4.168.)

some who remember that they were asked by their teachers to remain after the morning assembly and were interrogated about mail they might have received from the United States. Many, however, were apparently able to go on living normal lives. Burying deep in their minds the knowledge of their American birth and citizenship, they sought to behave like children who had been born in Japan. Like other children in Japan then, they grew up to become military-minded young people. Quite a few young Nisei boys, filled with the hope that someday they would triumph over American enemy soldiers, lived as Japanese and learned judo and kendo.

Nisei who were in their teens when the war broke out had to make a more conscious effort to prove their loyalty to Japan. People around them were more aware that they had been born in America. Japanese could afford to feel some generosity toward the Nisei in the early days of the war, while Japan was winning one victory after another. But once Japan began to lose the war, they began to treat "American-borns" as if they were spies. For this reason, Nisei had to demonstrate faithfulness to the Emperor and loyalty to the Nation. It was not unusual for American-born youth of Japanese parentage to apply for the pilot-training corps, the Naval Academy, or the Military Academy.

The Issei in the United States were asked to swear loyalty to a country that refused them citizenship and interned them. Furthermore, the federal government demanded not only that Nisei swear allegiance to the United States but that they prove their allegiance with their own blood by enlisting in the war effort. As many Nisei saw it, they were being forced to aim a gun at the motherland of their parents. The loyalty oath plunged Japanese in the camps into fear and confusion. In California's Manzanar Relocation Center, a riot broke out, and shootings caused quite a few casualties. Nine thousand Issei and Nisei were labeled "disloyal." Some Issei refused to sign the loyalty oath and demanded to be repatriated. Many Nisei also answered "No" and thereby surrendered their citizenship. Between September and October 1943, these resisters were branded "disloyal" and placed in isolation at Tule Lake, a camp located on the border between Oregon and California.

Some Victims of "Friendly Fire"

In August 1945, Sadako Obata was six months pregnant.[6] She lived only 500 meters from the hypocenter, in Nishikuken-cho. Because her husband was in military service and stationed in Hiroshima City, Sadako was living with her elder sister and year-old nephew. She was in the kitchen after breakfast when a blinding flash struck her eyes. She heard a tremendous noise and lost consciousness. When she came to, it was to find herself plunged in stygian gloom. Her body was pinned under the crushed house, and she could not move, for a piece of wood had skewered her cheek.

"Help!" Sadako heard her sister cry out; the cry was followed by screams from her nephew. With unbelievable agony, she finally succeeded in pulling the splintered wood from her cheek. Devouring flames were approaching, and the only thing she could do was to flee, leaving her sister and the child behind.

Sadako spent the night on a riverbank near Yokogawa, overcome by thirst. She drank some drops of the black rain that had started to fall. On the third day of her survival, she was carried by truck to her father's house in Kabe. At last, the wound on her face was treated (a large scar remains). Her husband, who had been exposed to the bombing at the parade ground, had suffered no apparent injury. He came to Kabe to find Sadako. Within about ten days, he began to spit blood and soon died.

Sadako's younger sister-in-law, a Red Cross nurse who had dressed her wound, also died. Sadako was left alone. She carried the bodies of her husband and sister-in-law into the hills for cremation. Her elder sister, who had somehow crawled out of the ruins by herself, managed to struggle to an aunt's house, only to die there shortly afterward. Her elder sister-in-law also perished.

Sadako was born in 1925, the daughter of a farmer in the small southern California town of San Juan, and came to Japan with her parents at the age of fourteen. Her parents returned to the United States shortly afterward, leaving Sadako in a girls' school with her elder sister. She later learned that her parents as well as her brothers and sisters had all been sent to Poston Relocation Center in Arizona.

To Yoshika Ishigame, a seventeen-year-old student at the time of the bombing, Japan had always remained an alien country.[7] If her grandfather had not decided to go back to Hiroshima after his retirement in 1938 and taken her with him, she probably would have spent her youth as Jane Ishigame in Jerome Relocation Center in Arkansas after the outbreak of the war between Japan and the United States. That's where her mother (born in Hiroshima Prefecture) and her five brothers and sisters ended up. Jane was born in Fresno, California. Her father, a Kibei Nisei from Hilo, Hawaii, had spent his adolescence in Japan and then returned to the United States. At the outbreak of the war, he was farming in Fresno. He was separated from his family and confined in a camp in Santa Fe, New Mexico.

In her fourth year at Yasuda Girls' School, Jane was mobilized to work at the needle-manufacturing factory of Kowa Sewing Machines, at the foot of the Yokogawa Bridge, only one kilometer from ground zero. There had been an air raid warning early in the morning. Just when she had returned to work at the machines after the "all clear" had sounded, Jane's surroundings lit up suddenly, as if a flash had been set off. That's all she remembers. When she recovered consciousness, she saw dead friends all around her. Only four or five managed to crawl out from beneath the crushed roof. She fled under large drops of black rain. Somewhere, she sat beside a hut with a friend until evening. There, she remembers being fed with the juice of cucumbers from a field. Then the two were taken by cart to what seemed like a rural elementary school. Many people around her died one after another. Then the father of a friend of hers who lived in a neighboring village happened to come by, searching for his own daughter. He saw her name tag and the badge on her breast. "Why, this is the Ishigame daughter!" he realized, and took her back with him. When she returned to her home, everyone was discussing plans for her funeral.

At that time, Kaz Suyeishi was in her nineteenth year, the year known to Japanese as *yakudoshi* and traditionally regarded as unlucky.[8] Kaz had been brought up so perfectly a native Japanese that it was natural for her to use that classical Japanese word, *yakudoshi.* For although she had been born in Pasadena, California, where her father was on business, the whole family returned to Japan within a year after Kaz's birth. During the war, Kaz completed advanced studies at a girls' high school and in 1945 was working as a member of a girls' volunteer corps at the Kannonmachi branch of Mitsubishi Heavy Industries. On the day of the atomic bombing, however, she happened to be resting at home, recovering from a fever. At the moment of the flash, Kaz covered her eyes with her hands and threw herself flat on the ground. Something fell from above and struck her very hard across the hips. Everything became terribly quiet. All was gray and gloomy. Then her mother appeared with her hair in disarray, followed by her father, who was bleeding from his head and arms. In the afternoon, her younger brother made his way back from Hiroshima First Middle School. His white shirt had been turned chocolate brown by blood. When the black rain started to fall, she and her younger brother rushed to the shelter, crying in panic, "Watch out! The enemy is spreading gasoline!"

Afterward, Kaz's gums began to bleed, and she suffered from a high fever. She strained herself taking care of her father and brother, who were both close to death. After they recovered, Kaz was bedridden for half a year.

Aya (Judy) Enseki was exposed to the bomb while walking from her house to a nearby field.[9] Thanks most likely to the parasol she happened to be carrying, she hardly suffered any burns. Her two-year-old American-born son was not hurt either. Perhaps that allowed Aya to remain calm enough to observe the mushroom cloud. "It was huge," she recalls, "with a pure white rim. But in the center, the glaring red smoke was seething turbulently."

Aya was born to a farm family near Delano, in central California, the fifth of eight children. Her maiden name was Judy Misono. In early 1942, before she was moved to a temporary assembly center in Fresno, Judy met and married a young Kibei Nisei who had been brought up in Hiroshima. It was sympathy rather than love, she says, that made the nineteen-year-old "country girl" decide to get married. In September of the following year, two months after she had given birth to a child in the Manzanar Relocation Center, Judy received notification that she and her husband were on the list of those allowed to return to Japan aboard the second exchange ship. Judy had no desire to go to Japan. America was home. But she left Manzanar with her child to accompany her husband, who renounced his American citizenship. Via Poston and Gila camps, both in Arizona, Judy left Phoenix for New York. From there, the *Gripsholm,* a Swedish vessel, took them to Goa, India, where they were transferred to the *Teia Maru,* a Japanese ship. They reached Hiroshima on a military ship in the spring of 1944. Shortly afterward, her husband was drafted and left to serve in Manchuria, where he was taken prisoner by Soviet troops.

While America was seething with excitement over imminent victory, some in the United States heard the news of the atomic bombing of Hiroshima with quite different emotions. They were the Issei and Nisei Americans of Japanese descent. As Michi Weglyn writes:

> For the Issei and Nisei still trapped in Tule Lake, the atomic incineration of a quarter of a million kindred fellow humans in Hiroshima ushered in the final nightmare stage in a sequence of injustices which had issued forth from the order to evacuate. One-third of the segregant population were either natives of Hiroshima or had relatives living there, hundreds of them war-stranded Nisei.[10]

In deep grief, the Hiroshima-born Issei prepared a memorial service for their children and other relatives whom they assumed had been obliterated by the atomic bomb.

Many Nisei GIs had families and relatives in Hiroshima who were killed by the atomic bomb, but there were those who counted themselves lucky enough to find parents, brothers, sisters, and relatives from whom they had long been parted and to share their military supplies with loved ones who were enduring hunger.

Sadako Obata was one of the beneficiaries. Sadako, injured by the atomic bomb during her sixth month of pregnancy, dragged herself to a relative's house in the countryside, where she delivered a baby girl in December. Having already lost her husband from radiation disease, she had to go through all the hardships alone. In the midst of her predicament, her brother, a Nisei soldier stationed in Japan, came to see Sadako. They met after seven years. "After that," she recalled, "people around me started to treat me much better because my brother brought food supplies and other various necessities with him."

Many Nisei living in Japan obtained jobs with the occupation forces. After finding a job in General Headquarters (GHQ) with the help of a cousin who worked as a civilian for the occupation forces, Judy Enseki left for Tokyo on the special occupation forces' train. For Nisei who still remembered enough English, there were many opportunities available to work as interpreters and in other positions.

Many Nisei chose not to remain in Japan for long. Fifty Nisei sailed on the President Line's S.S. *Marine Lynx,* which anchored at San Francisco on June 6, 1947. Among them was Sadako Obata. She had sailed after having given away her baby daughter, who was exposed to the bomb *in utero.* She landed alone on the shores of her motherland after an absence of seven years. The headline in the *Rafu Shimpo,* a Japanese-language newspaper in Los Angeles, described her return to the United States as follows: "Pitiful Miss Obata—Scars of Atomic Bomb Burn."[11]

Strangers in Their Homeland

The number of Nisei who left occupied Japan to return to their homeland, the United States, reached its peak in 1948. Of the perhaps five thousand who had returned to the United States by that year, three thousand went to Southern California.

These Nisei chose to seek a new life in the United States—the country that had given them birth and yet attacked them with the fire of Satan—for reasons that were complex. America was their homeland. But to those who had spent their formative years in Japan, it was nevertheless a foreign country. For many, Japan was still their spiritual home. Yet many willingly went back to the United States. The Japanese-American *hibakusha* who returned to their homeland were a minority in every sense of the word. In their own families, and in the small Japanese-American community, they were isolated and alienated. They were "forgotten Americans."

Pasadena-born Kaz Suyeishi went from Japan to Hawaii to study dressmaking. Doctors in Japan had once given up on her because her physical condition, caused by radiation exposure, was so precarious. But by the time she arrived in Hawaii, she was much improved. In Kaz's words:

> About a year after I came to Hawaii, large colored spots began to appear on my arms and I had a high fever and loss of weight. I thought it might have something to do with my being away from home. My doctors told me that I was homesick and I should go back to Japan. After a month of rest on another island, however, I became well again. After [I] return[ed] to Honolulu, a Caucasian man in his fifties pointed his finger at me and said, "You bombed Pearl Harbor and killed our boys." That really reminded me that I was a victim of the atomic bombing and I wanted to tell him that, but my English wasn't good enough. I struggled to communicate to him with all sorts of gestures but from that time on, I became depressed. A rash developed all over my body. Dermatologist and internist alike kept saying it was because I was homesick.
>
> My parents wrote and told me to come home but I had come all the way to Hawaii with no small pains. I was determined to see my birthplace and even go to college in America. In 1952, I did go to college in Pasadena, where I had been born. I was told that my English was the worst in the history of that college. At that time I was physically OK, but within six months I was once more in the same condition. As a part of my speech class, I had to go to different places and in my broken English introduce myself to many Americans. When I said I came from Hiroshima they all asked me about the atomic bomb. At first, I was a little hesitant but I told them honestly about my experiences. During the daytime, I wasn't consciously upset, but every night I had nightmares. I panicked. At first, my hands and feet were numb; then I had a pressing sensation around my heart and difficulty in breathing. These were the same symptoms I'd had in Hiroshima. Three days out of five I had to rest. This lasted for about a month, and finally, in 1955, I returned to Japan.

A Call to Commemorate the Day the Victims Escaped Death

On August 6, 1965, in *Rafu Shimpo* and *Kashu Mainichi,* the two Japanese-language newspapers in Los Angeles, the following notice appeared:

> "A call to all Hiroshima and Nagasaki A-Bomb Survivors"
> A meeting will be held to organize a Hibakusha friendship association (temporary name). Those who are interested, please contact:
> Shuji Okuno SY 1–1576 or
> Kaname Shimoda AN 2–3250

Kaname Shimoda was born in Sacramento and received his A-bomb baptismal when he was fourteen.[12] He had come back to the United States by virtue of his enlistment in the U.S. Army at the age of twenty-seven. According to Ernest Arai (Japanese name: Satoru), a Hawaii-born (Third-generation Japanese-American) *Sansei* who was also a hibakusha and a friend of Shimoda, the initial interest in forming a group was to have a drinking fellowship of kindred spirits.[13] These people had somehow come to believe that alcohol could lessen, if not cure, the aftereffects of the atomic bomb. Ernest Arai's father had had telltale spots on his body and was on the verge of death when he began drinking to excess. He claims that it was this drinking that cured him. Whatever the virtues of alcohol may have been, the hibakusha shared common problems and sought commiseration in an alien land. Fellow survivors of the mushroom cloud would get together and drink themselves into a stupor so they could forget the past.

According to Japanese custom, only men normally engage in drinking bouts. However, those who responded to the notice through telephone calls were predominantly women, Japanese-born wives of U.S. citizens rather than Kibei citizens. Tomoe Okai, who had lost her first husband to the bomb, had remarried a Nisei and in January 1962 had come to live in Los Angeles.[14] Immediately after her arrival in the United States, she felt herself growing physically weak, and in September of that year, she returned to Hiroshima for a thorough physical examination and diagnosis. While she was still in Japan, Tomoe began to suffer from the effects of the A-bomb, and the doctor in charge informed her that every internal organ was affected. An American doctor who examined her in the United States told Tomoe that she was merely suffering from nervousness, not from aftereffects of the A-bomb detonation.

When she talked to other similarly troubled hibakusha, Tomoe learned that others had found American doctors utterly lacking in knowledge and understanding of the atomic bomb syndrome. Needless to say, there was a language barrier, yet what made the hibakusha most uneasy was the ignorance and unsympathetic attitude of American doctors. Survivors tired easily; they often fainted; vomiting was frequent; they lost their balance easily; they had nosebleeds and bloody discharge that would not stop. These were some of the effects they all suffered—both the adult hibakusha and those of their children who had been exposed to the bomb.

The first meeting of the Hibakusha Friendship Group was set for a day toward the end of August 1965. Only six people gathered for the first meeting: Kaname Shimoda and Shuji Okuno, the initiators; Shimoda's friend Ernest Arai; and Tomoe Okai, Shin'ichi Kato, and Chizuko Farbatera. Before the war, Kato had been active as a newspaper reporter in Los Angeles. He was sent to Japan from the detention camp in Missoula, Montana, on the first exchange ship. He returned to Hiroshima and was working on the *Chugoku Shinbun,* a Hiroshima newspaper, when the bomb fell on the city. Both his younger brother and sister died in the holocaust.

After the war, he returned to Los Angeles to newspaper editing and compiling a history of Japanese immigrants in the United States. After his return, he had served as a vice president of the Hiroshima Ken Society (a fraternal association of those who have common roots in Hiroshima Prefecture), never revealing to anyone that he had gone through the A-bomb initiation. His rationale was that "these people [Japanese in America] hate to talk about the atomic bomb; they feel they are permitted to live in this country through the condescension of Americans and they should not mention anything that their benefactors do not wish to hear." The only reason Kato came to the meeting was that it had been organized as a gathering for small talk among fellow survivors. He had known Tomoe Okai since her Hiroshima days.[15]

The Hibakusha Discovered

The apprehension of the hibakusha is rooted in the knowledge that, at any time, latent effects of the bombing might strike. High medical expenses and the language handicap simply aggravate the situation. Seven years after the Hibakusha Friendship Group met, some hibakusha turned their efforts to seeking government financial assistance for their medical care.

With the help of a member of the staff of Congressman Edward Roybal, a Mexican-American representative from East Los Angeles, and Dr. Thomas Noguchi, East Los Angeles County chief medical examiner–coroner, they drafted legislation in 1972 to provide medical aid to the hibakusha in the United States. Bill H.R. 17112 was introduced in the House of Representatives but died soon after. On January 24, 1973, it was reintroduced in the Ninety-third Congress as H.R. 2894. Its provisions were as follows:

> To provide reimbursement to individuals for medical relief for physical injury suffered by them that is directly attributable to the explosions of the atomic bombs on Hiroshima and Nagasaki, Japan, in August 1945, and the radioactive fallout from those explosions.
>
> *Be it enacted by the Senate and the House of Representatives of the United States of America in Congress assembled* that (a) the Secretary of the Treasury shall make payments out of any money in the treasury not otherwise appropriated, to any citizen of the United States or any individual who has been admitted to the United States for permanent residence who establishes to the satisfaction of the Director of the Office of Emergency Preparedness that he suffered a physical injury that is directly attributable (1) to the explosions of either of the two atomic bombs in August 1945 or (2) to the radioactive fallout from those explosions. Such payments shall cover expenses incurred after the date of enactment of this Act in the United States, as defined by section 102 (2) of the Disaster Relief Act of 1970 (42 U.S.C. 4402

(2)), by such citizen or individual for the remedial treatment of such injury, including hospital, doctor, and similar medical expenses.[16]

This bill, which was introduced as an amendment to the Disaster Relief Act, provided reimbursement only for future medical expenses. It did not provide reimbursement for past expenditures, even though claimants may have been forced to sacrifice all their possessions to fight the disease. It did not include compensation for the loss U.S. citizens suffered by an act of war on the part of their own government. Yet even this modest bill died in committee.

Dr. Noguchi and the hibakusha then sought support at the state level. For this purpose, they established four new chapters of the hibakusha organization: San Francisco, East Bay, San Jose, and Sacramento. These were organized as the Northern California Committee of Atomic Bomb Survivors in the United States. In March 1974, Kanji Kuramoto became the president.

You Were Our Enemies!

A public hearing on the hibakusha aid bill was held in Los Angeles on May 4, 1974, before the California State Senate, Subcommittee on Medical Education and Health Needs. For the U.S. hibakusha, this was the first opportunity for those cursed by history to express publicly to their mother country their unique agony and desperation.[17]

Five hibakusha took the witness stand and testified on their unforgettable memories of that day and their continuing nightmares. Most attempted to suppress their emotions and testify as calmly as possible. Two of the five testified in Japanese. Dr. Thomas Noguchi, Los Angeles County chief medical examiner–coroner; Dr. Sidney Marks, associated with the Atomic Energy Commission; and Dr. Jack Kirschbaum, formerly with the Nagasaki Atomic Bomb Casualty Commission, also testified, as well as various state officials. Because many of the hibakusha and their supporters who attended the hearing did not understand English, a volunteer interpreter translated the testimony into Japanese.

Senator Mervyn Dymally, chair of the Subcommittee on Medical Education and Health Needs, presided. The first witness was Ernest Arai:

> I was born in January 1935, in Honolulu, Hawaii; my parents were also born in Hawaii. In 1940, my father had to leave for Japan and we all went with him. Later we came to the United States. I was ten years old, and I will never forget the atom bomb in Hiroshima. I was about two miles away from the center when I heard an airplane. I looked for it; a little boy's curiosity. I saw three spots in the sky, then suddenly I saw the spot explode and a few

seconds later I heard a loud noise. I didn't know how long I was unconscious, but I awoke in the dark. When I got home I discovered that half of my face, my left arm, my right hand, and my right leg were burned. My mother had to nurse me for four months. The next spring, a G.I. doctor examined me and found my white blood corpuscles were only 500. For a couple of years, I felt very weak and was prone to fainting spells. At twenty-one, I came to the United States and went to school for two years, then I started gardening, but I still felt weak. I could work only a couple of hours and had to rest for a couple of hours.... About five years ago, my brother opened a service station, so I became an auto mechanic.... One day I mentioned to one of my customers that we survivors have to pay all our medical bills with no aid from the government. He showed me his I.D. card which had entitled him to have all his medical bills paid by the United States government. His father was a Marine who had died in Vietnam, so he and his mother received these benefits ... his mother for the rest of her life. I began to wonder why we didn't have similar benefits. Had I been fighting for the Japanese I wouldn't have expected to receive anything even if I was an American citizen; but I am an American citizen who had not been allowed to return to the United States; I was only a little boy.

Arai's statement, which he tried to make as calmly as possible, meant that although he had no choice but to remain in Japan during the war, he was an American citizen. Therefore, he strongly believed he had the right to receive compensation for damages incurred as the result of acts of war conducted by his government.

The next witness was Tomoe Okai, president and founder of the Committee of Atomic Bomb Survivors in the U.S.A. She testified about her efforts to organize and obtain aid for the victims. She explained that, in Japan, the atomic bomb survivors received free medical treatment, whereas in the United States, none is provided. Hibakusha are forced to pay high fees for medical examinations and treatment, and American doctors lack experience in treating radiation illnesses. If a person is known to be a hibakusha, some life insurance companies will refuse to provide coverage. She stated that the distressed victims would be able to obtain some peace of mind if only they could be provided with the same kind of medical treatment for radiation illness that is provided to Japanese citizens. She concluded by saying, "I sincerely hope that this kind of medical care is given to the atom bomb survivors in the U.S. so that they may be able to live in peace with this understanding and cooperation."

Kanji Kuramoto, chairman of the Northern California Committee for Atomic Bomb Survivors, called the dropping of the atomic bomb "the greatest crime ever committed by human beings." He related his grief-stricken and futile attempts to locate his father in the ruins of Hiroshima. He stated that although he was a secondary victim of the bombing due to exposure to residual radiation, he had been blessed with good health and a happy family after returning to the United States. At first, he said, he had tried to forget the tragedy of the bombing, but he was now extending his efforts to help others because he understood the agony of the hibakusha, who were completely deserted by the American and Japanese communities. He noted that the fewer than one thousand survivors in the United States, less than half of whom live in California, face difficulties with English and are politically powerless. For thirty years, they have been ignored. "Please give them the aid they truly need. They cannot wait any longer. Please set up a program similar to the one instituted in Japan."

The last of the scheduled witnesses was George Morimoto. "I am speaking for my wife, Shigeko, who is too nervous to speak to you today." The statement he read on her behalf told of how she became a bomb victim as a twenty-one-year-old Japanese citizen. Not only had she lost the function of her right hand, but she had been discriminated against while trying to find work after coming to the United States. Her testimony revealed that the mental state of the hibakusha was one of powerlessness and disappointment. At that time, her husband's health insurance covered her medical expenses. But when he retired, there would be no insurance, and there was always the danger that he would lose his job. In Japan, Shigeko was able to receive free medical treatment at the Atomic Bomb Hospital, but now she was living in America, and it was almost impossible for her to go back to Japan for treatment.

After the California Senate public hearing of May 4, 1974, a working group was formed to draft a bill. Seven months later, the bill, dated December 2, was submitted under the title Senate Bill 15 (SB 15). Cosponsors were Senators Mervyn Dymally and Alfred H. Song, while State Assemblyman Bill Greene was listed as an author. S.B. 15 called for the establishment of an Institute for Research and Treatment for Nuclear Radiation, to treat victims of atomic radiation among the residents of California. These victims were to receive treatment at no cost.[18]

This bill was the product of much painstaking work. Although it acknowledged the existence of hibakusha by stating, "There exist approximately 500 citizens or permanent residents who suffer the physical and psychological effects of radiation," neither the word *Hiroshima* nor *Nagasaki* ever appeared. The bomb itself was not mentioned, and reference was made only to "any California resident who suffers from atomic radiation as a result of exposure to atomic rays due to any wartime activity."

These lacunae were intended to forestall the "Hiroshima complex," which lurks in the depths of the American mind. It was considered important not to pursue the question of responsibility on the part of the U.S.

government but to require free treatment of the illnesses caused by the atomic bombing. Therefore, the drafters chose not to mention Hiroshima or Nagasaki in the bill.

The second strategy employed in the bill's language was to combine the plight of hibakusha with that of workers in nuclear industries who were also exposed to radiation. Operation of nuclear power plants had already started in California. Therefore, the emergence of nuclear accident victims could be anticipated. In the State Senate public hearing, Dr. Franz Bauer, dean of the School of Medicine of the University of Southern California, testified as a "staunch supporter of nuclear development which was recognized to be safe and efficient"[19] but also stressed the need for a statewide comprehensive safeguard system for workers in the nuclear industry as well as for the general population, which might be subjected to radiation. It may be questionable logic to combine past victims (hibakusha) and future victims, making them all beneficiaries of medical treatment at public expense, but it was thought to be a wise strategy to define victims of nuclear radiation as widely as possible in an effort not to focus solely on nuclear weapons.

In hearings on the bill in Sacramento, hecklers shouted, "These people were our enemies!" Kuramoto recalls that, at that moment, he began to shiver uncontrollably. "What a statement!" he thought. "Were we the enemy? No, we couldn't be. We were born in America and we only happened to be in Japan when the war broke out and so couldn't just return to the U.S.A. How can they call us enemies when we were injured by our own country's A-bomb?" But more than one person called the hibakusha "enemy."[20]

"They were our enemies. Why should we help these people?" two legislators opined. In vain, another legislator stood up and said, "I have a friend who is an American-born Japanese. Because of the war, he wasn't able to return to the U.S. However, he's a U.S. citizen."[21] When the vote was taken, S.B. 15 was defeated, 7 to 4. The official reasons were, first, that the state did not have a big enough budget and, second, that the cost of compensating hibakusha should be borne by the federal government.

Two days later, on June 4, hibakusha went to remonstrate with the legislators who had voted against the bill, especially those who called them "enemies." However, they were met with hard hearts and the response, "I will not change my idea that you were our enemies. I do not see any need of changing it."[22]

Judy Enseki was one of those who spoke with the legislators. She explained her personal feelings about the bomb in an interview:

> How do I feel? I feel nothing. I don't have any feelings about the atom bomb, nuclear power, anything. You know, you cannot just isolate one kind of

weapon. To me no one weapon is bad. I wouldn't like to be burned with napalm or stabbed with a bayonet. Unless we become civilized to the point [that] we are outlawing man's inhumanity to man, that's where you have to start.

You are not going to make a gentlemen's agreement. You're not going to use any gas or insecticides, so you're not gonna use [the] atom bomb. . . . What is the purpose of it all, if you don't want to be kind to your fellow human beings? Choosing your weapons is not the way to go. That's missing the point altogether. Let's learn to reason together, not be so greedy. Let's understand each other's problems, you know. I am not bitter at all about the bomb. I don't know if it is because of [my] Japanese upbringing or my own philosophy which comes probably from my father, you know, my parents. In fact my parents were happy people.[23]

In the summer of 1976, Judy was director of the Suicide Prevention Center in Los Angeles, living life fully as an American citizen, apparently free from mental or physical injuries caused by the bomb.

Jane Ishigame (later Iwashika), who was severely injured by the bomb, returned to the United States alone in 1948:

From the beginning it was my intention to come back to the U.S. I had no emotional attachment to Japan. All my friends were dead. My elder sister went back to the States earlier, and my grandfather told me he had some money over here so I could go to school. I did go to school, but it didn't work out well. I had to work to earn my living. Then I got married and I couldn't continue school any more. I came back to Los Angeles in 1948 and married my husband in 1950. My health was always bad. I was in bad shape in the morning and evening, and this lasted until about 1960. I gave birth to my first child in 1951. I was still feeling sick. I did not think of the atomic bomb at all then. The second child, born in 1953, was a girl. Even if I didn't feel well, I would crawl to work by sheer willpower. I would probably have become permanently bedridden if my husband had been too nice to me. I had heart trouble until several years ago; even before marriage I went to a dermatologist because of [a] skin rash; my bowels are in bad condition and I cannot walk straight. In 1957 I was diagnosed as having tuberculosis and was hospitalized for seven months. I showed no sign of improvement and my doctor asked me why I came to the hospital. I had my teeth pulled out in 1960 and all my teeth you see are false teeth. My arm was dislocated from the shoulder by the bomb and I put it back myself but since I didn't do it right, I had to have an operation later and have a pin inserted to connect the bone and the muscles. I have myopia and presbyopia, and my nose is bad, too. I wonder what my husband saw in me to marry!

But everything has been free of charge for me because I have been working at a supermarket and I was covered by group medical insurance. However, the insurance does not cover you unless you work full-time, forty hours a week. In my work, I had to keep standing all day long.

My face was awful with lots of scars when I was in Japan. I thought of committing suicide many times when I saw young girls looking beautiful. I was only eighteen or nineteen then. I had no friends and I was very lonely. I had parents but they were almost in name only. But these are all things of the past. I am living now trying to find delight in my own children. Of course I have worries and hardships, but I think I can stay in bed if I feel sick. You have to believe in your own willpower. When someone tells you you are sick, you feel like a sick man, really. I don't believe in any religion, but I have faith in myself.

The meaning of the atomic bomb experience to myself, you ask? That really changed my whole life, I think. I don't know whether for the better or for the worse. But I think you can say it changed my life for the better in the sense that it made me capable of fighting for myself. When I get sick I scold myself and call myself a weakling. What do I think of the atomic bomb? That was war. You ought to think that way. It is the will of God that a person has to die. Christ had to die, too, didn't he? To die is not at all a scary thing.[24]

Jane Iwashika exhibits a kind of tranquillity of mind similar to the calm after a storm. However, the suffering she has been through since she crawled out of the hell brought about by the atomic bomb until she reached this state of mind is beyond imagination. With her strong will and the support of her understanding husband and two children, she has been able to survive. The problems of the hibakusha are most apparent in those who do not have such support and inner strength to help them go on living.

We have considered testimonies of hibakusha who are pursuing their lives with a positive outlook. By contrast, consider a voice filled with bitterness against the atomic bomb. This is an unusual fragment of testimony, because the deeper and more intense the grudge they feel, the less the hibakusha are inclined to speak. Sadako Shimazaki (formerly, Sadako Obata) was in her thirty-first summer in America. After giving up her daughter, an *in utero* hibakusha, for adoption, she has not gone back to Japan even once since she returned to her homeland.

I came back alone in 1947. After they got out of a camp in Poston, my father became a gardener in San Mateo, south of San Francisco, so I came home to join them. About then, my blood pressure dropped low and I felt giddy. That reminds me that my doctor told me that I had anemia after I gave birth to my child. After graduating from sewing school in Los Angeles, I married a Nisei here. His former wife had died after she gave birth to a child, so we had similar situations. It was as much as twenty-five years ago that we came to Monterey Park. Since my husband was running a grocery shop here, we had hoped to build a home. But we were the first Japanese who came here and racial discrimination was quite strong. Often intimidating letters were put into our mailbox. After [our] marriage, a girl was born first. She was well in the beginning, but her health deteriorated when she was about fifteen and she started to faint often.

Then a baby boy was born to us, but he had ill health since birth and his joints broke very easily because of hemophilia. He often stayed away from school, but he was smart and got A's in all his subjects. He is brilliant and in fact he graduated from UCLA on a scholarship. Now he is the one who is in the hospital.

I had two operations for breast cancer, and now I have developed cancer in my bones. Bone cancer gives me great pain but I am enduring it because I am told that I am not dying right away. I couldn't sleep at night because of the pain, so I went to a doctor and he told me I had cancer in many parts of my bones. There is a spot on my lung, but we do not know if it is also cancer. The fragments of glass that got into my body by the atomic bombing still come out of my body now and then, so it could be just one of them, too.

When I ask my doctor if my son's and my own ill health has something to do with the atomic bomb, he says, no, it doesn't. My son's hemophilia is a rare disease. Nobody else in my family ever had it. That disease is more commonly seen among the Russian and British royal families who have interbreeding marriages, so I hear it is also called a royal disease. We make jokes in our family, saying that we are a royal family. . . .

Fortunately, my medical expenses are covered by insurance from the Kaiser Foundation, thanks to my husband's work. My husband says jokingly that he might be kicked out of the program, but so far he hasn't. My son's case is different, though, so we have to pay hospital costs. Blood transfusion alone costs one thousand dollars a day. When we get free blood from someone, it's fine, but otherwise we have to buy blood. The operations have cost us thirty-four thousand dollars so far. This time, my son was supposed to stay in the hospital for only eighteen days, but actually today is the fourth week and I am worried. My son's disease is a "crippling disease," to which Medi-Cal applies, but this covers only fourteen days and I wonder if the doctor is going to give his approval to the necessity of an extension.

We have two more younger sons and our youngest is a daughter. All of them are fairly well. While I was giving birth to the children I was fine, but afterwards I had to commute to doctors because of gastric ulcer and gallstones. Doctors tell me I am nervous. Well, probably they are right, because X-rays show nothing wrong with my body. But I wonder why this kind of thing happens to me alone. It is all over now. I feel that if I had not been taken to Japan, this would never have happened to me, but I don't blame anyone. I went to the hospital many times, and when I found out I had cancer for the second time, I cried like mad, thinking, "this is all because of the atomic bomb."

The more you think about atomic bombs, the more scared you get. I wish there had never been atomic bombs. Any kind of bomb is terrible, but this one is especially scary because of what it does even after the explosion. There is no end to it. The future is very uncertain, and I get scared thinking what will happen. I have made great efforts to forget it and not to have bitterness against it after the war, but I think of it every time I get sick. Many questions arise inside my mind as to the atomic bomb—"Why Hiroshima? Why me?"[25]

"Don't eat the snow. It may contain radiation," worried adults said, but children inno-
cently ate snow at the epicenter anyway. As in America, Japan experienced a baby boom
after the war, as young adults started families and began to rebuild their lives. Parents
who were in Hiroshima and Nagasaki in August 1945, including American Nisei, worried that their experience as hibakusha would impart some terrible genetic taint to their
children, even those born after the war. (Sasaki Kenichiro photographed the ruined dome
scores of times between 1945 and his death in 1980. This photo is from 1950. Ienaga, 2.53.)

An Appeal to President Carter

Kanji Kuramoto wrote a long letter in January 1978 to President Jimmy
Carter requesting federal assistance for American hibakusha. It concluded
with the following words: "I am appealing to you to open your heart to aid
these people in the spirit of true love."[26]

To his surprise, a reply dated February 8, 1978 came from an unex-
pected quarter—Edward M. Featherstone, chief of the Japan desk in the
State Department. It began with the opening remark, "The White House has
asked me to respond to your letters to President Carter." Kuramoto wondered whether President Carter believed that the A-bomb survivors in the
United States were Japanese nationals. With this doubt in mind, he read
further and soon felt as if a wall had suddenly sprung up in his path:

It has been the longstanding policy of the United States Government, however, not to pay claims, even on an ex-gratia basis, arising out of the lawful
conduct of military activities by U.S. forces in wartime. This policy is based
on such considerations as the absence of any legal liability and difficulties in
locating, singling out and determining the relationship of the A-bomb experience to current health problems. Additionally, the very great length of time
which has passed since the bombing would cause practical difficulties for
any investigations.

In accordance with this longstanding policy, the United States has not, as
you know, been directly involved in the treatment of those who were affected
by the atomic bombs. This work has been primarily carried out by the Japanese Government and Japanese medical institutions.

This letter was an assertion of nonresponsibility of the United States
government toward the atomic bomb victims, on the grounds that the dropping
of the bombs was a justifiable act of war. If any medical aid was to be given,
such aid should therefore come from private sources or from welfare agencies.

A matter of grave concern was that the U.S. government might be holding the erroneous view that the U.S. atomic bomb survivors were Japanese
nationals. Feeling that dealing with the matter was beyond his ability,
Kuramoto immediately contacted Harry I. Takagi, then acting as the representative of the Japanese American Citizens League (JACL) in Washington.
Takagi wrote a letter of protest to the White House, as follows:

Dear Mr. President:
. . . Mr. Kuramoto is dissatisfied with Mr. Featherstone's reply, because
(1) Mr. Featherstone showed no recognition of the fact that he was dealing
with an American citizen, and (2) Mr. Featherstone's office appears to be one
which deals principally with the affairs of Japanese in Japan, rather than with
the rights of *American citizens of Japanese ancestry*. Mr. Kuramoto is not
alone in his feelings; we who are loyal American citizens wish to be so
recognized and treated as such, and not confused with citizens of a foreign
country.

The letter also mentioned that the Japanese government had initiated a
law to provide medical treatment free of charge to the atomic bomb survivors and continued, "If the Japanese government has seen fit to do this on a
humanitarian basis, can your Administration, with its emphasis on human
rights, do any less?"

For the U.S. A-bomb survivors to receive medical aid from the U.S.
government would be the ultimate proof of their citizenship. The concluding remark in the same letter—"If it is considered necessary to refer this
letter to another office, please do *not* refer [it] to the State Department
Office of Japanese Affairs"—carried the weight of history, felt deeply not

only by the atomic bomb survivors in the United States but by all Japanese-American citizens.

The White House never replied.

Washington Comes to Los Angeles

There were new grounds for hope for the hibakusha in 1974. Norman Y. Mineta became the first Nisei from the mainland elected to the House of Representatives. He became a cosponsor of the bill that had originally been introduced by Congressman Edward Roybal, and with his sponsorship, the Japanese American Citizens League supported passage of the bill.

Congressman George E. Danielson, from a Los Angeles suburb, assumed the chair of the Judiciary Subcommittee on Administrative Law and Governmental Relations dealing with the case. Through Danielson's efforts, the first congressional hearing on the hibakusha aid bill was held in Los Angeles on March 31, 1978, six years after it had first been introduced.

The subcommittee consisted of seven members, but only Danielson was present that day. On the platform with Danielson were two other congressional cosponsors of the bill, Edward Roybal and Norman Mineta. Danielson allowed them to question the witnesses, although neither was a member of the subcommittee. Since all three California Democrats were in favor of the bill, the hearing was conducted in a congenial atmosphere.

Seated in the front row were Kuniko Jenkins and her parents. Jenkins had experienced the atomic bomb explosion in Hiroshima at the age of nineteen, while she was on duty as an intern nurse at the Army Hospital in Hiroshima.[27] She bears facial scars, which are a vivid and constant reminder of her tragic experience. She is happily married to an American veteran who once worked in a military medical institution. The functioning of her lungs had deteriorated so much that she required six inhalations of oxygen daily. Yet she came all the way from San Francisco to testify. No airline would allow her to carry her oxygen tank on board, and her husband could not get off from work to drive her. But she was so determined to be present that she drove all the way to Los Angeles herself, bringing her aged parents in the back seat as her aides. It takes ten hours for a healthy person to drive from San Francisco to Los Angeles. But Jenkins and her parents stayed overnight in Fresno and, stopping several times along the way, took two whole days to come to Los Angeles. Her doctors would not give her permission to speak on the witness stand, so when she took the stand, her testimony had to be read by another person.

The chairman, who looked like a warm-hearted gentleman in his early sixties, made the following announcement at the start of the hearing:

The idea of the Bill is to provide that for U.S. citizens and permanent residents who are suffering from radiation sickness of one type or another, . . . the U.S. Government, in the future, for future incurred expenses, pick up the cost of paying for that type of treatment. . . . There is one other tremendously important aspect of the bill, from the scientific point of view[:] there really is no one central bank of information on how radiation sickness affects people, how it should be treated, where, when, and so forth; and if this bill did become a law, it might make it possible to accumulate such a bank of information which could be held in reserve against the day that conceivably it might be needed again. Hopefully, we never will, but . . .

The United States government has always maintained that the atomic bombing during wartime was a legal and morally defensible military action. Therefore, American citizens who were survivors of the atomic bombs in Hiroshima and Nagasaki could not claim damages caused by the bombing as such. They were simply requesting financial aid for the medical treatment of symptoms caused by late effects of radiation that might strike them as they grew older. This was a very moderate request considering all they had had to endure through the years, and it took great courage to get the movement started. This public hearing was an attempt to prove, through the testimony of survivors themselves and their supporters, that the government had a responsibility to provide financial aid for their health care.

The first witness was Dr. Noguchi, who had been the leader of the supporting organization for the hibakusha in America. His testimony consisted of historical and medical observations regarding the problems facing survivors of the atomic bombings and a powerful appeal for passage of the bill. He concluded his testimony by saying, "We are not talking about health care for Japanese or for foreign subjects. We are talking about health care for Americans—the quiet Americans who have suffered for many years conditions directly attributable to the atomic bombings. I do not need to belabor this. The logic is very clear. It is the only purely humanitarian standpoint."

Following the questioning of Dr. Noguchi, the second witness, Samuel Horowitz, M.D., was called. Dr. Horowitz said, "I am particularly proud to announce to you that both the California Medical Association and the American Medical Association have endorsed [H.R. 5150]." Dr. Horowitz concluded his testimony by suggesting an addition to the bill to make available annual physical checkups for all hibakusha who would be covered by the bill.

It was almost an hour since the hearing had begun. Kuniko Jenkins was quietly inhaling oxygen. It was time for testimony from the survivors themselves. The first was Judy Enseki. Anyone who had seen Judy Enseki two years before would have been shocked when she stepped to the witness stand. In the summer of 1976, she had not looked at all like a hibakusha. Working hard as director of the Suicide Prevention Center in Los Angeles, she seemed in the prime of health. Now, however, she had lost weight, and her pallor was ominous. Was this because of nervousness?

From the witness stand, Judy Enseki testified about her present condition. "I am currently under treatment for anemia and thyroid problems," she stated. "My group medical policy at my place of work does not cover the cost of treatment, since this type of anemia is treated with vitamin-type injections and medication, and the policy does not cover preventive care."

Responding to questions, Enseki testified that her health care expenses at that time amounted to $700 a year and neither her present group insurance nor the Blue Cross insurance policy she once had covered treatment for such blood diseases as anemia or leukemia. (By 1980, Judy Enseki, who had been one of the healthiest and best-adjusted survivors, was hospitalized with cancer. She died on August 21, 1980.) Her case provides vivid evidence of the hazards and uncertainties many survivors face as they grow older.

It was Kuniko Jenkins's turn. She walked slowly past her concerned parents to the witness stand, carrying her oxygen tank. The entire hearing room was hushed. Judy Enseki read Jenkins's testimony for her: "[I]n some ways, I am very fortunate. I have been married to a wonderful man, who accepted me even knowing that I had survived the atomic bombing of Hiroshima. My husband is retired from the military, and I have been able to receive medical treatment without undergoing the extreme financial suffering that many survivors in the U.S. have had to face." She described vividly the scene of the atomic bomb explosion, her miraculous survival, and the days following the tragedy and closed her testimony by saying: "We ask for your help in supporting H.R. 5150, and we hope, above all for world peace." Her aged parents listened to her attentively with their eyes closed. They might not have understood her words, and yet they understood everything. Kuniko returned to her seat and immediately turned to her oxygen.

The last hibakusha to testify was Kanji Kuramoto, president of the Committee of Atomic Bomb Survivors in the U.S.A. He took the witness stand to share the plea of survivors who have been discriminated against in every aspect of their lives, from insurance policies and employment to marriage, just for being survivors. "The issue," Kuramoto concluded, "is whether the American Government can assist a small number of the American survivors living today." Of this testimony, Congressman Roybal remarked, "It is sad. It is moving, and I hope that it is read throughout the nation."

Following Kuramoto's testimony, Dr. Mitsuo Inouye, president of the

Southern California Japanese American Medical Association, took the witness stand. Mitsuo Inouye had been drafted into the U.S. Army from the Heart Mountain Relocation Center. His two elder brothers were already serving in Europe. When the war broke out, his parents had been anxious to go back to Japan, but their children stopped them. If they had returned, Inouye might very well have been one of the hibakusha. By the same token, any one of the U.S. hibakusha could have been serving in the U.S. Army and escaped the bombing had fate not led them to Japan. Any one of them could have been on either side of the ocean. That is the key to a real understanding of this problem of the hibakusha. It is one that touches not only Japanese-Americans but the entire human race. At the conclusion of his testimony, Dr. Inouye quoted the famous lines of John Donne:

> No man is an island, entire of itself; every man is a piece of the continent, a part of the main; if a clod be washed away by the sea, Europe is the less, as well as if a promontory were, as well as if a manor of thy friends or of thine own were; any man's death diminishes me, because I am involved in mankind; and therefore never send to know for whom the bell tolls; it tolls for thee.

Dr. Inouye thus brilliantly cast the hibakusha problem as a matter involving the entire human race. When he finished his testimony, it was already past twelve o'clock, the time scheduled for adjournment.

Hidden American Hibakusha

The hearing in Los Angeles had great significance even though the bill never left the Judiciary Committee. The American hibakushas' continuous efforts to appeal to the Congress to listen to their voices was finally realized at this hearing.

Over the years, the United States has been producing a great many "hibakusha," and this fact is being "discovered" belatedly. A large number of civilians and soldiers of the U.S. Army were present at the nuclear tests in Nevada during the 1950s. On January 25, 1978, the House of Representatives' Commerce Subcommittee on Health and Environment held three days of hearings and listened to the testimony of U.S. soldiers and scientists who had participated in the nuclear tests twenty years earlier. From 1946 to 1964, a total of 183 nuclear tests were carried out in the atmosphere by the U.S. government. Up to and including 1957, civilians and infantry units participated in 18 nuclear detonations. A total of 450,000 soldiers, scientists, and civilians participated in all nuclear tests. Many of them were not even provided with radiation-film badges to measure radiation exposure. It is even more shocking that very few follow-up surveys were ever made on the health of those who participated.[28] At about the same time as the hearings on "Operation Smoky," alarming results of research on the dangers of "low-level" radiation were made public. This study revealed a very high incidence of cancer among workers at the Hanford nuclear weapons facility.[29] On February 19, 1978, the *Boston Globe* reported that an alarmingly high rate of deaths from cancer had been observed among workers at the Portsmouth Naval Shipyard, a federal nuclear submarine plant.[30]

American hibakusha survivors of Hiroshima and Nagasaki felt more comfortable in joining with these hibakusha than they did in joining with Japanese ones. An American hibakusha activist said:

> They are foreigners and we are Americans, even though we have the same Japanese face. In addition, our country dropped the atomic bombs. They may not have any trouble back in Japan for what they have done here. Not all Americans think of their activities here as something disagreeable or even offensive, but some do. And we are the ones who have to face this negative atmosphere. We are neither accusing the U.S. government of having dropped the bombs nor demanding compensation for it. We are simply asking the government to pay the medical expenses for the atomic bomb disease which might occur to us at any moment.[31]

The basis for unity among hibakusha cannot be found here. It is easy to criticize the attitude of the American hibakusha as a manifestation of their unawakened social consciousness. What the American survivors are desperately seeking, though, is to be accepted as American citizens, not only in principle but in practice, through passage of the medical assistance bill. In other words, they are asking the government to bridge the gulf between their feelings and the separation they suffered from the mother country in the war.

On March 30, 1978, a day before the Los Angeles hearing, the Japanese Supreme Court made a historic decision in the case of Son Gin Doo, a Korean atomic bomb survivor who had entered Japan illegally in order to receive medical treatment for his atomic bomb disease. He was granted the right to obtain a hibakusha identity card.[32] How did this news affect the American hibakusha and their friends? The Japanese government had admitted responsibility and guaranteed the right of medical treatment to a non-Japanese hibakusha, even one who had entered the country illegally. Why, then, cannot the U.S. government provide the same treatment for its own citizens who happen to be survivors of the atomic bomb? The American atomic bomb survivors must find an answer for this simple question by themselves before they can accept the importance of unity between hibakusha in Japan and in the United States. Fifty years after the bombs were dropped on Hiroshima and Nagasaki, these hibakusha have yet to receive assistance from their government.

America, the country that dropped the bombs, refuses to recognize the responsibility it bears toward those of its own citizens who were the victims of its bombing policy. By contrast, Japan, the target of the bombing, has accepted that responsibility. American hibakusha are among the beneficiaries of the Act to Give Medical Aid to Survivors, not because they are descendants of the people of Japan but because they are "atomic bomb survivors"—survivors of the first nuclear war.

Notes

1. Takeda, Junichi, *Zaibei Hiroshima Kenjinshi* (History of the Hiroshima people in the Americas), (Los Angeles: Zaibei Hiroshima Kenjiushi Hakkojo, 1927), 47.

2. *Ozawa vs. United States*, 1922.

3. Interview with Shibama Tazu, former Hiroshima Jogakuin Girl's High School teacher, May 20, 1978, Hiroshima.

4. Takeda, *Zaibei Hiroshima Kenjinshi*, 132–39.

5. Maisie and Richard Conrat, *Executive Order 90666: The Internment of 110,000 Japanese Americans* (San Francisco, CA: Historical Society, 1970); Michi Weglyn, *Years of Infamy: The Untold Story of America's Concentration Camps* (New York: William Morrow, 1976).

6. Interview with Sadako Obata (Shimazaki), June 21, 1976, Monterey Park, CA.

7. Interview with Yoshika Ishigame (Jane Iwashika), June 28, 1976, Los Angeles.

8. Interview with Kaz Suyeishi, June 16, 1976, Los Angeles.

9. Interview with Judy (Aya) Enseki, June 18, 1976.

10. Weglyn, *Years of Infamy*, 339.

11. *Rafu Shimpo*, June 9, 1947.

12. Interview with Kaname Shimoda, September 11, 1977.

13. Telephone interview with Ernest (Satoru) Arai, June 19, 1976, Los Angeles.

14. Interview with Tomoe Okai, June 17, 1976, Los Angeles; January 21, 1978, Tokyo.

15. Interview with Shinichi Kato, March 4, 1977, Hiroshima.

16. The text of H.R. 2894 was provided to the author by the courtesy of Kanji Kuramoto from his personal papers. Interview with Kuramoto, June 12, 1976, San Francisco.

17. Record of Hearings at the California State Senate Sub-committee on Medicine, Education, and Welfare, "Health Problems of Atomic Bomb Survivors," May 4, 1974.

18. The text of SB 15 was provided by Kanji Kuramoto.

19. Record of Hearings at the California State Senate.

20. Kuramoto Interview.

21. Kuramoto Interview.

22. Kuramoto Interview.

23. Interview with Judy Enseki.

24. Interview with Jane Iwashika.

25. Interview with Sadako Obata (Shimazaki).

26. A copy of this letter, Edward M. Featherstone's reply, and Takagi's response, were provided by Kanji Kuramoto.

27. This section is based on the author's personal observations of the Los Angeles hearings as well as the official report, *Payment to Individuals Suffering from Effects of Atomic Bomb Explosions:* Hearings before the Subcommittee on administrative law and governmental relations of the committee on the Judiciary, House of Representatives, 95th Congress, Second Session on H.R. 8440, March 31 and June 8, 1978. Serial No. 43. Government Printing Office, 1978.

28. "Effects of Radiation on Human Health," hearings before the subcommittee on Health and the Environment of the Committee on Interstate and Foreign Commerce, U.S. House of Representatives, January 24–26, February 8, 14, 19, 28, 1978.

29. Harold L. Rosenberg *Atomic Soldiers: American Victims of Nuclear Experiments* (Boston: Beacon Press, 1980), 151–2.

30. *Boston Globe*, February 19, 1978.

31. Kaz Suyeishi, interview, August 26, 1978.

32. *Asahi Shinbun*, March 31, 1978.

12

Remembering Hiroshima at a Nuclear Weapons Laboratory

Hugh Gusterson

Like you, I longed for a memory beyond consolation, a memory of shadows and stone. Each day I resisted with all my might against the horror of no longer understanding the reason for remembering. Like you I forgot. Why deny the obvious necessity of remembering? Listen to me: I know it will happen again.

—*Hiroshima Mon Amour*

How do American nuclear weapons scientists remember Hiroshima and Nagasaki? This chapter explores the ways in which the destruction of these two cities in 1945 is remembered in Livermore, a picturesque California town of about sixty thousand that is home to one of America's two nuclear weapons laboratories. The Lawrence Livermore National Laboratory, the younger of America's two nuclear weapons laboratories, is where the neutron bomb and the warheads for the MX and Cruise missiles were designed. I spent almost three years in Livermore, from 1987 to 1990, trying to understand its weapons scientists as a cultural

This chapter is adapted from my article "La Bombe par ceux qui la Font," in *Hiroshima: Cinquante Ans,* ed. Maya Todeschini (Paris: Autrement, 1995). It is based on research funded by a Mellon New Directions Fellowship and by a Social Science Research Council (SSRC)–MacArthur Foundation Fellowship in International Peace and Security. I am grateful to Mark Selden and Laura Hein for their comments as I was writing this, and to Art Hudgins and Cynthia Nitta for helpful comments on an earlier draft, which was presented to the American Anthropology Association meetings in 1988. My thanks also go to the scientist who appears here in the pseudonym *Tom* and to Bart Bernstein for the many hours he has spent improving my understanding of the issues discussed here.

anthropologist.[1] Although it was at America's other nuclear weapons laboratory, Los Alamos, that the bombs dropped on Hiroshima and Nagasaki were designed, some of the older scientists at Livermore did work on these bombs, and as the foundational drama of the atomic age, the atomic bombing of Hiroshima and Nagasaki is an important subject of memory and anxiety for scientists and ordinary citizens in Livermore. This chapter examines the carefully controlled, sanitized ways in which Hiroshima and Nagasaki are normally remembered in Livermore, if they are remembered at all, as well as attempts by peace activists, largely from the nearby city of San Francisco, to disrupt ordinary patterns of remembrance.

The wider context for this story is the United States itself, where the remembrance of Hiroshima has in recent years become increasingly disputed. In 1994–1995, as Americans prepared to commemorate the fiftieth anniversary of the bombing, disputes over the memory and meaning of Hiroshima became particularly inflamed. The disputes of 1994–1995 focused on plans by the Smithsonian Institution's National Air and Space Museum in Washington, D.C., to mount a major exhibit around the refurbished *Enola Gay*, the plane that dropped the bomb on Hiroshima on August 6, 1945, and on plans by the U.S. Postal Service to issue a commemorative stamp bearing a picture of a mushroom cloud and the caption, "Atomic bombs hasten war's end, August 1945." After months of conflict during which veterans' groups and some congressional representatives complained about the text of the planned Smithsonian exhibit, winning changes that then provoked an outcry from many professional historians and peace groups, the Smithsonian's curators canceled the whole exhibit except for the display of the *Enola Gay* itself, which, in the words of one conservative critic, would now be displayed "like Lindbergh's plane, with silent reverence."[2] Plans for the stamp were canceled in December 1994 after the Japanese government and some American citizens complained that it was tasteless and offensive.

At the heart of the dispute over the postage stamp and the Smithsonian exhibit were two concerns. The first concern is with the representation of bodies. Critics of the exhibit complained that the curators were planning to mount graphic, heart-rending displays of the devastation caused by the bomb—including, for example, photographs of charred bodies and the display of a schoolchild's shredded uniform and melted lunch box. The critics wanted the focus of the exhibit to be on the American bodies saved by the bomb, not on the Japanese bodies lost to it, and they wanted all these bodies to be represented more as numbers than as sentient people. Meanwhile, the mayor of Nagasaki, criticizing the planned American postage stamp, made the exactly equal and opposite complaint that the abstraction of the design erased the fact that "beneath that mushroom cloud, hundreds of thousands of noncombatant women and children were killed or injured on the spot."[3]

The second concern is with the rationality of the decision to bomb Hiroshima. According to the "official story," the bombing of Hiroshima was rational and even compassionate in that, in the long run, it saved lives, Japanese as well as American, by shortening the war and sparing the need for an invasion. The Smithsonian exhibit touched a nerve because it asked whether racism and a lust for vengeance, not just pure reason, influenced the decision to bomb Hiroshima and because it questioned the accuracy of the arithmetic upon which the decision to drop the bomb was supposedly based. By thus questioning the first act of the nuclear age—the American creation myth of the nuclear age—the Smithsonian exhibit raised questions about the popular assumption in the United States, a society whose politics are broadly permeated by the rhetoric of technocracy, that Americans have a special role as rational and moral custodians of nuclear weaponry.

As we shall see, these same two issues—the picturing of the body in Hiroshima and the (ir)rationality of the bombing—permeate the entangled layers of representations and counter-representations of Hiroshima in Livermore, a city where the bombing of Hiroshima has never lost its contemporary relevance.

Hiroshima in the Laboratory

Hiroshima and Nagasaki are not much discussed at the Livermore Laboratory, but when they are discussed, the hallmark of the dominant discourse is its tonal quality of distance and abstraction. The central axiom of this discourse is the claim that the atom bombing of Japan was rational, even merciful, in that it brought the Second World War to a swift end, thereby saving more lives than it cost. This claim tends to be treated as self-evident common sense by laboratory scientists, and it has served as a historical anchor for the cold war ideology of nuclear deterrence, according to which nuclear weapons, despite their terrible destructive power, are weapons that save lives: they saved lives in 1945 by ending World War II, say laboratory employees, just as they saved lives after 1945 by deterring World War III.

Here is an example of Livermore's dominant discourse on Hiroshima from the autobiography of Herbert York, a physicist who worked on the Hiroshima bomb and went on to become the first director of the Livermore Laboratory:

> [In 1945,] the suffering and the misery caused by the war in Asia and the Western Pacific continued unabated. War-related deaths in China already

numbered in the neighborhood of 20 million, and that number continued to grow as the Japanese expanded their holdings in that unfortunate country even while they were falling back in the Pacific. The goal of the [Manhattan] Project thus narrowed simply to ending the war at the earliest possible moment.[4]

What is remarkable about this statement is the location of the speaker. Although York was participating in the military effort of the most powerful of the warring nations, he speaks about the war as if he were observing its misery from a lofty and compassionate distance; and he speaks not of beating an enemy but of ending a war. The putative objectivity of this discourse is the source of its strength. Claiming to transcend the dichotomy between victims and executioners, it invokes the aura of universal common sense to legitimate the bombing of Hiroshima and Nagasaki as an act that was in everyone's interest.

The most striking instance of the discourse's success in legitimating the bombing is contained in a story run by a Livermore newspaper, the *Valley Herald*, on the anniversary of Hiroshima in 1982. The story profiles Miyako Matson, a survivor of the Nagasaki bomb who married an American dentist and settled in the Livermore Valley, where, we are told, she owns a hot tub and volunteers for the local Cub Scout group. She remembers vividly that day back in 1945 when she saw thousands of people staggering like zombies around the ruins of Nagasaki, some with their eyes melted out of their sockets. She spent hours brushing the maggots off people and painting their radiation burns with white paint. In the years after the bombing, her father, her uncle, and her aunt all died of cancer. Now she, too, suffers from a burning stomach, malfunctioning kidneys, and constant fatigue. She fears she also is about to die of cancer. However, in the words of the journalist, Miyako says that "the two atomic bombs prevented an even greater loss of lives. She believes nuclear weapons designed by the Lawrence Livermore National Laboratory are a necessary evil."[5] Miyako has, in this journalist's account, accepted the laboratory's narrative of Hiroshima and Nagasaki, together with its representation of the meaning of her suffering.

Although most Livermore scientists would surely have compassion for Miyako's story if they read it, the suffering of the people at ground zero tends to be absent, repressed even, in laboratory discourse about Hiroshima and Nagasaki. This discourse, in keeping with the broader impersonal discursive norms of Western science itself, represents the victims of the atomic bomb from a distance as numerical aggregates rather than in terms of their individualized suffering.[6] This is true whether the scientists are discussing the politics of the bombing or, in a more explicitly technical frame, its physical consequences. It can be seen most clearly in the distanced, disciplined, and unemotional ways in which nuclear weapons scientists learn to talk about Hiroshima and Nagasaki as sources of scientific information about the effects of nuclear explosions. Today's scientists at Livermore are heirs to information gathered by Manhattan Project scientists who visited Hiroshima and Nagasaki almost as soon as the bombs had been dropped. At a time when American officials were confiscating photographs and censoring news reports that might tell the outside world about the human effects of the bomb, these scientists went to Hiroshima and Nagasaki to turn the dead and injured bodies of the Japanese into bodies of data.[7] For example, they used measurements of the shadows of people, burned into buildings and into the ground by the bomb's flash, to calculate the altitude at which the bomb had exploded. They also used Japanese casualty figures, together with a mathematical formula called "the Standardized Casualty Rate," to calculate that Little Boy, the bomb dropped on Hiroshima, had killed and wounded people 6,500 times more efficiently per pound delivered than conventional high-explosive bombs would have done.[8] American scientists spent subsequent years keeping careful track of Japanese casualties, trying to document the exact numbers killed and wounded by the initial flash, blast effects, the fireball, instantaneous radiation effects, and subsequent cancers.[9]

We now know that, in addition to studying Japanese bodies affected by the first two atomic bombs, American scientists also, after the war, experimented with radioactive substances on hundreds of Americans—usually sick, poor, incarcerated, conscripted, or mentally retarded Americans. To give just a few examples: terminally ill hospital patients were injected with plutonium, uranium, and other radioactive compounds; mentally retarded children were fed radioactive breakfast cereal; prisoners' testicles were irradiated; and American soldiers were positioned close to atomic explosions in the Pacific or at the Nevada Nuclear Test Site, where they were forced to march into the mushroom clouds to evaluate their physical and psychological reactions.[10]

Needing still more bodies on which to experiment, scientists turned to animals. For example, scientists at the Nevada Test Site experimented with pigs—picked because their skin most closely resembles humans'. The pigs were strapped into position at precisely selected distances from a nuclear detonation and their skin carefully photographed as it was charred by the nuclear fireball and flash. Each pig wore a protective garment over about 80 percent of its body so that the protective capability of these garments and the effects of nuclear explosions upon exposed flesh could be studied from the marks burned into the pigs' bodies.[11]

In the 1950s, American scientists experimented with more than eight hundred beagles, feeding them strontium 90, irradiating them with cobalt 60, or injecting them with radium. The dogs' deaths were carefully recorded and studied in an attempt to better understand the effects of radioactive fallout. Scientists even went to the extreme of implanting plastic portholes in the sides of cows that grazed on the Nevada Test Site, so the radioactive contents of the cows' stomachs could be monitored.[12]

These mammalian bodies have served as texts from which to read the precise nature of the bomb's power and have thus been indispensable in constructing the regime of simulations that has grown up around nuclear weapons. Scientists have arduously metamorphosed the mutilated and suffering bodies of these people and animals into tidy bodies of data used in myriad strategic calculations. Such data are used to help calculate the efficiency of radiation and other nuclear weapons effects in killing and injuring enemy bodies and to devise measures aimed at protecting friendly populations against an enemy's nuclear weapons. Although nuclear war planners are principally interested in destroying enemy missiles, command and control facilities, and factories rather than in killing people per se, a nuclear war would inevitably involve enormous human casualties, and these casualties are integrated into the calculations made by war planners.

Michel Foucault and Elaine Scarry have both argued that mutilated bodies, spectacularly inscribed with marks of power, possess a unique ability to produce "effects of truth."[13] Thus, the bodies of executed prisoners display the power of the sovereign who executed them and reinforce the authority of the laws they transgressed; diviners often use animal entrails in proclaiming the unknown known; oaths are frequently solemnized across the dead bodies of animals; and wars settle contested national truth claims with the blood of the dead. In a similar way, American (and other) scientists use mutilated human and animal bodies, reincarnated as bodies of data, to help display the military power of those who control nuclear weapons and to certify the realism of elaborate scenarios about hypothetical nuclear attacks—attacks that have not yet happened, and may never happen, but whose outcome is believed to be predictable despite strong historical evidence that the course of war is rarely predictable. These elaborate scenarios about the effects of "nuclear exchanges" form the basis for national arms-procurement policies, arms-control negotiation policies, and civil defense policies, as well as for national leaders' stratagems of threat and bluff in international crises. Such scenarios have been important in the regulation and replication of hierarchies of dominance in the international power structure.

Yet there is a problem here. Even as injured bodies are necessary in order to make real the bomb's power and to construct stable regimes of

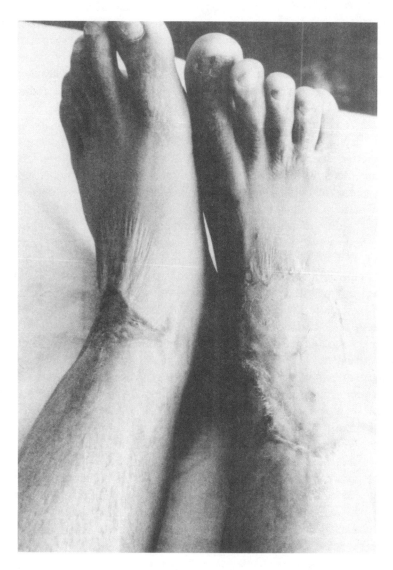

Healing feet of an un-named middle-school boy in Hiroshima Children's Hospital, undergoing reconstruction surgery. Images such as these can evoke either empathy or a stance of scientific distance, depending on the perspective of both the photographer and the viewer. In the context of a Pentagon analysis of nuclear destruction or a physicist's attention to the effects of heat and blast, the latter stance predominated. However, this photographer was famous for his elegant and loving photographs of Buddhist statuary, often tightly focused on hands or feet. Viewers familiar with his work would have been struck by the identical reverence with which he treated both subjects and thus been far more likely to view this image empathetically. (Photograph by Domon Ken. 1957. Ienaga, 3.39.)

truth around that power, still the mutilated bodies of atomic bomb victims have an incendiary, subversive potential that, at the same time, makes them dangerous. These bodies, mishandled, can excite feelings of sympathy and terror that work to undermine the nuclear state. The discourse on the effects of nuclear weapons is perched on a razor's edge between the bomb's need for bodies to display its power and the laboratory's need to discreetly conceal those bodies if that power is not to be inflammatory. Thus, in nuclear scientists' representations of Hiroshima, the body, even in its presence, has an absent quality.

Take, for example, nuclear scientists' photographs of Hiroshima and Nagasaki survivors. These photographs feature close-ups of burns, mangled limbs, and exposed tissues that are often taken from the back or focus so closely on ravaged flesh that the race, age, and sex of the victim are unclear. In these photographs, human bodies are metamorphosed into body parts and pieces of human matter—fragments of bodies that have been fragmented by the weapons but also, in the act of documentation, by the photographers whose cameras separate limbs from bodies as definitively as the bomb itself did. Although the images are of damaged human bodies, these bodies are seen from so close up that the effect is distancing. This is a mode of representation that, in its attention to detail, objectifies damaged bodies, makes them disappear, and impedes sympathetic identification with the people who inhabit them.

In laboratory culture, the disciplined, unemotional attention to detail is crucial. For example, one older scientist who had worked on the Manhattan Project showed me a photograph of a Hiroshima victim's burned back. "You see the spotty burns on this woman's back," he said. "When the bomb went off, she was wearing a white dress with black flowers on it. Each burn on her arm and back is where there was a black flower. The black absorbs the heat, and the white reflects it." This scientist had learned to read this woman's damaged body as a text, to translate the marks of her pain into the laws of physics.

The same scientist later became annoyed with me when I showed him a paper in which I had written that many people in Hiroshima were "vaporized" by the bomb. He pointed out that the correct term was *carbonized*. "That's the problem with nonscientists: you are so sloppy with detail," he added.

This scrupulously precise attention to detail is vital to the successful execution of scientific experiments and scientific analysis. It is surely one of the marks of a good scientist. Still, it has collateral effects. When one's concern is focused on being precise about whether a body was vaporized or carbonized, when one's gaze is studying the pattern of the burns across the back, when the shadows on the wall become signatures of the bomb, then the body—the person in the body, the pain in the body, the subjectivity of the body—has begun to disappear. It is not impossible to combine these ways of seeing: to hold together in one's consciousness at the same time a dispassionate interest in the origins of the pattern of burns along the back and an awareness of the pain that radiates through another person's being from each of those marks—and indeed, doctors in the physicians' movement against nuclear weapons in the 1980s sought to combine these two modes of awareness in precisely this way, allying their expertise as medics with the empathic compassion of the professional healer.[14] Still, at Livermore, operating outside the context of a healing mission or a critique of nuclear weapons policy, this way of representing the victims' bodies has a more distancing, fragmenting effect.

The distancing and dismembering effects of such ways of representing the injured body are nicely illustrated by this passage from *The Effects of Nuclear Weapons,* a Pentagon book widely used by nuclear weapons scientists and defense planners:

> The general interactions of a human body with a blast wave are somewhat similar to that of a structure as described in Chapter IV. Because of the relatively small size of the body, the diffraction process is quickly over, the body being rapidly engulfed and subjected to severe compression. . . . The sudden compression of the body and the inward motion of the thoracic and abdominal walls cause rapid pressure oscillations to occur in the air-containing organs. These effects, together with the transmission of the shock wave through the body, produce damage mainly at the junctions of air-containing organs and at areas between tissues of different density, such as where cartilage and bone join soft tissue.[15]

In the same chapter of this book, the destroyed bodies of hundreds of thousands of people are recomposed in the form of tables with such titles as "average distance for 50% survival after 20 days in Hiroshima," "tentative criteria for direct (primary) blast effects in many from fast-rising, long duration pressure pulses," "probability of glass fragments penetrating abdominal wall," and so on. The latest edition of the book features a pouch at the back containing the "nuclear bomb effects computer"—a circular slide rule that enables the reader to calculate "1–99% probability of eardrum rupture" or "probability of a glass fragment penetrating 1-cm of soft tissue" if they know the strength and distance of a nuclear explosion.

This portrayal, abstracted from the experience of Hiroshima and Nagasaki victims, has a generic quality. It is not about any particular body, but about the body in general. The observer is not located anywhere and has no

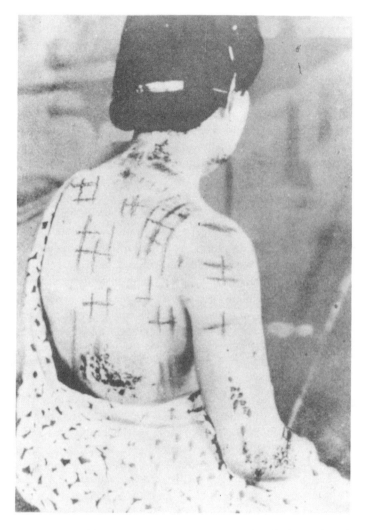

The black patterns on this Hiroshima woman's clothing absorbed more heat than did the white background, creating distinctive burn patterns on her back. Images such as this one of just part of an un-named woman's body have been used in different contexts to achieve very different ends. Many such photos appeared as scientific data in U.S. Defense Department studies of the impact of the bomb. However, the Peace Memorial Museum in Hiroshima relies heavily on the same images to tell the story of the bombing from the hibakusha perspective. The same dual vision has occurred in the United States. The National Air and Space Museum curators originally planned to use this photo in the Enola Gay exhibit in order to humanize the hibakusha but later censored it under pressure. Nonetheless, this same photograph is displayed in the Smithsonian National Museum of American History's exhibit "Science in American Life." (Photograph by Matsushige Yoshito. Ienaga, 1.28.)

acknowledged relationship with the disassembled body. And the body we see here is presented not as a person but as a set of components that undergo mechanical interactions with blast waves and glass fragments. Instead of wounds, we have *damage,* a word usually reserved for inanimate objects such as buildings and machines. These are words that dismember. They illustrate the way the dominant discourse at the laboratory repeats and conceals in the displaced realm of language the physical obliteration of human bodies at Hiroshima and Nagasaki.

An Encounter at the Boundary of the Laboratory

In the 1980s, antinuclear protesters from the communities around Livermore feared that the suffering of people in Hiroshima and Nagasaki was a prefiguration of our own suffering to come in a terrible war. The protesters, like the scientists, used the bombing of Hiroshima and Nagasaki as the first chapter in a narrative of the nuclear age, but where the scientists' story of life on the stable plateau of mutual deterrence figured the bombing of Japan as a culminating inoculation against further violence, the protesters used Hiroshima and Nagasaki more prefiguratively to renarrate the nuclear age as an inflationary spiral of apocalyptic violence. The protesters believed it was essential to recover the experience of the people in Hiroshima and Nagasaki in order to prevent its repetition. To this end, every year on the anniversary of Hiroshima or Nagasaki, the protesters converged, and still converge today, on the laboratory to make the holocaust symbolically real. They stenciled shadows on the Livermore sidewalks as a reminder of the Japanese who were instantly evaporated by the bombs; in memory of Sadako, the *hibakusha* girl who died while trying to fold a thousand paper cranes, they decorated the laboratory fence with origami cranes; they carried photographs of Hiroshima victims—photographs that pictured them as people who had been damaged, not as abstract body parts; one year, they re-enacted the bombing, falling to the ground where they lay writhing, moaning, and screaming as loudly as possible until laboratory scientists on the other side of the fence emerged from their offices to see what was happening; another year, they carried signs saying "Hiroshima 1945, Livermore 19??."

It was at such a protest, in 1988, that I met Tom,[16] just as a Methodist minister's voice was booming through the loudspeakers that "in no way, under no circumstances, can the use of a nuclear weapon ever be considered close to being an act of Christian love. Yet this nation ... founded on Judeo-Christian principles, is the only nation that has used a nuclear weapon." Tom, a weapons scientist and dedicated member of the Church of

Latter-day Saints, was a captive of the crowd. His car was blocked in front by a boisterous group of protesters sitting in the road to sever access to the laboratory; behind, a long line of traffic prevented him from turning back. As he sat there, already late for an important meeting inside the laboratory, two protesters sauntered over to talk. He looked suspiciously at the buttons on their faded denim jackets —"Another Dyke for Peace"—and when they asked why he worked at the laboratory, his reply was as predictable as it was meaningless to them: "Because I believe in peace," he said through half-clenched teeth. As the protesters continued to quiz Tom, I watched the rage spread through his body. His arms were trembling, his fists clenching and unclenching. Meanwhile, the driver of the car next to him was starting to rev his engine menacingly, as if preparing to charge the protesters sitting just a foot in front of his bumper. Tempers were fraying, and the peace demonstration was on the edge of turning violent.

A week later, I interviewed Tom in his home. Like most scientists at the laboratory, Tom said he worked on nuclear weapons because the world is anarchic and dangerous and only the weapons are strong enough to keep a stable peace and prevent the loss of millions of lives. Speaking more like a world governor than a cold warrior, he said:

> You get back to what's the justification of ever having used or ever using nuclear weapons at any point. Do they cause less suffering or less destruction at the time that they were used or not? And the whole justification would be that it could put an end to it quicker. And that's the justification in the original use of the bombs at Hiroshima and Nagasaki. And it has to be.

"So do you think," I ask, "that Jesus Christ would sanction the use of nuclear weapons in some instances?" He answers without hesitating: "In some instances, yes."

The philosopher George Hogenson has argued that deterrence theory is rooted in an attempt to reclaim the perfect, infallible, transcendent rationality that Leibnitz and the Cartesian philosophers identified with God.[17] Tom says that Jesus came to earth to teach "fundamental truth." For Tom, who is both a Christian and a scientist, Jesus Christ represents a transcendent unification of perfect rationality and perfect compassion. Christ's is a compassion that, fortified by rationality, does not flinch from tough choices. Tom's Christ, the Christ who would bomb Hiroshima in order to save lives, would have no difficulty with Dostoievsky's famous question: Would it be permissible to torture a child in order to end all human suffering?

Tom's statement is a classic example of the way in which the dominant discourse at Livermore phrases moral questions in pragmatic and rationalist terms.[18] It is the scientists' discourse of choice for discussing the bombing of Hiroshima and the continuing manufacture of nuclear weapons—though usually without the Christian inflection. This discourse of pragmatic rationalism is only one of two discourses in Livermore used to defend the bombing of Hiroshima, however. While the scientists talk about rationality and the greatest good of the greatest number, there is another discourse that celebrates emotion, revenge, and power. It is a discourse of populist emotion. Each year around the time of the protests, the letters pages of the Livermore newspapers abound with examples of it. "We had plenty of reason to bomb Japan. Remember Pearl Harbor," says one letter.[19] Another says:

> All we hear about is how terrible the A-bomb was that we dropped on Hiroshima forty years ago. Yes, it was terrible but we hear very little about what the Japanese had done in the years before the A-bomb. . . . We don't hear about the rape of China, the dirty sneak attack on the Pacific fleet at Pearl Harbor, the 1,100 sailors and Marines still on the bottom of Pearl Harbor in the USS *Arizona* and the Philippine Bataan Death March.[20]

At first sight, there appears to be a perfect synergy between the scientists' discourse of pragmatic rationalism and this more down-to-earth discourse of vengeance. The two discourses converge in legitimating the bombing of Hiroshima and Nagasaki while diverging in phrasing the legitimacy of the bombing in both technocratic and more populist terms. The divergence between the discourses reflects the binary nature of Livermore itself, which has traditionally been a small town with a nuclear weapons laboratory implanted into it. However, we should not be deceived by the scientists' rationalist discourse into believing that they have entirely set aside the motives of other mortals. Although Livermore's scientists have a clear preference for the rationalist discourse when discussing the bombing of Hiroshima and Nagasaki, they are not immune to the lures of anger and vengeance, and this introduces a hairline fracture within their ideological world that has the potential to split open the entire ideology of nuclear deterrence.

You will recall that Tom presented the immense power of nuclear weapons as a means of disciplining the unruly, anarchic tendencies in international relationships. "Remember the kamikaze pilots?" he asked me.

> How do you deal with those people? The two bombs convinced the Japanese that further resistance would be fruitless, saving lots of lives on both sides. . . .
>
> [Today] we must create a lasting peace. The question is: How do we do this with so many would-be Hitlers running loose in this world?

But this was not all that Tom had to say. Throughout the interview, he was deeply troubled by two things. First, he was upset that the U.S. government had, the previous day, bombed Iranian oil platforms in the Persian Gulf. He saw this as a reckless and irrational act of escalation. Second, he was upset by his own anger at the protest where I had met him. Four times in the interview, he returned, almost obsessively, to this theme:

> I had feelings like, doggone it, I want to drive right on through there and things like that, which I don't want to exercise again. I think that the better way to feel . . . is to keep in better control of what you want to do. . . . Anger's a valid feeling and often motivates, but I got angrier than I probably in retrospect feel like I should have done. I was more angry than I wanted to be.

Finally, at the end of the interview, I said I thought he was so upset by his anger at the protest because it suggested we might not be rational and controlled enough to make deterrence work if such a small thing could anger him so greatly. He nodded sadly.

In his article "Nuclear Weapons and the Dark Side of Humankind," the psychiatrist John Mack says, "[N]ot far below the surface in each of us are impulses of hatred and violence which can be aroused with a minimum of provocation." He goes on to quote the Indian novelist Salman Rushdie: "[W]hat-must-on-no-account-be-known is the impossible verity that barbarism could grown in cultured soil, that savagery could be concealed beneath decency's well-pressed shirt."[21]

Throughout his interview with me, Tom was struggling with what lay beneath his own well-pressed shirt. He was wrestling with the problem that we need nuclear weapons to fend off the irrational violence of others, but we may not ourselves be rational enough to be trusted with them.

Nuclear weapons have bestowed on human beings godlike powers and godlike responsibilities. Despite the attempts of deterrence theorists and military strategists to devise a perfectly rational system for the management of these weapons, we are, after all, merely human. That dilemma—how human beings might wield the powers of gods—is what perplexes Tom. "What we really need," he said, sounding as utopian as the protesters who so angered him, "is to generate a true Christlike love and concern for each other. . . . That's a difficult thing to do."

Conclusion

The dominant discourse on Hiroshima and on the postwar nuclear arms race, both inside and outside the Livermore Laboratory, rests upon certain kinds of repression. In particular, the dominant discourse represses sympathetic picturings of the victims of nuclear war, and it represses questions about the rationality and infallibility of those who control nuclear weapons. Many antinuclear activists sense these points of vulnerability and hence use tactics in their protests that apply pressure to these areas of weakness, particularly by resurrecting the suffering bodies of the victims. The planned exhibit at the Smithsonian in 1995 outraged veterans' groups and conservatives precisely because it balanced its celebration of Hiroshima with pictures of the suffering bodies of atomic bomb victims and with questions about the beneficent rationality of the American victors. For this reason, it had to be repressed. Tom, in exploring with me his anger at a Hiroshima Day protest at the gates of the laboratory, found that the protest evoked troubling questions for him about the rationality and reliability of humans as custodians of the bomb—questions with which he struggled in our interview through the prism of Christian narratives of divine perfection and human imperfection. Although he did not question the bombing of Hiroshima, his emotional reaction to a protest questioning prevailing rationalist explanations of Hiroshima did lead him to question the indefinite viability of nuclear deterrence itself as a regime.

If we are to avoid a repetition of Hiroshima, it will not be by repressing exhibitions about it that displease us. Nor is it likely to be, I am sorry to say, by becoming more Christlike. Instead, we must confront honestly our predicament as imperfectly rational beings entrusted with weapons capable of doing terrible things to other people on an almost unimaginable scale. We must be reminded of our fallibility, and we must be reminded of the terrible destruction nuclear weapons inflict. For this reason, strange though it may sound, protesters perform a service for the scientists at the laboratory, and the Smithsonian curators rendered a service to the American people.

Notes

1. See Hugh Gusterson, *Nuclear Rites: A Weapons Laboratory at the End of the Cold War* (Berkeley: University of California Press, 1996).

2. Charles Krauthammer, "Exhibit Distorts Historical Context of the A-Bombing of Japan," *Albuquerque Journal,* August 21, 1994.

3. Quoted in T.R. Reid, "U.S. A-Bomb Stamp Called 'Heartless,'" *Washington Post,* December 3, 1994.

4. Herbert York, *Making Weapons, Talking Peace: A Physicist's Odyssey from Hiroshima to Geneva* (New York: Basic Books, 1987), 23.

5. M. Myslinski, "Memory Haunts Nagasaki Survivor," *Valley Herald,* August 6, 1982, 1.

6. On Western science's historical antipathy to emotional, personal, situated accounts of the natural world, see Evelyn Fox Keller, *Reflections on Gender and Science*

(New Haven, CT: Yale University Press, 1985). In a fascinating autobiographical account of his socialization as an engineer, Pepper White recalls hearing as a graduate student that one of his friends had gassed herself to death in her car. His first reaction was to calculate in his mind the flow of carbon monoxide and the time it would have taken to kill her. It was at this moment that he realized he'd been resocialized by his training at MIT, saying to himself, "[T]hey've got me." (Pepper White, *The Idea Factory: Learning to Think at MIT* [New York: Plume Books, 1992], 255.) Mark Selden (personal communication), foregrounding the roots of this objectifying impulse in the culture of science itself, points out that Japanese scientists represented the suffering bodies of A-bomb victims in strikingly similar terms—though they did also criticize their American counterparts for treating the A-bomb victims like guinea pigs and for studying their symptoms without offering treatment.

7. On U.S. censorship of news about the bombing, see Glen Hook, "Censorship and Reportage of Atomic Damage in Hiroshima and Nagasaki," *Multilingua* 7, (nos. 1–2): 133–58; and Greg Mitchell, "Hiroshima Day," *Progressive,* August 1994, 27–28.

8. Richard Rhodes, *The Making of the Atomic Bomb* (New York: Simon and Schuster, 1988), 734.

9. See Catherine Caulfield, *Multiple Exposures: Chronicles of the Radiation Age* (New York: Harper and Row, 1989); Committee for the Compilation of Materials on the Damage Caused by the Atomic Bombs in Hiroshima and Nagasaki, *Hiroshima and Nagasaki: The Physical, Medical, and Social Effects of the Atomic Bombings* (New York: Basic Books, 1981); Samuel Glasstone and Philip Dolan, *The Effects of Nuclear Weapons* (Washington, DC: Department of Defense and Energy Research and Development Administration, 1977); James Neel et al., "Delayed Biomedical Effects of the Bomb," *Bulletin of the Atomic Scientists* 41, no. 7 (1985): 72–75; and Theodore Postol, "Nuclear War," *Encyclopaedia Americana* (1987), 519–32.

10. See Carole Gallagher, *American Ground Zero: The Secret Nuclear War* (Cambridge, MA: MIT Press, 1993); Howard Rosenberg, *Atomic Soldiers: American Victims of Nuclear Experiments* (Boston: Beacon Press, 1980); Eileen Welsome, "The Plutonium Experiment," *Albuquerque Journal* pamphlet, 1993.

11. Some footage of this gruesome experiment can be seen in the 1982 documentary film *Dark Circle*. The documentary footage is also incorporated into a fictionalized recreation of the events in the 1989 Hollywood film *Nightbreaker*.

12. McClatchy News Service, "History Has Glow in Desert," *Tri-Valley Herald,* November 13, 1994, A1; Robert Norris and William Arkin, "Hot Dogs," *Bulletin of the Atomic Scientists* 46, no. 10 (1990): 56.

13. Michel Foucault, *Discipline and Punish: The Birth of the Prison* (New York: Vintage Books, 1979); and Elaine Scarry, *The Body in Pain: The Making and Unmaking of the World* (New York: Oxford University Press, 1985).

14. My thanks to Laura Hein and Mark Selden for this point.

15. Glasstone and Dolan, *Effects of Nuclear Weapons,* 548.

16. This name is a pseudonym.

17. George Hogenson, "The Cultural Embeddedness of Deterrence" (paper presented at The Mind at War conference, University of California at Berkeley, November 12, 1988).

18. Specialists in nuclear ethics refer to this position as "consequentialism" because, instead of focusing on the morality of the means employed, it stresses the morality of the consequences achieved by actions that, although unethical in themselves, may become ethical in the context of their consequences.

19. *Livermore Valley Herald,* August 20, 1982.

20. Ibid., August 18, 1985. Another letter, this one to the director of the Los Alamos

Science Museum in 1995 from Bill Hudson, said, "I would like to see photographs of the bombing of Pearl Harbor, the Bataan Death March, Marine casualties at Tarawa, some of the 6,821 Marines who were killed off Iwo Jima, the ships sunk by Kamikaze planes off Okinawa, and a BIG MUSHROOM CLOUD OVER JAPAN [capitals in original]. The Japanese started the war, we ended it." *Livermore Valley Herald*, 1995.

21. John Mack, "Nuclear Weapons and the Dark Side of Humankind," *Political Psychology* 7, no. 2 (1986): 223–33.

IV

Afterword

国のため

13

Learning about Patriotism, Decency, and the Bomb

Laura Hein

I have been thinking about World War II and the bomb my entire life. When we visited my grandparents, we always talked about the war. Both my parents were born Germans first, Jews second. But as the decade of the 1930s wore inexorably on, they all began to realize that this was no longer allowed. In both families, it was the women who organized, cajoled, and insisted on the move. My Swiss grandmother—Ilse, my father's mother—enticed my grandfather out of his Freiburg home and his legendary garden. I have never seen that garden, but I know of its roses trellised along a wall, its grape arbor shading a picnic table, and the sweet-smelling fruit trees because I have seen the shadow gardens—first in Binghamton, where my grandparents lived; then in my father's two gardens in Massachusetts; and then, the palest ghost of all, in my own Chicago backyard.

But it was in a front room of the house, overlooking the street rather than the garden, that she first decided they had to leave. She was changing her youngest son's diapers when she caught the words being sung by a group of Nazis as they marched by. I have only heard it in translation, and I have always wondered whether its meaning could somehow manage to be less chilling in German. "Wouldn't it be good to see Jewish blood dripping from the points of our knives!" Ilse looked down at her baby and finished the Nazis' thought. For all of us, hearing and telling that story many times over the years, the punch line was that, even then, they stayed on. My father was born on September 1, 1932, and they did not leave Germany until 1936.

My grandfather was reluctant. Germany had been good to him. He had left his Prussian village where the baker owned the only oven and the blacksmith made all their tools by hand. (They are good tools, too. My father still digs his garden with them.) My grandfather's parents must have had ambitions for him from the start. They named him Siegfried, although everyone called him Friedel. He went to high school and university and passed the exams to become a doctor. In the photos from his years at the university, he lounges on the grass in his fraternity uniform proudly, even arrogantly. He was one of only fourteen Jews to become a doctor in Freiburg before the Second World War, according to a doctoral student who wrote to my grandmother a few years ago. I once asked him if he studied hard, since the exams were given only once a year and the temptation to loaf must have been strong. He told me yes, because his father sold a plot of land each year to pay his fees. He had accepted responsibility for a triple alchemy: land into healing skills, country boy into urban sophisticate, and half-assimilated Jew into German.

My grandmother was born and raised a city girl—her grandparents were among the very first families to move into the cathedral town, barred to Jews until the 1860s—and we all admired her easy sociability. That must have been one of her attractions for my grandfather. Even so, when they first talked about leaving Europe, he wanted to go to Palestine and be a farmer again—that was something he knew how to do in any language. But Ilse said no, she was not cut out to be a farmer's wife.

By 1933, Friedel had achieved all his goals and fathered three children. It was not just that he did not want to leave his country, his medical practice, his home. He simply could not imagine the horrors that were to come. At one point, he remembered later, he actually said, "How bad can it get? They aren't going to kill us all, you know!" Germany was civilized, and such barbarism was outside the realm of possibility.

Friedel had served in the Great War as a doctor and an officer. He was lucky to be sent to France and not the eastern front and was proud to be a veteran. Once, when I was very young, he told me that he and his fellows would smash the necks of wine bottles and drink straight from the bottles. I loved the thought of my quiet, gentle grandfather so daring and so willing to break the rules. I only realized later that they were pillaging French homes. But the disturbing elements of his story paled next to those of his father-in-law. He, too, looks extraordinarily mild in his photographs. He served as the censor in a prisoner-of-war camp. His job was to read the mail of the Italian soldiers and throw out all the letters that revealed their hunger and cold. But he only learned later, after the war, why so many of them wrote about their pleasure in meeting Count Ugolino in the camp. He had never read Dante and didn't know that Ugolino inhabited a special circle in hell because he killed and ate his own children after their enemies had locked them together in a tower to starve. The family moral of that story was that a good classical education will save you from many embarrassments. But there was another moral, too: if only the Second World War had been like the First, my family could easily have stayed on, been good Germans all their lives. It is hard to know whether that knowledge should bring me shame or pride.

My grandmother probably used that story and its reassuring message that cultured and educated people live in Italy to convince my grandfather to give up his practice and start over again in a new country and a new language. She was always good at languages and loved Italy. My grandfather passed the medical exams all over again in Italian, as he had to later, for a third time, in English. Now that my cousins are adults, we also invoke his example when we have to learn something new. Jews and other refugees trained early for the postmodern economy. Best to learn a skill that you can carry in your head.

They settled down in Boliasco, a small town outside of Genoa. They spent three years there and planted another garden. My father once told me that, in the late summer, the long flight of steps up to the door were covered in tomatoes, cut in half and left out in the strong Italian sun to dry. There they learned that individual acts of courage save lives. My grandfather walked into the bank one day and was surprised when the manager rushed out and asked him into his office. Friedel thought the manager was acting oddly, especially when he didn't seem to have anything special to say. Only then did he notice the letter, strategically placed by his chair, freezing the bank accounts of all Jewish depositors, as of the following day. When he walked back out into the bank lobby, he withdrew all his lire. I've always admired that provincial bank manager. He must have been a cautious man—a bold one would have just blurted out the news—but he acted with decency and generosity that day.

They started trying to leave for America that night. But by late 1938, this was not so easy. The worst moment was when the American doctor in Naples proclaimed that my uncle John and aunt Ruth had trachoma and so could not have visas. My grandfather protested to the consul: he was a doctor; he knew they were healthy. The consul brushed him off with an answer all of us remember every time we negotiate through a big bureaucracy: "We never change our mind, even when we are wrong." They were most worried for John, who would be drafted if war broke out, as it would one year later.

In February, my grandfather went on alone to New York, and my grandmother, who still had Swiss citizenship, took the kids to her mother's apartment in Zurich and reapplied for visas on the Swiss rather than the German quota. The Swiss government functionaries, kindred spirits to the American ones, were happy to help a local girl who spoke their own dialect. German supplicants did not fare as well. John was her stepson and they were not sure she would be able to include him, but they didn't have any other ideas.

They were very lucky. They sailed for America in April 1939. Officially, they were not even refugees, but immigrants. I always imagined them traveling light, one breathless step ahead of the Nazis, until I heard the story of their piano being unloaded on the docks at New York. I can't remember whether it slipped off its rope and smashed into pieces or whether my grandmother just watched in fear that it would. They brought lots of their heavy, dark furniture with them, and the feather beds with satin covers, which always slid inexorably off our beds during the night, so that when we visited in winter we woke up freezing cold.

My mother and her family left Europe earlier, in 1937. This time, it was her grandmother who insisted they leave. I remember my great-grandmother Hedwig very well. She was the oldest and most powerful person I had ever met. When we visited her, I felt compelled to sneak into her bedroom and open the closet door, just to see the unbroken row of black dresses hanging there. They were so dark they seemed to absorb all the light. There was one navy blue one with tiny white flowers, but I never saw her wearing it. Uroma Hedwig always caught me and scolded me for invading her private room. She lived with my grandparents when I first met her. I remember Hedwig in permanent war over the household with her daughter-in-law, and even at five, I knew she had won control of the kitchen. My mother remembers her softer, thwarted of her independence by death after death after death. But my father shares my memory of her as one part flesh, nine parts indomitable will. I was six when my grandmother sickened and died of colon cancer very suddenly at age fifty-four. Then, serenely, Hedwig moved out into her own apartment. That's why I think she could have done so twenty or ten years earlier.

Hedwig's two brothers, Julius and Emil Oppenheimer, had moved to New York as young men and married Americans, and Hedwig had visited many times before. So when the family decided to leave Europe, they were the obvious people to sponsor them in America. Hedwig went ahead to make plans and choose a place for everyone to live. It was a long trip because Julius, now widowed, had moved to California, where his sons Robert and Frank lived. Meanwhile, my grandparents, Alfred and Liselotte, took grim little Sunday drives across the border to Holland, leaving some money every time. My grandmother sewed her jewelry and valuable papers into the furniture, clothes, and toys. My mother says that all her belongings crackled with secrets when she touched them, even her teddy bear. Now that I have small daughters of my own, ripping open that bear and filling it with grown-up mysteries—stocks or property deeds—seems ruthless to me.

But perhaps she was just more clear-eyed than I am. By 1938, Jewish children were already implicated in the adult world in ways far more disturbing than my grandmother could devise.

Only my grandmother's mother stayed behind. She killed herself when the Gestapo started to take all the Jews away, I learned many years later. Suicides bring out stories of previous ones, I have noticed. Gradually, my family has revealed a startlingly long list. Some, like my maternal great-grandmother, preferred it to Dachau. Others chose death out of a more private despair. But I can understand why *hibakusha* are often reluctant to tell their stories to their children or to the world. It seems a very familiar decision.

While they traveled across the Atlantic, Julius died. Hedwig was to have lived with him. In 1940, she traveled back to Europe to meet her sister, Selma, in Holland and bring her to the United States, where they planned to share an apartment. Selma died during the journey. I wonder whether my grandmother would have left Germany if she had known she would have to share a kitchen with her mother-in-law for the rest of her life. Probably, but I wonder. That emotional tug-of-war was so much easier to imagine than the hell Germany soon became. How do you know when it is time to leave? When do you give up on your country?

With Julius gone, Robert stood as their sponsor. They settled into American life in Berkeley while Alfred retook all the certification exams and began an obstetrics practice. Everyone learned English. My uncle Hans immediately chose Lefty as a nickname. Everyone still calls him that today. (His cousin Wolfgang, who spent the war years in England, was transformed into David.) Even so, Lefty and my mother were tormented on the school bus as "Mr. and Mrs. Hitler." They worried that German-Americans would be evacuated from the coast after all the Japanese-Americans had been rounded up. Worse, they might be repatriated. Like all other "enemy aliens," they had to surrender any cameras and shortwave radios. They were even less religious than my father's family and happily participated in American Christmas and Easter. Their garden was a wonderful place to hunt Easter eggs. Its terraces began with a sunny, narrow lawn on top and dropped down to a mysterious, shady bottom. Each level had its own delightful smells, descending from roses to lemon trees.

Then, Robert disappeared off to do government work. Later, they found out he was heading the top-secret laboratory at Los Alamos and building the atomic bomb. Frank left a little later. He went to Oak Ridge, Tennessee, where they enriched the uranium for Little Boy. His job was to devise evacuation routes if something went very wrong. Frank was at Alamogordo with Robert when they tested the Nagasaki bomb for the first time. I don't remember Robert at all, but Frank was an intensely interesting person—and passionately committed to making science accessible to everyone. He and his wife, Jackie, were committed antifascists and, indeed, "premature antifascists" in the contemporary code for Communist Party members. They quit in disillusionment sometime in the 1940s, but this was one of the reasons Robert lost his security clearance in 1954. Frank lost his job, too, at the University of Minnesota, and his family spent some lean years in Colorado in the 1950s, growing corn and beans out back so they would be sure of food for dinner. Patriotism has always been a tricky thing to count on in my family.

Frank died of lymph cancer in 1985. As my brother pointed out, after a lifetime of chain smoking and building nuclear bombs, what else can you expect? Science and especially physics—the queen of sciences—was Frank's true love to the end. If the men at Los Alamos were all like Frank, it is easy to imagine them pushing aside questions of how the bomb would be used once they had been seduced by the sweet challenge of making it work. Before they started, the Manhattan Project was to stop Hitler. Afterward, nothing else mattered as much as the science itself. Decades later—incredibly, to me—Frank still believed that scientific knowledge is intrinsically liberating. His lasting legacy is the Exploratorium in San Francisco, the pioneer interactive science museum, and a place that does indeed offer science as excitement and drama. When I go there, I can see why he never gave up, despite everything.

I find it odd that so many people think of Robert as mystical. Only an extremely practical person could run something as complex as the Manhattan Project. Administration, as my mother told me years ago, is really glorified housework. Mainly, it involves making money and time stretch the farthest and figuring out ways of getting people who annoy each other to cooperate. Taking care of a couple of kids is the perfect training. Robert must have learned how to organize people the hard way, starting with grown-ups. But by all accounts, he was a very quick study.

Robert was also extremely ambitious, although less for fame and fortune themselves than for the general opinion that he truly deserved them. That sort of ambition is a little classier and a little easier to live with than are the garden-variety kinds. But in the end, he missed his moment—when he could have used all his brains and urbane charm to argue against annihilating two cities full of people. I've always thought Frank was the luckier brother. The bomb rode more lightly on his shoulders, not because he was just a junior scientist then but because he lived a little closer to his convictions.

When my mother visited me in Japan, she wanted to go to Hiroshima on

August 6. We did go there later, but I took her to the Marukis' home and art museum on the anniversary instead. The atomic-bomb artists hold a Quaker-style meeting and testimony every year, followed by potluck dinner in the garden. Afterward, everyone carries lighted paper lanterns down the hill to the river and floats them away in remembrance of those who died. The people there looked just like the ones at American peace rallies: the women a little less manicured than average, the men a little less kempt, the children striking an incongruous note in their T-shirts blaring out the current rage in kid fashion. I think it was Ninja Turtles that year, those irradiated inventions of two guys who made a fortune out of their nuclear-era teenage sensibility, a fascination with Japanese martial arts, and fervent desire to quit working at Amherst's most infamous employer, the pickle factory. It felt good to mark the anniversary with people who give some of their life, if just a little, to the daunting task of trying to get people to act with compassion toward one another.

The Hiroshima celebration just seemed so large and impersonal, and especially then, when the unregenerate nationalist Nakasone Yasuhiro was prime minister, a stage for people to give insincere speeches and smile into the cameras. I thought so even more when we came to Hiroshima a few days later and all traces of the huge crowd were already gone. It was just another ugly modern Japanese city, baking in the August sun. It was so hot there; it must have been excruciating in 1945 even for those who were not wounded. All the water must have been tainted, too. So many people waded into the rivers to cool their burns, then died. But fifty years later, the ground no longer yields its harvest of bones. Traveling to Hiroshima is mainly a journey of imagination.

Now that I teach about Japan and the war, every year I watch my students react in the same way. They are fascinated by the idea of the bomb: it is always my most successful class. But like many others, they find it almost impossible to focus on the impact on the people who lived in Hiroshima and Nagasaki, despite all the material I give them. Their discussion skims past the hibakusha and veers instantly back to America. They are riveted most of all by the plight of the decision makers—President Harry Truman, the military leaders, and the scientists. They are drawn to Robert because he, more than anyone else involved with the project, seemed to be haunted by his actions. The most thoughtful students always linger on his complicated story. Robert is a tragic figure, inside family memory even more than in his public life, but my students offend my sense of proportion. They leap to explore his personal dilemma while determinedly avoiding the hundreds of thousands of other sad stories that began in Hiroshima and Nagasaki fifty years ago. They know the atomic story must have a tragic end, and Robert gives them one to substitute for all those other tragedies in Japan. Even now, Robert is letting them off the hook, both with his acquiescence in 1945 and with his later distress. In ways no one could anticipate, he really was the perfect choice to head the program. He gave his fellow Americans an easier way to live with the bomb; it is no wonder we still find his example so compelling.

About the Authors

Laura Hein teaches Japanese history at Northwestern University, specializing in postwar economic and political history. She is the author of *Fueling Growth: Energy and Economic Policy in Postwar Japan* (1990); "Growth versus Success" in Andrew Gordon, ed., *Postwar Japan as History* (1993); "In Search of Peace and Democracy," *Journal of Asian Studies* (1994); "Japan and the West Revisited," in *Diplomatic History* (1996); and editor of a special issue of the *Bulletin of Concerned Asian Scholars,* "Remembering the Bomb: the Fiftieth Anniversary in the United States and Japan" (1995).

Mark Selden is the author of *China in Revolution: The Yenan Way Revisited* (1995) and *The Political Economy of Chinese Development* (1993), co-author of *Chinese Village, Socialist State* (1991), winner of the Joseph Levenson Prize of the Association for Asian Studies, and co-editor of *The Atomic Bomb: Voices from Hiroshima and Nagasaki* (1989). He teaches sociology and history at Binghamton University and edits the M.E. Sharpe series Japan in the Modern World.

Sadao ASADA is Professor of International History, Political Science Department, Doshisha University. He is the editor of *Japan and the World, 1853–1952: A Bibliographic Guide* (1989). His book *Ryotaisenkan no Nichibei kankei* (Japanese-American relations between the wars: naval policy and the decision-making process), which received the Yoshino Sakuzo Prize, will appear in English translation.

Monica Braw is a historian, foreign correspondent and novelist. She began covering Asia in 1969 and received her Ph.D. in history from the University of Lund in 1986. She is the author of thirteen books, including several on Japan, as well as novels and short story collections. Besides her native Swedish, her work has been published in Finnish, German, English, French, and Japanese.

John W. Dower is Elting Morison Professor of History at MIT. His books include *Japan in War and Peace* (1994) and *War Without Mercy: Race and Power in the Pacific War* (1986), winner of the National Book Critics Circle Award and Japan's Ohira Prize. He was executive producer of the documentary film *Hellfire: A Journey from Hiroshima,* an Academy Award nominee.

Lane Fenrich teaches American cultural history at Northwestern University. He is the author of *Envisioning Holocaust: Mass Death and American Culture, 1945–1995* (forthcoming) and "The *Enola Gay* and the Politics of Representation" in the *Bulletin of Concerned Asian Scholars* (1995).

Hugh Gusterson is associate professor of anthropology and science studies at MIT. He is the author of *Nuclear Rites: A Weapons Lab at the End of the Cold War* (1996). His articles have appeared in *The Bulletin of Atomic Scientists, Technology Review, Tikkun,* and *The Journal of Contemporary Ethnography.*

Ellen H. Hammond teaches on Japan and the United States at Chiba Keiai College near Tokyo. Long interested in the efforts by Japan's Ministry of Education to control the way the war is presented in school textbooks, she was intrigued by the similar efforts by the Ministry of Health and Welfare. She most recently co-authored (with Laura Hein) "Homing in on Asia: Identity in Contemporary Japan," *Bulletin of Concerned Asian Scholars* (1995).

George H. Roeder Jr. teaches history at the School of the Art Institute of Chicago. Among his recent publications are "Censoring Disorder: American Visual Imagery of World War II," in Lewis A. Erenberg and Susan E. Hirsch, eds., *The War in American Culture* (University of Chicago Press, 1996): an extended essay on "The Visual Arts" in Stanley Kutler, ed., *Encyclopedia of the United States in the Twentieth Century* (1995); and *The Censored War: American Visual Experience During World War II* (1995).

Michael S. Sherry teaches U.S. history at Northwestern University. He is the author of *The Rise of American Air Power: The Creation of Armageddon* (1987), which won the Bancroft Prize for Distinguished Books in American History and Diplomacy for its innovative blending of cultural and military history. His most recent book is *In the Shadow of War: the United States since the 1930s* (1995).

SODEI Rinjiro teaches politics and history at Hosei University in Tokyo, specializing in the United States and the U.S.-Japanese relationship. He has been chronicling the American political scene since 1960. His many books include the prize-winning *Makkaasaa no nisen nichi* (Two thousand days of MacArthur) (1974) and *Yumeji no Amerika* (Yumeji's America) (1994). His English-language articles include "Satire under the Occupation: the Case of Political Cartoons," Thomas Burkman, ed., *The Occupation of Japan: Art and Culture* and "Hiroshima/Nagasaki as History and Politics," *The Bulletin of Concerned Asian Scholars* (1995).

Lisa Yoneyama, born in Urbana Illinois and raised in Kyoto, teaches Cultural Studies and Japanese Studies in the Literature Department of the University of California, San Diego. She is the author of "Taming the Memoryscape: Hiroshima's Urban Renewal," in Jonathan Boyarin, ed., *Remapping Memory: The Politics of Timespace,* 1994, and the forthcoming book *The Dialectics of Memory/Hiroshima.* Her recent article on Hiroshima exploring storytelling as a critical practice appeared in *Shiso* (1996).

YUI Daizaburo teaches contemporary history, particularly of the United States, Japan, and their twentieth-century relationship, at Tokyo University. He is the author, among other works, of *Sengo sekai chitsujo no keisei* (The formation of the postwar world order) (1985), *Mikan no senryo kaikaku* (The unfinished reforms in occupied Japan) (1989), and *Nichibei senso-kan no sokoku* (Controversy over views of war between Japan and the United States) (1995).

Index

Page numbers in italic indicate photographs

B

C